D0984085

Puritan Poets and Poetics

Puritan Poets and Poetics

Seventeenth-Century American Poetry in Theory and Practice

PETER WHITE, *Editor*

Harrison T. Meserole, *Advisory Editor*

THE PENNSYLVANIA STATE UNIVERSITY PRESS
UNIVERSITY PARK AND LONDON

For
John Nau
facing westward

Library of Congress Cataloging in Publication Data

Main entry under title:

Puritan poets and poetics.

Includes index.
1. American poetry—Puritan authors—History
and criticism. 2. American poetry—Colonial period,
ca. 1600–1775—History and criticism. 3. American
poetry—New England—History and criticism.
4. Puritans—New England—History—17th century.
5. Poetics. I. White, Peter, 1947–
PS153.P87P87 1985   811'.1'09   85-6366
ISBN 0-271-00413-4

CONTENTS

FOREWORD

A century ago, alert readers of Moses Coit Tyler's history of American literature from the beginnings to the Revolution could perceive within Tyler's generally severe assessment of that body of writing a gleam of quiet enthusiasm for specific authors and texts: some praise, with reservations, for Anne Bradstreet's art, for example, and delight, without reservation, in William Wood's *New Englands Prospect*. The signals were clear. Within the canon of our earliest literature were to be found poetry of genuine stature and prose of robust quality to be read with pleasure and studied with profit. Given the acuity of Tyler's judgment, particularly in his savoring of Wood's address to the "mind-travelling reader" of the *Prospect*, it is not untoward, I think, to suggest that Tyler would have relished Edward Taylor's poems had they been available to him.

Taylor, of course, has emerged as America's foremost early poet since his poems were brought to light a half-century ago and began immediately to attract an energetic and wide-ranging body of scholarship and criticism which has shown no sign of abating. Equally important, interest in Taylor has encouraged students of the period to re-read and re-assess the work of Taylor's contemporaries and immediate predecessors not only in New England but also in the Middle and Southern Colonies, and to return to manuscript and document depositories in search of poetry and prose by seventeenth-century Americans not yet known to us.

Traditional aspects of scholarship—bibliographical, historical, biographical, editorial—have served us well in our study of the era, and there is demonstrable need for these efforts to continue as we seek to extend our knowledge of those writers who stand at the wellspring of American literature. But there is equally demonstrable need for new approaches in criticism which either re-evaluate earlier stances or pursue directions so far un-çonsidered. Both the traditional and the new are represented among the twenty-two essays in this volume.

To act as advisory editor for this collection has been for me at once an illuminating and a chastening experience. It is a pleasure to be educated by one's former students, as I have been by a number of the contributors to this volume, and by one's colleagues who here pursue in considered argument some ideas I once touched upon but left undeveloped. At the same time, to act, in effect, as spokesman for the company of senior scholars whose work Peter White properly acknowledges in his Preface gives one pause indeed, not least when it is recognized that the late Richard Beale Davis and I were to have shared this responsibility. One can only hope that the collection as published reflects to a modest degree the vision Dick Davis offered in its preliminary planning.

Harrison T. Meserole

PREFACE

The chapters in this book, all newly written, represent a summary view of the work of scores of dedicated scholars of American culture who in recent decades have sought new ways of looking at the intellectual history and the aesthetic practices of our colonial past. Each contributor has moved confidently into his or her subject in the secure knowledge that there is intrinsic merit in the poetry of the Puritans, that there is an active, professional interest in this material in the United States and abroad, and that there is much we still need to know about our earliest writers of verse. Writing from such an advantageous position, the contributors to this collection have succeeded in shedding the defensiveness of the pioneering scholars in our field in favor of a new assertiveness which aims to explain, to clarify, to weigh and balance judgments, and to make more subtle discriminations. This book, then, demonstrates clearly the progress that critics have made in assessing the artistic theories and literary products of early America.

With generous and thoughtful assistance from Professors Roy Harvey Pearce, Sacvan Bercovitch, Harrison T. Meserole, and the late Richard Beale Davis, I set out to design a book on the Puritan poets which might serve several useful functions. The primary aim of this collection is to survey comprehensively for students of American literature the major poetic issues, ideas, themes, individuals, and genres of the period between 1630 and 1730 in New England, or in other words the century between the Great Migration and the death of Edward Taylor in 1729. Obviously, the goal is well beyond the reach of any one book. Yet, by isolating those issues which have received the most consistent attention and those fruitful enough to demand further exploration, and by identifying experts who have distinguished themselves in concentrating upon particular subject areas, I concluded that a single volume could serve as a companion, a guide, or a handbook to the most important material in the field. Students can find excellent examples of the elegy, anagram, acrostic, or meditation in Meserole's *American Poetry of the Seventeenth Century* and other anthologies, but to what single source might they go to learn more of the backgrounds, the context, the range and limits of these literary forms as they were practiced in seventeenth-century America?

All of the contributors to this book regularly teach early American literature on the college or university level, and they know the frustration of presenting material in piecemeal fashion, of the hours spent reproducing articles from journals and chapters from books, many of which are not appropriate for under-graduates or even graduate students because they are written for specialists and assume familiarity with the poet, the genre, or the controversy. My first aim was to make a body of knowledge available to interested students.

My second objective was to offer more advanced students and scholars, both in intellectual history and literary studies, something more than the mere repe-tition or condensation of older ideas. Each contributor, therefore, was asked to write a chapter which first surveys our knowledge of a particular idea, genre, or individual poet and then strikes its own course into deeper, more informative, critical, interesting, or controversial waters. In general, the chapters aim to sort out the opinions of the past while they advance literary scholarship in colonial American studies. In that respect, this book moves beyond bibliographical sur-veys, checklists, reference guides, and outlines—all necessary but limited resources. A good number of the chapters provide provocative and challenging theses; some offer radical reassessments made possible by a deliberate distancing from the subject; some demonstrate the value of newer critical approaches and methods; and some illustrate the continuing utility of traditional investigation and analysis.

As editor of this collection, I have not only learned from my colleagues, but I have learned about them. I have seen the discipline and patience required to master such fields as the history of rhetoric, the esoterica of alchemy, or the intricacies of typology, all part and parcel of the "character" of the colonialist. The contributing authors have cooperated with me, with the advisory editors, with the able staff at Penn State Press, and with one another. Through every stage in the writing of this book, I have counted upon my colleagues for a collaborative effort in which contributors—no matter what their critical orien-tations—would work together to unravel the poetics of the Puritans. With endur-ing patience and cheerfulness, with insight and humor, each of these authors has shown a sensitivity and a commitment that I deeply appreciate.

Early in this project I benefited from the advice of Richard Beale Davis, Leon Howard, and Calvin Israel now greatly missed by everyone represented in this collection. Whatever merit rests in this book reflects the wisdom of these advisors and teachers. Professors Brom Weber (University of California, Davis), Robert Secor and Harrison T. Meserole (The Pennsylvania State University), and Alan Pope (Berlin, Germany) have been instrumental in helping all of us to focus our ideas, to be precise, and to be comprehensive. How may one thank a colleague who voluntarily reads an 800-page typescript, not once but several times, cor-recting and commenting extensively?

Such a volume as this one can be produced only if the editor has daily support from his colleagues at home. I wish to thank the Research Allocations Committee, University of New Mexico, and especially my advisors and friends: Professor Hamlin Hill, Chairman of the Department of English; Professor Marta Weigle, Chair of the Department of American Studies; and Professors George Arms, Lee

Bartlett, and Sam Girgus. Ms. Maria Warren and Ms. Katherine Albert skillfully helped me prepare the manuscript for the press. My special gratitude is extended to Ms. K. T. Martin of the English Department for her extraordinary effort in corresponding with contributors during my leave, for her organizational skills, and for her selfless devotion to our work.

LIST OF ABBREVIATIONS USED IN THE TEXTS AND NOTES

AL	*American Literature*
AQ	*American Quarterly*
Bercovitch, *Jeremiad*	Sacvan Bercovitch, *The American Jeremiad* (Madison: University of Wisconsin Press, 1978)
Bercovitch, *Puritan Origins*	Sacvan Bercovitch, *Puritan Origins of the American Self* (New Haven: Yale University Press, 1975)
Bercovitch, *Typology*	Sacvan Bercovitch, *Typology and Early American Literature* (Amherst: University of Massachusetts Press, 1972)
Bradstreet, Ellis	John Howard Ellis, *The Works of Anne Bradstreet* (Gloucester: Peter Smith, 1867, 1962)
Bradstreet, Hensley	Jeannine Hensley, *The Works of Anne Bradstreet* (Cambridge, Mass.: Harvard University Press, 1967)
Bradstreet, McElrath and Robb	Joseph R. McElrath and Allan P. Robb, *The Complete Works of Anne Bradstreet* (Boston: Twayne Publishers, 1981)
Bradstreet, Norton	Charles Eliot Norton, *The Poems of Mrs. Anne Bradstreet (1612–1672)* (New York: The Duodecimos, 1897)
Daly, *God's Altar*	Robert Daly, *God's Altar: The World and the Flesh in Puritan Poetry* (Berkeley: University of California Press, 1978)
EAL	*Early American Literature*
Grabo, *Christographia*	Norman S. Grabo, Edward Taylor's *Christographia* (New Haven: Yale University Press, 1962)

Israel, *Discoveries*

Calvin Israel, *Discoveries and Considerations: Essays in Early American Literature and Aesthetics Presented to Harold Jantz* (Albany: State University of New York Press, 1976)

Jantz, *First Century*

Harold S. Jantz, *The First Century of New England Verse* (Worcester, Mass.: American Antiquarian Society, 1944; rpt. New York: Russell & Russell, 1945)

Keller, *Taylor*

Karl Keller, *The Example of Edward Taylor* (Amherst: University of Massachusetts Press, 1975)

Lewalski, *Poetics*

Barbara Lewalski, *Protestant Poetics and the Seventeenth-Century Religious Lyric* (Princeton: Princeton University Press, 1979)

Lowance, *Canaan*

Mason I. Lowance, Jr., *The Language of Canaan: Metaphor and Symbol in New England from the Puritans to the Transcendentalists* (Cambridge, Mass.: Harvard University Press, 1980)

MHS

Massachusetts Historical Society

Meserole, *Poetry*

Harrison T. Meserole, *American Poetry of the Seventeenth-Century* (University Park: The Pennsylvania State University Press, 1985; originally published 1968)

Miller, *Mind*

Perry Miller, *The New England Mind: The Seventeenth Century* (1939; rpt. Boston: Beacon Press, 1961)

Miller and Johnson, *Puritans*

Perry Miller and Thomas H. Johnson, *The Puritans: A Sourcebook of Their Writings* (New York: American Book Company, 1938)

Morgan, *Family*

Edmund S. Morgan, *The Puritan Family* (New York: Harper and Row, 1966)

Morison, *Life*

Samuel Eliot Morison, *The Intellectual Life of Colonial New England* (1936; rpt. Ithaca: Cornell University Press, 1963)

Murdock, *Literature*

Kenneth B. Murdock, *Literature and Theology in Colonial New England* (1949; rpt. New York: Harper and Row, 1963)

Murdock, *Paul*

Kenneth B. Murdock, *Handkerchiefs from Paul* (Cambridge, Mass.: Harvard University Press, 1927)

NEHGR

New England Historical and Genealogical Register

NEQ

New England Quarterly

NYHS

New York Historical Society

Pearce, *Continuity*

Roy Harvey Pearce, *The Continuity of American Poetry* (Princeton: Princeton University Press, 1961)

PAAS

Proceedings of the American Antiquarian Society

PMLA

Publications of the Modern Language Association

Scheick, *Will and Word*

William Scheick, *The Will and the Word: The Poetry of Edward Taylor* (Athens, Ga.: University of Georgia Press, 1974)

Sewall, *Diary*

M. Halsey Thomas, *The Diary of Samuel Sewall, 1674–1729* (New York: Farrar, Straus and Giroux, 1973)

Silverman, *Poetry*

Kenneth Silverman, *Colonial American Poetry* (New York: Hafner Publishing Company, 1968)

Stanford, *Taylor*

Donald E. Stanford, *The Poems of Edward Taylor* (New Haven: Yale University Press, 1960)

Tyler, *History*

Moses Coit Tyler, *A History of American Literature, 1607–1765* (1878; rpt. Ithaca: Cornell University Press, 1949)

Waggoner, *Poets*

Hyatt H. Waggoner, *American Poets from the Puritans to the Present* (Boston: Houghton-Mifflin, 1968)

White, *Tompson*

Peter White, *Benjamin Tompson, Colonial Bard: A Critical Edition* (University Park: The Pennsylvania State University Press, 1980)

WMQ

William and Mary Quarterly

INTRODUCTION

Puritan Poets and Poetics reveals that the early Protestant settlers of New England were in love with language and ideas. The men and women of seventeenth-century New England were searching piously or playfully for the means of expressing their beliefs about human nature, art, God, love, war, and the wilderness. They were consciously harnessing the powers of ideology and mythology, or systematically employing the structures of logic and rhetoric, or taking a whimsical delight in the "re-creations" of witty language. Some of the poets, exercising their talents in various poetic forms, were striving to break through the abstractness inherent in Reformation dogmatics, or alchemical science, or the vicissitudes of Western history. These New Englanders were attempting to break down the thoughts of their age and reassemble them in terms and shapes more appropriate to their mission in the new world. In a sense, their poetry was aimed at bringing their values into sharper focus, through the reordering and enlivening of concepts they considered important truths—there was a providence in a name, a meaning in death, a lesson in nature, and a laugh in foolishness.

Part I of this book examines the major theoretical questions raised by Puritan poetics: what did the Puritans conceive as the proper relationship between literary expression and theology or dogmatics; upon what cultural resources and methods did they draw to produce their art; and how did particular individuals, notably Edward Taylor, practice a poetics within the intellectual framework of American Puritanism? Jayne K. Kribbs begins this section with a brief survey of the more practical concerns of the early writers, outlining the evolution of printing and publishing in the colonies.

Mason I. Lowance, Jr., accepted the demanding task of organizing and condensing the aesthetics of the Puritans and recapitulating the classic and the contemporary critical reactions to Puritan poetry. Lowance demonstrates that collectively we are coming to realize that Puritan poetry was grounded in the Reformation's reliance upon the biblical Word, dependent upon the concrete and sensual imagery of the world, governed by standard rules and practices of the time, and guided by a rational system of accommodating Divine Truth to the human mind. Further reinforcing the notion that the Bible functioned for the Puritans as a kind of literary and historical handbook, Karen E. Rowe traces the Puritans' reliance upon the hermeneutic art of reading the Old Testament for signs of messianic fulfillment, spiritual truth, and historical-mythological justification for their errand into the wilderness.

Michael P. Clark and Lynn M. Haims offer two essays on Puritan aesthetic theory and practice that might be read as companion pieces, and should, I think, be read as examples of the new and original directions of scholarship in our field. Drawing upon the insights of modern semiotics, Clark argues that the Puritan poet deliberately and heroically hung suspended in the ontological gap between the visible and the invisible worlds, between the "hieroglyphic" signs of the corporeal world and the spiritual truths of the next world. The poem, therefore, takes on a sacramental character; writing was "an act of faith that was as aesthetic as it was religious." Lynn M. Haims also sees the Puritan poet as grappling with his desires to unite the world with the Word, "to make literal and palpable the abstractions of Covenant Theology." Haims tackles the commonplace notion that the Reformation, and in particular the American Puritan version, stripped the church once and for all of iconographic, "idolatrous" worship. Edward Taylor's *Gods Determinations* is the primary text Haims uses to illustrate how the poet achieves the verbal and theotrical counterpart of the "graven images" forbidden in doctrine and ecclesiastical service.

Jesper Rosenmeier sheds new light on the function of poetry in Edward Johnson's *Wonder-Working Providence of Sion's Savior* through a detailed examination of the role of memory in sixteenth-century English Puritanism. The Reformation, Rosenmeier claims, brought about a shift in the definition and use of the faculty of memory from the classical idea of the artificial and mnemonic method to the more natural, affectionate, and persuasive means of summoning Protestant heroes from the grave to an "eternal presence" on Christ's battlefields in New England.

Also working through the backgrounds of Puritan poetry, Cheryl E. Oreovicz calls our attention to the poets', especially Edward Taylor's, knowledge of alchemy, the ancient "philosophy" of chemical transformation and transmutation. Taylor, above all, argues Oreovicz, was able to articulate poetically and faithfully the genuine content of the most recent developments in "chemical philosophy."

Two articles answer the just demands for further re-assessment of the contribution and image of women in Puritan poetry. Although they approach the topic from different directions, both Pattie Cowell and Cheryl Walker remind us that the seventeenth-century cultural environment enforced upon women "patterns of humility" and the stature of "marginality." Yet, Cowell shows, despite all the obstacles, eleven early New England women poets from Anne Bradstreet (b. 1612) to Abigail Dennie (d. 1745) produced a body of mostly private poetry intriguing in its depiction of frontier struggles, individual attitudes, aesthetic concerns, and religious ends, regardless of its range of artistic accomplishment. Overcoming limited and unequal opportunities for education, social pressure to conform to normative expectations, and rural isolation, among other discouragements and deterrents, these women poets relied upon an independence of mind and spirit, an unquenchable ambition, or a loving counsellor or model to devote themselves to poetry for its "rich ideas, great and unconfin'd."

Cheryl Walker's "In the Margin: The Image of Women in Early Puritan Poetry" argues that Puritan women were regularly ignored, de-personalized, or minimalized out of the male, public poets' heroizing of the errand into the wilderness. When the communal spokesmen for New England imposed their mythological and ideological framework upon the Massachusetts Bay Colony, they almost uniformly minimized the actual sacrifices of women and their contribution to the building of Zion—physical, moral, spiritual, and intellectual. Women are regulated to the periphery of this "sacred history," thrust from the center to the margins of the communal mission.

In Part II, I have attempted to identify the Puritan poets whose careers are worthy of separate critical treatment—Anne Bradstreet, the Danforths, John Saffin, Edward Taylor, Benjamin Tompson, and Michael Wigglesworth.

Playing with our modern American English the way Taylor himself played with his own dialect, Karl Keller in his "Edward Taylor, the Acting Poet," wittily sketches the "creation" of Edward Taylor—the "making" of an American poet—from Thomas H. Johnson's discovery of the first manuscripts, through the early critical debates, the editing and re-editing, the exaggerated claims, and the close analyses, to the recent studies which place Taylor in his intellectual and theological milieu. The problem of Edward Taylor, as Keller calls it, is how to account for this "bad writer's" ability to delight us and to explain "what makes his art work and play for us." Among other dramatic roles, Taylor plays the fool, the clown, beggar, the pitiful one in variously nostalgic, sentimental, and melodramatic performances.

Rosamond Rosenmeier would agree with Keller that the habits of mind and belief predominant in unsettled Massachusetts or Connecticut are now very distant and remote, but she believes that Anne Bradstreet's "serious, inventive, and purposeful" artistic manners and methods can be retrieved to assist us in understanding her "prophetic art." Bradstreet's persona foresees the merger of the things of this world with the next, using biblical language and the voice of the afflicted sufferer to serve as the "scribe" of the Holy Spirit.

John Saffin, seventeenth-century merchant, lawyer, judge, and poet, was one of the century's most prolific and gifted poets and experimented with a greater variety of forms than any other contemporary writer. Kathryn Zabelle Derounian sees Saffin as one of the period's most worldly and genial writers, a poet who could elegantly express the intricacies of human relationships and his love of beauty, sometimes through exploitation of the dramatic and sometimes through more quiet, rational contemplation.

Robert Daly's essay on the Danforths, like Robert Secor's later chapter, remarkably revises and enhances our knowledge of early American almanac verse. Daly reads the Danforths' work closely and in context to see "the mixing of local, biblical, classical and scientific referents neither as a curious idiosyncrasy nor as a lapse in sensibility and decorum but as a part of a deliberate and coherent poetics." Daly locates the source of their poetics in their observance of Samuel Mather's injunction to discriminate between "graven images" and God-sanctioned typology and further in their admiration and emulation of Vergil's redefined sense of his role as *vates,* a public "seer" who weaves together local, historic, and mythical elements into a poetry which claimed New England as the culmination of Vergil's Arcadia and biblical Israel, of secular and sacred history.

Alan Pope's "Petrus Ramus and Michael Wigglesworth: The Logic of Poetic Structure" supports Perry Miller's famous thesis that seventeenth-century New Englanders were decisively influenced by Ramean logic. Pope finds that Wigglesworth used Ramean syllogistic reasoning to compose the debates between Christ and the sinners in *The Day of Doom* and that Wigglesworth used the major divisions of Ramus' "Invention" to structure the ten meditations and the concluding hortatory in *Meat Out of the Eater.*

My chapter on Benjamin Tompson's *New Englands Crisis* further establishes, I believe, the point that every author stresses in this section of the book: the major poets of colonial New England were artists who drew upon a variety of sources for their forms and materials. Here I advance the idea that Tompson used European engravings and Italian poetry to portray the native Americans as cannibals and infidels. Like his contemporaries, Tompson was inventive, eclectic, and purposeful.

Part III treats colonial poetry from a categorical or generic point of view with chapters on almanac verse, the anagram and acrostic, baroque free verse, comic poetry, Latin verse, and the Puritan meditation.

Robert Secor's "Seventeenth-Century Almanac Verse" offers some genuinely startling information about the frequency of verse in annual publications. Reliable literary historians like Samuel Eliot Morison, Perry Miller, Thomas Johnson, and Harold Jantz have indicated or suggested that verse was regularly included in the Harvard (or Cambridge) almanacs throughout the century. Secor's survey adjusts this view and, just as importantly, shows how colonial almanac-makers differed from their European counterparts by being educated "true lovers of mathematics and the stars," astronomers not prognosticators catering to popular demand.

One of the advantages of covering Puritan poetry by genre is that some authors, like John Fiske, the justly celebrated anagrammatist, were not prolific enough to deserve separate treatment in Part II but did compose a few works which survive as the best examples of particular poetic forms. Jeffrey Walker adheres to the traditional critical estimate of the function of the anagram and the acrostic, but his approach is liberal and inclusive. These forms allowed the poet to scrutinize Providence, to order life and art, but, further, to exercise wit by the microscopic analysis of language to assemble a multiplicity of meaning, to take delight in their discoveries, and to celebrate the nuances of linguistic "rediscoveries."

In "Baroque Free Verse in New England and Pennsylvania" Harold Jantz, a specialist in both Germanic and early American literature, takes us on a scholarly adventure through the ages, across continents, and even into the historic recesses of critical theory about our colonial literature. Jantz believes that the neo-Latin and vernacular verse inscription deserves to be treated by colonialists as a poetic form, as the form has traditionally been regarded in Europe. In the late Renaissance, poets turned the ancient Roman monumental inscription into a new literary genre; yet, Jantz argues, it appears that Francis Quarles and the New England colonists reinvented the vernacular verse inscription on their own, independent of any outside influence. This "very unusual and courageous act of employing a modern language in this genre" was followed in the first part of the eighteenth century by the equally innovative act of using free verse for satiric, political, and parodistic purposes. Jantz believes that our literary historians, like their German counterparts, have been reluctant to take these American Baroque poems seriously and have instead repeated the mistaken notion that the colonists suffered from a "cultural lag."

In a sense, Robert Arner's essay on wit, humor, and satire in early American verse also attacks the "cultural lag" theory. Arner shows that the colonialists immediately hit upon and developed many of the comic themes and techniques that are uniquely American and have since become traditional in our literature and popular culture. In Sarah Knight's humor he finds the culmination of earlier seventeenth-century trends, including, for instance, the comic characterization of the American Indian, the culturally deprived, the talkative and taciturn Yankee, the shrewd Yankee trickster, and the country bumpkin. Knight's work also contains many of the stylistic techniques commonly employed by the earlier wits (Morton, Ward, Johnson, Tompson, Tulley, Josselyn, Danforth, and Alsop), such as mock-epic language, surprising and unusual metaphors, interplay of high manners and low speech, pidgin English, and proverbial declarations.

Even the casual student of early Americana could quickly surmise that the elegy was the most important and frequently composed poetic form in seventeenth-century New England. Given this fact, it is embarrassing, remarks William J. Scheick, that dubious critical notions about the elegy persist, among them that the elegy in New England was only communal or regional and not personal and that the quality of New England works evidences our provinciality. Scheick points out that many critics have over-simplified and generalized the issues: they have ignored much of the English poetry in order to make easy distinctions— but misleading ones—among the English and American elegies, and they have overlooked the poets' relationship to the decreased, their audience, and the community. Thus, both old and new world elegies emphasize the communal significance with a public rhetoric to address the "reader directly as a participant in a ritual occurring during a communally relevant moment." But, striving for subtler and more meaningful distinctions, Scheick advances the idea that the

New England funeral elegy sometimes merges its social function with a configuration of the self: an "ideal collective self against which the audience is to measure itself."

Lawrence Rosenwald's objective in writing about the Latin verse of the American Puritans is to present concisely his assessment of their attachment to that language and culture. He concludes: "Seldom is a Puritan poet wrestling with, embracing, saturated in, possessed by a Roman poet or a Roman poem. (The one exception is a systematic preoccupation with the *Aeneid*.) The literature of ancient Rome is more a resource for the Puritans than an influence. It is inert." What then were the Puritans doing with Latin? Rosenwald speculates that ancient languages "were the means of asserting the coherence of a restricted society. . . . It functions somewhat like trade jargon, thieves' argot, and the sacred language of priests." Far from condemning the Puritans for their impersonal use of Latin, Rosenwald believes that they refrained from changing ancient Latin to express their contemporary mind and instead used their fluent, classical Latin to "bind together those to whom it was accessible."

Ursula Brumm takes up Norman Grabo's challenge to define and analyze the Puritan devotional literature which channels emotion into verbal structures. After tracing Cotton Mather's biographical emphasis upon meditation and Thomas Hooker's more philosophical preparatory contemplations, Brumm looks at the meditational works of Anne Bradstreet, Edward Johnson, Philip Pain, and Michael Wigglesworth, using as her standard the determination of whether the poet in the traditionally Protestant way "ties meditation to salvation, the infusion of grace and faith." Edward Taylor's meditations represent the crowning achievement in the American-Protestant meditative tradition. In "an extraordinary variety of configurations which determine the individual structure" of each of his poems, Edward Taylor used the meditational form to concentrate all of his "intellectual and emotional effort to understand the mysteries of the Christian religion, his own existence and ultimate destination, and the order of the whole cosmos. . . . His meditations constitute the most intricate and concentrated exploration of word and meaning to be found in all American literature."

Puritan Poets and Poetics consists, then, of new chapters on the widest range of subjects possible in a single volume. The contributors are all intensely interested in widening and deepening our awareness of a rather remote and different age. Now, allied with cultural and intellectual historians, linguistic and aesthetic theoreticians, and American Studies interdisciplinarians, literary critics are truly examining the seventeenth century from exciting new points of view. One can see in this book, for instance, that the writers have used their knowledge of Renaissance rhetoric and philosophy, classical Latin, post-Renaissance alchemy, Reformation theology, metaphysical English poetry, historical biography, domestic and cultural history, feminist scholarship, and semiotics to reveal some intriguing aspects of the Puritan mind and its poetic practices.

I
PURITAN AESTHETICS
AND SOCIETY

1 PRINTING AND PUBLISHING IN AMERICA FROM DAYE TO ZENGER

JAYNE K. KRIBBS

God's providence carried the Puritans safely to Massachusetts Bay to establish a new Jerusalem in their promised land. Through His grace they built homes and churches and formed their civil government. Thereupon, wrote one chronicler, "One of the next things we longed for, and looked after was to advance *Learning*, and perpetuate it to Posterity . . . ,"[1] clearly signalling the early settlers' high regard for education. In practical terms, Puritan preachers had to be trained to unravel the mysteries of God's word revealed in the scriptures, and congregants needed to understand their ministers' teachings in order to lead informed, Godly lives. Accordingly, in 1638, a parcel of land in Cambridge was set aside for a college. Several months later when the Board of Overseers learned that John Harvard had died bequeathing his entire library and half of his estate of seven or eight hundred pounds to the school, they named the college after him.

Additional funds for the college were raised by, among others, the Reverend Mr. Jose Glover, who apparently had hopes of becoming its first president. However, nearly coincident with John Harvard's death was Glover's death aboard the ship *John* as it made a rough Atlantic crossing from London. Among the possessions left to Glover's widow were a wooden printing press and several fonts of type for use at the college. Widow Glover, who, ironically, did marry Harvard's first president, Henry Dunster, saw to it that America's first press was delivered to the college. Although it was first installed in a makeshift shed beside the president's house, it clearly had great value for the Puritan leaders. The continued spread of the gospel to the people of New England was imperative, and with their own press, they could be sure that their holy mission found expression in their own printed sermons, catechisms, and other religious tracts. And, of course, they also recognized the practical importance of the press in turning out the orders, laws, and other kinds of governmental documents necessary to the routine operation of the colony.

Late in 1638 Stephen Daye and his son Matthew, Glover's pressmen, had their first assignment: to print "The Freeman's Oath," a statement prepared by government officials—the original draft in John Winthrop's handwriting is extant—for the male citizens of Massachusetts Bay Colony. It read, "I do solemnly bind myself in the sight of God, when I shall be called to give my voice touching any such matter of this State, in which freemen are to deal, I will give my vote and suffrage as I shall judge in mine own conscience may best conduce and tend to the public weal of that body, without respect of persons, or favor of any man."[2] Although this pledge seemed to hold more sentimental and traditional than legal significance for Massachusetts officials, it did, to some degree, permit them to control membership in the colony and to retain their positions of authority over the citizens. Both this oath and the second issue from the press, Captain William Peirce's *Almanack* for 1639, were put to sturdy use. No copy of either survives.

English America's first book and the first publication from the Cambridge press to survive into the twentieth century is *The Psalms in Metre, Faithfully translated for the Use, Edification and Comfort, of the Saints, in Publick and Private, especially in New England* (1640). The *Bay Psalm Book,* as it is more familiarly known, is listed among the world's most important books not just because it is America's first or that only eleven known copies are extant, although these are certainly reasons enough, but also because it was so frequently reprinted here and in England.[3] The first printing of 1700 copies sold quickly, as did an extraordinary fifty-four other editions published before 1760. That its authors—Richard Mather of Dorchester and John Eliot and Thomas Welde of Roxbury—should insist upon using their particular translation of the Psalms of David when numerous other editions were available to them may seem rather curious until we remember that they believed they were God's chosen people, that He had guided them into the wilderness for His own especial purposes.[4] What better way for them to follow the injunctions of Holy Writ than to render the psalms for themselves, to adapt them to their special spiritual mission?

Their particular translation, though a noble attempt, failed to accomplish precisely what it intended—to provide a lyrical, singable, metrical version of the psalms. After reading the work in manuscript, Thomas Shepard, obviously not impressed with the rhyming, wrote this humorous quatrain to his friend Richard Mather:

> you Roxburough poets take this in Time
> see that you make very good Rhythme
> And eeke of Dorchester when you the verses lengthen
> see that you them with the words of the text do strengthen.[5]

Shepard was not the only one to find fault with the *Bay Psalm Book.* Over the years this poetry by committee met with harsh criticism, but none as sharp as Moses Coit Tyler's in his *History of American Literature:* "Sentences wrenched about end for end, clauses heaved up and abandoned in chaos, words disembowelled or split quite in two in the middle and dissonant combinations of sound that are the despair of such poor vocal organs as are granted to human beings. The verses, indeed, seem to have been hammered out on an anvil, by blows from a blacksmith's sledge."[6] For some years the faithful of New England struggled with the music and the text until Henry Dunster, Harvard president and the colony's Hebrew scholar, along with Harvard tutor Richard Lyon, undertook the job of retranslating the psalms.

By the time their manuscript, *The Psalms, Hymns, and Spiritual Songs of the Old and New Testament* (or more simply the *New England Psalms*), was ready for publication in 1651, the operation of the printing press had passed into the hands of Samuel Green. Although not trained in typography, Green soon found his way, and for forty years continued to print the religious and governmental documents that had been the staple of the Dayes' work.[7]

As early as 1654 Green began parparations to print what was to be one of colonial America's most unusual works. The Commissioners of the United Colonies, who acted as agents for the corporation in England for propagating the gospel among the Indians in New England, charged Green with printing the Indian Bible. Under the guidance of the Reverend John Eliot, who had devoted his life to the conversion of the Narragansetts and Algonquians, Green finally began setting type for the Bible in 1660, with Eliot proofreading and correcting the sheets as they were pulled from the press. The job was made easier by the arrival of a second press and type fonts and by the addition of three men to the staff: Marmaduke Johnson, a skilled London printer summoned to Massachusetts specifically to work on the project; James the Printer, a native American Indian converted to Christianity who helped Eliot with the language and with setting type; and Hezekiah Usher, Boston merchant and bookseller who acted as the liaison between the Commissioners and the Corporation, kept all accounts, and provided the materials (paper, type, ink, etc.) for the printing. By the time this unique project was finished in 1663, their modest little print shop at Cambridge had become the most famous in the English-speaking world, including England.[8]

Work on Eliot's Indian Bible did not progress without interruption, however. In addition to the orders and laws, Harvard College theses, and an occasional sermon or broadside, Green and Johnson printed early America's second "best seller," after the *Bay Psalm Book*. In 1662 they put out nearly 1800 copies of Michael Wigglesworth's *Day of Doom*. The entire edition was sold out within the year. Richard Crowder, in his biography of Wigglesworth, notes that one of every thirty-five people bought a copy and circulated it among family and friends. It was literally read to pieces. Ministers used the *Day of Doom* as text for their sermons. Children memorized it completely. Broadside versions appeared in every corner of the land.[9] With reprintings at the Cambridge press and in England, this rendering of Calvinist theology into galloping verse became for a century one of New England's most widely read books after the Bible.

After the Wigglesworth poem and the final effort to complete the Indian Bible in 1663, Green and Johnson again turned their attention to a routine of theses, primers, almanacs, and sermons, certain of which deserve mention as particularly important to our understanding of New England life and letters: John Cotton's *A Discourse About Civil Government in a New Plantation* (1663), and his *Spiritual Milk for Babes in Either England* (1668), and Samuel Danforth's *Astronomical Description of the late Comet or Blazing Star* (1665). The first history of the colony to be printed in America, Nathaniel Morton's *New-England's Memoriall*, appeared in 1669, followed in 1670 by the first American biography, Increase Mather's *The Life and Death of that Reverend Man of God, Mr. Richard Mather*.

Also in 1670 Michael Wigglesworth carried the manuscript of another poem— more ambitious, in fact, than *The Day of Doom*—from his home in Malden to the press in Cambridge. The four-thousand-line *Meat Out of the Eater: Meditations Concerning the Necessity, End, and Usefulness of Afflictions unto God's Children All tending to Prepare them For, and Comfort them Under the Cross,* was the longest American poem published at the time. Like his previous work, *Meat Out of the Eater* sold extraordinarily well. Our earliest extant copy of the poem is the fourth edition dated 1689, and we know that Wigglesworth tinkered continuously with the original text, altering a word here and there, correcting obvious punctuation errors, and changing and adding several references in the margins. His final revised version was not published until twelve years after his death, however. The title page of the fifth edition, 1717, states that the text had been "Corrected and Amended by the Author, in the Year 1703."[10]

With Samuel Green and Marmaduke Johnson, as with the Dayes before them, the small wooden hand press groaned under the relentless necessity of printing those religious and civil documents intended to hold the colony together; therefore, what was not printed in Cambridge becomes as historically important as what was printed there. Unlike the clergy, especially the Mathers (the "great Mather copy-factory," according to critic John T. Winterich), who rushed their sermons into print, the upper-class colonists frowned upon having their writings (especially their poetry) published, thinking it a nasty business, "on a par with the theater, or even lower in social status."[11]

Concerning the writing and printing of verse in seventeenth-century America, Harrison T. Meserole has observed that "there were strictures against too consummate an attention to poetry. 'A little recreation,' asserted Cotton Mather, was a good thing, and one should not contemplate an unpoetical life. But to turn one's mind and energies wholly to the composition of verse was to prostitute one's calling, to risk opprobrium, and most important, to lose sight of the proper balance God envisioned for man on earth."[12] In spite of this, Meserole continues, approximately 250 New Englanders tried their hands at writing poetry. One need only look at the Puritan histories, journals, diaries, and letters to discover a considerable quantity of verse touching on numerous topics. Religion was, unquestionably, the most pervasive subject, yet poets also chose to explore love, Indians, the land, and sea voyages as poetic topics.[13] It is clear that people were not at all hostile to poetry, but enjoyed it thoroughly. Often poets would pass handwritten copies of their verse among family and friends for comment. Broadside elegies on the death of a loved one were also common during this time and were given to mourners as commemorative tokens and gratefully received. As Meserole points out, "It is not really possible to speak of *a* seventeenth-century audience for verse. There were varied audiences, ranging in age from school children to septuagenarians, in occupation from farmers to college presidents, and in size from a single person to whole communities."[14]

If authors wanted their compositions to be read by a wider audience, perhaps by critics and other intellectuals, as was the case with Anne Bradstreet's *The Tenth Muse* (1650), they sent their manuscripts to London to be published. Publishing in London also meant a less expensive and a more aesthetically pleasing final product in terms of typography and paper quality. As late as 1726, Cotton Mather, who had little reason to complain about printing practices in America, remarked in a letter to Thomas Hollis in London: "One reason why your servants the commissioners here did no more to bear the expense of publishing [a Mather treatise] in this country, was not only because it would be very great, much beyond what it would be in London, but also because it would be much better done, and (which may appear a little surprising!) much *sooner* at London than at Boston."[15]

Over more than thirty years the shop at Cambridge ground out an astonishing 157 titles. The demands placed upon it from a rapidly growing and changing population caused Marmaduke Johnson to petition for permission to sever his partnership with Green and move his press across the Charles River to Boston. In May 1674, the General Court "granted that there may be a printing Presse elsewhere then at Cambridge," and with that Johnson set up the first commercial press in America. He died, however, before he could actually begin printing, and ownership of the press went to John Foster. From the moment he established his shop "over against the Sign of the Dove," it was a place of firsts. Not only was his press the first to be free from dependence upon the College, but Foster himself was America's first native-born printer and engraver. Our earliest known woodcut is a portrait of Richard Mather, executed by Foster in 1670. His "Mapp of New England" in William Hubbard's *Narrative of the Troubles with Indians in New-England* (1677) is our first book illustration. In 1676 he published what has been called America's first epic, a poem about America by a native-born American—Benjamin Tompson's *New Englands Crisis. Or a Brief Narrative, of New-Englands Lamentable Estate at present, Compar'd with the former years of Prosperity* . . . (which also seems to have been the first American book to be reprinted in England). The first medical treatise published in America was issued from Foster's press in 1677 as a broadside—*A Brief rule to guide the common people of New-England how to order themselves and theirs in the small pocks, or measles.*

But of all his firsts the most important for students of early American literature is the second edition of Anne Dudley Bradstreet's poems, *The Tenth Muse*

(London, 1650), published by Foster in 1678 with the title page reading: *Several Poems Compiled with great variety of Wit and Learning, full of Delight. . . . By a Gentlewoman in New-England. The Second Edition, Corrected by the Author, and enlarged by an Addition of several other Poems found amongst her Papers after her Death.* This slender volume, published six years after Bradstreet's death, reflects a more mature, polished reading of her poetry. Numerous changes were made in the wording and, in several instances, entire sections were deleted and substituted. Modern textual editors argue convincingly that a number of these alterations may not have been the work of Bradstreet herself but of the talented, loving friends who prepared her manuscripts for publication.[16] In "The Author to her Book," Bradstreet does make clear, however, that she did revise her work. She describes *The Tenth Muse* as the "ill-form'd offspring of [her] feeble brain," her "rambling brat":

> Yet being mine own, at length affection would
> Thy blemishes amend, if so I could:
> I wash'd thy face, but more defects I saw,
> And rubbing off a spot, still made a flaw.
> I stretcht thy joynts to make thee even feet,
> Yet still thou run'st more hobling then is meet;
> In better dress to trim thee was my mind,
> But nought save home-spun Cloth, i' th' house I find. [11–18]

For the six years that John Foster operated his press in Boston until his death in 1681, he produced consistently high quality work from the manuscripts of more New England authors than any other printer in the seventeenth century. Some historians speculate that had Foster lived beyond the age of thirty-three and continued to issue such fine works and engravings, Benjamin Franklin might well not now be known as America's foremost printer but as "the second Foster."

Although out from the shadow of Harvard College, Foster's press, like Green's, was watched by a board of Censors, appointed expressly "For the preventing of Irregularyties and abuse to the authority of this Country, by the Printing Presse." No person or persons, they decreed, shall "presume to print any Copie but by the allowance first had and obtayned under the hands of such as this court shall from tjme to tjme Impower . . . to survey such Copie or Coppies and to prohibit or allow the same according to this order; and in case of non observance of this order, to forfeit the Presse to the Country and be disabled from Vsing any such profession within this Jurisdiction for the tjme to Come. . . ."[17] Thus, the government maintained control over printing well into the eighteenth century. In 1711, for example, perhaps as the result of Cotton Mather's concern that the Church's influence in the colony was weakening, the General Court passed "An Act against Intemperance Immorality and Profaneness and for Reformation of Manners." Fining and pillorying were the swift and sure punishments for anyone caught "composing, writing, printing, or publishing . . . any filthy, obscene, or profane song, pamphlet, libel or mock sermon, in imitation or in mimicking of preaching, or any other part of divine worship."[18] And if such harsh enactments weren't enough to deter some foolhardy printer, a cross word or a dark scowl from the mighty Mathers would.

Few dared tempt such an unhappy fate in Massachusetts Bay until 1686, when a brash, enterprising printer/publishers/bookseller named Benjamin Harris descended upon Boston. By 1690 he drew the wrath of the Censors when he failed to obtain a license to publish the colony's first newspaper. The first issue of *Public Occurrences both Foreign and Domestick* (printed by Richard Pierce), dated 25 September 1690, was also its last. What particularly annoyed the Puritan fathers was not just that Harris had defied their authority but also that one of his articles attempted to undercut the government's uneasy peace with the Narragansetts, and another called into question the morals of French King Louis XIV. Not daunted by this setback, and ever out for the main chance, the flamboyant Harris tried his luck with another publishing venture later that year. This time, with *The New England Primer*, he won.

The idea for the *Primer* did not originate with Harris, but with John Gaine, a noted London printer at the time. Gaine's book, *The New England Primer, or Milk for Babes,* issued in London in 1683, incorporated much of John Cotton's earlier published catechism, *Spiritual Milk for Babes in either England. Drawn out of the Breasts of both Testaments for their Souls Nourishment. But may be of like use to any Children* (1668). Harris's reprint of Gaine's *Primer*, containing his own revisions, became an immediate bestseller. Like the *Bay Psalm Book* and the *Day of Doom* before it, *The New England Primer* was memorized and thumbed to pieces. For decades it formed the very heart and soul of every child's moral and spiritual education, from "In Adam's fall / We sinned all" to "Zaccheus he / Did climb the tree / Our Lord to see." In the century and a half following Harris's original issue, this "Little Bible of New England," as it was often called, sold between six and eight million copies, making it the most read book in colonial America after the Bible.[19]

After publishing numerous almanacs, sermons, religious pamphlets, and civil documents, and after serving one year as the official government printer, Harris apparently decided that Boston was just not city enough for his enthusiastic schemes, so he returned to London where he took up quarreling in print with the likes of Alexander Pope and Jonathan Swift. John Dunton, himself a printer and one-time friend of Harris, characterized the man this way: "He is so far from having any dealings with Truth and Honesty, that his solemn word, which he calls as good as his bond, is a studied falsehood, and he scandalizes Truth and Honesty, in pretending to write for it. . . . [T]here is very little of wit or honesty in him, but what he hath stolen from . . . his own hypocritical heart. His employment, or rather livelihood, is to blast other men's credit, and to steal their copies."[20] John Dunton's assessment notwithstanding, Benjamin Harris's place in the history of publishing in America is secure because he is the last prominent printer of the seventeenth century (without a doubt its most colorful), because he published our first newspaper, and because he compiled and issued a primer that became the wellspring for children's literature in the United States.

As if all this weren't enough, we must also credit Harris with being the seventeenth century's most successful bookseller. By the time he opened shop in 1686 "over against the Old Meeting House in Cornhill," bookselling had already become an integral part of the town's social and intellectual life. Beginning with Hezekiah Usher, who in 1647 was the publisher/bookseller for the *Bay Psalm Book*, nearly all printing was done for the booksellers who, in effect, commissioned a piece, supplied the capital for its publication, and sold it in their bookshops. The indefatigable Cotton Mather often took advantage of this system by "inviting" booksellers or acquaintances—among them John Winthrop, Thomas Bradbury, Thomas Prince, and Mrs. Gurdon Saltonstall—to contribute several pounds toward the publication of his most recent sermon or philosophical treatise. On 15 November 1717, for instance, Mather wrote to John Winthrop: "If you do this poor sermon the honor of passing thro' the press, the sooner the better. (Perhaps Mr. [Eleazar] Philips might order the press which he [is] more particularly master of, to do it out of hand.) . . . This minute [Thomas] Crump (who is Mr. Philips's printer) happens to come unto me upon an errand. And he tells me that if you think fit to have the work done, in a large, fair, decent character (which is all he has unemployed) he will with all his heart immediately go on the service proposed. But I entirely leave all to your descretion."[21] Mather did not see his manuscripts through the press or read proofs (authors rarely did in those days), nor did he expect "royalties." He, like other authors, was content that the work was published and that he could have some gratis copies to distribute.

Booksellers would also use the occasion of a natural disaster, a murder, or the death of an eminent divine to solicit verses from one of the town poets to be published as a broadside for a quick sale and an easy profit. Timeliness was the key to sales, so the verse as well as the typesetting often showed marks of extreme haste; the paper generally was of inferior quality and decorative borders and emblems were ordinary.

For the faithful of New England especially, the bookseller also filled an important social need. The obvious, acceptable gathering place for social chatter and good will was the local bookshop, and many shopkeepers, like the ever-enterprising Benjamin Harris, obtained licenses to sell "Coffee, Tee and Chucaletto."[22] While sipping their drinks, people could browse among shelves crowded with books from London—religious works, primarily psalm books, sermons, catechisms, and occasionally historical, medical, and navigational texts, dictionaries and law books, as well as books from American authors, mostly by the Mathers and their friends. Many of these shops also stocked stationery supplies from England—ink, ink pots, quills, parchment and paper—and advertised for sale such goods as "whalebone, live geese feathers, pickled sturgeon, chocolate, Spanish snuff, &c."[23]

In 1704 Boston booksellers advertised for sale for the first time another most unusual item—a newspaper. Fourteen years after Harris's abortive attempt, Bartholomew Green, who had learned the printing trade from his father at the Cambridge press, published (this time "By Authority") *The Boston News-Letter,* a weekly that appeared on Mondays. Although published by Green, the paper was managed by James Campbell, the local postmaster, and this arrangement continued for an extraordinary eighteen years. Green assumed complete responsibility for the *News-Letter* in 1722. With several changes in name, the paper was continued by Green's successors until 1776 when British troops stormed Boston.

When William Brooker was appointed postmaster for Boston in 1719, he began the publication of America's second successful newspaper in the colonies, *The Boston Gazette,* and engaged James Franklin as his printer. Several months later, however, Philip Musgrave replaced Brooker as postmaster, and Samuel Kneeland replaced Franklin. Encouraged by his friends to begin another newspaper free of the postmaster's (and thus the government's) hand, Franklin issued another weekly in 1721, *The New England Courant.* The short essays he published in imitation of the *Tatler* and *Spectator* quickly drew displeasure from Boston's civil and religious leaders, Cotton Mather not the least among them. Public censure and a month in prison did not turn Franklin away from what the authorities deemed "scandalous libels." He evaded the legislature's order to cease publication by using his younger brother's name on the imprint: "Boston, printed and sold by Benjamin Franklin, in Queen Street, where advertisements are taken in." Not long after James initiated this change in 1723, the younger Franklin took leave of his brother to try life for himself in Philadelphia. The *Courant* continued to be published several years longer under Benjamin's name, but James eventually tired of Boston and removed to Newport, Rhode Island, with his printing equipment. Here he established that colony's first press in 1727, and in 1732 its first newspaper, *The Rhode Island Gazette.*

Nearly forty years before Benjamin Franklin stepped onto the Market street wharf and about the time that Benjamin Harris staked out Boston, printing began in Pennsylvania. William Bradford was among the first emigrants from England, settling in the area in 1682, just one year after William Penn had been granted his charter from King Charles II. About 1685 a press and several fonts arrived from England, and soon afterwards the Quaker Bradford printed *An Almanack for the year of the Christian account 1687,* the earliest known work from a Pennsylvania press.

What Bradford did not have ready access to, however, was paper. Like other printers in America, he ordered his supply through a London agent, most of it coming from the continent, the finest quality coming from Holland. What Bradford sorely needed was a light-weight stock that he could use for almanacs, handbills, forms, and government reports—ideally from a source that would free him from dependence on foreign paper altogether. So, in 1690, with William Rittenhouse and other shrewd young businessmen of Philadelphia, Bradford built America's first papermill on a branch of Wissahickon Creek near Germantown. It served his printing needs and the needs of many other colonial printers who followed in the 109 years of its operation.[24]

It took nearly a century after Stephen and Matthew Daye set up their press in Harvard Yard for the print shop to become a permanent fixture in eight of our colonies—Massachusetts, Pennsylvania, Maryland, New York, Connecticut, Rhode Island, Virginia, and South Carolina. All those who operated the equipment learned early that so long as they acceded to government strictures they remained at peace with local officials. In fact, they seemed generally to occupy a quietly respectable place in the community. We know, for example, little or nothing about approximately twenty of the more than fifty printers who are listed in Charles Evans' *American Bibliography*. It was possible, says Robert Harlan, "to be a printer and obscure": "The printer was not only born and trained into a pattern of conformity; he also worked to retain that image. He was civic-minded, serving as town clerk, or perhaps as a member of the militia. He established diverse interests in the business community. He belonged to the predominant religious sect of his community, even when this called for rapid conversion (William Bradford's conversion to the Anglican church occurred shortly after his arrival in New York). The printer's politics were 'correct' and within the mainsteam."[25]

At the end of this first century of printing, one man did emerge from a comfortable anonymity, this "neutral" place, to challenge the authority of government control over printing and publishing. The German-born John Peter Zenger began his career in 1720–21 in Maryland, moved next to Philadelphia, and finally settled in New York in 1728, where for a short time he apprenticed to William Bradford. He was neither an extraordinarily gifted craftsman nor a likely hero, but the country's attention focused on him in 1733 when he was summarily jailed by action of Governor William Cosby and his council. The charge against him was "printing and publishing several seditious libels" in his newspaper, *The New-York Weekly Journal*. Zenger was acquitted by a jury.[27]

From the moment that Jose Glover's wooden hand press printed "The Freeman's Oath" in 1638, religious leaders of Massachusetts Bay understood the role of the press in enlightening and shaping the public mind. The fact that for nearly forty years all printing was done under the scrutiny of the Board of Censors is testimony to the press's powerful influence. Of the more than three hundred works published in Boston and Cambridge between 1638 and 1738, approximately seventy percent were sermons and other religious readings; the remaining thirty percent were largely laws, proclamations, almanacs, and non-religious pamphlets. Unquestionably, those works that supported and explained the faith of the good people of New England became the era's best sellers. Whatever they may have lacked in typographical appearance and paper quality, they clearly made up for in their timeliness of expression and usefulness to the daily lives of the colonists. Not just in New England, either, but in the colonies to the south as well, the printing press provided the cultural, intellectual, civil and religious foundation for the rapidly growing and expanding country. Despite its modest (some would argue crude) beginnings, the press profoundly shaped the progress of colonial affairs and had a far-reaching influence in the continued development and spread of new ideas.

NOTES

1. From an anonymous pamphlet entitled *New England's First Fruits* (1643), quoted in Samuel Eliot Morison's *Builders of the Bay Colony* (Boston: Houghton Mifflin, 1958), p. 188.

2. Quoted in John Tebbel, *A History of Book Publishing in the United States.* Vol. I: *The Creation of an Industry, 1630–1865* (New York: Bowker, 1972), p. 5.

3. For the printing history of the *Bay Psalm Book,* see George Parker Winship's *The Cambridge Press, 1638–1692* (Philadelphia: Univ. of Pennsylvania Press, 1945), pp. 22–23.

4. Between 1620 and 1640, eighty-eight editions of the Bible were in print, six separate prose editions of Psalms, and 135 editions of a metrical version of the Psalms; ibid., p. 23.

5. Jantz quotes these lines in his *First Century*, p. 21, from a scrap of paper in Increase Mather's handwriting.

6. (New York: G. P. Putnam's Sons, 1879), I, 276.

7. Green died in 1702 at the age of 86, leaving behind him, as one scholar put it, "the guarantee in his sons and their descendants that the art of printing which he had learned from such an unpromising beginning, would be carried on in his name." Timothy, Bartholomew, and Samuel, Jr. learned printing early on at their father's Cambridge press and passed that knowledge on to their sons. See Tebbel, *History of Book Publishing,* p. 21.

8. See Ola Winslow's *John Eliot "Apostle to the Indians"* (Boston: Houghton Mifflin, 1968), especially chapter 11, "The Indian Bible," pp. 137–47.

9. *No Featherbed to Heaven: A Biography of Michael Wigglesworth, 1631–1705* (Ann Arbor: Michigan State Univ. Press, 1962), p. 121.

10. Ibid., 259.

11. Tebbel, *History of Book Publishing,* p. 15.

12. Meserole, *Poetry,* p. xviii.

13. Ibid., p. xx.

14. Ibid., p. xxi.

15. Kenneth Silverman, ed., *Selected Letters of Cotton Mather* (Baton Rouge: Louisiana State Univ. Press, 1971), p. 412.

16. Bradstreet, McElrath and Robb.

17. By order of the General Court of Massachusetts, 19 October 1664; quoted in Isaiah Thomas's *The History of Printing in America,* 2nd ed. (Albany NY: Joel Munsell, 1874), I, 58–59.

18. Robert D. Harlan takes up the issues involved in the censorship of colonial presses in his *The Colonial Printer: Two Views* (San Marino, CA: William Andrews Memorial Library, 1978). It seems that printing and publishing in Massachusetts were not entirely free of government controls until about 1755.

19. See Charles F. Heartman's *The New-England Primer Issued Prior to 1830* (New York: Bowker, 1934).

20. *The Life and Errors of John Dunton, Citizen of London* (New York: Burt Franklin, 1969), II, 465–66.

21. Silverman, *Selected Letters of Cotton Mather,* pp. 236–37.

22. One of the best studies of the booksellers trade is Worthington Chauncey Ford's *The Boston Book Market, 1679–1700* (Boston: The Club of Odd Volumes, 1917).

23. Thomas, *History of Printing,* I, 227.

24. The history of papermaking in America is well-documented. The best sources are Lyman Horace Weeks's *History of Paper-Manufacturing in the United States, 1690–1916* (New York: The Lockwood Trade Journal Co., 1916), Dard Hunter's *Papermaking in Pioneer America* (Philadelphia: Univ. of Pennsylvania Press, 1952), and George E. Miller and Thomas L. Gravell's *A Catalogue of American Watermarks, 1690–1835* (New York: Garland, 1979).

25. Harlan, *The Colonial Printer,* pp. 27, 28.

26. John T. Winterich, *Early American Books & Printing* (Boston: Houghton Mifflin, 1935), p. 98.

27. For a detailed account of these proceedings, see Livingston Rutherfurd's *John Peter Zenger: His Press, His Trial, and a Bibliography of Zenger Imprints* (New York: Dodd, Mead & Co., 1904).

2 PURITAN WOMEN POETS IN AMERICA

PATTIE COWELL

Cotton Mather remarked as early as 1712 that many New England women "have wrote such things as have been very valuable; especially relating to their own experiences." But even in Mather's day, most such works were unknown, a situation he explained by pointing to the circumspect behavior of the writers themselves: "they have been patterns of humility. They have made no noise; they have sought no fame. . . ."[1] Puritan women in seventeenth-century New England left no sermons or histories, no public tracts in which we may explore their lives and concerns. With the important exception of Anne Bradstreet (who was first published without her knowledge), their writings were private, for themselves or for a limited audience of family and friends.

Though it was not a public poetry, the verse of Puritan women proves intriguing for many of the same reasons as the more public work of their male contemporaries: for an exploration of a people experiencing a new world, for the revelation of individual attitudes and struggles, for the adaptation of verse to religious ends. Although the poetry varies enormously in quality, even the lesser works present something of the complex environment which has made Puritan culture so fascinating. This survey of eleven early New England women poets—Anne Bradstreet (1612?–1672), Anna Hayden (1648–post 1720), Sarah Knight (1666–1727), Mary English (1652?–1694), Sarah Goodhue (1641–1681), Grace Smith (fl. 1712), Mercy Wheeler (1706–post 1733), Abigail Colman Dennie (1715–1745), Susanna Rogers (b. 1711?), Mary French (fl. 1703), and Jane Turell (1708–1735)—will explore both their cultural environment and their verse. Perhaps our investigation will allow some of them to break the "patterns of humility" they have maintained for so long.

THE MATERIALS OF VERSE

Seventeenth-century New Englanders found themselves on the frontier. For some the shock was enormous. Anne Bradstreet's memoir for her children recalled that her first view of America discovered "a new world and new manners, at which [her] heart rose." But Bradstreet's rebellion was soon quelled by force of will: "after [she] was convinced it was the way of God, [she] submitted to it and joined to the church at Boston."[2] Others may have found such submission more difficult. One wonders, for example, if Dorothy Bradford's death by falling (jumping?) overboard from the *Mayflower* was occasioned by her spending six weeks looking at the barren sand dunes of Cape Cod, meditating on the infant son she had left behind. One can only imagine how Margaret Winthrop received her husband's first letters from Massachusetts Bay Colony, with their typical refrain: "be not discouraged (my dear wife) by anything thou shalt hear from hence, for I see no cause to repent of our coming hither. . . ."[3] The material conditions under which Puritan women lived, their faith and doubts, their education or lack of it, and their status bear direct relation to their verse, for the verse of Puritan women, like that of other cultures, was shaped by its environment. How did the "new world" appear to Puritan women? What sacrifices were made, what opportunities created as they adapted to New England?

The popular proverb "Houses where no women be are like deserts or untilled land"[4] reflected the value of a woman-centered family to the English colonists.[5] New economic and legal conditions for women mark one measure of that value. Labor shortages opened areas of employment outside the home, and women who continued to work at home (as most did) found recognition for the economic value of their work. Existing sex ratios—more men than women—in the early settlements further increased the economic status of women. Perhaps as a result of these forces, legal protections for women were strengthened.[6] Marriage contracts, for example, were viewed under colonial law as reciprocal agreements which carried enforceable obligations for both husband and wife. Furthermore, it became legal in many of the colonies for a woman to make prenuptial contracts or trust arrangements that would preserve her rights to her property even after marriage. Though the Puritans imported a patriarchy as part of their cultural baggage, Puritan women were accorded a status unknown to their British counterparts, or to their eighteenth-century successors for that matter.

Supplementing such economic and legal advantages, the religious base of Puritan culture assured women of at least spiritual equality with men. However temporal roles might differ, piety's requirements applied to all: the isolation, even loneliness, of the Puritan relation to God exacted the same minute soul-searching of women as of men. The risks and the rewards were identical. To a degree, Puritan theology even extended this spiritual status to women's roles in marriage. Some discussions of Puritan marriage—not all, of course, emphasized mutuality rather than hierarchy. William Secker's often reprinted sermon *A Wedding Ring Fit for the Finger* (1658), for example, described Eve as "a parallel line drawn equal" with Adam and suggested that relationship as a model for readers. Samuel Willard's *Compleat Body of Divinity* (1726) eschews Secker's argument by analogy for a more direct statement: "of all the orders which are unequals, [husbands and wives] do come nearest to an equality, and in several respects they stand upon even ground. These do make a pair, which infers so far a parity."

These theoretical statements regarding the status of Puritan women provide only limited insight into the "new world" available to them, however. The "promised land" was not so easily obtained for women: the practical business of daily life continually reminded them of their "place" in the patriarchy and in God's temporal providence. The economic opportunities outlined above disappeared as the population increased. Legal rights were seldom invoked because few women were informed about them. Political rights for women were almost totally absent from the beginnings of settlement. Even spiritual equality proved more elusive than Puritan theology might indicate. Samuel Willard, for example, tempered his discussion of women in the family. For the sake of stability, he argued, "God hath . . . made an imparity between [husband and wife], in the order prescribed in His Word." For women, the "new world" was perhaps not so new.

Such material and spiritual conditions affected all Puritan women, regardless of class. But one additional factor particularly important for women poets bore direct relation to class as well as to gender: education. Though New England established a public school system in the seventeenth century, girls seldom had access equal to that of boys. Initially, girls could attend only during the summer when boys were doing field work. And when they did attend, they were offered a substantially different curriculum than boys, one which prepared them only for the tasks of domestic economy. Cotton Mather's *Ornaments for the Daughters of Zion* (1692) outlined the essential education of a Puritan girl:

> Such is her industry, that she betimes applies herself to learn all the affairs of housewifry, and besides a good skill at her needle, as well as in the kitchen, she acquaints her self with arithmetic and accomptantship, [perhaps also chirugery] and such other arts relating to business, as may enable her to do the man whom she may hereafter have, good and not evil all the days of her life.[7]

Women's education changed little from Mather's prescription until late in the eighteenth century when theorists like Benjamin Rush and Judith Sargent Murray openly argued that women's intellectual inferiority was more a function of education than of biology.

Several women poets were atypical cases: they obtained unusually extensive educations. Before emigrating to Massachusetts, Anne Bradstreet had access to private tutors and to the library of the Earl of Lincoln, for whom her father worked. Jane Turell and Abigail Dennie, daughters of the Reverend Benjamin Colman of Boston's Brattle Street Church, were carefully educated by their father. He participated in a regular epistolary exchange with Jane as a method of encouraging her writing, responding with warm praise, for example, to an early poem she had written: "Joy of my life! is this thy lovely voice? / Sing on, and a fond father's heart rejoice."[8] In addition to such family-based educational opportunities, Sarah Knight's mercantile activities and Mary English's marriage to well-to-do merchant Philip English gave them at least access to the books and leisure essential to a literary education.

There were, however, some pressures from which even the fortunes of class could not protect Puritan women poets. Women who chose to pursue literary avocations took considerable social risk. They might recall the case of Anne Yale Hopkins, who "had written many books," none of which survive, but who was reported by John Winthrop to have "fallen into a sad infirmity, the loss of her understanding and reason." Winthrop's journal entry for April 13, 1645, concluded that

> if she had attended her household affairs, and such things as belong to women, and not gone out of her way and calling to meddle in such things as are proper for men, whose minds are stronger, etc., she had kept her wits, and might have improved them usefully and honorably in the place God had set her.[9]

Literary women who did not fear for their reason might well have feared for their reputations. Thomas Parker, minister of Newbury, Massachusetts, probably spoke for his culture when he published an open letter to his sister, Elizabeth Avery, in England on the occasion of her book's publication: "Your printing of a book, beyond the custom of your sex, doth rankly smell."[10] Small wonder that not one Puritan woman poet voluntarily published her work.

Such attitudes openly and frequently expressed by community leaders must have created a strong deterrent to women writers, a deterrent probably reinforced by their own internalized sense of limited potential. How were literate women to respond to Edward Johnson's veiled allusion to Anne Hutchinson which contrasted "silly women laden with diverse lusts" and "those [men] honoured of Christ, induced with power and authority from him to preach . . ."?[11] How many encountered Nathaniel Ward's suggestion that women of fashion wore "drailes [long, trailing headdresses] on the hinder part of their heads" because they had "nothing . . . in the fore-part, but a few squirrels brains to help them frisk from one ill-favour'd fashion to another"?[12] How might women poets have reacted on reading Ward's "commendatory poem" at the publication of Anne Bradstreet's *Tenth Muse, Lately Sprung Up in America* (1650): "It half revives my chill frost-bitten blood, / To see a woman once, do ought that's good . . ."? Given such an audience, it is no surprise that even Bradstreet's fine collection of poems acknowledged in "The Prologue" that "Men can do best, and women know it well"; Bradstreet asked only "some small acknowledgement" for herself.[13]

THE VERSE

The networks of women poets that were to develop in eighteenth-century Boston and Philadelphia were unavailable to earlier generations. Despite what seems today like close geographic proximity, Puritan women poets were isolated figures, isolated from one another and from an audience beyond immediate family and friends. Some common features of their verse can be observed, of course: most adopted conventional poetic modes—elegy, acrostic, anagram, hymn, biblical paraphrase, invocation, quaternion, dialogue, various types of occasional pieces. Most developed religious themes. But it is as individuals that these poets' contributions must be weighed. Though Puritan women poets shared a great deal by the accidents of time, place, and gender, their work is not monolithic, nor are their skills as poets.

The most talented and prolific woman poet in seventeenth-century New England was, of course, Anne Bradstreet. Two editions of Bradstreet's poems circulated in early New England: *The Tenth Muse, Lately Sprung Up in America* . . . (London, 1650), containing her early quaternions, elegies and dialogues, and *Several Poems, Compiled with great variety of Wit and Learning, full of Delight* . . . (Boston, 1678), a much revised and expanded second edition. Many of the later poems moved away from the public themes of the 1650 edition to private themes of illness and health, of childbirth and the deaths of children, of love for her husband and gratitude to her father, of faith and the questions it raised. Her long poem "In reference to her Children, 23 June 1656," for example, detailed the complex responsibilities and joys of raising eight children to adulthood:

> O would my young, ye saw my breast,
> And knew what thoughts there sadly rest,
> Great was my pain when I you bred,
> Great was my care, when I you fed,
> Long did I keep you soft and warm,
> And with my wings kept off all harm,
>
> . . . .
> You had a Dam that lov'd you well,
> That did what could be done for young,
> And nurst you up till you were strong,
> And 'fore she once would let you fly,
> She shew'd you joy and misery;
> Taught what was good, and what was ill,
> What would save life, and what would kill? [p. 181]

Disdaining temptations "to sing of wars, of captains, and of kings," Anne Bradstreet sought in her mature poems to avoid "encroaching upon others conceptions, because [she] would leave [her children] nothing but [her] own."

Whether Bradstreet's work inspired other Puritan women to write is difficult to determine, but her verse circulated in New England well into the eighteenth century.[14] Her poems had such continued appeal that a reprint of *Several Poems* appeared in 1758. A handful of eighteenth-century verses suggests Bradstreet's direct influence, and if other Puritan women achieved neither her skill nor her audience, surely they were emboldened by her example.

Nine such women poets may be discussed as a group because their extant works are so few. Anna Hayden left two poems; Sarah Knight left a half dozen, all but one of them in her well-known *Journal*. From each of the others, only a single poem remains. For the most part, the verse of these Puritan women is patterned on conventional seventeenth-century genres and rooted in religious and domestic duty. Mary English of Salem, Massachusetts, for example, wrote an acrostic prayer on her own name.[15] Anna Hayden of Braintree, Massachusetts, produced two rough elegies, one of them to her brother, poet Benjamin Tompson.[16] Worried that she would not survive the delivery of her ninth child, Sara Goodhue of Ipswich, Massachusetts, prepared her family for her death: "O dear heart," she wrote to her husband, "if I must leave thee and thine here behind, / Of my natural affection here is my heart and hand."[17] She was right to prepare: she delivered twins but died herself, as the title page of her *Valedictory and Monitory Writing* (1681) records. Grace Smith of Eastham, Massachusetts, offered similar comforts to her family in *The Dying Mother's Legacy* (1712), seeking to provide "a perpetual monitor" for their spiritual behavior:

> My children dear, whom I did bear;
> O lend your ear to my instructions:
> [Let] not vain toys nor worldly joys
> Shut out these my directions. . . .

Mercy Wheeler of Plainfield, Connecticut, also spoke from her deathbed, but having no children of her own, she took a larger audience and made *An Address to Young People, Or . . . Warning from the Dead* (1733). These deathbed pieces contain only a few lines of verse, their authors and/or transcribers preferring to cast the bulk of the message in prose.

Beyond these themes of religion and family, however, early New England women poets sometimes recorded vignettes of their lives and culture. Sarah Knight's travelogue of her horseback journey from Boston to New York in 1704 is a well-known example.[18] Her occasional verses discarded religious interpretation of her experiences in favor of simple descriptions of events and people. She cursed a slovenly innkeeper:

> May all that dread the cruel fiend of night
> Keep on, and not at this curs't mansion light.
> 'Tis Hell; 'tis Hell! and devils here do dwell. . . .

She berated a group of noisy drunkards:

> I ask thy aid, O potent rum!
> To charm these wrangling topers dumb.
> Thou hast their giddy brains possest—
> The man confounded with the beast—
> And I, poor I, can get no rest.

And she cast a sympathetic glance at the incredible poverty she found among rural settlers:

> These indigents have hunger with their ease;
> Their best is worse behalf than my disease.

If Sarah Knight presents a moving example of back-country hunger and struggle, some Puritan women provide equally painful glances (seldom more) at their own lives. The story of Benjamin Colman's rebellious daughter, Abigail ("Celia"), is suggested in a verse letter she wrote to her sister, Jane Turell, in 1733.[19] An an eighteen-year-old runaway from her parents' home, she confided in her older sister:

> To you alone I venture to complain;
> From others hourly strive to hide my pain.
> But Celia's face dissembles what she feels,
> Affected looks her inward pain conceal.
> She sings, she dresses and she talks and smiles,
> But these are all spectators to beguile.

Financial difficulty forced Abigail Colman back into her father's household in 1734, but her verses clarify the heavy psychological toll of that loss of autonomy.

Other Puritan women detailed more public griefs. Susanna Rogers' lament for her slain fiance, Jonathan Frye, killed in 1725 during a skirmish with Indians in Maine, sought to celebrate Frye's bravery and to comfort his parents, but it reminds us as well of her personal loss.[20] Mary French's verse summary of Puritan precepts was written from captivity.[21] Taken prisoner by Indians in 1703 during a raid on Deerfield, Massachusetts, and held by the French in Canada, she wrote a spiritual message for her sister, also in captivity and apparently under pressure to convert to Catholicism:

> Many there fell by bloody rage,
>   When we were left behind.
> Let us be silent then this day
>   Under our smarting rod.
> Let us with patience meekly say,
>   It is the will of God.

That final line was a frequent motif for Puritan verse, a motif further elaborated by the only woman other than Anne Bradstreet to leave a substantial body of poetry: Jane Colman Turell.[22] If much of her verse is conventionally religious, Turell's extant work suggests, nevertheless, a wide range of poetic interests and a remarkable skill. Like Bradstreet, Turell began writing very early; almost from infancy she acquired a local reputation as a prodigy. Benjamin Colman's paternal concern for her education created an environment in which she learned by her second birthday to "speak distinctly, knew her letters, and could relate many stories out of the Scriptures."[23] Chronic ill health, inclining her to sedentary activities, led her to supplement her father's instruction with wide reading. Access to Colman's large library enabled her to explore works of theology, history, and literature, an avocation for which (as her husband later remarked) "the leisure of the day did not suffice, but she spent whole nights in reading" (p. 78).

To practice her writing skills, Turell developed a regular correspondence with her father. Their epistolary dialogue frequently involved the exchange of verses, the earliest of which was apparently a hymn she had written before her tenth birthday. Throughout her life, Turell submitted samples of her verse to Colman for "correction." Perhaps sensing his daughter's overwhelming need for his approval, he mingled criticism with praise: "Nor be discourag'd [by my corrections], but instructed," he wrote in a 1725 letter to his daughter; "it is your learning time, and I am not asham'd of my pupil" (p. 71). Until her marriage, and perhaps even after, Colman was the most influential member of his daughter's small audience.

That audience grew by one in 1726 when Jane Colman married her father's theology student, the Reverent Ebenezer Turell of Medford, Massachusetts. Their marriage resulted in four children, none of whom reached adulthood. The physical strain of repeated childbearing for one whose health had never been strong, coupled with grief at her children's early deaths, produced one of Turell's most moving poems, her ["Lines on Childbirth"]:

> Thrice in my womb I've found the pleasing strife,
> In the first struggles of my infants life:
> But O how soon by Heaven I'm call'd to mourn,
> While from my womb a lifeless babe is torn. . . . [p. 103, ll. 5–8]

After her marriage, despite the new duties involved in running a household and maintaining the social obligations of a minister's wife, Jane Turell continued her regular writing habits. Her husband noted that she kept to a daily reading program and "once in a month or two" undertook "some new essay in verse or prose" (p. 79). Much of that work remained among her private papers at her death, forming the principal source for Ebenezer Turell's *Memoirs of the Life and Death of . . . Mrs. Jane Turell*, signatured with Benjamin Colman's *Reliquiae Turellae, et Lachrymae Paternae . . .* (1735). Until that posthumous publication of selected poems, letters, and daily excerpts, Turell's audience had been limited to friends and family, from whom she apparently received much encouragement. The Reverend John Adams' "Epistle to . . . Mr. Ebenezer Turell, Occasioned by the Death of His Late Virtuous Consort" spoke for Turell's friends: "Few were her words, but chose [chosen; well-chosen?] and weighty too, / We could not blame, but griev'd they were so few."

Despite so favorable a reception among friends, Turell never risked the "blame" of a larger audience. Only those works which her husband Ebenezer chose to include in his *Memoirs* were ever published. The mass of books and manuscripts that he carefully preserved was apparently dispersed in the nineteenth century, leaving only a small body of her work. And from that body, Ebenezer Turell had deliberately omitted her "pieces of wit and humor, which if publish'd would give a brighter idea of her to some sort of readers" because in his judgment "her heart was set upon graver and better subjects, and her pen much oftener employ'd about them" (p. 86). Paraphrases of the psalms and canticles, presumably the works most likely to please her father and husband, make up fully a quarter of the published poems. Even Turell's poem on her mother's death touched only briefly on her grief: "Ah dearest, tenderest parent! must I mourn, / My heavy loss." Instead her emphasis was conventionally didactic, on death's lesson for the living: "O quickening spirit! now perform thy part, / Set up thy glorious kingdom in my heart . . ." (p. 105). As a consequence of Ebenezer's censorship, Turell's moral preoccupations dominate her extant work.

Yet, despite religious concerns that sometimes (by Ebenezer's account) bordered on fanaticism, Jane Turell demonstrated an uncommon devotion to poetry for its "rich ideas, great and unconfin'd" (p. 74). She was, after all, the product of an extensive classical education as well as the daughter of a clergyman, and her verse only partially reflected conventional Puritan themes. Early neoclassical influences pervade the couplets she favors and the non-religious themes she explores, themes of rural living, local affairs, grief, personal ambition, and praise for other poets. She occasionally invoked her Muse as well as her Maker:

> Come gentle Muse, and once more lend thine aid,
> O bring thy succor to a humble maid!
> . . . .
> Instruct me in those secret arts that lie
> Unseen to all but to a Poet's eye. [p. 74, ll. 1–2, 11–12]

Her literary goals were hardly modest.

And neither were her personal goals. Ebenezer Turell's *Memoirs* noted that "she was sometimes fir'd with a laudable ambition of raising the honor of her sex, who are therefore under obligations to her . . ." (p. 78). Poems which openly acknowledge that ambition are interspersed among poems of happy domesticity. Writing from Medford to her father in Boston, for example, Turell issued "An Invitation into the Country, in Imitation of Horace."

> Though my small incomes never can afford,
> Like wealthy Celsus to regale a Lord;
> No ivory tables groan beneath the weight
> Of sumptuous dishes, serv'd in massy plate:
> . . . .

> But though rich dainties never spread my board,
> Nor my cool vaults Calabrian wines afford;
> Yet what is neat and wholesome I can spread,
> My good fat bacon, and our homely bread,
> With which my healthful family is fed. . . .
> . . . .
> This I can give, and if you'll here repair,
> To slake your thirst a cask of autumn beer,
> Reserv'd on purpose for your drinking here.
> 　　　　　　　[pp. 84–85, ll. 11–14, 33–37, 44–46]

Though Turell invoked conventional pastoral themes, the images of frontier living are realistic and personal. Significantly, nowhere in the sixty-four-line poem does she suggest to her father any enticements outside the traditional feminine sphere. Food, drink, bed—these she offers, but never conversation, companionship, or poetry.

Her poems of aspiration form a sharp contrast to such scenes of domesticity. Apparently the Reverend John Adams had overlooked these pieces, since he noted as a mark of virtue that Turell was "free from ambition." But careful readers learn otherwise: at seventeen, Turell had written to her father that she strove to ". . . raise / Her song to some exalted pitch of praise" (p. 66). She pleaded with her muse to let her participate fully in the poet's experience:

> O let me burn with Sappho's noble fire,
> But not like her for faithless man expire.
> And let me rival great Orinda's fame,
> Or like sweet Philomela's be my name.
> Go lead the way, my muse, nor must you stop,
> 'Till we gave gain'd Parnassus shady top:
> 'Till I have view'd those fragrant soft retreats,
> Those fields of bliss, the muses sacred seats.
> I'll then devote thee to fair virtues fame,
> And so be worthy of a poet's name. [p. 75, ll. 13–22]

Interestingly, the models Turell lists here are all women: Sappho, Katherine Philips (the "matchless Orinda"), and Elizabeth Singer Rowe ("Philomela"). The importance of female models is further emphasized in her sonnet "On Reading the Warning by Mrs. Singer":

> Surpris'd I view, wrote by a female pen,
> Such a grave warning to the sons of men.
> Bold was the attempt and worthy of your lays. . . . [p. 73, ll. 1–3]

That other women could write, and write boldly, was at least part of Turell's inspiration. The pleasure with which she read women poets perhaps hints at the terrible loneliness of the attempt to balance cultural expectations with literary pursuits.

Jane Turell and Anne Bradstreet articulate most directly the desire of many Puritan women to grasp "a poets pen" without suffering the lash of "each carping tongue."[24] Women's poems of distress, of ambition, of travel, of frustration, of family provide us with materials for expanding our narrow views of Puritan poetry. Additionally, the work of these eleven women may explain in part the increasing numbers of women poets in eighteenth-century America; they may have made literary pursuits easier for their immediate successors, for poets Sarah Moorhead, Martha Brewster, Mercy Warren, Judith Murray, and others. It is impossible to be sure, of course; records of the reading of eighteenth-century women poets and of book sales and circulation are woefully inadequate. But the number of women poets increased as the Revolution approached, and one may not be far afield in suggesting that Puritan women poets provided an impetus. Even Jane Turell, for all her "timorous" temper, undertook her writing boldly: "O let me burn with Sappho's noble fire. . . . / And so be worthy of a poet's name." Later poets must have found the example, if not the verse, hard to ignore.

NOTES

1. Cotton Mather, *Awakening Thoughts on the Sleep of Death* (Boston: Timothy Green, 1712), pp. iii–iv. All quotations have been presented with modern English usage as to capitalization, spelling, and typography.

2. Bradstreet, Ellis, p. 5.

3. John Winthrop to Margaret Winthrop, July 23, 1630, in *Letters from New England: The Massachusetts Bay Colony, 1629–1638*, ed. Everett Emerson (Amherst: University of Massachusetts Press, 1976), p. 46.

4. Quoted in Roger Thompson, *Women in Stuart England and America: A Comparative Study* (Boston: Routledge and Kegan Paul, 1974), p. 10.

5. Extended discussion of Puritan family life and patterns of family governance are available in Morgan, *Family*; Levin L. Schücking, *The Puritan Family* (1964; trans. New York: Schocken, 1970); and John Demos, *A Little Commonwealth: Family Life in Plymouth Colony* (New York: Oxford University Press, 1970).

6. Richard Morris, "Women's Rights in Early American Law," *Studies in the History of American Law* (New York: Columbia University Press, 1930), pp. 126–200.

7. Cotton Mather, *Ornaments for the Daughters of Zion* (Delmar, N.Y.: Scholars' Facsimiles & Reprints, 1978), p. 83. This facsimile reprints the third edition (1741).

8. Benjamin Colman, *Reliquiae Turellae, et Lachrymae Paternae . . . : Two Sermons Preach'd at Medford, April 6, 1735. . . . To Which Are Added Some Large Memoirs of Her Life and Death, by Her Consort, the Reverend Mr. Ebenezer Turell. . . .* (Boston:

S. Kneeland and T. Green for J. Edwards and H. Foster, 1735), p. 64. Ebenezer Turell's *Memoirs* are available in facsimile in *The Poems of Jane Turell and Martha Brewster* (Delmar, N.Y.: Scholars' Facsimiles & Reprints, 1979).

9. John Winthrop, *The History of New England from 1630–1649*, ed. James Savage (Boston: Little, Brown and Co., 1853), II, 265–66.

10. Thomas Parker, *The Copy of a Letter Written by Mr. Thomas Parker . . . to His Sister, Mrs. Elizabeth Avery . . . Touching Sundry Opinions by Her Professed and Maintained, November 22, 1649* (London: John Field, 1650), p. 13.

11. Edward Johnson, *Wonder-Working Providence of Sions Savior in New England, 1628–1651*, ed. J. Franklin Jameson (1910; rpt. New York: Barnes and Noble, 1959), p. 28.

12. Nathaniel Ward, *The Simple Cobler of Aggawam in America*, ed. P. M. Zall (Lincoln: University of Nebraska Press, 1969), p. 26.

13. Bradstreet, Ellis, p. 85. All textual references are to this edition.

14. Pattie Cowell, "The Early Distribution of Anne Bradstreet's Poems," *Critical Essays on Anne Bradstreet*, eds. Pattie Cowell and Ann Stanford (Boston: G. K. Hall, 1983), pp. 270–79.

15. Mary English, [Acrostic], in George F. Chever, "A Sketch of Philip English . . . ," *Essex Institute Historical Collections*, 1 (1859), 164.

16. Anna Hayden, "Upon the Death of . . . Elizabeth Tompson" and "Verses on Benjamin Tompson," Murdock, *Paul*, pp. 6–7, 20–22.

17. Sarah Goodhue, *The Copy of a Valedictory and Monitory Writing . . .* (Cambridge, Mass.: James Allen, 1681), p. 7.

18. Sarah Knight, *The Journal of Madam Knight* (New York: Garrett Press, 1970), pp. 19–24.

19. Abigail Dennie, ["Lines by Mrs. Abigail Dennie"], *NEHGR*, 14 (April 1860), 170.

20. Susanna Rogers, "The Mournful Elegy of Mr. Jona[than] Frye, 1725," *NEHGR*, 15 (January 1861), 91.

21. Mary French, ["A Poem Written by a Captive Damsel . . ."], in *Good Fetch'd Out of Evil . . .* , ed. Cotton Mather ([Boston: n.p., 1706]; rpt. [Boston]: n.p., 1783), p. 24.

22. This material on Jane Turell is adapted from a longer essay—Pattie Cowell, "Jane Colman Turell: 'A Double Birth,' " *13th Moon*, IV, 1(n.d.), 59–70—by permission of the publisher.

23. Ebenezer Turell, *Memoirs of . . . Mrs. Jane Turell*, signatured with *Colman, Reliquiae Turellae . . .* , p. 61. All subsequent page references to this volume are in the text.

24. Bradstreet, Ellis, p. 101.

3 RELIGION IN PURITAN POETRY: THE DOCTRINE OF ACCOMMODATION

MASON I. LOWANCE, JR.

Perry Miller most clearly articulated the popular conception of Puritan poetry as didactic, theological verse. In his well-known introduction to the anthology he produced with Thomas Johnson in 1938, he argued:

> At no point does the literary thought of the Puritans reflect the trend of the times more exactly than in their views of poetry. When Milton, searching for a worthy epic theme, finally chose to write on the fall of man, he was himself but following a trail that had been already blazed. Davenant had said that poetry "is as all good Arts subservient to Religion," and Abraham Cowley, greatly admired for his learning, had begun *Davideis,* a sacred epic. The famous preface to Cowley's *Poems* remarks that "he who can write a *prophane Poem well* may write a *Divine one better.*" Puritans were agreed that subjects other than moral and divine were unworthy of serious treatment. It was as inheritors of the Renaissance and of the metaphysicals that Puritans conceived of poetry as a learning or a moral philosophy directed toward the highest ends within the conception of man; and believing such, they viewed mere versifying as a pleasant accomplishment for leisure hours. The Puritans who compiled the *Bay Psalm Book* saying that "God's altar needs not our polishing"; the men who "attended Conscience rather then Elegance, fidelity rather then poetry," were in part tacitly acknowledging their inadequacy as poets, not belittling the power of verse—into which, after all, they were fashioning their thoughts. . . . Thoughtful Puritans essayed verses often enough, and recommended poetic composition as good training for the young. . . .[1]

Miller's assessment may appear to be excessive, but he had good reason for reaching such absolute conclusions. In the expressions of critical theory found in Puritan New England there are many direct statements to support Miller's comprehensive view, the best known of which is Cotton Mather's long essay on poetry that he delivered at Harvard in 1726, *Manuductio ad Ministerium*. In this disjunctive piece, Mather warns:

I proceed now to say that if (under the guidance of a Vida) you try your young wings now and then to see what flights you can make, at least for an epigram, it may a little sharpen your sense and polish your style for more important performances. . . . All your days make a little recreation of poetry in the midst of your more painful studies. Nevertheless, I cannot but advise you, "Withhold thy throat from thirst." Be not so set upon poetry as to be always poring on the passionate and measured pages. Let not what should be sauce rather than food for you engross all your application. Beware of a boundless and sickly appetite for the reading of the poems, which now the rickety nation swarms withal; and let not the Circean cup intoxicate you. But especially preserve the chastity of your soul from the dangers you may incur by a conversation with muses that are no better than harlots. . . .[2]

And throughout his *Psalterium Americanum* (Boston, 1718), Cotton Mather defends the rhythm and meter of each verse by developing the association between poetic expression and the didactic purposes of prose writing. For example, in his discussion of Psalm 1, he remarks "Behold the *Psalter*, beginning like the *Sermon* of our Saviour, with a Discourse on the Supreme and Final Happiness of Man." It is therefore little wonder that Perry Miller would conclude his discussion of Puritan poetry by asserting that,

It is as writers of prose that the Puritans' literary art finally must be judged. Prose was the vehicle for their finest thoughts; it was the one by which they assisted a whole people to a realization of the powerful idiom at hand for all men to use. . . . The problem of poetic composition seldom absorbed their attention, but in so far as they were gentlemen trained in the manners of their day they were alert to the changes of taste, and adapted themselves, especially in the later Puritan era, to the current modes. Prose, on the other hand, was the vehicle for their ripest thoughts and their deepest emotions. A flat, awkward, cumbrous style is rarely encountered in their treatises or sermons; the color of their rhetoric was absorbed from the world they knew about them. . . . The Puritans more than others shaped that learning and enthusiasm to the idiom of language with a clarity, directness, grace, and freedom from eccentricity that rendered incalculable service to English prose.[3]

Miller's views are reinforced by other modern readers, like Kenneth B. Murdock, whose *Literature and Theology in Colonial New England,* originally a series of lectures, has done much to disseminate the view that all Puritan poetry and prose eschewed aesthetic style for a rigorous expression of truth:

The real power of a piece of writing came not so much from the pleasure it provided as from the truth it contained. Nevertheless, the Puritans were forced to grope for their theory of literature, and constantly one feels in Puritan literature a conflict between a desire to convince and persuade by the readiest means available, and the determination never to cross the line into pleasing the sensual man in such a way as to enslave, even momentarily, the spirit to the flesh.[4]

In keeping with such a generally acknowledged literary philosophy was the modern acceptance of a doctrine of "plain style," by which the Puritan aesthetic was easily explained to be a compromise with beauty, at best. In William Bradford's *Of Plimouth Plantation*, we find that he has attempted to write a "plaine stile; with a singuler regard unto the simple trueth in all things." This emphasis on prosaic plainness is echoed in Samuel Morison's *The Intellectual Life of Colonial New England*, where we find:

A Plain style naturally appealed to plain Puritans; and among all the native New England writers . . . the Plain style prevailed. But this does not mean that they cultivated plainness for its own sake, or consciously sacrificed art in writing. In what he wrote and did, the New Englander used as much art as he was capable of. In architecture and silverware this is perfectly evident . . . but it remains to be proved in letters. Even the religious service of the primitive Puritans seemed to some of the native-born too bald.[5]

Before the proliferation of Puritan studies that commenced in the late 1950s and 1960s, few modern scholars addressed the problem of the relationship between religion and art (as it appears in Puritan writing) without agreeing with Murdock, Miller, and Morison. This is, after all, a formidable triumvirate, and agreement with acknowledged authority is always easier than the rigorous labor required to challenge accepted studies, even when they are wrong. One very bright spot of illumination appeared in 1956, in Spiller and Thorp's *Literary History of the United States*, where the editors concluded that

The Puritan author, ever striving to make his books useful, recognized that they could be so only when they presented truth understandably and attractively. He chose his methods from those which seemed to have proved useful in practice and also to be in accord with God's laws. Art was a means, not an end; but the New Englander's realization that some degree of artistry was required if his writing was to be effective made him a careful workman and led him to develop a definite, although limited, theory of style.[6]

In the varied genres of Puritan poetry—the elegy, the hymn, the psalm, the poetic paraphrase, the epic, the lyric, and of course, the meditation—the Puritan was struggling to reconcile art and truth in such a way that the medium would not become the message, but that the message might be conveyed effectively. Art was essential to this creative process, and we have too long taught our students that for the Puritan writer, art should always instruct while not pleasing. This dictum, after all, echoes Dr. Johnson, not Michael Wigglesworth or Edward Taylor. Yet some of the Puritan efforts at an effective reconciliation were exaggerated distortions of art and truth paraded as theology in the guise of literary theory. The Preface to the *Bay Psalm Book* (1639), for example, offers an excellent paradigm of critical absolutism which succinctly gives modern readers an inaccurate view of Puritan practice:

> The singing of Psalmes, though it breath forth nothing but holy harmony, and melody: yet such is the subtilty of the enemie, and the enmity of our nature against the Lord, & His wayes, that our hearts can finde matter of discord in this harmony, and crochets of divison in his holy melody.[7]

Another appears in Thomas Hooker's Preface to *A Survey of the Summe of Church Discipline*, where we find

> That Plainnesse and perspicuity, both for matter and manner of expression, are the things, that I have conscientiously indeavoured in the whole debate: for I have ever thought writings that come abroad, they are not to dazle, but to direct the apprehension of the meanest, and I have accounted it the chiefest part of Iudicious learning, to make a hard point easy and familiar in expression.[8]

Neither poetry nor prose was thought to be original in conception or expression; rather, each was designed to contribute to the generic proofs of God's divine activity on earth, and each was to be a support of truth already demonstrated by its existence in Scripture.

The revisionist position—that literary art was an essential part of Puritan expression in poetry and prose, and that the creative genius of man could well serve the Divine purposes of his creator—has been widely recognized among scholars of Puritanism in the 1960s and 1970s. Three critics, Barbara Lewalski, Robert Daly, and Kenneth Silverman, have addressed the problem discussed here: that a misconception about the role of art in Puritan expression has dominated our study of Puritan poetry since the 1920s when Perry Miller first began to issue corrective notions about the regressive viewpoints of Vernon Louis Parrington and James Truslow Adams. Miller, Murdock, and Morison have done much to establish the importance of New England Puritanism in the evolution of American cultural history, but their misconceptions about art and truth in

Puritan verse are only now being rectified by such writers as Lewalski, Daly, and Silverman, and by my own *The Language of Canaan.*

In her 1979 book, *Protestant Poetics and the Seventeenth-Century Religious Lyric,* Barbara Lewalski examines in detail the traditional sources of this aesthetic theory, the "Protestant poetics" that governed the writing of such divergent poets as Donne, Herbert, Vaughan, Traherne, and Taylor, the "primary exemplars of a Protestant aesthetics of the religious lyric." She clearly shows how the new Protestant approach to poetry was anchored in a sound knowledge of the principles of biblical exegesis:

> We should approach Augustinian aesthetics not in medieval but in Reformation terms, taking account of the important new factor introduced by the Reformation—an overwhelming emphasis on the written word as the embodiment of divine truth. In this milieu the Christian poet is led to relate his work not to ineffable and intuited divine revelation, but rather to its written formulation in scripture. The Bible affords him a literary model which he can imitate in such literary matters as genre, language, and symbolism, confident that in this model at least the difficult problems of art and truth are perfectly resolved. My proposition is, then, that far from eschewing aesthetics for a rhetoric of silence or a deliberate anti-aesthetic strategy, these poets committed themselves to forging and employing a Protestant poetics, grounded upon scripture, for the making of Protestant devotional lyrics. . . . Puritan worship focused exclusively upon the Bible for readings and sermon texts. Such constant communal reading and hearing was surely a major means by which poets became conscious of the poetic elements of scripture, and of the models it might present for Christian lyric poetry.[9]

Robert Daly also argues that the Puritan poet was not a monastic ascetic who mortified the senses. in *God's Altar,* he notes that

> Taken collectively, the critics have written that the Puritans were hostile to art and consequently produced none whatever. Or, they have maintained that the Puritans produced art consisting merely of religious abstractions, art that ignored or condemned the physical world and the concrete images needed to render it. Even if the Puritans were not opposed to art or to naturalistic imagery, we are told, they objected to the use of sensuous or even sensual imagery to illustrate religious doctrine; they considered the use of sensuous appeals in religious art peculiarly Catholic and avoided it. Finally, those critics who allow the Puritans a rudimentary imagistic art assert that it was never symbolic, that for the Puritan the gap between the visible world of creation and the invisible Creator was too great to be bridged by symbol; the creatures could tell depraved man

nothing whatever of the infinite, inscrutable God about Whom the Puritans predicated nothing.[10]

Daly's essential argument is very different from Barbara Lewalski's, and he goes on to show how *sensual imagery*—Biblical and otherwise—fills the lines of Puritan verse, despite opinion to the contrary. "If we advert to the poetry itself," he suggests, "we find that the world's body, the physical world sensorily perceived, inspired many Puritan poems and that such poems, though not divorced from considerations of that other world, are filled with an undisguised appreciation of this one" (pp. 8–9). Anne Bradstreet and Edward Taylor are the principal subjects in this brief investigation, but the viewpoint which Daly shares with Lewalski—that Puritan verse owes much to a common tradition of imagery and style which was essentially derived from the biblical writers—does not receive the full attention it deserves, and the biblical focus is lost in the ensuing discussion.

Kenneth Silverman has addressed the problem and is emphatic in his defense of the Puritan aesthetic. In his anthology, *Colonial American Poetry*, he provides an introduction to "Puritan Verse" that contains this clear statement:

> Two common explanations for the aesthetic failings of Puritan verse are that its writers, inhibited by their piety, regarded poetry as an ornament, as mere heightened prose; and that the wilderness was an unfavorable environment for poetry. These arguments have been applied to colonial verse as a whole. Yet the first is false, the second dubious. The Puritans thought of poetry as a superior form of discourse, mainly because of its importance in the Old Testament. Although William Bradford damned as lascivious the verse tacked on Thomas Morton's maypole, the Plymouth leader wrote two long pious poems of his own. Nor had religious conservatism among Puritan writers any bearing on literary merit. The best Puritan poet, Edward Taylor, was of the orthodox, orthodox. . . . The Puritans knew English verse of the period, especially George Herbert's, which they loved to quote; Francis Quarles contributed translations for the *Bay Psalm Book*.[11]

The approach to "Protestant poetics" that Barbara Lewalski has exhaustively examined is suggested when Silverman asserts that the Puritans "accepted current literary ideas and modified them when they pleased. They never rebelled, in fact, against the standard critical theory of their time. One often cannot distinguish Anglican from Puritan theory or practice" (p. 33).

What, then, do the Puritans in New England share with the Anglican Protestants in England? What essential characteristics of religious art, or what doctrine of religion-in-art, particularly poetry, do we now perceive that for several centuries was lost from view? A good place to begin is with the Doctrine of

Accommodation, a moral and aesthetic principle which the Protestant writers derived from Augustine of Hippo. It is accommodation that Daly sees in the Puritan use of sensual images. But it was much more than a simple arrangement of uses and means. Accommodation implied that the Divine Author was employing the writer in His service, and that the universe of language and imagery was available to the poet who sought to reconcile art and truth in his verse. As George Herbert would say in *Jordan I:*

> Who sayes that fictions onely and false hair
> Become a verse? Is there in truth no beautie?
> Is all good structure in a winding stair?
> May no lines passe, except they do their dutie
> Not to a true, but painted chair?

Biblical truth, already revealed and understood to be the authoritative word of God, was also expressed in literary forms which the Puritans were at liberty to imitate, even create. The Doctrine of Accommodation allowed them a great range of freedom in following the biblical example, which was itself rich in metaphor and symbol, and steeped in the highly figurative "language of Canaan."

The notion that literature should be logical and clear was derived from the writings of Peter Ramus, a French, anti-Scholastic, and anti-Aristotelian logician of the sixteenth century. The Puritans adopted aspects of the Ramean logic because it seemed to offer good rules for expository prose. But the primary source for Puritan literary theory came from Augustine and Calvin.

Calvin had taught that Scripture does not always plainly express what God is, but adapts the understanding of him to human capacity. This process of adapting the Divine to the human is labeled accommodation, and the two most significant Puritan writers in England during the seventeenth century, Bunyan and Milton, both practiced accommodation as a literary mode. The "wayes of God to man" are accommodated to the reader of *Paradise Lost,* and Bunyan's spiritual experience is made clear through the narrative of Christian's odyssey.

Essential to the Doctrine of Accommodation is the use of "types" in describing the spiritual experience of an individual in terms of all mankind. A representative is no more than an example, and the Puritan examples were derived from rhetorical practices of the late Middle Ages and Renaissance, the use of *exempla* and the writing of emblem books. The morality play *Everyman* employs types as characters, and this method of type-characterization prefigures Bunyan's assigning of specific values to his characters in *Pilgrim's Progress.* If the medieval writers used "types" to set examples of moral ways of life, the Puritan writers developed their narratives into statements about the journey through earthly life that the elect Christian experiences. Abraham became more than an Old Testament hero; he is a type of Christian pilgrim, an individual selected by God for the fulfillment of a predetermined Divine purpose. "Christian" is not only the hero of Bunyan's powerful epic of the Christian life; he is also a type of Christian *perigrinus,* or wanderer, who seeks the way from the earthly city to the City of God.

The use of types and accommodation was not an exclusive invention of the Renaissance and Reformation. St. Augustine employs accommodation in his *De Civitas Dei,* but unfortunately his allegorical method is so complex at times that contemporary readers required an explanation, which Augustine provided in the "Defense of Obscurity" in *On Christian Doctrine.* Similarly, St. Thomas Aquinas believed that "poetry uses metaphors to depict, since men naturally find pictures pleasing. But sacred doctrine uses them because they are necessary and useful" (*Summa,* I. Q. i, Art. 9). The medieval church erected elaborate theories of literature and art that employ both allegory and typological symbolism, utilizing rational and scholastic approaches to perpetuate doctrine through art in all forms. What the Puritans inherited, or rather *selected,* from the medieval church was the belief that art should be purposefully didactic, and that literature especially should contain only enough art to guide one to the truth. A good example of this attitude is found in Milton's *De Doctrina Christiana,* where the Puritan poet acknowledges the accommodated nature of Scriptural teaching:

> Our safest way is to form in our minds such a conception of God, as shall *correspond with his own delineation* and representation of himself in the sacred writings. For granted that both in the literal and figurative descriptions of God, he is exhibited not as he really is, but in such a manner as may be within the scope of our comprehensions, as he, in *condescending to accommodate himself to our capacities,* has shown that he desires we should conceive. For it is on this very account that he had lowered himself to our level, lest in our flights above the reach of human understanding, and beyond the written word of Scripture, we should be tempted to indulge in vague cogitations and subtleties.[12]

It is beyond the scope of this essay to examine the role of figural writing or typological symbolism in Puritan poetry. (See Karen Rowe's chapter in this volume, and Lowance, *Canaan.*) The point is that for the Puritan, the onus of interpretative responsibility was on the individual, who was accountable directly to the Divine Author for his response to Scripture. In medieval and Catholic theology, however, the church established interpretative modes, and accommodation was a rational, even a Scholastic method of establishing doctrinal principles through art and symbolism. The once sacred mysteries of the medieval church became explicable in terms of earthly examples, although the Reformation thinkers always maintained a healthy agnosticism about such ultimate questions as the knowledge of one's election. If consubstantiation superseded transubstantiation as a belief about the condition of the Host, assurance of one's salvation was ultimately in the hands of the Almighty, and mortal Puritans could hardly venture to grant each other certainty of election. The Doctrine of Accommodation assisted in explaining the ways of God to man; however, it rarely gave the Puritan special powers for understanding spiritual mysteries. Whatever revelations were accommodated to mankind came only because God had willed it so: "The Lord gave him [man] an excellent faculty in making abstruse things plain, that in handling the deepest mysteries, he would accommodate himself to vulgar capacities, that even the meanest might learn something."[13]

In interpreting Scripture, Milton was firmly committed to what H. R. MacCallum calls "epistemological accommodation," that is, a resting in the words and images of Scripture, not seeking to penetrate behind them. In poetic practice, however, Milton employs MacCallum's alternative, "social accommodation." As epistemological accommodation defines the limits of human comprehension, social accommodation stresses condescension to an audience's limitations and has the effect of inducing the student to read between the lines, to "penetrate behind the veils of imagery to the hidden meaning."[14]

Within the two basic definitions of accommodation, then, must be distinguished two complementary thrusts: the one bringing truth down to earth, and the other gradually raising the earthly mind to heaven. The first of these Geoffrey Hartman calls "initiatory."[15] Kathleen Swaim notes that "In *Paradise Lost* generally, but especially in Book III, condescension to audience or human limitations is regularly complemented by stretching exercises of the mind and imagination. Similarly, accommodation is at once a closing and an opening, a builder of reader confidence and a provocation of inquiry."[16] It is clear that "accommodation" was a very important literary principle for the Puritan reformers; in Milton's theoretical statements and practice, accommodation of God's Divine Wisdom to the capacities of man constitutes the rationale for his own literary epic and for the Divine drama through which the ways of God to man may be known.

It is ironic, perhaps, that this kind of critical thinking about imagery and literature got the Puritans into trouble with the literary authorities, almost to the degree that their religious views had caused them trouble in the Anglican establishment. Roland Frye notes that "in the century after his death, the visual elements of Milton's poetry were more often praised than condemned, but quite as significant are the kinds of condemnation that developed during this period. Adverse criticism maintained that Milton was far too concrete and explicit in his description of spiritual subjects."[17] It is significant that the Doctrine of Accommodation saved Milton and other Puritan poets from immersion in this critical reaction, since through accommodation and the language of biblical typology, discussed fully elsewhere in this volume, the Puritans were able to have their cake and eat it, too. While critical themselves of the medieval allegorical extravagances and the Anglican habits of mind by which natural objects were given elaborate spiritual significances, the Puritans developed a "literal" and "spiritual" method of reading Scripture, so that the wisdom of God could be accommodated to human capacity through language, metaphor, and art without introducing so much "human ingenuity" that the "truth" was lost in "artistic" elaboration. The reformers, in short, insisted that God did the speaking, the writing, and the painting. Man was simply the instrument through whom accommodation performed God's will. Thus Frye is able to conclude:

> Most early critics did not read Milton in this unfavorable way, and showed little or no embarrassment over his physical presentation of spiritual realities, because Christendom had long employed a doctrine of *accommodation* by which objects and actions could be interpreted according to their spiritual significance rather than their literal meaning. That understanding of *accommodation* (found alike in the Fathers of the Church and in the Protestant Reformers) continued to be influential, but it was subject to gradual and steady erosion during the eighteenth century and thereafter. Along with erosion, we see more and more signs of embarrassment, both among some of the faithful and among others, over the physicality of many of Milton's descriptions. An increasingly literal understanding of the Scriptures in some circles thus combined with a heady suspicion of mythology in the Age of Reason to condemn Milton for a too detailed visualization of his supernatural scenes.[18]

The mandate which all Puritan poets followed—in England and in New England—was that literature should be didactic, precisely because it was an extension of Scripture, a reflection of God's revealed will and Divine wisdom, so that any "art" which detracted from the "truth" it sought to reveal would inherently be suspect of an intrusion of human ingenuity. The various doctrines of accommodation allowed tremendous flexibility in bringing to literal description a spiritual or even allegorical meaning.

Similarly, the attention to clarity in style was a departure from a more general movement in English letters toward plainness in prose. In 1700 English writers were being judged for clarity and simplicity, and the efforts of Jonathan Swift to establish an Academy of Language represent the attitude of many writers toward the simplification of language. There is little doubt that Puritan theories helped to form these attitudes toward language. Although simplification of style was sought as a means to Divine truth, the result in writing was that many moved away from the highly stylized formulae of the Restoration prose writers, who were generally denounced for having corrupted the English tongue.

Allegations of simplicity and stringent dogmatism simply do not hold up when a wide spectrum of the verse itself is examined, though of course isolated examples of artless, versified dogma may be easily found. Michael Wigglesworth's *Day of Doom*, probably the most popular poem ever produced in America, if measured by the ratio of copies available to the population, is clearly a doctrinal epic which does much to clarify the intricacies of Calvinistic doctrine that often baffle modern readers and even may have confused laymen in the seventeenth century. Doggerel, "rolicking fourteeners" describe its style, and yet, when read aloud to a class of undergraduates, it is as effective an instrument for communicating the anxiety that lay beneath dogmatic Puritan assurances as any lecture by a sociologist or psychologist. The poem may want art by modern standards, but its fusion of verse form appropriate to the subject and style appropriate to the audience make it good reading, even today, when presented properly.

The setting of the narrative piece is cosmic; the poem purports to be the Judgment Day, and its universality and scope remind one of the last Judgment of Michelangelo on the wall of the Sistine Chapel in Rome. The work contains a central, didactic message: one should always be prepared for the Last Judgment. Metaphorically, it depicts the world in a dormant state of rest before it is suddenly shocked into that Final Day. The condition of the earth and its people is described in terms of a small community that has just settled down from an evening of gaiety. Allusions to the parable of the "Wise and Foolish Virgins" show how the poet has taken his theme directly from Scripture:[19]

Wallowing in all kind of sin, vile wretches lay secure:
The best of men had scarcely then their Lamps kept in good ure.
Virgins unwise, who through disguise amongst the best were number'd,
Had closed their eyes; yea, and the wise through sloth and frailty
      slumbered. [St. 2]

The action moves swiftly from this dormant state to the sudden introduction of light and the commencement of the Judgment:

For at midnight brake forth a Light, which turn'd the night to day,
And speedily an hideous cry did all the world dismay.
Sinners awake, their hearts do ake, trembling their loynes surpriseth;
Amaz'd with fear by what they hear, each one of them ariseth. [St. 5]

Finally, Christ enters and sends the doomed off to eternal Hell-fire. This is *the* Puritan poem best exemplifying the tragic vision of the afterlife for those not elect for salvation.

Ye sinful wights, and cursed sprights, that work Iniquity,
Depart together from me for ever to endless Misery.
Your portion take in yonder Lake, where Fire and Brimstone flameth:
Suffer the smart, which your desert as its due wages claimeth. [St. 201]

The doggerel lines, and the clumsy use of the Latinate suspension, for example, the suspension of the verb until the close of the sentence, as in the concluding line of the stanza above, add to the severity and dread that the poem's subject impose.

> For day and night, in their despight, their torment's smoak ascendeth.
> Their pain and grief have no relief, their anguish never endeth.
> There must they ly, and never dy, though dying every day:
> There must they dying ever ly, and not consume away. [St. 210]

It is clearly revealing of the Puritan taste in poetry that the first edition of this poem, totally eight hundred copies, was exhausted within one year of the printing. This means that during that year, 1662, one in every twenty-five persons living in New England had purchased a copy.

The theological message of this poem is clear. As Hyatt Waggoner put it: "The Puritans valued poetry for its usefulness—but not in any crude, utilitarian sense. They would not have understood an art for art's sake doctrine, not because they had contempt for art but because for them life was all of a piece and lower values should properly be subordinated to higher ones. The use of poetry was to help one live well—and die well. For this purpose, even the simplest poetic memorial of the humblest versifier might serve."[20] Through biblical metaphor and symbol, the Puritan poet was able to unite art and truth, beauty and theological reasoning. No Puritan writer except John Milton was as effectively able to reconcile these artificially opposed forces as Edward Taylor. It would require an extensive study of Taylor's work to prove this assertion. Moreover, recent critical treatment of Taylor has amply demonstrated that his relationship to English writers of the period, both Puritan and Anglican, establishes his work as broadly Protestant and neither biblically "Puritan" nor artistically "metaphysical." "This Metaphysical–Puritan dichotomy pointed up by the critics is, I think, a false one for Taylor, who stands in the line of Donne, Herbert, Vaughan, and Traherne as a Protestant poet practicing a Protestant poetics," says Barbara Lewalski, and it is clear that Taylor understood the most complex and sophisticated rhetorical strategies of seventeenth-century writers, including the extremely intricate distinctions between allegorical and typological exegesis as the Puritans have inherited and modified these rhetorical modes.[21] For Taylor, both the allegorical and typological modes were ways of expressing the personal significance of Christ, but he is careful, following the distinctions established by Samuel Mather, to maintain allegory and figural topology as different vehicles for expressing the same essential substance. For example, the Second Series of *Meditations* is thematically divided to exhibit the different rhetorical techniques in separate sequences of poetry. *Meditations* II, 1–30, specifically treat Old Testament typology, while texts from the Canticles, and poems treating the subject of Christ as bridegroom and the church as bride, are found throughout *Meditations* II, 115–53, the poems specifically designed to exhibit the allegorical significance of that Old Testament dispensation of Christ. The meditations in between these two specific groups, II, 31–114, are essentially the central panel in a triptych, and in this group—flanked on one side by typology and on the other by allegory—Taylor concentrates on themes expressing Christ's superiority to the types and the salvational value of the believer's identification with the Saviour's personal presence. It is the most mystical segment of the three groups and relies more on the metaphysical mode of *discordia concors* than either the Canticles allegory or the typological group. In this central panel, the spiritual and corporeal elements seem mystically fused, and for Taylor, this represents, metaphorically, the theantropy accomplished when the spirit became flesh in the incarnation. The same theme is expressed in Meditation I, 8, brilliantly developed from the text "I am the Living Bread" (John 6:51), where the poet creates conceits and invokes analogies in the finest "metaphysical" tradition to articulate the subtleties of his doctrine of the sacrament.

Puritan poetry, then, does not allow the oversimplifications and generalizations that have characterized critical approaches to the seventeenth century. Even much post-war study rehearsed the dogma of the early twentieth century, and it has only been very recently that scholars recognized the full value of the Puritan achievement in their reconciliation of the fundamental tensions between religion and art in verse. John Milton understood this issue, and has given us perhaps the supreme expression of this reconciliation in his own writing, both the poetry and the prose, which can often serve as a gloss on the verse. But at least until the 1960s, students of American literature were not according New England Puritanism the same measure of credibility for this astonishing achievement. The response to Herbert's query, "Is there in truth, no beauty," must surely lie in the extraordinary work of Edward Taylor just as clearly as it is represented in the writings of Milton. For Puritan New England, the gross distinctions we have drawn between "truth" and "art" were resolved by adherence to the biblical model, and, in Taylor's poetry especially, we have abundant evidence that the religious truth of Scriptures could be artistically and beautifully crafted into contemporary verse form.

NOTES

1. Miller and Johnson, *Puritans,* I, 77–78.

2. Cotton Mather, *Manductio ad Ministerium,* (1726), as quoted in Milton B. Stern and Seymour L. Gross, *American Literature Survey: Colonial and Federal to 1800* (New York: The Viking Press, 1975), pp. 131–32.

3. Miller and Johnson, *Puritans,* I, 78–79.

4. Murdock, *Literature,* p. 50.

5. Morison, *Life,* p. 151.

6. Robert E. Spiller and Willard Thorp, *A Literary History of the United States* (New York, 1956), p. 54.

7. Cotton Mather, John Mather, and Richard Mather, *The Bay Psalm Book* (Cambridge, 1639), p. 14.

8. Thomas Hooker, *A Survey of the Summe of Church Discipline,* quoted in Miller and Johnson, *Puritans,* II, 673.

9. Lewalski, *Poetics,* pp. 6–12, passim.

10. Daly, *God's Altar,* pp. 4–5.

11. Silverman, *Poetry,* pp. 32–33.

12. John Milton, *De Doctrina Christiana,* quoted in *The Columbia Milton* (New York, 1934), 14, pp. 31, 33.

13. Increase Mather, *Life of Richard Mather,* quoted in Miller and Johnson, *Puritans,* II, 494.

14. In Milton's own words, accommodation is the mediated vocabulary through which human beings, because of their "imperfect comprehension," can be said to "know" the transcendent God. I am indebted to my colleague at the University of Massachusetts, Kathleen Swaim, for this central suggestion and phrasing. For an extended discussion of Milton's comments on accommodation in *Christian Doctrine,* see Leland Ryken, *The Apocalyptic Vision in Paradise Lost* (Ithaca: Cornell University Press, 1970), pp. 7–33. Especially to the argument about accommodation in its various forms see pp. 19–24. For the Latin original of the *De Doctrina Christiana* passage (but the same translation) see *The Works of John Milton,* ed. Frank A. Patterson et al. (New York: Columbia University Press, 1933), XIV, 30–33.

15. See Geoffrey Hartman, "Adam on the Grass with Balsamum," ELH, 36(1969), reprinted in Geoffrey Hartman, *Beyond Formalism: Literary Essays 1958–1970* (New Haven: Yale University Press, 1970), p. 136. Later in this essay, Hartman speaks of the opposite of accommodation as "conflagration, a burning up of restrictive mystery, an opening up of man, and a cleansing of the doors of perception," in sum an apocalypse (p. 137). Again, Professor Kathleen Swaim has provided these references.

16. See Kathleen Swaim, review-essay on contemporary Milton criticism, to be published in *Philological Quarterly.*

17. Roland M. Frye, *Milton's Imagery and the Visual Arts: Iconographic Traditon in the Epic Poems* (Princeton: Princeton University Press, 1978), p. 10.

18. Ibid.

19. Michael Wigglesworth, "The Day of Doom," Miller and Johnson, *Puritans,* II, pp. 587, 588, 602, 603.

20. Hyatt H. Waggoner, "Puritan Poetry," *Criticism,* 6 (1964), 291–312.

21. Lewalski, *Poetics,* p. 389. See also Lowance, *Canaan.*

4 PROPHETIC VISIONS: TYPOLOGY AND COLONIAL AMERICAN POETRY

KAREN E. ROWE

Paradoxically, visions of America's destiny began with a retrospective appeal to biblical visions of Israel's journey out of Egypt into Canaan—the promised land. That New England Puritans would turn to the past in order to illuminate their present and future would not have seemed idiosyncratic for this band of religious immigrants exiled in uncharted territory. These crusaders shared with the apostle Paul a concept of providential history interpreted as an extended pattern of foreshadowings and fulfillments. Whether Old Testament prophecies were surpassed by Christ's incarnate excellence, recapitulated by the founding of a New Jerusalem in America, or absorbed as spiritual patterns by each Elect soul hoping to travel the thorny Calvinist path to salvation, the motive remained fundamentally the same—to see in the unfolding of human lives the working out of God's providence. Typology, the hermeneutic art of reading divine signs, or more precisely Old Testament persons, events, ceremonies, and objects, as prefigurations of Messianic fulfillments became one method common among covenant theologians, historians, and poets in New England from 1620 through the eighteenth century. Typology, in short, provided the justificatory mythos for the Puritans' errand into the wilderness.[1]

Appeals to Mosaic types dotted the poetry of early promotionalists for whom the immigrants were Israelites, brought out of English bondage into a New Canaan. When later in the seventeenth century the fertile garden seemed again a perilous wilderness, elegies identified dying patriarchs as veritable Moseses, Aarons, and Joshuas and expressed the Puritans' nostalgic yearning for their former faith and prophetic vision. As the vision of a spiritual kingdom on earth gave way to the eighteenth century's nascent nationalism and an intensified millennialism, poets and historians linked Old Testament prefigurations, New Testament revelations, and America's destiny to an apocalyptic glory yet to come. In contrast to these public voices of chroniclers and elegists, meditative singers, among them Edward Taylor and Samuel Davies, in private journals sought out biblical types as sacred models for the soul's solitary trials. Figural persons and events set forth exemplars to be imitated, or as Davies depicts Solomon, to serve as a "Royal Preacher" and "skillful Guide, made by Experience wise," and rich with "costly Med'cine for mis-judging Eyes."[2] As participants in the cyclic fulfillment of Old Israel's mission, these devotional poets offered living testimony to the fruition of Christ's new dispensation. But while New

Englanders en masse took plough in hand to cultivate the frost-bitten sod, confessional poets, through intensely private meditations, prayers, or Davidic psalms, retraced the briar-strewn ascent to redemption, the striving for assurances of divine election, the epithalamic hope of marriage with the Bridegroom in Heaven. Schoolmasters, housewives, governors, merchants, lawyers, and preachers— these poets testified to the living resonances in New England of a biblical typology that provided our Puritan forbears with symbolic patterns on which to model their lives, build their society in a New Jerusalem, and in the process create an American poetic tradition.

The ancient hermeneutic method which we identify as typology inaugurated a distinctive mode of Christian symbolism. Adopting the classic terms "skia" (shadow) and "typos" (type) in Heb. 10.1 and Rom. 5.14, Paul interpreted Old Testament events, persons, and ceremonies as signs which prefigured Christ's fulfillment *forma perfectior* and new covenant with the apostolic Church. Since the evangelists' desire was to link Israel's heritage with the Messiah's advent, all types, it was affirmed, possessed an historical verity as persons or events truly existent in the world. But, according to Paul in Col. 2.17, Hebraic law and ceremonies also served as "a shadow of things to come," for which the substantial "body is of Christ," who made manifest the redemption through grace masterminded by God. The Gospels and Pauline epistles, therefore, emphasized the type and antitype as historical actualities, God's progressive revelation of a redemptive plan, and consequently the acceptance of Moses' saga as a literal account (albeit prophetic) of the Chosen people. Under the Church Fathers, medieval scholastics, and Catholics until the sixteenth century, multiple allegorical readings of Scripture, which relied more upon Platonic than chronologic leaps from text to divine truth, often subsumed fundamental historical significances. But with their demand *ad fontes*, a return to original sources, the Reformers reasserted a concept of spiritual meanings as inseparable from or contained within the Bible's single, literal sense. Spearheaded by Luther and Calvin, later seventeenth-century Protestant theologians restricted their "symbolic" readings to identifiable types whose ultimate antitypes are the incarnate Christ, His benefits to the Church under a new dispensation, and the Second Coming.

Clear enunciations of Protestant theory and practice appeared in a flood of seventeenth-century guidebooks, most notably William Guild's *Moses Unvailed* (1620), Thomas Taylor's *Christ Revealed* (1635), and Samuel Mather's *The Figures or Types of the Old Testament* (1683), the latter widely disseminated in the New World.[3] Samuel Mather invokes the painter's draft and dark glass, traditonal metaphors used by exegetes from Chrysostom to Calvin, to differentiate the Law from the Gospel, that is, shadowy "*Mosaical Ceremonies*" from "*Christ* the Body and Substance." In Col. 2.17 the Apostle, according to Mather, alludes "to the rude Draught and first delineation of a Picture by the Painter, and to the full Perfection thereof, when drawn forth in all its Lineaments and Colours and whole Proportion. So the Shadow is the first rude Draught: but the Image is a more lively and exact Representation. So the dark Shadow is ascribed to the *Law*. The more lively Image to the *Gospel*. The Things themselves are in Heaven." Mather similarly interprets the "*Glass darkly*" of 1 Cor. 13.12 to emphasize his developmental concept of typology, since the metaphor aptly captures the sequence of God's Old, New, and eschatological dispensations. The legal types present merely shadows or sketchy outlines, the Gospel yields "the *very Image*" of "Things *as in a Glass*" or a painted portrait, but Christ in divine radiance will be unveiled only in Heaven where "*we shall see* [Him] *Face to Face*." This developmental pattern of progressively clearer dispensations provided the basis upon which New England Puritans claimed their covenant community as God's chosen successor to Israel and voiced their latter-day millennial prophecies.

Generally available biblical glosses of these metaphors together with the Great Awakening resurgent evangelicalism make it less surprising that as late as 1750 Samuel Davies (1723–1761), a Presbyterian missionary in Virginia and later President of Princeton, would contemplate God's transmittal through "the Channel of Thy Word" and "Sacred Emblems" of "sweet Instructions" to men of darkened vision (pp. 91, 92). Its jogging iambic tetrameter couplets notwithstanding, Davies' poem is a rarity in colonial verse because it so directly sets forth Puritan views of figuralism:

> Thro' various Types and Shadows dart
> Thy Glories on my ravish'd Heart;
> While far above created Sight,
> Thou sit'st enthron'd on Hills of Light.
>
> But say, shall Types and Figures still
> The Glories of Thy Face conceal?
> While these thick Shades Thy Beauty shroud,
> It breaks but faintly thro' the Cloud.
> I love Thine Image in a Glass;
> But Oh! to see Thy naked Face!
> Thyself I long, I pant to see;
> I turn mine Eyes in Quest of Thee.
>
> . . . .
> The Glories of Thy Face display,
> Tho' Life should for the Vision pay.
> O! let me die, opprest with Light,
> Rather than live without the Sight.

In "Sight thro' a Glass, and Face to Face," Davies annotates 1 Cor. 13.12 as he defiantly confronts the frustrating limits of human vision which cannot penetrate the clouded types shrouding Christ's beauty. Intensified by faint glimpses of the divine image in the glass, his longings escalate to a death wish—to be so transfused by light that he may behold Christ's naked face in Heaven where He sits enthroned upon hills of light. Commonplace oppositions between types and Christ, shadows and light, cloudy images and transcendent glories as well as the quest for inspired sight to read God's sacred emblems recur often as passing allusions in colonial poetry, but poets far less frequently develop the fundamental principles of typology.

Edward Taylor is the exception. In *Upon the Types of the Old Testament,* preached (1693–1706) in Westfield but never published, he imitates preceding exegetes by rigorously defining figural theory and, more important, writes thirty-six poetic meditatons to accompany his sermons.[4] In Sermon I he re–invigorates the metaphor of Christ's gospel portrait, finding that even a draught "drawn to the Life of the most Exquisit art in most Sparkling Colours in all the World, adornd with richest orient Gems" is but a "dull Shadow, & Smutty Lineament" of the "Lovely one . . . Christ Jesus."[5] Exclamatory epithets ("Oh! Golden Rose! Oh. Glittering Lilly White") and a plethora of "brightsome Colours," "Dazzling Shine," and "flaming Rayes of light" scintillate like fireworks throughout the poems to heighten Christ's "Transcendent glory sparkling cleare."[6] Fond of the portrait metaphor in part because it signifies a sacred artistry he seeks to emulate, Taylor characterizes Israel's patriarchs as "Choicest Saints" who are "Pictures" in which Christ is "portrai'd . . . in Colours bright" (II.ll.4, 5, 3), among them Joseph in whom "thou pensild out, my Lord, most bright / Thy glorious Image here" (II.7.35–36). In a striking transmutation of typology's focus on historical prophecy which culminates in the Messiah's incarnation, Taylor invokes a three-dimensional image of Christ as a "Choice pearle-made-Box" (II.50.23). This "Box, four thousand yeares, o'r ere 'twas made," was set forth "in golden Scutchons lay'd in inke Divine" by God, through "Promises, of a Prophetick Shade, / And in embellishments of Types that shine" (II.50.19–22). To the "Artists Hand" of God Taylor attributes the original sketch in "inke Divine" of Christ's image in Old Testament promises and types, but (much like Davies) he yearns now for celestial revelations—Christ the shining "Box of Truth" or the radiant Messiah's face (II.50.1, 43). Failing in this ambition so long as he inhabits the earth, Taylor reiterates a humbler plea for the eye of faith, surely essential for a Puritan poet who explicates types:

> Wilt thou enoculate within mine Eye
>   Thy Image bright, My Lord, that bright doth shine
> Forth in thy Cloudy-Firy Pillar high
>   Thy Tabernacles Looking-Glass Divine?
>   What glorious Rooms are then mine Eyeholes made.
>   Thine Image on my windows Glass portrai'd? [II.59.1–6]

Here Taylor reverts to the conventional metaphor of types as a "Looking-Glass Divine" in which to read prophecies set forth by Israel's journey, patriarchs, and ceremonies. His post-Reformation, pre-transcendental variation on the "eye-ball" as a receptor, a "windows Glass" to be imprinted with Christ's image, underscores the typologist's acute need for inspired vision. Other colonial poets often lodge similar request *pro forma,* but Taylor elaborates upon his desire to weld faith's sight to reason's light. In his verse we hear more sharply the poet's call for imaginative inspiration. The need to see spiritually in order to penetrate both prophetic signs and the Heavens corresponds with typology's inherent prom-ise of a double fulfillment. In the Old Testament smoky glass and shadowy portraits, the typologist and poet seek clues both to the lively Gospel image of a human Christ and also to "things themselves," that is, Christ's naked face irradiated by celestial splendor.

Samuel Mather's influential treatise not only defended Puritan theory, it also distinguished "meer *natural* or arbitrary similitudes" and parables from sacred types. The simile, a rhetorician's figure of speech or *"Typus arbitrarius,"* is merely an apt comparison, often humanly fabricated and used only occasionally. The *"Typus fixus & institutus,"* such as the ceremonial law, is *"instituted* and set apart by God," bears "something of *Christ* stamped and ingraven" upon it, and seals the "visible Promise" of God's ultimate exhibition of "Gospel Mys-teries." Together with many Protestant expositors, Mather acknowledged the descriptive power of metaphors, none more so than those drawn from the Bible's poetic books (Psalms, Canticles, Proverbs, Ecclesiastes, Job) so often para-phrased by fervent versifiers. Still, commonplace metaphors (sin as disease, Christ as the physician, grace as a curative tincture; man's spiritual pilgrimage; the Church as a flowering garden) lacked telling marks—divine institution, his-torical prophecy, and Christ's fulfillment—which distinguished types from ordi-nary tropes. Whereas Henry Vertue in *Christ and the Church: Or Parallels* (1659) and Benjamin Keach in *Tropologia: A Key to Open Scripture Metaphors* (1681) amply analyzed scriptural metaphors and similes, Mather restricted his compendium to established types.[7] He categorized legitimate types under two broad headings: Persons singly before (Adam to Moses) and under (Moses to Jehoshua) the Law, or in ranks (prophets, priests, and kings); and Things, both occasional types (Israel's deliverances from Egypt and Babylon, journey to Canaan, and destruction of God's enemies) and perpetual types or ceremonial law (Circumcision, sacrifices, purifications, holy places, festivals, and priests). Advocates of a conservative exegetical typology, such as Samuel Mather, Edward Taylor, and Davies, reaffirmed Puritan belief in the Messiah's fulfillment of all types, His abrogation of Old ceremonial laws to be superseded by "heart-worship," and hence the Christocentricity of scriptural history. In "The Law and the Gospel," Samuel Davies shrinks from "the Terrors of the Law" until "Jesus appears, and by His Cross / Fulfils His Father's broken laws" and promises "Salvation" to all those who heed the call, "BELIEVE, OR DIE. / Thee let the Glorious Gospel draw, / Or perish by the fiery Law" (pp. 93, 94). By fusing more closely prophetic types to the revelatory antitype, Puritan preachers thus treated the Bible as a unified text. They found in Christ the perfected Saviour which Old Testament *figura* adumbrated and exhorted the Elect to prepare spiritually, armed with faith and new hope, for His Second Coming.

In the charged political arena of England and the New World, however, figural patterns of prophecy and revelation took on a liberalized function which extended the concept of fulfillment beyond Christ and his Gospel teachings. Indeed, from Calvin to Samuel Mather, Puritan Reformers came gradually to view all history less as dualistic (the Gospel as opposed to the Law) and more as a continuum of progressively clearer revelations of God's will, each new dispensation more brilliantly anticipating the day of judgment. The extension stemmed in part from the assertion, according to Mather, that types related *"not only to the* Person *of Christ; but to his* Benefits, *and to all Gospel Truths and Mysteries, even to all New New-Testament-Dispensations."* By including Christ's benefits to His Church as on-going antitypal fulfillments, Puritan historians might then apply Old Testament prophecies to political events, whether the Protestant schism with Rome, defeat of the Spanish Armada, or the religious Civil Wars. Or as Barbara Lewalski observes, the "narrowing of the divide between the two Covenants" permitted Puritans to assimilate "events and circumstances of contemporary history—and even the lives and experiences of individual Christians—to the providential scheme of typological recapitulations and fulfillments throughout history."[8]

Nowhere more pervasively than in poetic lyrics of the Puritans' quest for a New Canaan in the American wilds, did recapitulative typology so nurture the mythos and ethos of a developing nation. Because they interpreted literally Christ's promise to his Chosen New Testament Church, Puritan chroniclers translated Old Testament types into models or prefigurations, for as John Wilson claims in his *Song of Deliverance* (1626), "what is there to Israel committed, / Hath a more large and general extent, / And to our present times may well be fitted."[9] Particularly in the extraordinary types of Israel's deliverance from Egyptian bondage (and later Babylonian captivity), God's guidance through the wilderness (crossing the Red Sea, manna from heaven, pillar of cloud and fire, and brazen serpent), and in Moses' vision of Canaan, the emigrants from England and the Netherlands found an inspirational pattern for their own sacred mission. Poetic chroniclers might elect to use the pattern as a simple analogy, a more developed correlative, or to proclaim New World colonists the recapitulative descendants of Israel. Regardless of the formulation, the "language of Canaan," as Mason Lowance christened it, became the fundamental rhetoric of America as it progressed from Christian commonwealth to revolutionary republic.[10] Moreover, embedded within the figural paradigm of deliverance were themes—the freedom from bondage and liberty of choice; the promise of a new world with boundless, untapped resources; and the millennial prospect of peace—which would permeate the literature of America's first two centuries.

In eighteenth-century landscape verse, the frontier became not Massachusetts but the forested domains of the Shenandoah Valley, the Blue Ridge Mountains, and the plains beyond. Yet the rhetoric of Canaan lingers, for instance, in the Reverend George Seagood's "Expeditio Ultramontana" (1729), when he alludes to the "chosen Band" led "as once did *Joshua* to the Promis'd Land" and to the millennial "Prospect sweet" when "the Sun of Peace shall [cast his rays?]" and "his Messias reign from Pole to Pole."[11] But abundant classical references and pastoral descriptions of the "verdant Earth" and "beauteous Landskip" which "charm'd his ravish'd Sight," overshadow religious allusions and make Governor Spotswood's Appalachian expedition into an heroic march "T'advance his Sov'reigns and his Saviour's name." Just as Seagood bows to King George, so also Roger Wolcott pays obeisance to King Charles in his 1725 "A Brief Account of the Agency of the Honourable John Winthrop, Esq; in the Court of King Charles the Second, *Anno Dom.* 1662. When he Obtained for the Colony of *Connecticut* His Majesty's Gracious CHARTER."[12] In this poem Winthrop, the Puritan governor, once lauded by Cotton Mather in 1702 as "Nehemias Americanus," prostrates himself "before his Princes Feet"; England, earlier compared to Egypt, becomes the "happiest Seat in *Christendom*"; and parallels between Israel's and America's nascent separatism become virtually neutralized. In a naturalized account of the stormy sea voyage, for example, "*Cloudy Chariots* Threatning take the Plains" (meteorological variant of Pharaoh's legions), "fervent Prayers for deliverence" yield a respite from "Winds" and "Waves" rather than from religious intolerance, and even Moses' vision from Pisgah where his eye "was well enabled to Discry / The Land of Promise in its full extent" becomes prelude to a classical catalogue of America's "*Excellent Fertility*" from which "Lady *Flora's* richest Treasure grows." Whether land lust, royalist sympathies, or political exigencies dictated the rhetorical shifts, the once elaborate correlations with Israel's quest had by the eighteenth century begun to lose the typological resonances so central to the seventeenth-century Puritans' myth of their wilderness errand.

While landscape poetry illustrates the eventual secularization of typal analogies, poetic chronicles and jeremiads reflect a persistent countervailing pull toward a religious ideology that gives rise to the Great Awakening and later millennial visions of America's destiny. Before the Halfway Covenant (1662), the promise of New England as Canaan or the New Jerusalem burned brightly. As Edward Johnson surveyed the founding of each new town (1628–1651), in his *Wonder-working Providence of Sions Saviour, in New England* (wr. 1649–1651), he interspersed poetic hagiographies to laud dissenting reverends who braved "boystrous Seas" to shepherd the Christian flock and, like Zachary Simmes "with *Moses* zeal stampt" to edify "Christ Churches in this Desert Land."[13] Each eulogy set forth the exemplary ecclesiastical conduct by which a minister, here the Reverend Francis Higginson of Salem, passed from this earthly wilderness to Heaven's crowning glory:

What Golden gaine made *Higginson* remove,
　From fertill Soyle to Wilderness of Rocks;
'Twas Christs rich Pearle stir'd up thee toile to love,
　For him to feed in Wilderness his flocks.
First Teacher, he here sheepe and lambs together,
　first crownd shall be, hee in the Heavens of all,
Christs Pastors here, but yet Christ folke had rather,
　Him here retaine, blest he whom Christ hath call'd.

Recapitulative typology, whether applied to the collective New England Israel or to individual leaders, encouraged a spiralling vision of future promise that led many settlers to expect the imminent Second Coming of Christ. Though Johnson's expectations wane as apostasy erupts in New England during the mid-seventeenth century, nevertheless, his poem establishes the early millennialism. Borrowing his parallels eclectically from Old Testament histories, Canticles, and Revelation, Johnson finds that compared to "the noble Acts *Jehovah* wrought, his *Israel* to redeem, / Surely this second work of his shall far more glorious seem," Christ will wreak vengence against "*Dagon* . . . the Beast" and "Satan and his subtil train," while He also adorns "his Bride in bright array" and calls "you his friends him to attend upon his Nuptial day." Johnson promises New England's Elect that "the day's at hand he will you wiser make," when "Kings you shall be" and behold "Christ exalted high," and he exhorts readers to "Apply your selves his Scriptures for to read" with "eyes enlightned" so "you shall see Christ once being come is now / Again at hand your stubborn hearts to bow." Already in Johnson's work of the 1650s, the beckoning hope of a new worldly Eden begins to give way to visions of Christ's enthronement "attended with his glorious Saints in Church fraternity" in a Kingdom not of this earth. As the New England errand seemed to founder on the shoals of materialism, land hunger, and political revolution, compensating visions of a New Jerusalem would increase—though fulfillment of this prophecy seemed always just beyond the horizon.

When second and third generation settlements (1660–1720) became fraught with Indian wars, heretical assaults on covenant theology, and an expanding trade economy, the belief in New England as a desert where the rose would bloom, the seat of a New Eden, gave way to jeremiads which warned of God's destruction of apostates in their midst.[14] In Mather's *The Figures or Types,* Israel's deliverance had been coupled with the converse type of God's destruction of his enemies (Egypt, Rome, Babylon). Now suddenly secular wolves were attacking the chosen flock from within, and fears of declension led to Michael Wigglesworth's famous *The Day of Doom* (1662), Benjamin Tompson's *New Englands Crisis* (1676), a second edition of John Wilson's *Song of Deliverance* (1680), and Cotton Mather's prose epic, the *Magnalia Christi Americana* (1702).

These complaints, modelled upon Jeremiah's lamentations, drew primarily from the types of Israel's lapses from God's worship in pursuit of heathen Gods. John Wilson's preface, which paraphrases Deut. 31, portrays the poet as a latterday Moses, charged like "that holy Shepherd, Isrells guide" to write a song of warning for the "Isralytish fry" to remind them of God's duality as merciful saviour and stern judge.[15] Much as the Hebrews "having eat their fill and waxen fat, / Unto strange Gods . . . their heart dispose" and "contemptuously provoke" Jehovah's wrath, so also, Wilson mourns, New England's Canaanites taste the "bitter root" of "falshood and rebellion." But since Christ's new covenant promises "Heav'n it self" as "another Canan . . . / Far better" to which "our Spirits should ere long be guided," Wilson tutorially exhorts erring "Children" to "consider well, / Gods Word," so "that we might well repent us of our sin" and "praise him, and our lives amend." Wilson chooses the mnemonic "fourteener" or ballad measure when he subsequently compares God's deliverances of England from the Spanish Armada, the 1623 Gunpowder Plot, and 1625 Plague to the Old Testament types of Pharaoh's defeat in the Red Sea, Samson's triumph over the Philistines, and God's pestilential punishment for "*David's* proud presumption." From retrospective types and England's recapitulative example, New England might learn its lesson, or so Wilson hoped. With laborious didacticism, in *The Day of Doom* Wigglesworth seeks prospectively to instill fear of Christ's Second Coming as the baleful Judge, while he counsels New England's saints to pray for the Redeemer's blessing.[16] In his lesser known *Meat out of the Eater* (1670), Wigglesworth also marshals Old Testament fathers (Joseph, Moses, Daniel, Noah, David, Jacob, Samson) as types of the "Suffering Saint" in order to preach a homely variant of the *felix culpa* theme: "Out of the Eater He / Will surely bring forth meat: / And Spiritual Good more sweet than honey / Out of affliction great."[17] To support his doctrine of sweet affliction, Wigglesworth also draws upon the antitype Christ, that "Blest-High-Priest" whose "Sufferings" on the cross provide the "Coppy-book / Whereon we often ought to look." Though *Meat out of the Eater* aims primarily to fortify God's individual saints, its "Conclusion Hortatory" foreshadows Wigglesworth's later apocalyptic predictions of communal doom: "Oh! let *New England* turn, / When gentler Warnings given; / Lest by our sins the Lord to use / Severity be driven."

Even nostalgic appeals in late-century jeremiads could not, however, stem the changing tide of America's destiny or its myth-making rhetoric. During the Revolutionary period, the language of Canaan served both to glorify Columbia's ambitious nationalism and also to project new visions of the long-heralded Millennium of peace. Writing his "Lines on the Massacre" (1770) of Boston civilians by British soldiers, James Allen (1739–1808) summarily retells how New England's "inspired patriarchs" fled from Pharaoh's "realms of bondage, and a tyrant's reign" by "freedom prompted, and the Godhead led" to settle upon America's "virgin soil."[18] But the figural litany reads like an oft-invoked tribal chant, less inspired by Puritan faith than by political exigency—to sound a battle cry "in freedom's cause" and in patriotic defiance of George III's imperialism. Similarly, in "M'Fingal" (wr. 1775–1782), a burlesque of British officers and Tory Sympathizers, John Trumbull only fleetingly, and then as stock similes, invokes the once pervasive types of the "Egyptian yoke," "brazen snake of Moses," "Red Sea waves in Israel's march," and "Jewish pole in Edom."[19]

Despite this subsuming of the Puritan myth of the New Canaan beneath national panegyrics on Columbia and a vogue for imitating Latin and Greek classics, Dryden, and Pope, American poets still drew inspiration from the Bible. Trumbull, for example, paraphrases Numb. 23 in his "Prophecy of Balaam" (1773), in which the seer "fill'd with prophetic fire" pours forth blessings upon "Fair, oh Israel," the "dwelling of the saints," over which "bright Judah's star ascending" will flame "destruction on the opposing world."[20] Trumbull draws no overt correlations, as his Puritan ancestors would have done. But since this biblical example predicts Israel's defeat of heathen nations, it is hard in 1773 not to extract a partisan message: trust in "God, their guardian God," who "o'er the favor'd host Omnipotence extends" will ensure America's triumph over Britain. Trumbull also assisted fellow nationalist, Timothy Dwight (1752–1817), by criticizing early drafts of America's first epic, *The Conquest of Canaan*, an agonizingly pedantic poem inspired by Milton's *Paradise Lost* but cast in Augustan heroic couplets. Not unpredictably, Dwight in 1785 dedicates this embellished paraphrase "To his Excellency, George Washington, Esquire, Commander in chief of the American Armies, The Saviour of his Country, The Supporter of Freedom, And the Benefactor of Mankind."[21] From Winthrop, the Moses who guides the original Puritan wanderers, to Washington, a conquering Joshua who founds the Republic—this transformation of biblical types from models for ecclesiastics to archetypes for generals and presidents marks the extent of a revolutionary secularism during America's first two centuries. By the eighteenth century, freedom meant not simply religious toleration but liberty from British tyranny; the "new world" had become not only a New Jerusalem to protect covenanting emigrants but also a nation to rival the Roman Empire; and the prospect of peace signified an end to Revolution and a vision of a prosperous, powerful Republic. The language of Canaan had yielded to the rhetoric of Federalism and the Enlightenment.

Even as politics progressively diverged from religion, new millennial expectations emerged, serving on the one hand to exalt America's destined progress toward national supremacy and universal peace, and on the other, to project eschatological rewards to compensate for increasingly worldly preoccupations with nature, science, and commerce. Chiliasm represented an extension of developmental typology, based primarily upon futuristic prophecies from Isaiah and Revelation which heralded Christ's Second Coming after Satan's downfall. According to Mason Lowance, "the Great Awakening extended this paradigm to the time of the American Revolution and enlarged what had been a parochial New England idea" of God's predestined salvation of the Elect "into a national conception of America as the location of Christ's millennial fulfillment."[22] Certainly Philip Freneau (1752–1832), in "The Rising Glory of America" (wr.1771), envisioned the Millennium as the capstone of America's growth. Not alone in his patriotic chiliasm, Freneau was joined by Connecticut wit Joel Barlow. Barlow, whose "Vision of Columbus" (1787) celebrated the Republic's birth with commonplace figural prophecies, could also in 1778 project a grander millennial "Prospect of Peace," when after "celestial spheres, / In radiant circles, mark a thousand years," the "Church elect" would "from smouldering ruins, rise, / And sail triumphant thro' the yielding skies."[23] These poets blended landscape vistas of a renewed Edenic pastoralism with latter-day Enlightenment science and Republican government—a strained mating of spiritual with political values which established America as the chosen seat for Christ's "Long and glorious reign on earth."

With less faith in a literal kingdom and greater skepticism about America's utopian grandeur, other poets searched the Scripture for promises of a spiritual millennium, one which would enable feeble men to transcend earthly vanities, even the Edenic charms of a democratic New Canaan. John Trumbull's "The Downfall of Babylon" (1775), a biblical "Imitation" of Isaiah and Revelation, sets forth the "great Apostle" John who "with sacred light inspir'd" proclaimed "future visions" of "Heaven descending in the beam of day" and "Destruction from the Almighty hand" sweeping "o'er thy guilty land."[24] Based upon the type of "The Law Given at Sinai," Thomas Dawes (1757–1852) also heeds the "potent trump" when "the heavens and earth expire, / And nature rolls in one devouring fire," as the redeemed alone "arise to flourish in eternal bloom" while all "Creation" sinks in "rude combustion o'er a flaming ball."[25] Less consumed with God's wrath, Samuel Davies in "The Messiah's Kingdom" (1752) finds Christ's rule of "Eternal Righteousness" on earth (as promised under the New covenant) merely a prelude to greater "Celestial Splendors from the Source Divine" after the Judgment Day (pp. 69, 76). The pastoral Eden which Davies visualizes does not, however, bloom amid America's plains, but rather flourishes as a spiritually reincarnate world, regerminated by the "heav'nly Branch from *Jesse's* sacred Root" (Christ) so that "the Desert blossoms like the fragrant Rose, / And there sweet *Leb'non's* flow'ry Beauty glows" (pp. 74, 75). Hence, while Freneau and Barlow patriotically herald a literal millennium, grounded upon America's scientific and commercial progress, Davies seemingly reverts to a more traditional transcendent vision, one compatible with the Puritan Fathers' belief that individual saints and the Elect Church would build a New Jerusalem, if not in this world surely in the next.

The hallmark which distinguished seventeenth-century recapitulative and millennial from exegetical typology was the ease with which poetic chroniclers leapt from Israel's deliverance or Isaiah's prophecies to contemporary events, leaving implicit the intervening agency of Christ as supreme antitype. Similar typological analogies, often as of similes or brief epithets, recurred throughout innumerable elegies written to commemorate New England's leaders. It was more the rule than exception to compose funeral verses or anagrams; John Wilson, John Danforth, and Benjamin Tompson made an avocation of it. Often recited at graveside services, perhaps with an epitaph to be attached to the pall, elegies were sometimes published, if not in histories such as the *Magnalia,* then as a broadside or in a local gazette. As first generation patriarchs passed away, elegists granted them a worldly immortality by extolling each decedent as a latter-day Moses, Joshua, Abraham, Jacob, Nehemiah, Solomon, Melchizedek, Josiah, or as a New Testament John, Paul, or Lazarus. Fearing a grief-induced dispersal of the "Mourning Flock" after John Cotton's death (1652), Benjamin Woodbridge, for example, reassures them that "though *Moses* be, yet *Joshua* is not dead," for "Renowned NORTON" will be "Successor to our MOSES" and a ministerial lineage sustained "Oh happy Israel in AMERICA."[26] Also conscious of connubial burdens shared by a "Mother in our Israel," poets frequently compared wives to Queen Esther, Dorcas, Sarah, the Shunamite, Abram's daughter, or Mary. John Danforth praised thereby the prototypal domestic piety of Elizabeth Hutchinson (d. 1712), who "the Bright Vertues of Good Wives & Mothers / Practis'd Her Self, and Cherished in others."[27] By identifying New England's patriarchs and matriarchs with Hebrew ancestors, grieving survivors reaffirmed the destiny of New Israel, led always forward by spiritually stalwart daughters and clerical sons.

For succeeding generations of Puritan ministers, Aaron, the High Priest appeared as a particularly appropriate correlative type. Benjamin Tompson (1642–1714) labelled Cotton Mather, Peter Hubbard, and Samuel Whiting all as Aarons, and in Whiting's case, used the High Priest's breastplate to extol the spiritual "Perfections" which "*this* Sacred *Father* bore" as "more Splendid far than ever *Aaron* wore, / "Within his Breast," because Whiting's "*Holy Vesture* was his *Innocence.*"[28] Among the ecclesiastical fraternity, it was also common to invoke the examples of David's lament for Jonathan, Jeremiah's for King Josiah, and Paul's for Timothy. As Anne Bradstreet's paraphrase of "David's Lamentation for Saul and Jonathan II Sem. 1:19" illustrates, David's elegy provided an oft-chosen precedent for Puritan memorial verses.[29] Ambivalent about the efficacy of poetry itself, yet struggling to shape his grief into a ceremonial form, Urian Oakes (1631–1681) also takes inspiration from "King *David*" who "in an Elegiack Knell / Rung out his dolours, when dear *Jona'than* fell" and with this "Soveraign, Sacret Poet" as his Muse endeavors "Now *Shepard's* faln, to write his Elegy."[30] Oakes' lamentation (1677) for Thomas Shepard, his "*Dearest Brother*" and "Inmost, Bosome-Friend," reveals strikingly the threat which all such deaths posed. "When such a Pillar's faln . . . / When such a glorious, shining Light's put out," Oakes reasons, "Well may we fear some Downfal, Darkness, Rout," and he questions, "Lord! Is thy Treaty with *New-England* come / Thus to an end? And is War in thy Heart?" Though originally protected by the God who guided Israel, the latter-day Chosen People yet perpetually feared lest through the gradual decimation of their leadership, New England's sacred errand would fail. By invoking Old Testament types, elegists assured the community that the lineage of its priests and prophets held constant from generation to generation.

In addition to reaffirming the Puritan's destiny, elegies—often written in diaries and journals—enabled mourners to vent private sorrows and to seek consolations. Accordingly, analogies between Old Testament types and New English saints not only established national ideals for public conduct but also set hagiographic models for personal lives (and deaths). Benjamin Tompson, for example, memorializes that "examplary Christian, Mary Tompson" (d. 1679) as a "Dorcas in our israell" and exhorts the bereaved to "follow her steps & imitate her life, / Who was a Virtuous virgin mother wife."[31] In a private notebook, John Saffin portrays "how Death is wellcom'd by the Saints" by listing Jacob, Joseph, Moses, David, Simeon, and Paul, who invite "our Constant imitation."[32] John Wilson's "Into Honnor," a funeral anagram for John Norton (d. 1663), similarly catalogues Old and New Testament figures as "rare Examples," if we "had the grace" to make us "worthy once / of that most glorious place."[33] Funeral lyrics thus encouraged a greater personalism that oftentimes led poets to eulogize ministers and mothers not simply as contributors to the collective good but also as moral exempla for individual saints. Still it must have seemed a grotesque reincarnation, like hearing voices from the grave, to read aloud Wilson's first-person dramatic accounts of William Tompson's (d. 1666) and Joseph Briscoe's (d. 1657) deaths. In the anagram for Tompson, the deceased delivers his own memorial, paralleling his experiences of doubt and redemption to Jonah's: "With ionah now Ime Cast ashore; / The whale Could not me keep; / But in my sauiour iesus Christ, / I swetly fell asleep."[34] As later poems by Edward Taylor (II.30) and Philip Freneau also testify, Jonah's deliverance from the whale's belly furnished an apt type for Christ's resurrection from the grave.[35] Thus, William Tompson (as persona) climaxes his figural lesson by admonishing readers to "Concider Christ himself, / The prince of our salvation" who "from his hellish Torments all, / At last to heaven up taken / To highest glory."

The *imitatio figura* and *imitatio Christi* appeared frequently in typological sermons and treatises, usually as a moral "use" or instruction for the congregation. However, new world Puritans took this concept of imitation one step farther— beyond Old Testament types or Christ as Antitype to the Elect themselves. But what differentiates funeral lyrics from communal histories is the more overt insistence upon Christ's transforming agency, because only through a uniquely personal belief in the Saviour's power to redeem man from death could each saint hope for eternal life. Hence, Wilson's anagram, "Job cries hope," concludes with an appeal: "Remember what a Death it was that Christ / (Suffered for me) the Darling of the highest; / His Death of Deaths hath quite remov'd the sting."[36] Writing nearly one hundred years later, Davies set forth the "bright Example" of Samuel Blair's death (1751) for "bravest Emulation" by creating a baroque vision of Christ's crucifixion, "See! from his Hands and Feet his Head and Side /

Rivers of Blood and Mercy mingled glide," and calling sinners to "Believe and Live, there wash thy foulest Stains, / In this dear deluge from his bleeding Veins" (pp. 145, 149).

Because death generated natural anxieties about the fate of loved ones and the unknown beyond, memorialists responded by providing not only immediate apprehensions of Christ's redemptive mercy but also consoling visions of God's heavenly kingdom. As in a funeral sermon or Renaissance encomium, elegies might begin by mourning the lost soul, then eulogize his/her lineage, holy life, deeds, and virtues, and conclude with promises of a heavenly crown of right-eousness. At the moment of transcendence, even the loquacious Tompson finds himself speechless, "My soul with him doth rest, / Of joys & Consolations / Unspeakably posest," while Davies' persona in "The Soul releas'd by Death" discovers the "Joys Divine" of seeing "Thy Face at last, / O my Dear, incarnate God!" (p. 29) In the dramatic narrative of Elijah's "translation" into Heaven, Benjamin Colman finds the perfect figure for drawing hope from Samuel Wil-lard's death. Perhaps for Willard, too, the "Bright hosts of *Angels*" will line "the Heav'nly Way / To guard the *Saint* up to Eternal Day" and "a *Chariot* Bright / And *Steeds of Fire,* swift as the Beams of Light" will bear him aloft to be *"Enthron'd,"* where he will also wait with Elijah for the "more Illustrious *Second Coming* with his Lord."[37] In moments of loss, mourners thus sought consolation in biblical visions of angelic feast, seraphic hymns, crowns and thrones of glory, and God's naked face. Unlike chroniclers, who projected the Millennium as a culmination of America's national progress, elegists preferred spiritual Readings of Revelation, where the Judgment Day would herald the resurrection of redeemed souls, family reunions, and Christ's nuptials with his Bride—the Church. In death Puritan fathers, wives, children stepped forward momentarily from the anonymous panorama of social progress, and from these models (based upon the exempla of ancient types) survivors in this world's perilous wilderness draw comfort by anticipating a heavenly regeneration.

Drawing a proverbial lesson from Norton's passing, Wilson proclaimed, "His life was nothing but of death / a daily meditation, / And to his happy end, at last, / a solemn preparation." The need to prepare for death shaped not only each believer's life but also seventeenth-century meditative lyrics in which the saint confronted the spiritual torments of his earthly pilgrimage. Nicholas Noyes (1647–1717) extolled the efficacy of such "pious *Meditation*," which like Isaiah's *"Coal"* from the *"Holy Fire"* will "perfume, and purifie / Thy mind, and make it heavenly," refines "the *dross* and *tin*, / Makes *Gold* without, and *Gold* within," and "makes a *New man* of the *Old*."[38] Puritan insistence upon meditation, like a "Coelestial *Stone*" to transmute sin to sanctity, derived in part from a Reformed emphasis on applying scriptural paradigms to the self, so that each saint might discover Christ's saving grace within his heart. Protestant theologians rejected tropological readings of the types, that is, moral allegories spun out by medieval theologians, but they advocated instead applying the spiritual truths to personal lives. After annotating Adam, Enoch, Noah, and Melchizedek as "imperfect

Shadows of the Messiah," Mather, for example, counsels readers to "know these things, meditate and consider them more throughly, and improve Christ in these Discoveries for your Spritual good," and more particularly *"examine your selves, and try which of the two Adams* you are under," for *"Adam* and *Christ* divide the whole World." For some Puritans, including Philip Pain, Samuel Sewall, Davies, and Taylor, writing poetry became a vehicle for self-examination and for applying figural truths to their lives—an extension beyond preaching to practice.[39] The personal voice, spiritual trials and hopes, Old Testament types, and Christ's redemptive grace which characterized elegies appeared in heightened relief in Puritan meditations. Yet unlike memorialists who encouraged public emulation of Old Testament patriarchs as *exempla fidei*, private devotional poets focused primarily on the *imitatio Christi*. Davies, who wrote poems to accompany his sermons, lauds Christ as *"Prophet," "High-Priest,"* and *"Saviour-King,"* but it is to the *"Transcendent Excellency of* Christ," as the title suggests, that he directs attention with the refrain "to imitate the Blest above" (pp. 190, 191). More insulated from the public realm, contemplative poets gravitated toward a stricter exegetical typology, one less apt to find recapitulations in every national catastrophe or minister's death, one more apt to exalt the antitypal Christ robed in transcendent glory.

The most skilled of America's colonial poets, Edward Taylor (1642?–1725) epitomizes this conservatism among devotional typologists. From 1693 to 1706, he preached thirty-six sermons, *Upon the Types of the Old Testament*, modelled after treatises by Samuel Mather and Thomas Taylor. But Taylor's uniqueness stems from his habitual composition of preparatory meditations, in which he recasts homiletic doctrine, then applies it to his own sin-infected soul. The sermons and companion poems systematically survey typological theory (II.1– 2), the personal types from Adam to Jonah (II.3–13, 30) and ranks (II.14–15), the real things, or sacrifices, the temple, feasts, and purifications (II.16–28), God's extraordinary providences for Israel (II.29, 58–61), and the ordinary seals confirming faith, circumcision and Passover (II.70–71).[40] Compressed para- phrases of the sermons, the meditations cast into bold relief the bipolarity of typology, that is, the illuminating reciprocity between type and antitype, prefi- guration and fulfillment, the law and gospel. Like Luther and Calvin, Taylor reaffirms the continuity of God's revelations, but the historical dispensations are Old and New Testament, not contemporary providences in New England. Whereas elegists popularly use Aaron as an archetype for Puritan priests, Taylor instead locates the High Priests within the context of Jewish rituals and delineates the parallels with Christ:

> A'ron as he atonement made did ware
>   His milke white linen Robes, to typify
> Christ cloath'd in human flesh pure White, all fair,
>   And undefild, atoneing God most High.
>
> . . . .

> Aaron goes in unto the Holy place
>   With blood of Sprinkling and sprinkles there
> Atones the Tabernacle, Altars face
>   And Congregation; for defild all were.
> Christ with his proper blood did enter in
>   The Heavens bright, propitiates for Sin. [II.23.25–28, 43–48]

Such correlations, often metaphorically embellished, are the dominant method in Taylor's figural meditations. He proclaims, "Jonas our Turtle Dove, I Christ intend" (II.30.43); questions, "Is Josephs glorious shine a Type of thee?" (II.7.7); and exults, "I spy thyselfe, as Golden bosses fixt / On Bible Covers, shine in Types out bright, / Of Abraham, Isaac, Jacob, where's inmixt / Their streaming Beames of Christ displaying Light" (II.6.6–10). The "Golden Altar" figures forth Christ's "Eternall Plank of Godhead, Wed / Unto our Mortall Chip, its sacrifice" (II.18.25, 21–22), the "Temple" bespeaks the Son as God's new "Medium of Worship" (II.20.43, 50), and the "Feast of Tabernacles" foreshadows Christ's "Theanthropy" (II.24.61, 62). Taylor's antiphonal matching of antitype with type leads to a preordained conclusion—Christ's superiority. In Puritan doctrine, all personal types are superseded, legal ceremonies abrogated by new worship, and ancient purifications inferior to the Saviour's balm of "Sanctifying Grace" (II.27.58). Although revealed to us through the cloudier "Looking glass" of Old Testament personages and rituals, Christ ultimately becomes the shining model for imitation.

Unlike New World historians or elegists, Taylor resists a recapitulative typology and applies figural lessons instead to the spiritual life. For Taylor's Israel's Exodus does not herald the Protestant Reformation or Puritans' emigration. Rather "Isra'ls coming out of Egypt," Taylor writes, "is such a Coppy that doth well Descry / Not onely Christ in person unto us. / But Spirituall Christ, and Egypt Spiritually" (II.58.31, 32–34). Deliverance from "Egyptian Bondage whence gates Israel shows" equates with freedom from Satan's "Spiritual bondage whence Christs children goe" to seek a new covenant grace (II.58.35–36). Neither a Jeremiah nor a patriotic millenarian, Taylor envisions salvation as an intimate journey in which each human soul travels from this world's "Wilderness of Sin" to the heavenly Zion (II.58.113).[41] Israel's calling, Moses' parting the Red Sea, the forty years' trek, Marah's bitter waters—all mark the "interchanging Course" of "Providences, Honycombs and Stings" through which a holy pilgrim wanders until "here within Celestiall Canaan sings" (II.58.117, 119, 120). "Celestial Canaan" may signify the assurance of divine election or Heaven itself. Whatever the destination, Christ alone dispenses sanctifying grace. Taylor's remaining four poems on extraordinary types explicate the pillar of cloud and fire, manna, water from the rock, and brazen serpent, all prefigurations of Jesus, the "Churches King to guid, support, Defend" (II.59.26), the "Bread of Life"(II.60A.26), his blood the "Aqua Vitae Deare" (II.60B.26), and his presence a "Sovereign Salve" against the "Serpents bite" (II.61.33, 34). Taylor thus conceived of his meditations not only as Sabbath preparations for administering the Lord's Supper, but also as a life-long diary recording his spiritual quest. Hence, the developmental paradigm of typology is writ large in his patterning of the second series of *Preparatory Meditations,* where he begins with Old Testament prophetic types (II.1–30), progresses toward a New Testament Christological focus (II.31–114), and culminates with Canticles (II.115–165), in which he envisions the saint's eternal marriage with the Bridegroom.[42]

Edward Taylor cares little for historical immortality, and he endeavors instead to claim a place, however peripheral, in the providential schema of Christ's fulfillment. He promises "rent of Reverent fear / For Quarters" in God's Tabernacle (II.24.51–52); he calls the Lord to "let thy Deity mine Altar bee," so that he can offer "Myselfe, and services" as sacrificial atonements (II.18.55, 51); he yearns to be "thy Guest too at this Feast" of Pentecost "and live / Up to thy Gospell Law" (II.22.68, 69), and he beseeches Christ to "Cleanse mee thus with thy Rich Bloods Sweet Shower" (II.27.61). But marginal participation is only one way of personalizing the type and antitype. Habitually, Taylor's poems begin with pain-wracked confessions of sin, proceed through a figural analysis from which he draws spiritual hope, and climax with renewed dedication to imitating Christ's life. "Be thou my Samson, Lord, a Rising Sun, / Of Righteousness unto my Soule" (II.11.49–50), he prays, or "Make mee, thy Nazarite by imitation / Not; of the Ceremony, but thy selfe, / In Holiness of Heart and Conversation" (II.15.38–40). Contrary to usages in Puritan elegies or chronicles, Christ never drops from the typal correlation, because Taylor cannot conceive of a personal or providential history without the Saviour's presence. He comes closest to a correlative typology when he longs for an artistry comparable to Solomon's or David's and sufficient to create divine psalms rather than crude human syllabifications. His earthly tongue's "muddy Words" or "Goose quill-slabbred draughts" cannot satisfy his desire to create graceful praises (II.43.23, 15). Neither can he envision an after-life without poetry, as he anticipates his humble place among God's angelic host. If Christ tunes his heart's strings, then Taylor will offer his "Sacrifice of Praise in Melody" (II.18.64), "sing / New Psalms on Davids Harpe to thee" (II.2.41–42), and "with Angells soon / My Mictams shall thy Hallelujahs tune" (II.8.41–42). Taylor's devotional meditations thus dramatize one man's personal applications of figural truths and his beliefs that a life lived *imitatio Christi* prepares the Elect for the celestial paradise.

Among colonial poets Taylor was not alone in adopting David as the figure for the divinely inspired poet. Anne Bradsteet portrayed him as "rosy cheek musician," while Jonathan Mitchell (1624–1668) claimed, "David's affliction bred us many a Psalm."[43] A dedicatory poem to George Sandys' paraphrase of the psalms grants him unrivalled supremacy, since "Prophets are poets, to whose song to bring / More state, the prince of poets is the King / David, full of his

God and holy fire, / The chief perceptor of this sacred quire."[44] While devotionalists chose David as their model, elegists celebrated ministers as Aarons, and chroniclers acclaimed Moses as Israel's premier historian. Puritans believed in poets only in so far as they were conduits for transmitting God's Holy Word. Poetic embellishment was anathema, directly contrary to an emphasis on matter over manner, on sacred lessons more than their arraying in gorgeous imagery. Puritan poets thus turned to the language of Canaan and Old Testament types to create visions of New England's holy commonwealth as a New Israel, to herald pious patriarchs as correlates to the Hebrew fathers, and to glorify Christ as divine exemplum *forma perfectior* and the saint's spiritual guide. The reservoir of types provided the sustaining power of a God-sanctioned myth, one which placed the Puritan migration and each saint's spiritual journey within providential history and millennial revelation. Those imaginative visions of America's grand destiny resonate today, even in a world significantly altered from the theocracy of the Massachusetts Bay Colony.

NOTES

1. See Bercovitch, *Typology*; idem, *Puritan Origins*; and Earl Miner, ed., *Literary Uses of Typology from the Late Middle Ages to the Present* (Princeton: Princeton Univ. Press, 1977).

2. "SOLOMON. A Paraphrastical Poem on sundry Passages in the Book of Ecclesiastes," in *Collected Poems of Samuel Davies 1723–1761*, ed. Richard Beale Davis (Gainesville, Fla.: Scholars' Facsimiles & Reprints, 1968), p. 11. Subsequent references to poems by Davies are to this edition.

3. *Moses Unvailed, or those Figures which Served unto the patterne and shaddow of heavenly things, pointing out the Messiah Christ Jesus*, 2 pts. (London: G. Purslow for J. Budge, 1619 [part 1]–1620 [part 2]); *Christ Revealed; or the Old Testament Explained*, ed. W. Jemmat (London: M. F. for R. Dawlman and L. Fawne, 1635); and *The Figures or Types of the Old Testament* (Dublin: n.p., 1683). Samuel Mather's *Figures or Types*, 2nd ed. (London: For Nath. Hillier, 1705; rpt. New York: Johnson Reprint, 1969), is the basis for my discussion of Puritan typology throughout this chapter.

4. See Charles W. Mignon, "The Nebraska Edward Taylor Manuscript: 'Upon the Types of the Old Testament,' " *EAL* 12 (1977–78): 296–301.

5. Charles W. Mignon, "Christ the Glory of All Types: The Initial Sermon from Edward Taylor's 'Upon the Types of the Old Testament,' " *WMQ* 37 (1980): 299.

6. Stanford, *Taylor*, II.2.1; II.7.39; II.9.1; II.50.16; II.3.21. Taylor's *Preparatory Meditations* are cited in the text by series, number, and line.

7. Vertue, (London: T. Roycroft, 1659); Keach, (London: John Darby for Enoch Prosser, 1681).

8. Lewalski, *Poetics*, p. 129.

9. *A Song of Deliverance*, in Murdock, *Paul*, p. 28.

10. Lowance, *Canaan*.

11. In Silverman, *Poetry*, pp. 317–322. Seagood translated this poem into English from the Latin version by Arthur Blackamore and published it in *The Maryland Gazette*, no. 93 (June 24, 1729).

12. In Silverman, *Poetry*, pp. 222–34.

13. (1654; rpt. Delmar, New York: Scholars' Facsimiles & Reprints, 1974), pp. 89, 71, 166–68, 235–36, 167, as quoted in the text.

14. See Bercovitch, *Jeremiad*.

15. *Song of Deliverance*, p. 27–31, 63.

16. ed. Kenneth B. Murdock (New York: Spiral, 1929).

17. (Cambridge: S. G. and M. Y. for John Usher of Boston, 1670), pp. 17, 22, 49. See also Judg. 14:14 for the story of Samson's riddle from which Wigglesworth derives his title.

18. In *Specimens of American Poetry*, ed. Samuel Kettell, 3 vols. (Boston: S. G. Goodrich, 1829), 1:162, 163.

19. In Kettell, *Specimens*, 1:185, 191.

20. In *American Poems*, ed. Elihu Hubbard Smith (1793; rpt. Gainesville, Fla.: Scholars' Facsimiles & Reprints, 1966), pp. 22, 23.

21. In *The Major Poems of Timothy Dwight*, ed. William J. McTaggart and William K. Bottorff (Gainesville, Fla.: Scholars' Facsimiles & Reprints, 1969), p. 15. Dwight also wrote *A Dissertation on the History, Eloquence, and Poetry of the Bible* (New Haven: Thomas and Samuel Green, 1772) in which he defends the sublime poetry of Scripture.

22. See Lowance's fuller discussion of American millenialism in *Canaan*, p. 115–59.

23. In Smith, *American Poems*, p. 93. See Lowance's discussion of "Joel Barlow and the Rising Glory of America," *Canaan*, pp. 208–46.

24. In Smith, *American Poems*, pp. 25, 27.

25. In Kettell, *Specimens*, 2:36, 37.

26. "Upon the TOMB of the most Reverend Mr. John Cotton, late Teacher of the Church of Boston in New-England," in Meserole, *Poetry*, p. 411.

27. "Honour and Vertue Elegized in a Poem Upon an Honourable, Aged, and Gracious Mother in our Israel, Madam Elizabeth Hutchinson," in "The Poetry of John Danforth," ed. Thomas A. Ryan, *PAAS* 78 (1968): 161.

28. "Upon the very Reverend SAMUEL WHITING," in White, *Tompson*, p. 137.

29. In Bradstreet, Hensley, pp. 199–200.

30. "An Elegie upon the Death of the Reverend Mr. Thomas Shepard," in Meserole, *Poetry*, pp. 209–20; Silverman, *Poetry*, pp. 147–60. See chapter 20 of this book.

31. "A short memoriall & Revew of sum Vertues in that examplary Christian, Mary Tompson, who Dyed in march 22: 1679. penned for the imitation of the liveing," in White, *Tompson*, pp. 142, 143.

32. In *John Saffin: His Book*, ed. Caroline Hazard (New York: Harbor Press, 1928), p. 124.

33. "John Norton. Anagr. Into Honnor," in Murdock, *Paul*, pp. 91–97.

34. "William Tompson Lo my ionah slumpt Anagr 2," in Murdock, *Paul*, pp. 15–18.

35. See Freneau, "The History of the Prophet Jonah," in Harry Hayden Clark, ed., *Poems of Freneau* (New York: 1929), pp. 193–203.

36. John Wilson, "A Copy of Verses . . . on the sudden Death of Mr. Joseph Briscoe," in Murdock, *Paul*, pp. 82–83.

37. "A POEM on ELIJAHS Translation, Occasion'd by the DEATH of the Reverend and Learned, Mr. SAMUEL WILLARD," in Meserole, *Poetry*, pp. 348, 350.

38. "A Prefatory POEM To the Little Book, Entituled, Christianus per Ignem," in Meserole, *Poetry*, pp. 271–73.

39. Philip Pain created a series of *Daily Meditations: Quotidian Preparations for, and Considerations of Death and Eternity* (Cambridge, 1668), of which "The Porch," and sixty-four meditations are extant. See chapter 22 of this book. Samuel Sewall (1652–1730) is reputed to have written more than fifty poems, including elegies, epitaphs, and contemplations of the New England landscape and events, some published as broadsides. He also recorded verses from his friends in his commonplace book, now at the *NYHS*.

40. See discussions of Taylor and typology in Thomas M. Davis, "Edward Taylor and the Traditions of Puritan Typology," *EAL* 4 (1969–70): 27–47; Karen E. Rowe, "Puritan Typology and Allegory as Metaphor and Conceit in Edward Taylor's *Preparatory Meditations*" (Ph.D. diss., Indiana University, 1971); Robert Reiter, "Poetry and Doctrine in Edward Taylor's *Preparatory Meditations, Series II, 1–30*," in Bercovitch, *Typology*, pp. 163–74; Karl Keller, " 'The World Slickt Up in Types': Edward Taylor as a Version of Emerson," in Bercovitch, *Typology*, pp. 175–90; Lewalski, *Poetics*, pp. 388–426; and Lowance, *Canaan*, pp. 89–111. My conclusions about typological organizations in Taylor's sermons and poems are based upon the manuscript of *Upon the Types of the Old Testament*, to which this author has been granted access by the University of Nebraska Library.

41. See also Michael Wigglesworth, *Riddles Unriddled, or Christian Paradoxes Broke open . . . attached to Meat Out of the Eater* (1670), in which he offers a spiritual interpretation of the deliverance.

42. See my "Sacred or Profane?: Edward Taylor's Meditations on Canticles," *Modern Philology* 72 (1974); 123–38; and Jeffrey Hammond, "A Puritan *Ars Moriendi*: Edward Taylor's Late Meditations on the Song of Songs," *EAL* 17 (1982–83): 191–214.

43. Bradstreet, "Of the Four Humours in Man's Constitution," in Bradstreet, Hensley, p. 38; Mitchell, "On the following Work and Its Authors," in Meserole, *Poetry*, p. 412. Mitchell wrote the prefatory poem for Wigglesworth's *Day of Doom*.

44. "To Mr. George Sandys on His Paraphrase on the Sacred Hymns," in *The Poetical Works of George Sandys*, ed. Richard Hooper, 2 vols. (London: John Russell Smith, 1872), 1:lxxii.

5 THE HONEYED KNOT OF PURITAN AESTHETICS

MICHAEL CLARK

In one of the earliest studies of Puritan aesthetics Lawrence Sasek argued that it didn't exist, and critics have yet to refute that claim convincingly.[1] As Sasek showed, the Puritans were as little concerned about establishing a separate aesthetic as they were about establishing a separate church. Along with more secular artists, they simply accepted most of the traditions inherited from the Renaissance. The pedagogical and democratic assumptions behind the theological plain style did, of course, tend to emphasize the second half of the Horatian *dulce et utile* that was such a popular slogan, and the Calvinist proposition of the fallen world as a distorted reflection of the divine was especially compatible with the equally popular belief that human creative acts replicated the primal creation of the material world. This close correspondence between broad tenets of Puritan theology and more general fashions in aesthetics was often explicitly acknowledged. In the preface to his *Arte of Prophecying,* for example, William Perkins goes so far as to parallel religious and rhetorical arguments, juxtaposing postlapsarian humility with a classical epigram:

> Humane wisdome must be concealed, whether it be in the matter of the sermon, or in the setting forth of the words . . . because the hearers ought not to ascribe their faith to the gifts of men, but to the power of God's word . . . the minister may, yea and must privately use at his liberties the arts, philosophy, and a variety of reading, whilst he is framing his sermon; but he ought in public to conceal all these from the people. . . . *Ars etiam est celare artem.*[2]

The similarities between Puritan and other religious poets are even closer, as Barbara Lewalski has recently pointed out.[3] Like other seventeenth-century Protestants and Catholics as well, the Puritans drew upon a tradition of biblical poetics that included topics as various as the generic classifications of biblical modes by Jerome and Isidore of Seville, Cassiodorus's extensive list of biblical tropes, and Petrarch's analyses of metaphorical references to Christ. In addition to these more general sources, the Puritan poet had at his disposal the narrower vernacular and Protestant traditions popular in England, including emblem books, various meditative methods, commentaries on the "poetic" books of the Bible (Ecclesiastes, Proverbs, and the Song of Solomon), and a somewhat haphazard amalgam of Scholastic, Augustinian, and Reformist ideas regarding the connection between the visible world of man and the invisible world of God. Not even the objects of the Puritans' scorn were unique to them. Their rejection of elaborate tropes and allusive phrasing was part of a general rejection of Ciceronian formalism current in the earliest years of the seventeenth century, and the attacks on the theater for which the Puritans have become so notorious were hardly limited to any identifiable religious persuasion. In fact, the only feature of Puritan texts on aesthetics that can be considered uniquely their own is the historical reality behind allusions to the world as a wilderness in works by Puritans writing in New England.

The Puritans' lack of concern about differentiating their attitudes towards style and art from those of their contemporaries was accompanied by an apparent disregard of the inconsistencies in those attitudes. Of the few Puritans who explicitly wrote about aesthetics, most contradict each other and often themselves. Richard Baxter's warning that "the Truths of God do perform their work more by their Divine Authority . . . than by any ornaments of fleshy wisdom," for example, was no more typical than Richard Sibbes' praise for the writer who "studied by lively representations to help men's faith by the fancy." And if Ralph Cudworth was prone to the iconophobic rejection of a Catholic anthropomorphism that produced only "a Baby-god . . . which like little children, they have dressed up out of the clouts of their own fond Phancies," Thomas Taylor was equally ready to defend such uses of worldly imagery: "we have not only a sensual use of the creatures . . . but a spiritual; and profiteth not only our bodies, but our souls by them. Wherefore else did the Lord create them." Despite the popular stereotype of the Puritan as an austere ascetic who believed with John Preston that "the vale of mortality doth hide us, it covers *God* from use . . . as a weake eye is not able to behold the Sunne . . . no more can you see God in his Essence," many were willing to insist with Edward Taylor that we follow Christ in his parables and "illustrate supernatural things by natural." "If it were not thus," Taylor argued, "we could arrive at no knowledge of supernatural things, for we are not able to see above naturals . . . the Apostle argues invisible things from the visible. So that on this account there is argument enough, if we have but skill to take it and use it aright."[4]

These contraditions have bedevilled scholars for a century and have usually resulted in the reduction of Puritanism to only one of its several sides. In Moses Coit Tyler's early history of American literature, they led to his influential portrayal of the typical Puritan poet as a literate Eve, fully willing to obey the ascetic dictates of her upright provider, Puritanism, but too prone to fall for the Satanic whispering of that toad at her shoulder, Beauty. The Puritan, Tyler said,

> was at war with nearly every form of the beautiful. He himself believed that there was an inappeasable feud between religion and art; and hence,

the duty of suppressing art was bound up in his soul with the master-purpose of promoting religion. He cultivated the grim and the ugly. . . . Nevertheless, the Puritan did not succeed in eradicating poetry from his nature. Of course, poetry was planted there too deep even for his theological grub-hooks to root it out. Though denied expression in one way, the poetry that was in him forced itself into utterance in another.[5]

Following Tyler's example, early critics read Puritan poems as the spoils in a Manichean struggle between Puritanism and the wilderness on the one side and humanity on the other. "The more [the Puritans'] work is examined in the light of the hardships the colonists faced," Kenneth Murdock claimed, "the more impressive it becomes," striving for the empathic reading described by Tyler when, "in turning over these venerable pages, one suffers by sympathy something of the obvious toil of the undaunted men who, in the very teeth of nature, did all this." Later critics, however, have celebrated the failure of both Puritanism and the woods to cool a "hot poetic emotion" that "cannot always be kept within the limits of reasoned doctrine," a "universal craving for well-wrought mimesis" that stands as proof of the Puritans' "natural desire to make poems." True, the Puritans said they rejected the sauce for the meat, but such disclaimers were really a "strong suggestion that they had more liking than they dared to confess, or their principles allowed them to indulge, for the literary flights which they professed to scorn." So despite the austere aesthetics that emerges from the Puritans' own comments, "the Puritan never hated literature—or, for that matter, the arts in general. Rather, he feared that he might like them too much."[6]

These simplistic efforts to have the Puritans writing poetry in spite of their Puritanism resulted from the identification of Puritanism with a gnostic asceticism that ignored the existence, let alone the beauty, of this world. There is some evidence for that assumption, as Preston's claim that the world "covers *God* from use" suggests. Like Calvin, the Puritans believed that there was an irreducible difference between the visible and invisible worlds. The creation was God's book, but the fall had rendered it illegible by disrupting the human faculties and blinding man to the divine revelation that surrounds him. Not only did the fall create an ontological chasm between the divine and the human, it also posed an epistemological obstacle to the pursuit of God in this world:

> That Wisdom bright whose vastness for extent
>   Commensurates Dimension infinite
> A Palace built with Saphir-Battlement
>   Bepinkt with Sun, Moon, Starrs, all gold-fire bright
>   Plac'de man his Pupill here, and ev'ry thing,
>   With loads of Learning, came to tutor him.

But he (alas) did at the threashould trip
  Fell, Crackt the glass through which the Sun should shine
That darkness gross his noble Soule doth tip.
  Each twig is bow'd with loads of follies Rhime.
  That ev'ry thing in tutoring, is a toole
  To whip the Scholler that did play the foole. [II.41,ll.1–12][7]

But the Puritans also believed that God had redeemed man from this hopeless dilemma through two different manifestations of the ultimate unity between the visible world of man and the invisible world of God: Christ and the Scriptures. The Scriptures were "the interpreter of the book of nature in two ways," Jonathan Edwards said, "by declaring to us those spiritual mysteries that are indeed signified and typified in the constitution of the natural world; and secondly, in actually making application of the signs and types in the book of nature as representations of those spiritual mysteries."[8] Christ was the literal embodiment of that unity in his Incarnation, where his gift of "life Naturall" and "Spirituall Life indeed, / Peculiar to Rationalls also / [was] Contained as in a Seed" (II.90, ll. 37–40). So despite the disruption of man's faculties in the fall and the consequent inability to perceive the sympathy between the creatural world of the senses and the divine truth occasionally glimpsed by faith, the ontological gap between the visible and invisible worlds had been bridged by the example of Christ; and the epistemological difficulties of reading spiritual truths in the "hieroglyphic" marks of the corporeal world had been alleviated—though not obviated—by the Golden Key of the Scriptures.

The best recent criticism deals with the issue of this connection between worldly signs and their spiritual significance, usually focussing on the epistemological claims of separate metaphors and figures in the poems as illustrations of theological doctrine. Rather than opting for this world or the world to come, the Puritan now lives between them. For some readers, such as Lewalski, Katherine Blake, and Michael Reed, the connection finally eludes the poet, leaving him to emphasize the "gap between the human and the divine which the subtler, more sophisticated conceits of the metaphysical poets tend to bridge." Others, such as Robert Daly and William Scheick, argue that the Puritans were ultimately assured of that connection through their understanding of the symbolic properties of the world and the poetic use of that world in metaphor. However, even though these alternatives are more subtle and sophisticated than those presented by earlier critics, each still requires what is finally an arbitrary decision to accept some evidence and dismiss conflicting claims as aberrations. But in their theology, as I have suggested elsewhere, the Puritans insisted on having it both ways, defining their faith in an invisible world through a precise and systematic delineation of the limits of the visible. That the delicate balance of that dialectic was often lost in poems of celebratory naturalism or gnostic asceticism does not belie its existence.

As the following examples attest, the Puritans did not always choose between the theological antinomies of symbolic creation or mystical revelation that led to the contradictions in their aesthetics. Instead, at rare but magnificent moments, they struggled to earn their faith through a heroic refusal to ignore either their place in this world or their destiny in the next.[9]

For the Puritans, poetry was an especially efficacious means of embodying the paradoxes of their faith. Not only did Solomon's books and David's psalms provide scriptural precedents for the poet's work, but "God by his unfolding himself and his Mind to us in several kinds of Metaphorical terms, hath not only allowed, but sanctified our Use of the like."[10] Furthermore, in the Incarnation Christ had used the flesh as, in Taylor's words, "This Metaphor to make thyselfe appeare / In taking Colours," making of himself "a most Exact Coppy, written by the Deity of the Son of God, with the Pen of Humanity, on the milk white sheet of an Holy Life. . . . wilt thou not endeavour to Write by this Coppy?" And many of his fellow poets agreed, turning from the parabolic stories and metaphorical epigrams that had formed a biblical poetics out of Christ's speech to an emulation of His body, the flesh made Word.[11]

This turn in the poetic use of the Bible was made possible by the radical scripturalism of the Reformation. Most reformers moved the province of the Word from the Church to the Bible, and some had gone so far as to make of the Scriptures a totemic text that at times surpassed the status and power of Christ Himself. While few Puritans would have been willing to follow Luther in maintaining that the saving power of Scripture inheres in the physical writing rather than its incorporeal sense, they would have understood the vivid physicality of the text in Luther's dramatic assertion that the Pope could not "annul nor abrogate one single letter or dot in the Scriptures."[12] Neither Luther nor the Puritans held human writing in such high esteem, but it is nevertheless clear that this attitude towards scriptural language led the Puritans to value language— especially but not only that of the Bible—as a significant domain in itself independent of the supplementary, interpretive connection to the world that Calvin described. One pious Puritan, for example, was so inspired by the scriptural text "Moreover, the dog came and lapped up the water" that he named his own dog Moreover after its appearance in the Bible.[13] We will never know the fate of this unlucky dog, but it is not hard to imagine the attitude towards the Bible that is invoked by the ingenious irony behind this comical misreading. The very possibility of yoking together a dog and a conjunctive adverb the way one might name one's child Abraham, Faith, or even Seaborn demands a notion of language that accords it an ontological status equal to both the objective referents in this world and the spiritual concepts generally granted priority. In theory, at least, there was only a short jump from the reality of the word to the snuffling materiality of Moreover himself.

A similar attitude is evident in the more complex example of an anonymous anagram written to Thomas Dudley in 1645 (in Meserole, *Poetry*), where the author explicitly rejects the dependence of language on the world in the opening couplets. This literal hermeneutic was characteristic of Puritan observations on the most casual events.[14] Here, however, the text is the only "event," the collection of letters that makes up Dudley's name. Just as the word "moreover" took on an existence quite independent of its syntactical function in the previous example, so, too, do the letters of this anagram take on an existence that is independent of their morphemic function. The truth conveyed by this poem is not derived from the connection between words and the people and images to which they refer; it is derived within a domain developed by the movement of the letters as they pass from one word to another. The exclusively alphabetic nature of this domain becomes apparent in the last lines of the poem, when the dentals of "old" and "dye" are first juxtaposed to the labials of "must" and "men"—"old men . . . dye must"—and then shift across the space between the phonemes, making "must," "dust," "dye," and later, "lye" into virtual homonyms of each other and of Thomas Dudley. The semantic differences between "Thomas Dudley" and "ah! old, must dye" fade away as the phonetic distinctions between these words begin to blur, and we are left with literal proof that the life of "Thomas Dudley," both the man and the words, is contiguous with its dissolution.

A more serious use of language as a proof for theological doctrine can be found in many of Edward Taylor's *Meditations*. Here, the seventeenth-century fashion for *ploce, traductio*, and other tropes of repetition is often combined with paronomasia and alliteration to create a specifically linguistic network of evidence in support of the doctrinal content of the lines:

> Thou wilst mee thy, and thee, my tent to bee.
> Thou wilt, if I my heart will to thee rent,
> My Tabernacle make thy Tenement. [II .24, ll. 46–48]

> If thy Almightiness, and all my Mite
>   United be in sacred Marriage knot,
> My Mite is thine: Mine thine Almighty Might.
>   Then thine Almightiness my Mite hath got. [II. 48, ll. 37–40]

If God's comprehensive power can be manifest in the phonetic compatibility of "Almightiness" and "all my Mite," which bridges the gap between the infinity of God and the small speck of man, then grammar, too, can confirm a theological claim: "Thine mine, mine Thine, a mutuall claim is made. / Mine, thine are Predicates unto us both" (II. 79, ll. 31–32). And in II. 90, Taylor even exploits the distinction between such linguistic proofs and the rational forms of human thought, using the grammatical versatility of the word "them" to conflate spiritual and natural life in a way that defies the propositional structure of syntactic argument:

> Eternal Life! What Life is this, I pray?
>> Eternity snick snarls my Brains, thought on:
> Its the Arithmaticians Wrack each way.
>> It hath beginning, yet it end hath none.
>> IIe that hath been ten thousand years therein,
>> 'S as far from 'ts end, as when they did begin.
> . . . .
> Life Naturall (although Essentiall to
>> All Living things) and Spirituall Life indeed,
> Peculiar to Rationalls also
>> Contained are in Christs Gift as in a Seed,
>> Are both Adjuncted with Eternity
>> In that he gives them them Eternally. [II. 90, ll. 1–6, 37–42]

If an objective pronoun can achieve such a synthesis, it should then come as no surprise that Taylor can resolve the most crucial question of his connection to Christ through a grammatical marker:

> My Blessed Lord, that Golden Linck that joyns
>> My Soule, and thee, out blossoms on't this Spruice
> Peart Pronown MY more spiritous than wines,
>> Rooted in Rich Relation, Graces Sluce.
>> This little Voice feasts mee with fatter Sweets
>> Than all the stars that pave the Heavens Streets.
>
> It hands me All, my heart, and hand to thee
>> And up doth lodge them in thy persons Lodge
> And as a Golden bridg ore it to mee
>> Thee, and thine All to me, and never dodge.
>> In this small Ship a mutuall Intrest sayles
>> From Heaven and Earth, by th'holy Spirits gales. [II. 35, ll. 1–12]

In these examples, the grammatical and syntactic properties of words supplant their referential function. More often, though, the Puritans insisted on the interaction between the semantic and syntactic roles of a word. Drawing on the four-fold hermeneutic of Scholastic exegesis, they argued that the place of a word in a text established a connection between two different meanings or "senses," the spiritual and the literal. John Weems called this the "compound sense" of Scripture.[15] The worldly thing was a sign, its spiritual significance the signified; and the word in the text generated a "transaction" between them:

> The sense, therefore, of that Scripture [i.e., Galatians 4.22] is one only, namely, the literal or grammatical. However, the whole entire sense is

not in the words taken strictly, but part in the type, part in the transaction
itself. In either of these considered separately and by itself, part only of
the meaning is contained; and by both taken together the full and perfect
meaning is completed. . . . When we proceed from the sign to the thing
signified, we bring no new sense, but only bring out into the light what
was before concealed in the sign. . . . For although this sense be spiritual,
yet it is not a different one, but really literal; since the letter itself affords
it to us in the way of similitude or argument. . . . By expounding a
similitude, we compare the sign with the thing signified, and so bring
out the true and entire sense of the words.[16]

Conversely, to write that letter the sign and its signified had to be joined through
a ritual conversion of similitude into significance, as when Christ joined bread
and His body. In that instance, Samuel Willard said, Christ "used his wisdom
in the choice that he made; and because he appointed them to be signs, he made
choice of such things as are aptly joined in their nature and use, to be accom-
modable to such a signification. The Sacrament is appointed to represent the
sufficiency and suitableness of Christ for our spiritual life . . . [and] *Bread is
the Staff of Life*. . . ."[17] William Perkins could therefore call the Lord's Supper
a "sacramentall Metonymie" and claim that such a relation among word, thing,
and spiritual sense is the source of all the tropes and figures that poets draw
on.[18]

   That "proportionable resemblance" is not, however, the basis for their epis-
temological value. The world was not a sign in itself. Willard is careful to
maintain that the fact that worldly things "should signify these spiritual things,
and be used for that end, doth not flow from their Nature, but [Christ's] free
Designation." And because that designative ritual constituted the significance,
it had to be incorporated into our use of the sign. Though there must be a "Bodily
Eating and Drinking of these Elements," Willard says, "else they would not be
Sacramental, or used as Signs; though still there must be a Mystical Improvement
of these, else they will not obtain the Sacramental end and use of them" (p. 864).
In other words, the materiality of the signs must be recognized; otherwise, they
are not signs. (Implicit in this requirement, of course, is the Puritans' rejecton
of direct apprehension of spiritual truth.) But we must also recognize that the
signified does not inhere in the sign, because what makes the sign significant is
the freedom of and necessity for the designative act which joins sign and signified
in what John Cotton called God's "gratuitous and free covenant."[19] What is
needed to mystically improve the sign therefore is an exegesis that demonstrates
the priority of the designative gesture over the symbolic junction itself. So,
Willard says, if people would understand the Lord's Supper,

   They must be arrived to such a judgment, as to be able to distinguish
   between the Sign and the thing signified by it, else they cannot make

that practical Improvement of it, which is required of all such. They that cannot put a difference between Bread and Wine, and the Body and Blood of Christ, and understand the Sacramental union between one and the other in the Ordinance, ought not to be received. (p. 863)

The proper understanding of the designation here does not depend so much on Perkins' proportionable resemblance as on the reader's ability to perceive the difference between the corporeal referent of the word and its spiritual significance. When describing Christ's reference to Himself as a vine (John 15), Willard reminds us that "every similitude hath something defective in it, and the spirit of God useth many, because no one can fully adumbrate it." Christ compared Himself to a vine and its branches "to note the closeness and connaturalness" of the connection, "to let us understand, that by virtue of it, we derive all our life, and fruit from Christ, and receive the same sap of Grace from him, which is predicated in him. But yet there is this difference, the branches do grow naturally out of the Vine, and are of the same individual substance with it, whereas Christ and we are personally distinct, and we are put into him by an implanting" (p. 429). The passage from John 15 contains no such caution. It is Christ's speech, and the metaphorical affirmation is unqualified: "I am the true vine." Willard's interpretation establishes the spiritual meaning of the phrase only by putting differences into the homogeneous coupling of Christ and the vine; it is those differences that make a literal reading impossible and necessitate its "practical improvement." So, although the scriptural text was supposed to be the spectacles through which the text of the world would be rendered legible because of a "certaine agreement and proportion of the externall things with the internall," that similitude was established through words that contained hidden gaps that separated the visible and invisible worlds as ontologically distinct and epistemologically antithetical.

Edward Taylor dramatized that paradox in his meditation on John 6.53: "Unless ye eat the Flesh of the Son of man, and drink his blood, you have no life in you." He begins by describing his difficulty in properly praising the Lord because his meditations keep being interrupted by "Some toy or trinket slipping in between / My heart and thee." In the next stanzas we find that this trinket is the literal referent of the biblical words:

> Thou art Lifes Fountain and its Food. The Strife
>   Of Living things doth for Life Sake proceed.
>   But he that with the best of Lifes is spic'te
>   Doth eate, and drinke the Flesh, and blood of Christ.
>
> What feed on Humane Flesh and Blood? Strang mess!
>   Nature exclaims, What Barbarousness is here? [II. 81, ll. 9–14]

Taylor's revulsion at the cannibalistic overtones of the literal image invoked here points rather obviously to the solution. He quickly exposes the logical inconsistency of the literal reading of the image and draws the necessary conclusion:

> Christs Flesh and Blood how can they bee good Cheer?
> If shread to atoms, would too few be known,
> For ev'ry mouth to have a single one?

> This Sense of this blesst Phase is nonsense thus.
> Some other Sense makes this a metaphor. [II. 81, ll. 16–20]

He then completes his poem with a series of metaphors that are so outlandish that they parody the confusion between literal and spiritual senses that momentarily interfered in his meditation: "Christs works, as Divine Cookery, knead in / The Pasty Past, (his Flesh and Blood) most fine / Into Rich Fare, made with the rowling pin / His Deity did use" (II. 81, ll. 25–28).

The ludicrous discrepancy between the spiritual and objective referents of these words vividly illustrates Taylor's claim that "the Creatures field no food for Souls e're gave" (I. 8, l. 14). But since like most other Puritans Taylor also maintained that we must illustrate "supernatural things by natural," we cannot simply dismiss his frequent use of natural images as the consequences of some innate mimetic craving struggling against a gnostic faith in immediate, mystical communion. These different attitudes form a dialectic, not a contradiction. In *Gods Determinations* Taylor advised us to "Do all Good Works, work all good things you know / As if you should be sav'd for doing so. / Then undo all you've done, and it deny / And on a naked Christ alone rely."[20] And that is what he does in his poems, time after time justifying a natural image of Christ's supernatural deity only to undo it through a sudden denial:

> Glory, What art thou? tell us: Dost thou know?
>   Its native to our nature to desire
> To weare thy Shine. Our Sparkling Eyes bestow
>   Their kisses on the Cheeks thou dost attire
>   Our Fancies fed therewith grow lively briske.
>   Acts always lodged in happy glances frisk.

> Then Glory as a Metaphor, Il 'tende
>   And lay it all on thee, my Lord! to bring
> My Heart in Flames of love, its rayes out send
>   Whose Curled tops shall ever to thee cling.
>   But all the glory Sunbeams on them beare
>   Is but a Smoaky vapour to thy Weare. [II. 100, ll. 1–12][21]

The meiotic deflation of metaphorical references to Christ and the divine realm is a common property of Puritan poetics. It reflects the Puritans' insistence on both the epistemological efficacy of this world and the theological constraint of a spiritual significance whose infinity necessarily surpasses any finite expression. The insistent dissolution of the connections among words, their objective referents, and their spiritual uses is the poetic equivalent of "that practical improvement" of the sign called for by Puritan hermeneutics. The tropes are elaborate exegetical exercises, hermeneutic commentaries on themselves in which the images disintegrate under the pressure of their spiritual signified. As a result, unlike the miraculous gesture through which Christ's speech joined sign and signified, the self-reflexive words of the Puritan poet were doomed endlessly to retrace their frustrated path between the world to which they referred and the Word to which they aspired. Trapped within this narcissistic reflection of the finite boundaries of the poem, the poet can only lament the limits he would transcend:[21]

> I fain would Prize, and Praise thee, Lord, but finde
>   My Prizing Faculty imprison'd lyes.
> That its Appreciation is confinde
>   Within its prison walls and small doth rise.
>   Its Prizing Act it would mount up so high
>   That might oremount its possibility.
>
> I fain would praise thee, but want words to do't:
>   And searching ore the realm of thoughts finde none
> Significant enough and therefore vote
>   For a new set of Words and thoughts hereon
>   And leap beyond the line such words to gain
>   In other Realms, to praise thee: but in vain.
>
> Me pitty, pardon mee and Lord accept
>   My Penny Prize, and penny worth of Praise.
> Words and their Sense within thy bounds are kept
>   And richer Fruits my Vintage cannot raise. [II. 106, ll. 1–16]

The failure of language is a popular theme in Taylor's poetry and in that of other religious poets. It recalls the fundamental inadequacy of the human mind, and more specifically it emphasizes the Puritans' adamant refusal to accord to man more than a dim reflection of Christ's signifying power. "Our writers [must] substantially prove the sufficiency of the Scripture in matter necessary to Salvation," John Cotton said, "because we are forbidden to add ought to the Word written. . . . All shadows are now past, the Body being come. It is contrary to the Rule of the Gospel there should be such Types, Shadows, and Significations brought into the Service of God." "God did not forbid his own Institution of signs," Samuel Mather explained, "but only our own inventions."[22] Obeying that proscription often led the Puritan poet to rely on simple declaration rather than description, and to replace Taylor's failed metaphors with doctrinal clichés. The result was usually the very worst poetry produced by the colonists. At times, though, the formulaic character of doctrinal propositions served as an effective foil to the tortured, broken syntax in which a poet registered the mystery and doubt of human experience.

This contrast is most dramatic in Anne Bradstreet's poem on the death of her grandchild Simon (see Meserole, *Poetry*). The structure of the poem is entirely conventional. Like most other Puritan poems about loss, it moves from personal grief through a doctrinal consideration of the occasion as God's will and finally concludes in a resigned acceptance of that will. But Bradstreet earns that resignation here through a desperate struggle to force it into the language of her grief.

The bathetic and coy refusal to name the event of the first line—"fal'n asleep" instead of died—is reflected in the second line, which tends to undermine the extremity of the grief through the qualification of the life as an "Acquaintance short." Ordinarily, this opening couplet would lead immediately to a complete dismissal of the grief in a recognition of God's will, as it does in Bradstreet's poem on the death of another grandchild, Elizabeth: "Blest Babe, why should I once bewail thy fate, / Or sigh thy dayes so soon were terminate; / Sith thou art setled in an Everlasting state?" (in Meserole, *Poetry*). But not in the Simon poem, as "scarcely blown" introduces a sense of yearning and loss that is emphasized by the redundant but pathetic specificity of "the last i'th' bud." The next line extends this metaphor and tone with an inverted foot that stresses the verb "Cropt," which points to the devastating separation wrought by the hand of an Almighty power rather than directing our attention to where it has taken the flower (as "plucked" might here, as "setled" does in the poem on Elizabeth's death). After such a beginning, the tone of the poem overwhelms the doctrinal meaning of the second hemistich, making "yet is he good" sound much more like a question than a statement. This prominence of the emotional connotations of the language does, of course, contradict the subordinate status that human emotion and language are supposed to have, and the next line reminds us of man's proper role: "With dreadful awe before him let's be mute, / Such was his will . . ." and then the sudden interruption that at first sounds like another question—"but why"—is immediately corrected as it falls into the syntax of the rest of the sentence, "let's not dispute." Bradstreet then ends the eight-line sentence by focusing the tonal ambiguity of the poem's language in her iambic stress on the word "say," which suggests an abdication that sounds a cynical counterpoint to the proper conclusion: "With humble hearts and mouths put in the dust, / Let's say he's merciful as well as just."

Had the poem ended here, Bradstreet would have justified the stereotype of the Puritan poet who simply jammed down dogma on top of whatever human suffering momentarily escaped her doctrinal eye. But in the closing lines she legitimately resolves the tension between the suffering of the poem's language and its doctrinal sense through her invocation of "that perfect Copy," Christ. In the smooth syntax and relaxed balance of the fifth couplet, the losses/crosses rhyme and the crucifixion—with its overtones of despair and Christ's lamentation about the absence of God in the time of His own suffering—align the suffering of man with that of Christ, invoke the union of God and man in that figure, and allude to the merciful God that Christ brought to earth and who promised to return. Thus when Bradstreet moves into the confident resignation of the final couplet, leaving her pain behind and virtually erasing the language in the smooth regularity of the iambic rhythm and the bland, conventional phrasing, she has prepared for that move not through a denial of the earlier suffering and the language that embodied it but through a sacramental "use" of the experience that converts it into the metaphor of all metaphors. Edward Taylor said that Christ "died on the Cross to Cross out Sin," cancelling the opaque mask of His humanity and revealing the truth of His spirit; and in Bradstreet's poem the crucifixion is also the occasion that crosses the text, casting off the sensual dimension of the language and the feelings connected with it to render the doctrine through, in the words of William Ames, a "crucified phrase."[23]

This dramatic cancellation of the sensible basis of language and experience also informs John Fiske's anagrammatic elegy on the death of John Cotton (in Meserole, *Poetry*), though Fiske's tour de force lacks the magnificent pathos of Bradstreet's poem. Fiske begins his anagram by recasting Cotton's name "Kotton after the old English writ'g" because that spelling will give him his poem. But he seems to ignore this purely textual origin at first and develops his opening lines according to the connotations surrounding the various kinds of knots that the word "knot" refers to. Cotton is a "gurdeon knot [a small lump of crystalline brown sugar] of sweetest graces"; the connotations of hardness and sweetness of that knot are then separated into two other kinds of knots, "But we as in a honi-comb a knott/of Hony sweete, here had such sweeteness Gott / the Knotts and knobs that on the Trees doe grow . . ." and so on. The poem does not quite simply report on the world, however, for Fiske repeatedly applies the connotations of object-knots to immaterial nouns: "With Joy erst while, (when knotty doubts arose) / To thee we calld, o Sir, the knott disclose." This is a perfectly ordinary recognition of the metaphorical flexibility of the world's objects, but in a remarkable passage halfway through the poem (lines 35–46), Fiske addresses the difficulty of understanding and using those "natural" metaphors. Throughout a curious thicket of references, Fiske weaves together most of the objects to which his poem has referred into a compound image of the very act of reference itself. He claims that the knot in the tree is misinterpreted by most people because their attention rests on its sensible hardness and deformity instead (shifting objects) of its internal sweetness or meaning. What looks like a difficult aberration in this world is really an indication of an invisible benefit, a moral that is broadened to include even "knotty Learning" in the subsequent couplet.

Soon after characterizing the errors inherent in these "twigs loaded with follies Rhyme," Fiske abandons objects altogether as structural devices and turns to the language of his poem: "o knott of Hony most delightful when / Thou livd'st, thi death a sad presage hath ben / Have Ben?" he remarks, called from his mistaken meditation on the knot by the language just as suddenly as Keats would be called from his revery by the word "forlorn" in the "Ode to a Nightingale." "Yea is, and is, and is alas," Fiske continues, reminding us that the real, permanent truth signified by Cotton's death is revealed only in the words themselves as their connection to the historically limited, actual event of his death fails. This discovery leads Fiske to abandon his knots after one more rather abstract appearance ("that knotty pride" in the next line) and turn Cotton into a cloth and then into language, only to conclude that all images must be discarded. Realizing the folly of dressing his Grief in the velvet tongues and silken wits of worldly language, he calls upon "My wakened muse to rest, my moystned pen / . . . cease try no more, for Hee hath gayn'd his prize / His heavenly mansion 'bove the starry skie (ll. 89–92). And with a reproach to his muse to "Returne thee home and wayle the evills there," Fiske falls silent, relinquishing his words to the world as their subject is translated from his earthly home to a heavenly mansion.

Cotton's journey was a familiar one to the Puritans, as many gravestone carvings show. There, on the hard surface of the stone, fragile soul-images are repeatedly caught in flight from the entombed body to the starry heaven as a symbol of death's transitional function. But even in this most resistant of media, the hand of the Puritan artist rendered the evanescence of that flight by framing it within the empty space of a portal, dissolving the heavy mass of the gravestone into a pure sign of the transformation that the threshold marks. Death is thus a structural paradigm for Puritan art as well as a frequent theme. For although the Puritan artist knew that whatever vision and grace were available to him depended on his emulation of the copy of Christ, he also knew that he could never repeat the designative gestures by which Christ had inscribed the Word on the things of this world. He therefore resigned himself to an ironic inversion of those gestures, separating signs from their meanings by eroding the very images in which they met. And the model for that disruptive designation was the Crucifixion. The Incarnation may have been God's metaphor and the Last Supper the proof of that metaphorical power, but their truth had been made legible to man only on the Cross:

> Our lord . . . at the table where he took part of his last feast with the Apostles, with his own hands gave them bread and wine; but upon the crosse he gave his bodie to be wounded by the hands of the soldiers: that the sincere truth and the true sincerity which he had more secretly imprinted in the Apostles, might declare unto the world how the bread and wine

were his body and blood; [how] . . . the things signifying and signified should be called both by the same names.[24]

Like death, Puritan art was a liminal event poised at the limit of human experience and defining that limit in the act of transcending it. Fixed between the failure of human language and the Puritans' rejection of disembodied revelation, their art mirrored the divine translation of death by disrupting its own integrity as sign even as it made the collative gesture that would bind the world to the Word. It is not surprising, then, that near the end of "What a rocky heart is mine" (I. 36) Taylor prefaces the possibility of regenerate song with a plea for a purgative blood-letting through a typological wound that will open his heart like the side of Christ, broadens that cleft into a crevice in which his message is conveyed, and then locates the dance of spiritual praise in the largest opening of all:

> Thy Argument is good, Lord point it, come
> Let't lance my heart, till True Loves Veane doth run.
>
> But that there is a Crevice for one hope
> To creep in, and this Message to Convay
> That I am thine, makes me refresh. Lord ope
> The Doore so wide that Love may Scip, and play.
> My Spirits then shall dance thy Praise. . . . [I. 36, ll. 71–77]

Taylor predicated his accession to his place among the Elect on this series of widening gaps because he knew that there was no place for this dance of praise in the world of a text where "My tazzled Thoughts twirld into Snick-Snarls run" (I. 32), just as there was no room for eternity in the tangled world of time:

> Thou Stoughst the World so tite with present things
> That things to Come, though crowd full hard, cant in.
>
> These things to Come, tread on the heels of those.
> The presents breadth doth with the broad world run.
> The Depth and breadth of things to come out goes
> Unto Times End which bloweth out the Sun. [I. 36, ll. 41–46]

He also knew that that parallel between the limits of time and language was no coincidence. For Taylor and other Puritan poets, the literary devices that crowded their texts as well as the endless arguments about the sufficiency of metaphor and the nature of the linguistic sign involved the most fundamental issues of their lives. Christ was a metaphor; God the author; the world His text; and the typological time of His creation a manifestation of the partial disclosure and deferred revelation inherent in the symbolic properties of language. So, in an act of faith that was as aesthetic as it was religious, the Puritans confronted the twin limits of language and the world by opening their texts through the images that formed them in a ritual gesture which cancelled words and things in the sacramental hush of the poem: "I eate my Word," Taylor proclaimed in this same meditation; "I now Unsay my Say."

NOTES

1. *The Literary Temper of the English Puritans* (Baton Rouge, La.: Louisiana State University Press, 1961). Sasek said, "The literary theory of the puritans was never systematized and distinguished from non-puritan theory, largely because the puritans never rebelled against the standard critical theory of their times."

2. *The Works of that famous and worthie Minister of Christ . . . M. W. Perkins* (London, 1612), 2:670–71.

3. Lewalski, *Poetics*. Also see Sasek, ch. 4.

4. Baxter, *A Saint or a Brute* (London, 1662), prefatory letter; Sibbes, *The Complete Works of Richard Sibbes*, ed. Alexander B. Grosart (Edinburgh, 1862–64), l:ci; Cudworth, *A Sermon Preached Before the Honourable House of Commons . . . March 31, 1647* (Cambridge, 1647), pp. 25, 5; Taylor, *A Man in Christ, or: A New Creature. To which is added a Treatise, containing Meditations from the Creatures* (London, 1628), pp. 2–3; Preston, *Life Eternall, Or, A Treatise of the Knowledge of the Divine Essence* (London, 1631), p. 101; E. Taylor, *The Treatise Concerning the Lord's Supper,* ed. Norman Grabo (East Lansing, Mich.: Michigan State University Press, 1966), pp. 43–44.

5. *A History of American Literature* (New York: G. P. Putnam's Sons, 1878), 1:264–65.

6. Murdock, *Literature*, p. 31; Tyler, *History*, p. 276; "hot poetic emotion," "natural desire," and "never hated literature" in Pearce, *Continuity*, pp. 45, 18; "universal craving" in Norman Grabo, "The Veiled Vision: the Role of Aesthetics in Early American Intellectual History," *WMQ* 19 (1962): 449; "strong suggestion" in Murdock, pp. 46–47.

7. Edward Taylor, meditation forty-one, second series, in Stanford, *Taylor*. Subsequent citations to Taylor's poems refer to this text.

8. No. 156 in *Images or Shadows of Divine Things,* ed. Perry Miller (New Haven, Conn.: Yale University Press, 1948).

9. Lewalski, *Poetics*; Blake, "Edward Taylor's Protestant Poetic: Non-transubstantiating Metaphor," *AL* 43 (1971): 1–24; Reed, "Edward Taylor's Poetry: Puritan Structure and Form," *AL* 46 (1974): 304–12; Daly, *God's Altar*; Scheick, *Will and Word*. For my discussion of the dialectical nature of the theological basis for Puritan semiology see "The Crucified Phrase: Sign and Desire in Puritan Semiology," *EAL* 13 (1978/9): 278–93.

10. Robert Ferguson, *The Interest of Reason in Religion; With the Import and Use of Scripture-Metaphor* (London, 1675), p. 367.

11. Taylor: "this Metaphor" in II. 101, ll. 8–9; "a most Exact Copy" in Grabo, *Christographia,* pp. 34, 102. In the *Christographia* Taylor also explained why the incarnate Christ was called the Word: "Now he is call'd the word, from the prophetical office that he attended: for as a word is the Conception of the minde, and being Spoken declares the minde to others: So Christ being Conceived in the Fathers minde comes forth of the Fathers bosom, and declares what is the minde of the Father unto others" (p. 75). Cf. Scheick, p. 99, n. 9.

12. *The Keys,* trans. Earl Beyer and Conrad Bergendoff, in *Luther's Works* (Philadelphia: Fortress Press, 1955ff.), 40:334.

13. Reported in Silverman, *Poetry,* p. 37.

14. In studies of past events, this literalism led the Puritans to an emphasis on the concrete occasion that distinguished their typology from that of the long Scholastic tradition. See Ursula Brumm, *American Thought and Religious Typology,* trans. John Joaglund (New Brunswick, New Jersey: Rutgers University Press, 1970), esp. Ch. 3, and Bercovitch, *Puritan Origins,* esp. ch. 4.

15. Weems claimed that the "compound sense" is "not taken here to make two Senses out of one scripture (for that were contradictory:) but onely . . . two parts, literall and figurative, to make up one sense, which is fulfilled two manner of ways, Historicê and Propheticê in the type, and literally in the thing signified" (*Christian Synagogue, Workes,* 1: 229–30). Cf. William Perkins, *A Commentary or Exposition upon the Five First Chapters of the Epistle to the Galatians* (Cambridge, 1604), p. 346.

16. William Whitaker, *Disputatio de Sacra Scriptura,* trans. Fitsgerald (London, 1588), pp. 405–8.

17. *The Complete Body of Divinity* (Boston, 1726), p. 860. Subsequent page references refer to this text.

18. *The Golden Chaine,* in *Works,* 1:72.

19. *Some Treasures Fetched Out of Rubbish* (London, 1660), p. 49.

20. *Gods Determinations touching his Elect,* "Doubts from Satans Temptations Answered," ll. 83–86, in Stanford, p. 444.

21. Charles Mignon offers several more examples of this strategy in "Edward Taylor's Preparatory Meditations: a Decorum of Imperfection," *PMLA* 83 (1968): 1423–28.

22. John Cotton, *Treasure,* pp. 11–12, 17, 48–9; Samuel Mather, *A Testimony from the Scriptures against Idolatry and Superstition* (Cambridge, Mass., 1640), p. 6.

23. *The Marrow of Sacred Divinity,* sig. A$_4$ recto-verso. The phrase by Taylor is from *God's Determinations,* "Doubts from Satans Temptations Answered," l. 80, in Stanford, p. 444.

24. Perkins, *The Demonstration of the Problem, or Position,* in *Works,* 2:560.

6 PURITAN ICONOGRAPHY: THE ART OF EDWARD TAYLOR'S *GODS DETERMINATIONS*

LYNN M. HAIMS

Gods Determinations is poetry in sackcloth, its artistic aspirations only barely concealed by Taylor's cultivated roughness. Although the theater was anathema to Puritans, Taylor, an orthodox minister, composed an iconographic drama with Christ, Satan, and the Soul as its emblem-like characters and four dramatic units resembling the acts of a play. As a minister, Taylor was well aware of the Second Commandment, which forbade the making of "graven images," including "similitudes of things that are in heaven above" and "in the earth below."[1] John Cotton, who arrived in America in 1633, interpreted the Commandment strictly, as forbidding "not onely bodily Images (graven or molten or painted) but all spirituall Images also; which are the imaginations and inventions of men. . . ."[2] Taylor, some fifty years later, appears to have regarded the prohibition with ambivalence: he remained faithful to his theology yet in subtle ways reconstituted in his poetry the images his theology abhorred. The example of *Gods Determinations* suggests a typical pattern among Puritan artists and writers. Although they denounced as idolatrous the sensual aids to piety used by Catholics—their music, incense, flowers and palm branches, their painted images, statues and stained-glass figures of Christ and the Virgin—Puritans reintroduced their equivalents in subtle ways here in America. Puritan sermons resonate with theatrical rhetoric even as they denounce the theater; landscapes and still-lifes surface unexpectedly in the poetry of Benjamin Tompson and Anne Bradstreet; histories and biographies recall the exemplary lives of New England saints with the suspense and adventure of a novel.[3] Although Calvin had declared it idolatrous to represent the deity in corporeal form, some twenty of Edward Taylor's *Preparatory Meditations* explore and linger about the face and body of Christ.[4] In embellishing the texts of Revelation and Canticles, Taylor perhaps felt he was using the authorized imagery of scripture and that his art was not idolatrous; yet the erotic, anthropomorphic nature of the images suggests a strong personal need to visualize God in corporeal form. Puritan tombstones offer the most explicit evidence of American Puritans' need to create graven images. Only forty years after they arrived on this side of the Atlantic, Puritans began to carve onto their gravestones the images of "things in heaven above" that were forbidden in their churches—angels, birds, soul effigies, even the breasts of Christ.[5]

The artist's need to visualize his religion, to make literal and palpable the abstractions of Covenant Theology, is perhaps less surprising when we consider he was denied other avenues of expression: theater, belletristic poetry, painting and sculpture. With the Bible his principal source of imagery, the Puritan poet reconstructed the New Jerusalem with architectural exactness: fifteen thousand miles square, with gold-paved streets and twelve gates of pearl facing North, South, East, and West, glittering with gems.[6] Angels, demons and witches—the denizens of the Invisible World—were real and palpable beings;[7] Christ and Satan were familiar characters in sermons and treatises.

In *Gods Determinations* we observe the struggle of the artistic sensibility to create within the confines of scriptural prohibitions against imagemaking. The resulting form is a compromise, an ambivalent expression both of the potential range of the poet's imagination and feeling and also of elements that suggest control, restraint, discipline. In Taylor as a representative artist, we see the Puritans' fondness for charts and diagrams, for literal forms and finite numbers, for the visible designs of anagrams and acrostics, for the logic of Ramist dissections. Taylor's " 'artless' art," his "deliberate roughness," is an accommodated form that merges the more private aspirations of the Puritan artist with the posture appropriate for a humble Christian.[8] Taylor's souls, accordingly, sing in "broken notes," walk on "broken stilts," see dimly with eyes that "want Cleare Spectacles," or write with a pen that "jags" and "jars"; these metaphors of imperfection blend aesthetic and theological meanings to articulate man's flawed, mortal condition.

The thirty-five poems of *Gods Determinations* can be grouped into four large units which correspond roughly to the four-part running title, [1] *Gods Determinations touching his Elect*; [2] *the Elects Combat in their Conversion, and* [3] *Coming up to God in Christ* [4] *together with the Comfortable Effects thereof.*[9] The main character is, alternately, a single soul—that is, the Poor Doubting Soul familiar to seventeenth-century readers of religious tracts—and a group of reprobate souls who, similarly, all strive for grace. The simple, childlike quality of Taylor's sequence is deceptive. The poems are compressed and carefully structured; the metaphors are colorful and stylized. They are simple in the sense that Ernest Hemingway's prose and Emily Dickinson's poems are simple: they lack ornament and clutter. Taylor replaces the arid intellectuality of doctrine with the dramatic immediacy of fear, anguish, hope, joy.

Gods Determinations begins as a lament, reviewing the circumstances that led to man's "Lapst Estate." As it proceeds through the four sections, the Soul moves through distinct emotional stages: from mute panic to groaning to talking to singing, ending with lyrics in praise of Christ. As the sequence opens, the Soul is a miserable cripple, mired in filth, in a state of "pannick feare"; as it closes, he is transformed into a Saint, singing in Christ's coach, soaring upward to heaven. The first, second, and third sections combine narrative and dramatic modes, while the fourth is comprised entirely of lyrics. The various forms suggest a progression from the awkward rhetoric of mortals to the song of the saved. Two image systems—images of light and dark and musical images—translate Taylor's theology into aesthetic terms and dramatize the Soul's conversion.

The first section (poems 1–6) takes place against the background of man's fall from grace. The first poem, "The Preface," calls attention to God's greatness and the bountiful gifts He bestowed on "Nothing man," who by his sin turned "All to Nothing." Trapped by the realization of his guilt, the Poore Doubting Soul trembles in fear of punishment, when he is spied by Justice and Mercy, who then debate about what his fate shall be. Justice, the Old Testament God of Wrath, is determined to punish the sinner. But Mercy, the New Testament God of Forgiveness, sweetly assuages his anger and offers to take up man's debt if Justice will relent. By the sixth poem, the single soul has split into four groups. Of these, the first are Saints, and they enter Christ's coach at once. A second group is rounded up by Justice, a third by Mercy, and the fourth by their combined efforts. These sinners will undergo the painful work of "conversion" so that they can move closer to Christ.[10]

The second section (poems 7–22) dramatizes in a series of agons between the Soul and Satan the conversion process, an elaborate form of self-scrutiny. Satan accuses the remaining three ranks of sinners of succumbing to pride, hypocrisy, and carnal pleasure. His first two attacks are upon the sinners of the first Rank, "Traitors, Foes." At each assault, the Soul (alternately one and many) turns to Christ for succor, and Christ responds with reassurance and comfort. As the Soul's groans become more anguished, Christ's replies become more loving. Satan next accuses the Second and Third Ranks, sinners who have fled grace. He taunts them, using sophistical arguments to make them believe they are unfit to ask for mercy. The two groups lament their sinfulness in a choral exchange and, although both feel doomed, they console one another and pray for pardon. The souls now revert to a single persona, resolving to seek counsel from "Gods people," presumably a minister or one of the elect.

The third section (poems 23–28) comprises a dialogue between the Soul and a Saint, who offers the reassurance and advice Edward Taylor likely offered his own congregation at Westfield. The Saint sympathetically relates his own difficulties in resolving doubts about his eligibility to become a "Child of God" and exposes the wiles and deceptions of Satan. The Saint's charity and wisdom encourage the Soul to "Call on the Mighty God with all [his] might." And the Saint warns that too much timidity is a form of "presumption" since it implies a denial of Christ's invitation to come to the Lord's Supper. The third section is about "sanctification," which in Covenant Theology refers to the birth of a New Man, cleansed from the filth of sin. The process of "Coming up to Christ" is accompanied by Taylor's version of ministerial healing as the Saint coaxes the Soul to put on the "Wedden Garment" and become a full church member, that is, one whose soul has been wedded to Christ.[11]

In the final section (poems 29–35), the sinners of the Second and Third Ranks sing the praises of Christ as they enter the state of Grace and enjoy "the Comfortable effects thereof," announced by the fourth part of the title. Images of perfume, spices, and music dominate as the Soul enters the heavenly city "like a Bride all Gloriously arraide" and beholds Christ's garden. These lyrics are based upon the section of Canticles celebrating the wedding of Solomon to the Shulamite, which Puritans read as an allegory of the Soul's marriage to Christ. The richly sensual love poetry exchanged between the Shulamite bride and her beloved typologically figured the Soul's love for Christ. Thus Taylor's Soul wears the "Wedden Garment" and, like the bride in Solomon's garden, is overwhelmed with flowers, perfume, and spices. The final poem in this section projects the joy of the newly confirmed Soul in musical imagery as, soaring upward to glory, he hears the saints in Christ's coach who "With Hymns do offer up their heart."[12]

Like the Puritan limners who distorted proportions and used heavy, lined figures and two-dimensional, "flat" representations, Taylor achieves freshness and vigor with stylized dramatic figures. His craft is concealed by the childlike stance of his main "character," the Soul. Since the child embodies the essential nature of man's relation to God in religious literature, it is an apt artistic choice.[13] As an errant child, man reenacts his insubordination at Adam's Fall, his confused sense of God's decrees, his awe and fear of God's vengeance, his need for God's love and approval. Taylor's other characters resemble animated emblems. Justice, Satan, Mercy, and Christ appear in a bold, fresh context, transformed from theological abstractions to figures who posture and gesture in various tableaux. We are struck also by the basic cheer in Taylor's speaking voice, unlike the somber chant of Michael Wigglesworth in *Day of Doom* or the resignation of Anne Bradstreet in her family poems.

Taylor's adaptation of emblem art presents Justice, Satan, Mercy, Christ, and the Poor Doubting Soul as two-dimensional figures who strike "attitudes" and portray particular emotions associated with their theological roles.[14] Thus we have an angry Justice, a deceitful Satan, a loving Mercy and Christ, a fearful Soul. In poem three, Justice appears colored red, and labelled angry in a few sharp, deliberate strokes; she strikes an attitude of rage:

> Offended Justice comes in fiery Rage,
>   Like to a Rampant Lyon new assaild,
> Array'd in Flaming fire now to engage,
> With red hot burning Wrath poore man unbaild.
> In whose Dread Vissage sinfull man may spy
> Confounding, Rending, Flaming Majesty. [p. 391]

Satan is also presented as a lion, "belching fire." His deceptiveness is translated into visual terms: he wears an angel's coat to lure the Soul into greater sin:

> Off goes the Angels Coate, on goes his own.
> With Griping Paws, and Goggling Eyes draws nigher,
> Like some fierce Shagg'd Red Lion, belching fire: [p. 407]

Christ is portrayed as an idealized mother, gentle, loving, protective. In poem sixteen, He reassures the Soul:

> Peace, Peace, my Hony, do not Cry,
> My Little Darling, wipe thine eye,
>   Oh Cheer, Cheer up, come see.
> Is anything too deare, my Dove,
> Is anything too good, my Love
>   To get or give for thee? [p. 414]

These imaginative personifications appropriately suggest a distance between man and his Creator and a happy, intimate connection with Him. Man's fear of punishment for offending his God is similarly stylized:

> Then like a Child that fears the Poker Clapp
> Him on his face doth on his Mothers lap
> Doth hold his breath, lies still for fear least hee
> Should by his breathing lowd discover'd bee. [p. 389]

Taylor's characterizations are theologically precise, and they appear as well in his sermons. In his *Church Record,* Taylor defines church membership as an "adoption" of man into God's family: "Adoption is a gracious Act of God, passt upon a true believer in Christ, whereby, translating him out of Satan's famaly, as a Childe into his own houshould, he constitutes him a rightfull heire of all the privilidges of his own child" (p. 524).[15]

In *Gods Determinations* Satan also appears as a dog, an agent of Christ sent to shepherd sinners back into the Lord's fold. The Soul, harried by "this Cur that is so Curst," appeals to Christ to protect him. Taylor's diction and imagery are appropriately childlike:

> I know he is thy Cur, therefore I bee
>   Perplexed lest I from thy Pasture stray.
> He bayghs, and barks so veh'mently at mee.
>   Come rate this Cur, Lord, breake his teeth I pray.
>   Remember me I humbly pray thee first.
>   Then halter up this Cur that is so Curst. [p. 414]

Christ lovingly replies that Satan is a necessary prod to bring the beleaguered Soul closer to Himself:

> If in the severall thou art
> This Yelper fierce will at thee bark:
>   That thou art mine this shows.
> As Spot barks back the sheep again
> Before they to the Pound are ta'ne,
>   So he and hence 'way goes.
>
> But yet this Cur that bayghs so sore
> Is broken tootht, and muzzled sure,
>   Fear not, my Pritty Heart.
> His barking is to make thee Cling
> Close underneath thy Saviours Wing.
>   Why did my sweeten start? [pp. 414–15]

Satan's function is explained further by Taylor in a *Christographia* sermon: "Hence as his people have need, so persecutors are upon them. They are the Sheapheards Curs, that he lets out at the Sheep When they Wander and Scatter away from their own Walk: but when they are worried by these dogs to their right pastures, then the Shephard rates the Dog again."[16] The sweetness and cheerfulness—the charming *personality* of Christ—come as a delightful surprise to anyone familiar with Puritan theological tracts. We may suspect, along with Colacurcio and Keller, that Taylor was attempting to woo his hesitant Westfield congregation toward full church membership.[17]

Reinforcing the childlike attitude of humility and trust with which man must approach his God and enter the kingdom of heaven is Taylor's rendering of the Creation and Fall. The opening poem of *Gods Determinations* sets forth the Creation as a parade of images that might evoke the awe and wonder of a child (in Meserole, *Poetry*). Borrowing freely from Genesis and Job,[18] the poem arrests the eye with its rough mix of colors and shapes, a collage of large objects fashioned by artisans and of more delicate ones made by craftsmen and seamstresses. Taylor's use of domestic details—curtains and curtain rods, a quilt ball, selvedge, green ribbons, a bowling alley—delights with its spontaneous and fresh perception. The poem is organized around a question-answer pattern, perhaps based upon the children's catechism. The first nineteen lines develop the question, WHO made all these wonders?, while the next seventeen answer, MIGHT ALMIGHTY did these things.

Equally delightful is this pared-down account of Adam's Fall, or the breaking of the Covenant of Works, and the making of the Second Covenant, the Covenant of Grace, by which Christ redeemed man from eternal punishment. The 5-4-4-3 metrical pattern provides rhythmic interest as a backdrop for the "story":

When that the World was new, its Chiefe Delight,
One Paradise alone Contain'de:
The Bridle of Mans Appetite
The Appletree refrain'de.

The which he robbing, eat the fruit as good,
Whose Coare hath Chokd him and his race.
And juyce hath poyson'd all their blood,
He's in a Dismall Case.

None can this Coare remove, Poyson expell:
He, if his Blood ben't Clarifi'de
Within Christs veans, must fry in Hell,
Till God be satisfi'de.

Christ to his Father saith, Incarnate make
Mee, Mee thy Son; and I will doe't:
I'le purify his Blood, and take
The Coare out of his Throate. [p. 420]

In this simple retelling of the story of Adam in the garden of Eden, Taylor combines the techniques of the emblem poets and allegorists, reducing to a bold, concrete image an entire body of theological doctrine.

An important component in Taylor's art is his careful attention to structure. A fondness for symmetry and balance, for geometrical design, and for schematic renderings of abstract states reveals his technical control and gives *Gods Determinations* a distinctive shape. The sequence is divided into four parts, the first and last roughly equal in length. The first and last poems praise God, implying a completed cycle of ends and beginnings in God. "The Preface" poses the predicament of man's fall; the final poem offers a reciprocal solution—his ascent to heaven. A second kind of symmetry is presented in opposite sets of images— of color and music. Poem one reviews the historic past, developing the Calvinist view of man's fall, ending with an image of darkness, an implied downward movement, and a lament for man's hopeless condition:

But Nothing man did throw down all by Sin:
And darkened that lightsom Gem in him.
That now his Brightest Diamond is grown
Darker by far than any Coalpit Stone. [p. 388]

The final poem, "The Joy of Church Fellowship rightly attended," projects a contrasting vision of futurity. Here the lament has turned to joyous song, and darkness is replaced by light as the souls soar to heaven:

> Oh! joyous hearts! Enfir'de with holy Flame!
>   Is speech thus tassled with praise?
> Will not your inward fire of Joy contain;
>   That it in open flames doth blaze?
>   For in Christ's Coach Saints sweetly sing,
>   As they to Glory ride therein. [p. 459]

A more significant structural balance is achieved by the three parallel debates that focus the poem's argument in parts One, Two, and Three. In different voices and moods, three sets of debaters examine the question, Can man be saved?, and the poetic units oscillate between hope and doubt until they are resolved in the final, fourth section. In Part One, the contending voices are those of Justice and Mercy; in Part Two, of Satan and Christ; in Three, of Soul and Saint. Although the debaters change places, the paradigm is constant: Justice, Satan, and the Soul argue successively that *man is nothing and deserves to be damned,* while they are challenged by Mercy, Christ, and the Saint, who argue that *he is still precious to God and will be saved.* Together they elaborate the poem's dialectic: that although man has fallen and deserves punishment (a restatement of the Covenant of Works), he will be redeemed and forgiven (the promise of the Covenant of Grace) through Christ's intervention.

Not only does the poem's theological argument split in two, but such splitting is integral to Taylor's poetic method. "All mankinde splits in a Dicotomy," poem five announces—those who are saved and those who are left behind. The latter group is then divided into three ranks, which Satan clearly labels:

> You're the first Van that fell; you're Traitors, Foes,
> And Unto such Grace will no trust repose.
> You Second Ranck are Cowards, if Christ Come
> With you to fight his field, you'l from him run.
> You third are feeble-hearted; if Christs Crown
> Must stand or fall by you, you'l fling it down. [p. 403]

In similar Ramist fashion, Satan delineates the "Double Face" of sin: Poems eleven and twelve, "The Accusation of the Inward Man" and "The Outward Man Accused," develop the image of Sin's double face, and "anatomize" the reciprocal aspects of visible signs of hypocrisy and the more sinful hypocrisy of the heart. Upon the Soul's facial features Satan reads the signs of corruption: its "Wanton Eyes," its mouth, its ears, and its bodily carriage as well. Poem thirteen is organized around the marked responses of each part, a "Painted Sign-Post of a Wanton heart." The mouth lies and detracts from others; the ears were satisfied with "filthy squibs, and jears"; the eyes frowned on honest poverty; and the Soul did "Peacock up [itself] above [its] rancks." Poem fourteen continues the accusations, focusing on the Soul's ears, eyes, and voice:

> Thy Holy Conference is onely like
> An Empty Voice that tooteth through a pipe.
> Thy Soule doth peep out at thine Eares, and Eyes
> To bless those bawbles that are earthly toyes. [p. 413]

Similarly, the Soul's state of fear is given a literal, charted dimension as an army of "A thousand Griefs" overruns his body. To delineate his "Pannick feare," imaginary arrows point to dangers in every direction:

> He looks *within*, and sad amazement's there,
> *Without*, and all things fly about his Eares.
> *Above*, and sees Heaven falling on his pate,
> *Below*, and spies th'Infernall burning lake,
> *Before* and sees God storming in his Face,
> *Behinde*, and spies Vengeance persues his trace. [p. 389; italics mine]

In poem twenty-two, fear is again presented visually. The Soul is caught between the "Heavenly bliss" Adam knew and the "bottomless Abyss" he fears is his own destiny. A geometrical progression suggests God's infinite love in the debate between Justice and Mercy. As Justice doubts the sufficiency of Mercy's love for man, Mercy replies in the language of numbers, doubling and redoubling her amounts:

> MERCY: If more a thousand times too little bee
>   Ten thousand times yet more than this I'le do:
>   . . . .
> JUSTICE: Nay, this ten thousand times as much can still
>   Confer no hony to the Sinners hive.
>   . . . .
> MERCY: What, though ten thousand times, too little bee?
>   I will ten thousand thousand times more do.
>   . . . .
> JUSTICE: Yet this ten thousand thousand times more shall,
>   Though doubled o're, and o're for little stands.
>   . . . .
> MERCY: Though this ten thousand thousand times much more
>   Though doubled o're and o're for little go,
>   I'le double still its double o're and ore
>   And trible that untill I make it do. [pp. 392–93]

These geometrical expressions of love and the quasi-logical dissections of sin and fear typically reveal the Puritans' literal responses to abstraction and the intangibles of doctrine. They appear to add balance and symmetry to the sequence; they are the counterparts of the heavily outlined figures in limner art.

Gods Determinations is not, as some critics claim, merely didactic Congregational Church poetry.[19] Taylor's aesthetic fuses religion with art. Two image systems dramatize in color and music the Soul's transformation from despair to joy, his transition from earth to heaven. References to bright and dark in the first poem, "The Preface," announce Taylor's poetic method, underlining as it were the terms in which he will present the conversion process. The colors of grace are bright: white, gold, and silver. Man has "darkened that lightsom Gem in him," turning his "Brightest Diamond" into something darker than "any Coalpit stone" (p. 388). Mercy appears in a "milkwhite Robe of Lovely Righteousness" (p. 395) and carries a "golden scepter" (p. 396). She promises to recolor the tarnished Soul who has lain too long "among the pots" (p. 398):

> Thy Wings with Silver Colours I'le o're lay:
> And lay thy feathers o're with yellow gold. [p. 398]

In poem four, Justice and Mercy challenge the Soul to explain "How he his Cloath defild and how he fell?" Falling, of course, refers to Adam's sin, but Taylor recasts the familiar story in images of filth to acknowledge a specific doctrinal idea: that filth is the first stage in the conversion process.[20] Man, mired in mud, with quavering lips and trembling joints, attempts to answer; like Adam, he blames his "Mate" for his predicament:

> . . . my Mate procurde me all this hurt,
> Who threw me in my best Cloaths in the Dirt. [p. 398]

In poem six, sinners are "Like Pearls in Puddles cover'd ore with mudd," and in poem sixteen, Christ promises to "put away the Guilt thereof, / And purge its Filthiness cleare off." He refers, in a witty development of Taylor's metaphor, to regeneracy as a whitening, brightening process:

> But still look for Temptations Deep,
> Whilst that thy Noble Sparke doth keep
>   Within a Mudwald Cote.
> These White Frosts and the Showers that fall
> Are but to whiten thee withall.
>   Not rot the Web they smote.
>
> If in the fire where Gold is tride
> Thy Soule is put, and purifide
>   Wilt thou lament thy loss?
> If silver-like this fire refine
> Thy Soul and make it brighter shine:
>   Wilt thou bewaile the Dross? [pp. 417–18]

As the Soul reaches its darkest moment of self-doubt (poem twenty-two), images of filth proliferate. Satan has goaded the Soul into its greatest agony, and the Soul's self-loathing is apparent in its references to itself as "a Lump of Slime" and a "Durty Clod of Clay." The long second section ends with similar images of self-abasement, the Soul praying for "Some glimmerings of Hope . . . / In Mercies Golden Stacks. . . ."

The third section, a dialogue between the Soul and Saint, is about "sanctification," or a cleansing from the filth of sin.[21] The Soul confesses his "hearts black stain" (p. 434), admitting to the Saint that he is "pestred with black thoughts of Blasphemy" (p. 435). The Saint answers, in similar terms, that Satan raises "a Fog, or fude of thoughts most vile / Within the soul; and darkens all that ile" (p. 442).

Christ's promise to "whiten" the Soul in poem sixteen is fulfilled in the fourth section (poem thirty-one), where the soul appears as a bride in a dress of "Sanctuary White." As Taylor explains in his *Treatise Concerning the Lord's Supper*, the conversion process allows one to shed the "filthy rags" of sin in order to wear the robe of evangelical righteousness, the "wedden garment."[22] In this final grouping of poems, images of brightness and light dominate. The heavenly city dazzles the Soul: "How is this City, Lord, of thine bespangles / With Graces shine?" (p. 455). It beholds the "Golden Pipes" that water Christ's garden (p. 453) and marvels at the flowers "Spanglde like gold" (p. 456). In the culminating image, as the saints ride in Christ's coach, glory is projected as blazing flames:

> Oh! joyous hearts! Enfir'de with holy Flame!
> Is speech thus tassled with praise?
> Will not your inward fire of Joy contain;
> That it in open flames doth blaze? [p. 459]

All that glitters is gracious: heaven, Mercy, Christ, His coach. The Soul refers to "Grace's Golden, Life Enliv'ning Beams" (p. 431), and the Saint to the "Curious needlework of Providence / Embroidered with Golden Spangles Cleare" (p. 449), and the "golden Meshes of this Net" that guide the Soul toward Christ (p. 450).[23]

Music imagery and Taylor's shift in poetic style from the deliberately rough verse relating the Soul's struggles to the grace of the final lyrics complement the use of color in suggesting a progression from sin to salvation. Seven paeans to Christ comprise the final, fourth section of the sequence and present Taylor's most elaborate designs, the "music" of the Soul's joy as it approaches heaven. They are, in fact, variations on the theme of grace. Six of the poems are unified by a basic form—a six-line stanza, and a rhyme pattern *ababcc*—but each poem has its own stanzaic "shape" or number of metrical feet, and its own number of stanzas ranging from four to ten. In these lyrics, we become most acutely aware of Taylor's art. Images of flowers, spices, perfumes, and music predominate in this celebration of the Soul's marriage with Christ; the speaking voice becomes exuberant as it sings His praises.[24]

Only once before in the sequence has there been a comparable moment: in poem seventeen, "An Extasy of Joy . . . ," where the Souls of the first rank rhapsodize upon Christ's forgiveness. The final two stanzas of poem seventeen dramatize the transition from the "broken notes" of the unregenerate Soul as it travels toward heaven, to the "flaming Melodies" it will sing when it arrives. Taylor suggests the awkwardness of the hesitant Soul by slowing a packed line with an exclamation mark, three commas, and a question mark: "But oh! how slack, slow, dull? with what delay, . . ." As the Soul imagines itself in heaven, the speaking voice becomes joyous and there is a corresponding release of feeling:

> And at my journies end in endless joyes
> I'l make amends where Angells meet
> And sing their flaming Melodies
> In Ravishing tunes most sweet. [p. 421]

The final seven lyrics undergo a similar transition, using images of weight and confinement to suggest the oppressive nature of guilt: "Like to a Lump of Lead my sin / Prest down my Soul." Again, there is a swift release to suggest flight, and a concomitant shift in tone.

In poem thirty-four, the Soul prays to learn the melodies of grace. Feeling unfit to play, yet longing to, the Soul declares its love:

> But should these Praises on string'd Instruments
>   Be sweetly tun'de? I finde
> I nonplust am: for no Consents
>   I ever minde.
>   My Tongue is neither Quill, nor Bow:
>   Nor Can my Fingers Quavers show. [p. 457]

The images of inarticulateness that proliferate in this poem are images of man's mortal imperfection.[25] Not until the final, thirty-fifth poem, does Taylor offer his "song." Because theirs is not an earthly music, the saints in Christ's coach sing sweetly, rhapsodically:

> And if a string do slip, by Chance, they soon
>   Do screw it up again: whereby
> They set it in a more melodious Tune
>   And a Diviner Harmony.
>   For in Christs Coach they sweetly sing
>   As they to Glory ride therein.
> . . . .

> In all their Acts, publick, and private, nay
> And secret too, they praise impart.
> But in their Acts Divine and Worship, they
> With Hymns do offer up their Heart.
> Thus in Christs coach they sweetly sing
> As they to Glory ride therein. [p. 459]

Most probably, *Gods Determinations* was for Taylor one of his "secret" or "private Acts" of imparting praise. By casting the final poem as a hymn with a choric refrain, Taylor evokes the sense of a congregation in song, sharing, as Taylor's own church members ideally did, the sweetness of worship. The frequent references to singing, music, and hymns, as well as the buoyant affect of the speaking voice, bring poem and song even closer together as modes of joyful expression.

Taylor's rich iconography and his quasi-dramatic form suggest an intense need to visualize his religion and his God. In Taylor the need was apparently forceful enough to exact a compromise with the prohibitions against making "similitudes" of things religious in Exodus 20.4–5. The deliberately rough form of *Gods Determinations* and Taylor's denial of artistic talent—as painter, poet, or musician—suggest the accommodated product of religious sanctions and aesthetic strivings. Taylor's sequence reflects, on the one hand, the various influences that shaped American Puritan poetry generally, and which remained active well into the nineteenth century: the English religious lyrics of Donne, Herbert, and Crashaw; the Bible; the emblem poetry of Quarles, Wither, and Bunyan; the logical dichotomies of Ramism; the stark directness of the plain style; and the injunctions against religious image-making. On the other hand, Taylor's sequence reveals the passion, ingenuity, and wit of the Puritan artist whose imagination found a partial outlet in the rich visual imagery of scripture. *Gods Determinations* documents the poet's artistic aspirations, his playfulness, his sincere love for his God, expressed with integrity and skill within the narrow avenues of his religion. In the colorful personifications of Justice and Mercy, Christ and Satan, Taylor transforms the dry abstractions of Covenant Theology into a passionate rite of self-transformation: the agony of the Soul in its quest for grace.

NOTES

1. The editions of 1582, 1601, and 1616 of the Geneva Bible likely used by the Puritans stated the Commandment as follows:

> Thou shalt make thee no graven image, neither any similitude *of things* that are in heaven above, neither that are in the earth beneath, nor that are in the waters under the earth.

> Thou shalt not bow down to them, neither serve them: for I am the Lord thy God a jealous God, visiting the iniquity of the fathers upon the children, upon the third *generation* and upon the fourth of them that hate me.

Quoted in Daly, *God's Altar,* p. 45.

2. John Cotton, *A modest and Cleare Answer to Mr. Ball's Discourse of set forms of Prayer* (London, 1642), p. 17.

3. See Norman S. Grabo, "The Veiled Vision: The Role of Aesthetics in Early American Intellectual History," *WMQ,* 3d ser. 19 (1962): 499.

4. See Meditations II, 118–26, 137–40; 149–52 in Stanford, *Taylor*. Subsequent textual references to Taylor's poems refer to pages of this edition.

5. Calvin believed the Commandment forbade "the sun, the moon, and the stars, and perhaps birds," as well as images of "figured stone" by which men imagined they "have God in some measure visible. . . ." See *Institutes of the Christian Religion*, trans. Henry Beveridge, 2 vols. Grand Rapids: Wm. B. Eerdmans, 1966), I:413–14; and *Commentaries on the Four Last Books of Moses Arranged in the Form of a Harmony*, trans. Charles William Bingham, 4 vols. (Grand Rapids: Wm. B. Eerdmans, 1950), II:115–17. Photographs of these images appear in Allan I. Ludwig, *Graven Images: New England Stonecarving and its Symbols, 1650–1805* (Middletown, Conn.: Wesleyan Univ. Press, 1966).

6. See John Norton's description in *The Orthodox Evangelist* (London, 1654), pp. 343–53.

7. Examples include Increase Mather's *Angelographia* (Boston, 1696) and Cotton Mather's *Wonders of the Invisible World* (Boston, 1693). In *Kometographia* (1683), Increase Mather attempted to correlate blazing stars and other heavenly lights, signs of God's displeasure, with His punishments: war between the English and Dutch, a plague, fire, drought, and floods. In *Remarkable Providences* (1684), he presents "evidence" of the Invisible World by interpreting visible happenings: deliverances from danger at sea, prayers answered, remarkable effects of lightning, floods, hurricanes, and whirlwinds; relations of possessed persons and apparitions.

8. Pearce's apt phrase, in *Continuity*, p. 54; see also Louis B. Martz's "Foreword" to *The Poems of Edward Taylor*, xv.

9. Critics differ about the structural divisions of Taylor's sequence. See Robert D. Arner, "Notes on the Structure of Edward Taylor's *Gods Determinations*," *Studies in the Humanities* 3 (June 1973): 27–29.

10. See Stephen C. Lewis, "Edward Taylor as a Covenant Theologian" (diss., New York University, 1971), for discussion of the conversion process.

11. In the terms of Covenant Theology, the Wedden Garment enabled one to attend the "mighty sumptuous feast" of poem five in *Gods Determinations*. This was the sacrament of the Lord's Supper, celebrating the arrival of a half-way member into full church membership. A clear discussion appears in *Edward Taylor's Treatise Concerning the Lord's Supper*, ed. Norman S. Grabo (East Lansing: Michigan State Univ. Press, 1966), p. xiii.

12. Taylor's image of the golden coach with scarlet canopy that appears in poems three and five of *Gods Determinations* comes directly from Canticles 3:9–10: "King Solomon made himself a Chariot of the wood of Lebanon. He made the pillars ther of silver, the bottom ther of gold, the covering of purple." Alan Howard explains its typological meaning in "The World as Emblem: Language and Vision in the Poetry of Edward Taylor," *AL* 44 (November 1972): 363–64.

13. William J. Scheick has commented extensively on Taylor's use of the childlike stance as an expression of humility before God. See "Nonsense from a Lisping Child" in *Will and Word*.

14. Taylor's affinity with emblem poets has been discussed by Thomas E. Johnston, Jr., "Edward Taylor: An American Emblematist," *EAL* 3 (Winter 1968): 186–98; Alan B. Howard; Norman S. Grabo, *Edward Taylor* (New York, 1961), pp. 154–58; Jeff Hammond and Thomas M. Davis, "Edward Taylor: A Note on Visual Imagery," *EAL* 8 (1973): 126–31; and, most recently, Lewalski, *Poetics,* pp. 209–11.

15. Scheick attributes Taylor's stance in part to the familiar biblical exhortation, "Whosoever shal not receive the kingdom of God as a little childe, he shal not entre therein (Mark 10.15)." Quoted in Scheick, p. 130.

16. Grabo, *Christographia,* p. 229.

17. Michael J. Colacurcio, "*Gods Determinations Touching Half-Way Membership*: Occasion and Audience in Edward Taylor," *AL* 39 (1967): 298–314; Keller, *Taylor,* pp. 77, 18–82.

18. See John Gatta, Jr., "The Comic Design of *Gods Determinations touching his Elect,*" *EAL* 10 (1975): 121–43.

19. See Keller, pp. 129, 135, 77; Martz, p. xiii; and Sidney E. Lind, "Edward Taylor: A Revaluation," *AL* 21 (December 1948): 518–30.

20. See particularly Taylor's Meditation II.27 for a striking example of the speaker's filth contrasted with Christ's purity. Karl Keller identifies Taylor's scatological views with theological tradition, pp. 193–207; see also Bercovitch, *Puritan Origins,* pp. 14–15.

21. Taylor defines sanctification in his *Church Record:* "Sanctification is a Reall Change of State whereby the Person being cleansed from the filth of sin, is renewed in the likeness of God by the graces of the Spirit" (p. 540).

22. *Edward Taylor's Treatise Concerning the Lord's Supper*, p. 58.

23. The last two images appear in an early Taylor sermon as the "Golden Checker work of the Draw net of Providence." See Thomas M. and Virginia L. Davis, "Edward Taylor on the Day of Judgment," *AL* 43:540.

24. In the *Treatise,* Taylor specifically equates the wedding of the soul and Christ with music: "Oh! the joy that spreads itself then over the soul. Oh! how it then is filled with singing" (p. 160). In another sermon, Taylor describes the song and music the Soul encounters when it enters the heavenly kingdom: "God having made the Soule Such a glorious Musicall Instrument of his praises, & the holy Ghost having so gloriously Strung it with the golden wyer of grace, . . . & now the Soule beg[inn]ing to Sing forth its endless Hallelujahs unto God . . . singing most heart-ravishingly out the Glory of God in the highest strains."

25. In the *Preparatory Meditations,* references to man's ineptitude and insufficiency are frequent. While they demonstrate Taylor's ingenuity and wit, they also show his deliberate intent to portray man as striving to improve his devotional offerings and always failing because he is simply mortal. Poetically the disparity between man in his unregenerate state and man in the state of grace is represented by the contrasts implicit in speech and song, by man's inarticulate stammering and the ultimate music he sings or plays as a Saint. In this context, Taylor's "roughness" reveals his poetic control. See Daly's commentary on the insufficiency of language to articulate the condition of grace in *God's Altar*, pp. 162–99.

7 INVESTIGATING "THE *AMERICA* OF NATURE": ALCHEMY IN EARLY AMERICAN POETRY

CHERYL Z. OREOVICZ

The culture we know as American Puritanism placed a number of strictures on anyone inclined to the writing of poetry. Not one's own creative energies and abilities but God's were ever to be foremost. Not the stark beauty of the landscape appreciated for its own sake but the lessons to be derived from God's "second book" were to be glorified. For the constant endeavor was somehow to praise God as befit His majesty. Educative of the mind as well as the spirit, Puritan poems acquire much of their richness and power from a dexterous use of images and metaphors drawn from the storehouse most close at hand, the Bible. But there exists in many of these poems another complex of figurative language often overlooked by modern readers that infuses its special insight into the workings of Nature and Nature's God. This is the language of alchemy, the hermetic science whose long tradition admitted multiple and diverse manners of describing on one level the remarkable transmutation of lead to gold and, on a second level, the more glorious sense of union of alchemist and the spirit of all creative activity.

In many instances, alchemy enters American poetry as the very briefest of allusions. "A FUNERAL ELEGY, Upon . . . Mrs. Anne Bradstreet . . ." by John Norton II, is a case in point. Part of Norton's depiction of the universal grief attending the loss of this "Mirror of Her Age" includes reference to earth's current darkness as the extinction of "the great glory of the Skye / That gilds the starrs with heavenly Alchamy."[1] Ichabod Wiswall's substantial reflection on the dreadful lesson to be learned from the comet observed by many New Englanders in 1680 in part identifies the Judgment Day as "Heavens Firmament . . . melt[ing] like Lead." Vigilance, he has earlier observed, is vital, for the "Refiners Fire will soon kindle" to separate gold from the dross since "God's Furnace now in *Zion is*."[2] Benjamin Colman's parable of the "silly Fly" hoping to find transformation where only destruction lies argues much the same point. Colman's explication of the human equation reads thus:

> We little think of the intense fierce Flame,
> That Gold alone is Proof against the same;
> And that such Trash as we like drossy Lead,
> Consume before it, and it strikes us dead.[3]

Or, as a final brief example we might consider John James' tribute to John Bunyan, whose career proves "Brasse in to Gold Grace can transmute."[4] The point of these excerpts should be clear. Even those poets who elected to introduce only sporadically the language of alchemy's mysterious transformation had at least minimal knowledge of its process and its implications.

This is hardly surprising because the seventeenth century witnessed the rise of a growing number of readers and practitioners in the occult art. No evidence survives to suggest that any, save one, of the poets under discussion here busily manipulated the "elements" of Sulphur, Mercury, or the elusive Salt or that they experimented with the disputed number of philosophical "fires" vital to either effective transmutation or to discovery of the wondrous elixir of life. But each poet intimates some awareness of the chemical philosophy's existence.

Allen G. Debus, the foremost interpreter of the chemical philosophy,[5] has traced its origins to the recipes and traditions of the ancient crafts, such as the recipe for fabricating silver contained in the third century Leiden and Stockholm papyri, the early Greek concern with exploring the mysteries of the Creation (Plato and Aristotle), the Alexandrian combining of practical and abstract formulae whose texts are characterized by a "dominating religious aura," and, eventually, the Arabic contribution (mainly mathematic) to the tradition. Here we find a clear interest in alchemy by those principally interested in the study of medicine. By the mid-thirteenth century, Debus contends, it became possible for one like Roger Bacon to adopt as "his thesis [the premise] that alchemy and medicine were fundamentally united." With the Renaissance rediscovery of natural magic, the stage was set for the appearance of Paracelsus (1493–1541), whose theories form the wellspring of a dispute which lent impetus to the Scientific Revolution.

Paracelsus, a rebel to the core, set himself the task of refuting absolutely the validity of the writings of Aristotle, Galen, Avicenna—the pillars of scientific thought. He flatly denied the separate existence of matter and spirit, refused to admit the existence of the four elements—air, earth, fire, and water—as the basis for all things, and razed the barrier erected between "scientific" thinking and mysticism. Instead, he argued that experiment rather than authority be the test of a belief, that there is a true and vital connection between the macrocosm and microcosm, that an understanding of the chemistry of the universe is *the* key to understanding nature, medicine, everything. Beginning with the Spirit moving over the waters to create order from chaos, all is chemistry. As Walter Pagel has observed, for Paracelsus there must be "traffic between that upper world of the Spirit and the lower world of matter—a process with the uniform aim of redemption—redemption that is of the soul from the fetters of matter and of the spiritual spark that can be found hidden in matter everywhere. Thus the *Opus* of the alchemist is dedicated to such redemption as the perfection of metals will afford. To be successful, the process in the furnace must be accompanied by a corresponding purification of the soul of the worker. Hence the close relationship between Alchemy, Gnosticism and neo-Platonism. . . ."[6]

The natural philosophy of Paracelsus and his followers (many of whom, like von Helmont and Glauber, published extensively) was thus based on a two-book concept of nature. Priority was given to the Bible as the revealed word of God, but it was seconded closely by the book of nature, another sort of evidence of the Creator. And citing Ecclesiastes 38 as an authoritative source, these alchemists were wont to argue that "Since Holy Scripture teaches that medicines are created from the earth, it follows that the physician who does not understand natural philosophy as a whole cannot be truly learned in medicine."[7] Exegesis and chemical experiment provide the method to discovery of nature's universal system.

During the last decades of the sixteenth and early years of the seventeenth century, a flock of Paracelsian publications made it impossible for the establishment to ignore the clamor for reforms these texts demanded, and so it was that in 1603 a major confrontation occurred and ended with the Parisian Medical Faculty condemning the Paracelsians flatly. But the British scientific community was more receptive to these new ideas. While criticizing the more mystical aspects of natural philosophy, the respected London College of Physicians, as early as 1589, agreed that their proposed pharmacopoeia include a section on the new chemical medicines, effectively working a compromise between Galen's traditional medicine based on the humors and Paracelsian practice.[8]

The *Pharmacopoiea* did not appear in print until 1649. It is the work of Nicholas Culpeper, himself something of a hermeticist and translator of several alchemical texts. Thomas Johnson lists one of these, a translation of Simeon Partlitz's *A New Method of Physick* (1654) as well as Culpeper's *A Physicall directory; or a translation of the London dispensatory* (the promised *Pharmacopoiea*) in his catalogue of Edward Taylor's library (items number 58 and 147).[9] Reading Partlitz, Taylor would encounter such admonitions as these: "Medicine cannot want Alchymie, the one is so helpful, to another as man & wife, and therefore they ought not to be separated"; "A physitian cureth not only the body but the mind in some manner."[10] Taylor's possession of these texts in addition to the work of another Paracelsian, John Webster, author of *Metallographia; or an History of Metalls* (1641; Johnson's item 52) suggests how possible it is for Taylor to have paid some heed to the range of concerns this new chemical philosophy embraced. Given Taylor's eclectic reading tastes, it is, of course, risky to generalize such familiarity to other poets of his time and place. Nevertheless, certain clearcut instances can be cited.

One of the longest and most ambitious alchemical poems written anywhere at any time is *The Marrow of Alchemy* (London, 1654–55). Purportedly the work of Eirenaeus Philoponos Philalethes, this long (more than two thousand lines) poetic treatise is actually the product of George Starkey (sometimes identified as Stirke, Sturke), a 1646 graduate of Harvard College. Early in his college training Starkey became disillusioned with the type of education he was receiving and turned to alchemical experimentation. Borrowing from the library of his friend John Winthrop the Younger, Starkey read many accounts of the *Opus* by the revered adepts before becoming the star pupil of Dr. Robert Child the

Remonstrant and subsequently embarking on a career as a physician in London. By this time, like his honored van Helmont a self-styled "philosopher by the fire," Starkey's reputation was sufficient to gain his entry into London's "Invisible College" and the attention of Robert Boyle, Samuel Hartlib, and James Dury. A vehement Paracelsian and active penman, Starkey authored no fewer than seven alchemical studies in prose and some occasional poetry in addition to *The Marrow* before he met his death in 1665 treating the plague.[11]

As poetry *The Marrow* is far from great. Despite effort to bring order to his text by dividing the subject into two large Parts—one devoted to theory, the other to practice—and subdividing these into, respectively, four and three Books, Starkey is rambling, diffuse, often wordy and repetitive as he proffers his directions for the successful path to the Philosopher's Stone. To his credit, however, is the fact that his aim is high. Whereas his poetical predecessors had most often limited themselves to addressing but one portion of the *Opus* or elicidating one allegory or trope through which the secret of the process was communicated, Starkey wants to do it all and do it in a variety of images and allegories that most frequently are handled separately and distinctly.[12] His is an immense synthesizing effort.

The royal marriage (or hiereagamos) of Mercury and Sulphur (Spirit and Body), pictured in elaborate detail in *The Chymical Marriage of Christian Rosenkreutz*, is the dominant allegory. Attending Starkey's wedding too are the creatures—the threatening lions, the serpents, many types of birds, dark executioners, reviving founts, homunculi revealed when a magic egg hatches—that Rosenkreutz encounters during the nuptial celebration. Along with these, however, are introduced a variety of lesser, or more briefly handled, allegorical threads: versions of the dying God myth, of the son devoured by his own father, of heroic quests—for dragons, for the Golden Fleece, for the Grail. Pagan lore abounds, most notably in the story of Mars' unholy love of Venus, but also in the tales of Cadmus and Europa. And Christianity is represented by references to the journey of the Magi and the sacrificial death of the Saviour who appears as the Tree of Life. Juxtaposed or offered in counterpoint, these fall together in a truly Baroque whole.

While an uncharitable reading of *The Marrow* might charge its author with an utter loss of control over his material, I would suggest instead that the presence of the Baroque mode accommodates this multiplicity of undergirding allusions and the variety of voices which tell their stories. A petulant voice, for example, intermittently comes to the fore, as when, after reviewing the credentials of Geber, Calid, Bernard of Tresvne, and Flame, Starkey queries: "And what I cannot with my wit perceive, / Because they are removed from my Sphear," should I discredit another's knowledge by assuming "Because I cannot learn can he not teach?"(I, 1, ll. 175–80). Or occasionally Starkey is as patient as a schoolmaster who speaks in deliberate and simple analogues and breaks in to explain the esoteric in terms most mundane:

> Behold an Egge which when the Sun returns,
> In Spring the hen doth lay, how it by heat,
> From thing to thing by constant motion turns
> Or it till time a chicken doth beget,
>   Yet shake this Egge till you the matter hear
>   Within to jog, 'twill not hatch in a year. [I, 1, ll. 463–68]

For the most part, however, the voices are those of the experimenter and the occult poet. The "scientist" speaks of the requisite tools, of the proper positioning of a chimney, of the dual fire, the "water that will not wet the hands," the seed of nature, and the need to dissolve and coagulate—the traditional code of natural philosophy. In this passage, for instance, he explains how his procedure once ran amuck:

> This then [Mercury] I did project,
> Being with [Silver] first of all allai'd,
> It tinged fifty parts, I did direct
> My course this to imbibe, but assai'd
>   In vain, for why? I had it colled, so
>   To Imbibition foolishly did go. [I, 2, ll. 272–76]

The scientist's speaking of metals as coupling and drinking is colorful, but never to be mistaken for the voice of the poet. Our Mercury, Starkey explains,

> 'Tis *Saturns* off-spring who a well doth keep,
> In which cause *Mars* for to be drowned, then
> Let *Saturn* in this Well behold his face,
> Which will seem fresh, and yong, and tender, when
>   The souls of both are thus together blended
>   For each by other need to be amended:
>
> Then lo, a Star into this Well shall fall,
> And with its lustrous raies the earth will shine,
> Let *Venus* add her influence withall,
> For she is Nurse of this our stone divine,
>   The bond of all Chrystalline Mercury,
>   This is the Spring in which our Sun must die. [I, 4, ll. 356–66]

As a practicing chemical philosopher, Starkey can speak seriously, almost reverently, of silver as Venus, iron as Mars, of lead as Saturn, and "our Mercury" as the offspring. Such identifications, for him, point to universal truths intentionally rendered cryptically to guard against their meanings becoming known to anyone God has not intended to become initiated into the Art. Furthermore, because of the mythology they bring to mind, these deities call up a wealth of cultural associations that can be molded into the shape of real poetry. But, these few examples make clear, Starkey lacks the true poet's ear: meter often falters and rhymes are forced. Perhaps for him that is ultimately of little importance, for the message rather than the medium stands preeminent. Alchemy per se is Starkey's concern, not the uses to which alchemical thought and language may be put. In this respect he stands apart from other colonial poets who took up the subject.

A case in point is that of Nicholas Noyes who, on one occasion, agreed with what Edward Taylor more consistently alluded to: the *Opus* is but a metaphor. The contention arises naturally from the text in honor of which this prefatory poem is written, Cotton Mather's *Christanus per Ignem*, the Christian made by the fire (1702). For roughly half of this 118-line poem, Noyes elaborates on his theme succinctly stated in these couplets:

> There is a *Stone* (as I am told)
> That turns *all Metals* into *Gold*:
> But I believe, that there is none,
> Save pious *Meditation* [ll. 13–16][13]

"Matter," which the sometimes fickle senses bring to the Fancy, Noyes claims, "The *Fire of Meditation*" can burn in musing. This is the true Philosopher's Stone calling us to godliness. Thus are

> The *flame*, the *sparks, light, heat* and *motion*,
> . . . *Metamorphosed* to *Devotion*.
> If *Godliness* be *greatest gain*,
> And doth when Gold is dross, remain;
> Conclude this the Coelestial *Stone*.
> Out does the *Philosophick One*. [ll. 23–28]

The central section of Noyes' poem documents in sometimes ambiguous but always extravagant praise Mather's ability to track his thoughts—"the Sally's of our *Author's* Soul"—across the map of the universe. Soaring to heaven and then swooping down into hell, "*fir'd* with *zeal*, like *Lion* bold," Mather "Roars out" the message of God's wrath and the need to reflect properly now or know the certain torment awaiting.

Readers are urged to Mather's "Holy Fire," which lends light as well as heat to the striving soul "And will perfume, and purifie" the mind, making it "heavenly," since "like to like it generates." In terms analogous to the adept's desire to make of his laboratory an oratory, Noyes exhorts readers to convert hearth into altar and themselves into "Living *Sacrifice*[s]" on that altar. In this holy fire thus domesticated all spiritual "*Crudityes*" can be digested, all dross removed, the purest refinement made possible.

However, he warns, should the meditative process not conform to this pattern, if no "*New man* [is made] of the Old," the fire must be a false one, an "*Ignis fatuus*." No efforts at concealment will avail. Testing reveals the counterfeit and

> . . . thou prove *Silver reprobate,*
> Which God and man *reject,* and *hate,*
> And when the *Great Refiner* come,
> Thou prove a *Caput mortuum.* [ll. 103–6]

The alchemical imagery of Noyes' poem is no "dead Head," a worthless residue. Neither is it merely windowdressing. It functions within the terms of the poem and the role it is designed to fill. On the other hand, in so strictly limiting the alchemical parallel to meditation, Noyes reveals how casual is his understanding of the implications inherent in viewing the world as a chemical universe. Alchemy, for him, is constrained to the quest for the Philosopher's Stone.

Nothing suggests that Benjamin Tompson was as aware of the chemical universe as Starkey surely was. But when the time came to commemorate the death of John Winthrop the Younger with two "Black Parenthes[es] of woe," Tompson was capable of drawing on a more than superficial understanding of the Art. In both elegies Tompson praises the departed saint in highly conventional terms for his charity, humanity, and excellent sense. It is Winthrop as "*unimitable* Pyrotechnist," however, that forms the core of each elegy, as the poet locates Winthrop within the historical line of adepts and praises his subject's skills almost exclusively in terms of the marvelous cures which could be effected by possession of the elixir of life.[14]

"A Funeral Tribute" quickly establishes the criteria by which Winthrop's career is to be defined. He was, Tompson notes, "that most *Charitable* Christian, *Unbiassed* Politician," and philosopher by the fire. All three characteristics will be addressed during the course of the poem, although sometimes with only the haziest of distinctions between the first and the third, as is appropriate. After first placing Winthrop in the midst of that worthy New England triumvirate— Dudley, Cotton, and the elder Winthrop—Tompson pictures the colonies as bleeding patients conscious of the loss of their great physician, an exemplar of "Christian Modesty." "Yet," he continues,

> . . . Miracles set by, hee'd act his part
> Better to LIFE then Doctors of his Art.
> Projections various by fire he made
> Where Nature had her common Treasure laid.

Some thought the tincture *Philosophick* lay
Hatcht by the Mineral Sun in *WINTHROPS* way;
And clear it shines to me he had a Stone
Grav'd with his Name which he could read alone. [ll. 19–26][15]

The texture here is dense, for just as the opening lines of the passage may be read as referring strictly to Winthrop's medical knowledge, and just as the final couplet may be a direct allusion to the stone on which members of the elect may read their names (Revelation 2.17), the center of the passage suggests a submerged alchemical reading that requires reconsideration of the context. Those "Projections various by fire" point toward Winthrop's being a student and controller of nature's secret generative fire, the oxymoronic "common Treasure" which is the true primal material. Accordingly, the evasive "Some thought" he possessed the all-powerful potable gold (the adept's gold egg "Hatcht" by the earth's vital heat) gives way to a certainty that Winthrop's eyes only could read the cryptic message of the Stone.

Following a brief digression linking Winthrop with the Scaevolas, a Roman family famous for its jurors and orators, Tompson returns to regarding his subject as medic/metallurgist. In the sun god's art—the royal art of alchemy—Winthrop stood "alone." So attuned was he to Nature that she is portrayed as actively reaching out to him. "Earth's veins" "creep" toward him and "stop his plodding eyes" that he might learn not just the use of the metal itself but its "juice," its essence. Those punning "Christal Mountains" to which his feet lead him, certainly a reference to the lapis as Christ, bring us to the cloistered gems, earth's stars, on which Winthrop plies his "tools of th' Chymick trade." Then, in the climactic image of this section of the poem, Tompson imagines "His fruit of Toyl Hermetically done / Stream to the poor as light doth from the Sun." Winthrop himself is thus transformed into the life-giving sun, symbol of the gold he seeks.

Allusions to alchemical thought are less plentiful in the remainder of the elegy. Although Tompson pictures Winthrop manning the bellows that preserve the heat vital to successful transmutation, speaks of the failure of any "Artificial fire" to disturb his subjects' equinimity, and labels Winthrop "the Balsome of his Countries Health," what dominates is the idea that "this *Chiron*," "this healer *Luke*" possesses every virtue in the constellation and thus rightly belongs in heaven. Yet one final alchemical link is forged. With death "*Helmonts* lines so learned and abstruse" must be cast aside as Winthrop's eyes and ears strive only to comprehend God's harmony. The association with Jan Baptista van Helmont is a fitting one. A respected follower of Paracelsus and solid iatrochemical theorist, Helmont helped to sustain the dual inquiry into the mystical side of the chemical universe and its more rational, "purer" counterpart. Winthrop's close identification with him neatly summarizes the portrait the elegy is designed to sketch.

More one-sided is the picture emerging from the companion elegy, "Upon the setting of that Occidental Star." Here, with the exception of a few introductory lines and a concluding passage lauding Winthrop's diplomatic abilities and consistent righteousness, Tompson focuses on Winthrop as Artist. Initially there is some question as to whether or not this "special Favorite of the Most High," this *"Monarch* of Natures Secret" did in fact have knowledge of "the *Star* of GOLD*."* First the positive claim is made; then the possibility that "the World mistakes" is admitted. "But had he it," Tompson continues, Winthrop, like Moses, to whom he is briefly analogized, would know that revelations are not permitted to the herd. His very success at healing must stand as proof of Winthrop's climb on "the Stairs of Science" to its visionary heights.

From this point on, save for the tiniest of doubts that the Tincture exists, Tompson settles down to describe Winthrop's alchemical acts.

> Into his Thoughts Alembick we may think,
> He crouded Stars to make a Diet Drink.
> (I mean) Terrestrial Stars which in the Earth,
> Receive their vitals and a Mineral Birth: . . . [ll. 29–32]

Flighty, Protean Mercury he could force into stability; the alchemist's Salt he converted into "a Balsom better than all riches"; and Sulphur, in Winthrop's hands, became the antidote to all diseases. The materials needed to accomplish the *"ARCHIATRICK* ends" so announced, Tompson continues, in traditional terms, to trace the progress of the *Opus* in terms of various color changes. Winthrop knows his way around "the Philosophick sea" and can see in "the World" of the alembic the initial blackness (Nigredo) give way to "Glorious Light" as "rich Embroideries" (the multicolored *cauda pavonis*) appear. In nice replication of genuine alchemical tracts, the poet, without overtly signalling it, backtracks to offer another version of the same process. The "Homogeneal spark['s]" rebellion against the blackening, the budding or flowering of the gems which defy comprehension to any but "Natures grand Courtiers," are but synonyms for the previously described tingeing process. Knowing "the Womb" is identical to navigating the philosophic sea.

In theory, Winthrop's privileged knowledge of nature's secrets should have prolonged his life almost infinitely. So the obvious fact of mortality might disastrously undermine all the preceding praise for his skill. "But all his Art must lie, there's no Disease / Predominant, where he doth take his Ease." Tompson gracefully negotiates this treacherous thought. Having outlived by more than two decades his noted predecessor, Theophrastus (Paracelsus), Winthrop has proved himself "Hermetick," so much so that Tompson, in outrageous hyperbole, is quite satisfied to grant his preeminence over Hermes Trismegisthus himself:

> . . . first in Grace,
> Thrice great in ART, the next deserving place;
> Thrice High in humble Carriage, and who,
> Would not to Highest Meekness ready bow? [ll. 55–58]

In this way, Thrice Great Hermes provides Tompson with a sturdy bridge into the conclusion of the poem where those personal virtues which made Winthrop an admired governer, and which guarantee his sainthood, can be rehearsed. It is an apt ending to a tribute that is at once a playful elegy and a poem that expects of the reader a fair degree of knowledge of the chemical tradition— historical, theoretical, and rhetorical.

It remains, nonetheless, the province of the colonies' premier poet, Edward Taylor, to demonstrate how pervasively alchemical tropes and metaphors might be drawn upon to articulate the wondrous transformation from sick, sinful spirit to glorified soul. Nowhere is this reliance more evident than in Meditation 7, First Series, where he envisions his body as the vial awaiting transmission from the "Golden Still" (Christ's body) of the "Liquor" of proffered grace, animated and enflamed by His "Holy Love."[16] Numerous Tree of Life images, especially that of Meditation I, 29, may in a less overt manner be read as direct allusions to the alchemist's elusive Mercurius, existing as it does in both material and spiritual form, as both male and female, active and passive principle of the Great Work, and as conciliatory agent ultimately successful in uniting and perfecting all things. Indeed, viewed most loosely, almost every reference to distillation, herbal or chemical, falls under the domain of the new philosophy, as when in Meditation 47, First Series, Taylor begs to be treated with the juice of a "Waybred spring he finds," a balm to combat the venom of the spider's spit. Or when, in Meditation 149, Second Series, the poet finds in the spouse "Spirits of the Spirits Chymistrie."

Of greater interest, however, are poems containing more extended passages that intimate Taylor's chemical knowledge. One such poem is Meditation 160, Second Series. This is one of the Meditations focusing on the Lily of the Valley figure, here approached from the angle of Taylor's supplication that he be worked upon to become "Thy spirituall valie all divine" (l. 17).

> I am thy Vally where thy lilly grows
> Thou my White and Red blesst lilly fresh;
> Thy Active and thy Passive 'bedience do
> Hold out Active and Passive Right'ousness.
> Pure White and Red making a lovely grace,
> Present thee to our Love to hug and 'brace.
>
> The Medicinall Virtue of the lilly speake
> That thou my Lilly are Physician who
> Healst all Diseased Souls both small and greate.
> None dy of any Spirituall Sores that to thee goe.
> The Vally lilly then doth Emblemize
> Thy fitness for thy Mediatoriall guise. [ll. 19–30]

Christ as lily, the healing mediator between sinsick man and God's righteous justice, acts as Mercurius does in the *Opus*, reconciling the seemingly irrefutable differences between matter and spirit. As the lily, Christ-Mercurius partakes of both the pure white and the red tingeing powers, of both active and passive powers that make possible the atonement and redemption signalling spiritual well-being.

Another distillation flowing from God's "gracious Chymistry" (First Series, Meditation 34) appears in a meditation on the Rose of Sharon, First Series, Meditation 4. Four stanzas of this unusually long poem (eleven stanzas) are devoted to prove that "God Chymist is." The rosy elixir, "all Catholicons excell[ing]," is potent enough to purge whatever ill humors trap the soul, wound the body, or torture the conscience: "Its Cordiall, ease doth Heart burns Causd by Sin." All of stanza nine elaborates on the physical and spiritual unification apparent in the "Heart burns." For in stanza nine the picking, mangling, boiling of the flower to prepare the potion readily points to Christ's anguish on the Cross that the Resurrection might be accomplished, "this mangled Rose [rising] up again / And in its pristine glory, doth remain." In the language of the chemical philosophy, dissolve (destroy) that you might coagulate (regenerate). Or, as Taylor describes it in more obvious alchemical language in Meditation 49, Second Series, "Gold in its Ore, must melted be, to bring / It midwift from its mother womb." Gold's birth, its vitality, depends upon the action of "A fining Pot, and Test, and melting fire" as surely as the poet requires God's fire to refine him.

> In spite of disclaimers that he
>   Strike[s] [his] oare not in the golden Sea
>   Of Godhead Fulness, thine essentially.
> But in the Silver Ocean make my way
>   Of all Created Fulness, thine Most High [II. 47, ll. 7–11]

Taylor more than occasionally manages to find and realize chemical images that powerfully render the comfort and consolation attendant on a state of grace. Shaped and wielded by a master poet, the ideas and images of the chemical philosophy have never been so well expressed by another American poet.[17]

Each of these poets, major and minor, thus reflects a consciousness of a world-view that sees and attempts to comprehend this as a chemical universe. In this they show themselves men of their time, not somehow benighted or subject to the cultural lag so long believed to have afflicted those migrating to these shores. On rare occasions or with regularity, roughly or melodically, they responded to that world-view in their own distinct styles and for their own particular purposes. It would be pleasant to think they were familiar with the definition of iatrochemistry that terms it an "Investigation into the *America* of nature."[18]

NOTES

1. Text is that in Meserole, *Poetry*, p. 461, ll. 15–16.

2. "A Judicious Observation Of That Dreadful Comet," in Meserole, p. 442, l. 312; p. 439, ll. 195–98.

3. "A Quarrel with Fortune," in Meserole, p. 337, ll. 15–18.

4. "Of John Bunyans Life &c," in Meserole, p. 425, l. 2.

5. See particularly *The Chemical Philosophy: Paracelsian Science and Medicine in the Sixteenth and Seventeenth Centuries,* 2 vols. (New York: Science History Publications, 1977), on which much of the current summary is based. Cited within this paragraph are *Chemical Philosophy* I, 46, I, 6, and I, 19.

6. "Paracelsus and the Neoplatonic and Gnostic Tradition," *Ambix* 8 (1960): 129. For a detailed review of Paracelsian thought see Pagel's *Paracelsus: An Introduction to Philosophical Medicine in the Renaissance* (New York: S. Karger, 1958).

7. Debus, *Chemical Philosophy*, II, 334.

8. Debus surveys conditions leading to this compromise in "The Paracelsian Compromise in Elizabethan England," *Ambix* 8 (1960): 71–97, and "Guintherius, Libavius, and Sennert: The Chemical Compromise in Early Modern Medicine," in *Science, Medicine and Society in the Renaissance,* ed. A. G. Debus, 2 vols. (New York: Neale Watson Pubs., 1972), I, 151–65.

9. *The Poetical Works of Edward Taylor*, ed. Thomas H. Johnson (New York: Rockland Editions, 1939).

10. Quoted by F. N. L. Poynter, "Nicholas Culpeper and the Paracelsians," in *Science, Medicine and Society in the Renaissance*, I, 206.

11. For biographical information on this little known but intriguing character, see Ronald Sterne Wilkinson, "George Starkey, Physician and Alchemist," *Ambix* 11 (1963): 121–52, and Harold Jantz, "America's First Cosmopolite," *PMHS* 84 (1972): 3–25.

12. Undoubtedly influential negative models are those poems contained in the *Theatrum Chemicum Britannicum* (1652) edited by Elias Ashmole, a volume Starkey knew well. See, for example, "The Hunting of the Green Lion," "The Hermit's Tale," and "The Worke of John Dastin."

13. All citations of Noyes's poem refer to the text in Meserole, *Poetry*, pp. 271–73.

14. Winthrop's chemical investigations are documented in a number of letters included in the MHS *Winthrop Papers* (Boston: Merrymount Press, 1929–47). See especially the correspondence presented in vol. 3 (96–98, 290–92), vol. 4 (333–38), and vol. 5 (221–22, 241–42). For biographical information see Robert C. Black III, *The Younger John Winthrop* (New York: Columbia Univ. Press, 1966).

15. All quotations of Tompson's elegies are from the text in White, *Tompson*.

16. Citations of the Preparatory Meditations refer to texts in Stanford, *Taylor*.

17. For detailed readings of other poems revelatory of Taylor's interest in alchemy see my "Edward Taylor and the Alchemy of Grace," *Seventeenth-Century News* 34, ii–iii (1976): 33–36. Note also the alchemical references in First Series Meditations 9 and 48, and Second Series numbers 4, 5, 18, 31, 61, 62, 68B, 105, and 158.

18. Noah Biggs, *The Vanity of the Craft of Physick* (1651), quoted by Debus in *Chemical Philosophy*, II, 503.

8 IN THE MARGIN: THE IMAGE OF WOMEN IN EARLY PURITAN POETRY

CHERYL WALKER

The body of early colonial poetry has been read in the past as documentary evidence of Puritan life and thought. By and large, the aims of this poetry are public and communal, as many commentators have noted. Because of these aims, however, we are invited to expect certain features which usually belong to public verse—descriptions of the personalities and occupations of this community's members, for instance. Among the mostly male seventeenth-century poets, one does find a good deal of information about the intellectual life of the people, their physical hardships, and their inordinate luck; repeatedly one notices their shared concern with the meaning of the errand into the wilderness. Along with factual detail comes the insistent suggestion that the poet's personal preoccupations have become co-extensive with his vision of national destiny. However, feminist critics have provided us with evidence that the picture is considerably one-sided. "Public and communal" are defined in terms of a purely male vision of community. Woman's life and livelihood belong to the margin.

In Roxbury, Massachusetts, Benjamin Tompson's tombstone stands as a monument to the tripartite function of the colonial male poet. Tompson (1642–1714) rests beneath it as a "learned Schoolmaster & Physician & the Renouned Poet of N: Engl:"—a man concerned with intellectual life, physical hardship and the symbolic (specifically teleological) significance of place. A poet *of* New England is a poet who speaks for its communal concerns. New England is more than a habitat for Tompson and others: it is a premise full of ideological intensity. Puritan poets like Tompson had a vision of the way the community should look. Such poems as Tompson's "New Englands Crisis," Michael Wigglesworth's "God's Controversy with New-England" and Edward Johnson's "Good News from New England"[1] demonstrate the fervor with which the mission to build the city on the hill was undertaken. Elegies, too, were pared and pruned to exemplify the pattern of Christian piety. The poet grows in stature as he comes to speak for the public and political rather than the lyrical self. What Sacvan Bercovitch has persuasively argued for Puritan writers generally can be applied to the male poet in particular: "He earns his authority as communal spokesman not by his relation to any existent community, but by personal assertion. His myth is essentially projective and elite, the invention of expatriate idealists who declared themselves the party of the future, and then proceeded, in an implicit denial of secular history, to impose prophecy upon experience."[2] In other words, Bercovitch reveals that factual, "realistic" comprehensiveness was not what the Puritan poets intended.

We do indeed find "an implicit denial" of some elements of secular history in these poems. Specifically, there is a notable lack of references to the actual work performed by women, work which was absolutely essential to the on-going life of the community. Furthermore, most of the female figures who do appear in Puritan poems can hardly be distinguished one from another and display a singular lack of personal force. Catherine Dunn, in an essay entitled "The Changing Image of Women in Renaissance Society," shows that the courtly sonneteers of the 1590s portrayed English women as wily, strong, and well-educated.[3] However, the Puritans in America rarely explored these qualities in their female figures. Domestic life, when it appears at all, seems but the theme of a moment's idyll between bouts of real literary work, work which was conceived of as masculine and which was rendered in metaphors of masculine labor. Jonathan Mitchell speaks of composing "costly Verses, and most laborious Rhymes."[4] These poets are not thinking of the physical energy expended, surely, but of a comparable expenditure of psychic energy. Yet, the poet sometimes pictures himself as an energetic husbandman or pomologist in his poems, grafting himself onto native stock, ploughing deep so others may enjoy a rich harvest. Work of all kinds is masculinized in the poetry. Edward Taylor, then, is a genuine exception—a male poet who in poems like "Huswifery" uses female domestic work images for his sacred poetic conceits.

What kind of work did women actually perform? Page Smith, Laurel Ulrich, Lyle Koehler, and Mary Beth Norton have helped us revise our notions about the lives of colonial women.[5] They describe the limits placed upon female behavior and take differing positions on the strategies women adopted for achieving power. All agree, however, that women's work was vital to the survival of the fragile Puritan community. Other commentators have also contributed to this picture. Eugenie Leonard details the functions specifically assigned to women in the early colonial period.[6] They were needed for the maintenance of the house and other buildings, for keeping fires lit and constantly burning. They procured, processed, and preserved the food, made their own soap, and sewed the clothing of family and servants. (Since the average number of live offspring produced in families of this period was eight, we can conclude that women were usually pregnant or lactating while they performed these functions.) As the only midwives in the colonies, they played a central role in protecting the future of the colonial experiment, a future bound up in the new generation who the Puritan fathers felt represented the true test of communal success. In addition to the young, the old and the sick were women's responsibility. Frequently called upon in the event of death, it was women who dressed and laid out the victims of fevers, the casualties of childbed, the grandfathers. It is a mistake, however, to assume that female activities were limited to the domestic sphere. Wives were expected to share with their husbands the responsibilities of social and religious life. In fact, toward the end of the seventeenth century, women had become more active than men in church affairs, as Cotton Mather ruefully notes in his *Ornaments for the Daughters of Zion*.[7] Finally, a small but significant number of women occupied non-traditional positions as innkeepers, shopkeepers, ferryboat-runners, advocates, etc.[8]

This picture provides ample evidence for the belief that women were as necessary to the success of the errand into the wilderness as men. Furthermore, in the early migrations many of the women were, like Anne Bradstreet, cultivated and well-educated, capable of contributing to the intellectual life of the community as well.

We might easily expect, therefore, that the poetry of this fervently ideological community, trying to establish itself on ungenerous soil, would reflect the contributions, both real and potential, of its female as well as its male members. And women are not totally absent from the poems. Yet, when they do appear, their contributions are marginalized, trivialized, tokenized—made to seem as though they are not vitally necessary for the success of the community.

A brief comparison of elegies composed on the deaths of men and women may enhance the discussion by focusing on the difference in treatment given to male and female subjects. John Fiske (1608–1677) wrote elegies for John Cotton and Anne Griffin that have become staples in anthologies. Besides being considerably longer, the Cotton elegy is characteristic of male elegies in describing the ways in which the deceased had benefited the community. His work (here intellectual) is specified:

> Hee who the knotts of Truth, of Mysteries
> Sacred, most cleerely did ope 'fore our eyes [ll. 15–16].

Cotton's loss is described as a loss to the whole community.

> A Father in our Israel's cea'st to be
> Even hee that in the Church a pillar was [ll. 8–9]

His contributions were part of the foundation upon which the Puritan project was built and thus his death threatens all.

> Such was hee of such use in these last dayes
> Whose want bewayle, o, and alas alwaies [ll. 61–62]

In contrast, the Griffin elegy contains no line like "such was [s]hee of such use." We are told that the wife of Mr. Richard Griffin, dying at ninety-six, was blessed with grace and destined for heaven—a pattern of piety for all. Her death achieves its significance as a reminder of the transitoriness and paltriness of earthly life. Neither her personal characteristics nor her contributions are specifically mentioned. Her loss reminds us of our duty: "Her change, her Gayne to count." This loss does not threaten the community's well-being.

Elegies for both males and females were largely written according to conventions. My point here is not that Puritans intended to discriminate against women in their elegies but that their conventions reveal the relative status they accorded to male and female members of the community. Lonna Malmsheimer, in an article entitled "Daughters of Zion: New England Roots of American Feminism," shows that funeral sermons in early colonial New England mourned the loss of a woman as a loss to friends and family first. Only occasionally does a funeral sermon mention that a dead woman is a loss to the church. Sermons on male members describe their loss as a gap in the hedge, a ruined pillar, a loss in vital support for the whole commonwealth.[9] For example, Fiske uses the pillar image in his elegy for John Cotton.

Similarly, John Norton's elegy on Anne Bradstreet, though it proceeds for ninety-five lines, is eloquent in what it does not say. A woman so prominent, both because of her own works and because of her connections to such luminaries as Thomas Dudley and Simon Bradstreet, could well have inspired some personal recognition of her achievements in the service of the community. Yet John Norton II (1651–1716) has trouble writing about her in these terms. Though I doubt that he intended it, the poem is an entertaining example of hollow praise. As he goes through his conventional posturings about his inability to praise her sufficiently, he does indeed praise her insufficiently. "Her virtues were so great, that they do raise / A work to trouble fame, astonish praise," he tells us in lines seventy-three and seventy-four. In fact, we hear very little about what she actually did to deserve all this praise. Every future reader who reads her worth "in Fames eternal Almanack" will deplore her loss, Norton says. Thus, her loss will not be felt more keenly by those of her own time and place than by others. No mention is made of Bradstreet's loss as a threat to the survival of New England. Her communal significance is underplayed.

The one place in the poem where Norton begins to describe what it was about Bradstreet that made her so valuable is in lines seventy-seven and seventy-eight where he says:

> Her breast was a brave Pallace, a *Broad-street*,
> Where all heroick ample thoughts did meet

However, this is the only even slightly specific reference to her skills. Norton seems much more concerned with Bradstreet's effect on others than with what she was herself. Immediately after the lines quoted above, Norton tells us:

> That others souls, to hers, dwelt in a lane.
> Beneath her feet, pale envy bites her chain,
> And poison Malice, whetts her stinge in vain. [ll. 80–82]

Envy and Malice seem like a pair of spiteful women who want to compete with Bradstreet but find themselves overshadowed.

A similar reference to envy is made at the end of Nicholas Noyes' consolatory poem to Cotton Mather on the death of his wife, Abigail. Noyes (1647–1717) praises Abigail in a catalog of female virtues and then concludes by saying:

> More might be said: but lest I vex
> And stir the Envy of her Sex,
> I'le not proceed in Commendation,
> But leave her to their Imitation. [ll. 90–93]

The *Imitatio Christi* of male elegies may seem to be paralleled by references to Mary, Martha, Rachel, Deborah, and Dorcas in female elegies. Yet, since Christ is seen as central and these female figures as merely peripheral, the parallel does not really hold. Though prominent male figures are often said to arouse envy in the hearts of *all*, women are specifically said to be the envy of other women. Male standards are "universal." Female standards are particular to females only.

Though rarely, one does occasionally find an elegy which relates the actual functions performed by its female subject for the good of the community. Such a poem is Benjamin Tompson's memorial for his wife, Mary.[10] Tompson specifically describes the relationship he carried on with his wife as one governed by love:

> Tis hard to tell where love did beare such sway,
> Who twas Commanded or who did obey. [ll. 17–18]

Of course, by mentioning this fact, Tompson is invoking what we might call the "implied paradigm" in which wives obey and husbands rule. Tompson wishes to present his wife as "a sweet example to a Christian Town," exemplary because exceptional.

> Ask but the neighbour hood and they will tell,
> She was a Dorcas in our israell,
> Ready on every hand to run or spend
> To sick and pore to minister and lend.
> So amiable in her whole Convers,
> The least we Can is to lament her hearse. [ll. 35–40]

Tompson gives us some picture of what his wife actually did, but even he does not connect these duties with the health of the community. In his elegy for John Winthrop, Winthrop is described as "the Balsome of his Countries Health." All of New England mourns his loss. Mary is mourned by her family only. Her (female) children and their children are told:

Follow her steps and imitate her life,
Who was a Virtuous virgin mother wife. [ll. 79–80]

Furthermore, we must remind ourselves that in its specificity about women's contributions to the life of the commonwealth, this poem is an exception. We may conclude, then, that the poetry of the early Puritan Fathers contains an unconscious denial of the contributions of women to the vital secular life of the colonies. At first we might suppose that secular life was not an acceptable subject for Puritan poets, except in so far as secular and sacred could be shown to reflect one another. However, many Puritan poems record the secular occupations of male members of the community.

In addition, women also played an important role in church life. This, too, is rarely mentioned. "Good News from New-England" by Edward Johnson (1598–1672) is one of the few places where a woman appears in an active religious role in colonial poetry. Johnson briefly mentions a woman preacher as a member of the crowd which had gathered around the English ships bound for America. This woman preacher is presented not as a saint but as an instrument of Satan, an "errour brocher," possibly a figure for Anne Hutchinson, who was condemned by the Puritans for her Antinomian heresy. In Johnson's poem the woman preacher is one of several individuals who pretend to a false faith:

Up starts another from a crowd, of women, her admiring,
An able tongue in Scripture learn'd, to preach forsooth desiring,
With revelations strange, yet true, as Scripture them accounting [ll. 82–84]

Women, of course, were not allowed to preach, and this comment—"to preach forsooth desiring"—instantly identifies the woman as grievously in error.[11] She wishes to step out of the place assigned to women.

The place assigned to women as a class was the margin. To help us understand what this may mean, we can profitably use the work of the deconstructionist Gayatri Spivak, especially her "Explanation and Culture: Marginalia."[12] In this article Spivak suggests that the margin is needed by every elite in order to establish and privilege a political, cultural, or literary center. It is well to remember that the margin is the border, the rim, the verge. Without it, the center lacks definition. Often what is pushed to the margin gains by its displacement an extraordinary force. Since distance is always threatening to collapse, this force must somehow be recognized and even reinforced without allowing it to intrude on the center. As noted earlier, it is unfair to charge that the Puritans intended to oppress women through their politics or their literature. In fact, women may have been better off in America than they were in England, although Lyle Koehler's A Search for Power denies this.[13] The Puritans were simply bound by conventions. It was conventional to write elegies describing women in undifferentiated terms as images of piety and humility. It was conventional to extol men as leaders and thinkers whose loss threatened the entire fabric of society.

However, people both constitute and are constituted by conventions. Structuralists and semioticians have recently demonstrated the benefits of a holistic approach to culture, treating conventions as signs of unrecognized and unarticulated prejudices about the world, prejudices which are revealed in all kinds of structural patterns in the culture. There is considerable evidence that the Puritan fathers were uneasy with the important role played by women in the development of their theocracy. This becomes especially clear toward the end of the century when the strength of the theocracy was threatened from all sides.[14] Then their fears exploded in vicious attempts to scapegoat those who would not conform. However, the Puritan response to Anne Hutchinson, Mary Dwyer, and the "witches" provides only one kind of evidence. There are also clues to this uneasiness in Puritan writings on other subjects. To emphasize the paradigm of the "virtuous woman," as opposed to the powerful, intelligent, and Christ-like man, is to suggest the fear of what unvirtuous women could bring to pass: the destruction of hierarchy, collapsing of distances, erasing of distinctions (boundaries, margins) necessary for the preservation of a privileged order. The Puritans' world-view was hierarchical and based upon an intense need to keep order. The heavenly realm was not just superior to the earthly realm; it was categorically *different* from it. This difference, and the margin between the two realms which sustained it, prevented earthly disappointments from threatening the idea of a perfect transcendental world. One could not then deduce the nature of heaven from the nature of earth. In an analogous way, the marginalizing of female activities prevented the collapse of what were considered critical distinctions between male and female roles and sustained male supremacy. Ben Barker-Benfield spots a nice example of a male Puritan's fear of declassification in "Anne Hutchinson and the Puritan Attitude Toward Women." John Cotton predicted, according to Barker-Benfield, that Anne Hutchinson's teaching would lead to "promiscuous and filthie comings togeather of men and woemen without distinction or Relation of Marriage."[15] We call something marginal not only if it is barely within a lower standard or limit of quality but also if it pertains to the fringes of consciousness. John Cotton's fears equate feminine assertion with a breakdown in the sexual mores holding society together. This illustrates the way fringe elements tend to run together; they also tend to become infected by the furtiveness and disgust associated with subconscious desires.

Eve is the figure most often used to justify woman's subordinate position in the culture. She is also allied with Satan and the dark forces of evil that hover at the fringes of consciousness. As the first to fall, Eve is invoked to prove that woman is the "weaker vessel" and must be kept away from temptation. Since it was Eve who persuaded Adam to eat the apple, she is also seen as a potentially powerful seducer, Satan's handmaiden. Lonna Malmsheimer quotes a funeral sermon from a collection of 1640 in which a Puritan minister connects the threefold punishment of women to the threefold sins of Eve. Because Eve listened to the serpent, he argues, women have their sorrows and mental sufferings increased. Because Eve accepted the fruit, women in bringing forth their own "fruits" must endure the miseries of labor, ever threatening them with death. As the seducer of Adam, Eve is responsible for causing women to become subject to their husbands' rule.[16] Puritan sermons purport to find women too weak to be left to their own devices. Yet, in fact, arguments like these suggest fearful female strengths that must be held in check.

One way to reduce the potential threat of these strengths is to obscure women entirely. Michael Wigglesworth (1631–1705) in his *Day of Doom* seems to have forgotten women's very existence. As he scans the crowd of penitents with his mind's eye, he sees male faces—except for one place toward the end of the poem where mothers and wives are briefly introduced. Thus does mankind become men, of one kind only. Overt non-recognition is the first sign of marginality. The metalinguistic message is that women do not matter.

An even more striking example is Johnson's "Good News from New-England." Johnson provides one of the many records of secular activities engaged in by the colonists. Here, if anywhere, one would expect to find some recognition of women in the discussion of procuring food, providing shelter, confronting seasonal change. However, the economics of Johnson's world are purely masculine. Autumn is a season for husbandman and ploughman, winter for eager hunters and merchants. The "building, planting, and giving out of LANDS" details the beginnings of capitalism when Planters overproduced and exchanged capital for money. "Usefull men are highly priz'd," the poet tells us. They

Get all they can, sell often, than, and thus old Planters rise.
They build to sell, and sell to build, where they find towns are planting,
Till men no more the Sea passe o're, and Customers are wanting.

[ll. 337–39]

Even Johnson's depiction of populating "this howling desart Land" seems to require no female participation.

Although a profit margin decides commercial success or failure, the connotations of "margin" suggest superfluity. Thus, the word conveys the ambiguity we have noted in Puritan women's role. While fulfilling irreplaceable functions in the life of the community, women are rarely recognized in the poetry. It is precisely the *usefulness* of women which is ignored, though we are reminded that "usefull men are highly priz'd." The marginal role of women meant that, while economically indispensable, they were made to appear superfluous. Their births frequently were not recorded, and their church activities were masked.[17]

Widows represented one of the most powerful groups of women in the colonies. Once endowed with their "widow's third," they could be self-sufficient economically. According to John Faragher, they played significant roles in religious and communal life. Widows were particularly sought after as marriage partners and yet they married less frequently than widowers, especially if the widows were financially independent. Of those widowed at fifty or younger, eighty-four percent of the men remarried but only forty-four percent of the women. Men also remarried more quickly. The median lapse between marriages for widowers was less than twelve months, while it was three years for widows. Faragher concludes that many widows *preferred* to remain unmarried and could more easily do without the other sex than widowers could.[18]

One notes with interest, therefore, the poem by Henricus Selyns (1636–1701) called "Reasons for and against Marrying Widows " (in Meserole, *Poetry*). Selyns sets forth none of the widely discussed economic considerations (widows could provide money and property) and reduces the matter to a purely masculine weighing of sexual advantages. Selyns' humor obtains its sharp edge through its cynical presentation of women. The sexual overtones of swallowing the water in which another has drowned suggest the devaluation of an item by previous use, thus objectifying the female and rendering her value in market terms.

Though his terms of value and risk are essentially economic, reifying virginity in this case, Selyns chooses to avoid the overt economic issues connected with widows, issues that Benjamin Franklin would raise directly a little later. Though women are evaluated in terms which reflect economic or meta–economic considerations, Puritans often seem to pretend, as Edward Johnson does, that women have no place in the world of economic calculations.

Nathaniel Ward (1578–1652) is responsible for one of the most extensive diatribes against women published in the colonies. *The Simple Cobbler of Aggawam*[19] is noteworthy because it does consider women explicitly in terms of commercial considerations. The woman of fashion, and Ward seemed to feel there were many such, was a favorite target of Ward's satire. He wrote: "I look at her as the very gizzard of a trifle, the product of a quarter of a cypher, the epitome of nothing, fitter to be kickt, if she were of a kickable substance, than either honoured or humoured." Such emotional language suggests Ward's rage at the margin. Women's fashions are called "Deficients, or Redundants, not to bee brought under any Rule." Ward, of course, makes no mention of the positive economic role played by women in the colonies or elsewhere. According to him, women mainly drain the economy, producing nothing, while men are forced to "pay so many Taylors Bills."

Ward is comparatively open about his intentions to use writing as a way of reinforcing a marginal status for women, as we can see by the language play associating women and their fashions with composition: "I rather thought it meete to let them stand by themselves, like the *Quae Genus* in the Grammar." A blank space surrounding a written text is, of course, a type of margin. Ward thinks a good woman, like a good text, deserves "a fair margent." By choosing not to record women's accomplishments, by giving them a wide margin, the male poets reinforce the importance of men's affairs. Particularly in the economic sphere, where female support in the household and around the farm was a precondition for success, the lack of acknowledgment of women's work is striking. However, by this very act of linguistic politics, the real force of women is covertly recognized.

Economic advantages were part of the appeal of the New World from the very beginning. And the Puritans understood very well the temptation to consider earthly advantage before heavenly duty. The first generation of Puritans had preached against luxuries, just as they had hoped that by keeping women in their place they could preserve a hierarchical order. By the end of the seventeenth century, it was clear that they had failed to achieve the pure form of theocracy the Founding Fathers envisioned. More and more members of the community were falling away from the church and responding to economic incentives— breaking the Sabbath, hiring heathen workers without care for their souls. In addition, women were becoming bolder, especially in the church, and their numbers on church rolls threatened to make them a potent force. The time had arrived to make some concessions to devout women even as those who threatened the patriarchal structure were severely chastised.

In 1692 Cotton Mather published *Ornaments for the Daughters of Zion: Or the Character and Happiness of a Vertuous Woman*. The strategy of Mather's essay is interesting. He takes to task those who have denigrated women in the past: "The petulant Pens of some froward and morose Men, have sometimes treated the Female sex with very great Indignities. . . . Yea, 'tis not easy to recount how many licentious writers have handled that them[e], *Femina nulla bona*, No woman is good!"[20] He also praises New England women for their intellectual and literary achievements, a far cry from John Winthrop's opinion that Ann Hopkins should have "attended her household affairs, and such things as belong to women, and not gone out of her way and calling to meddle in such things as are proper for men" by writing many books. (Mr. Hopkins, the governor of Hartford, had moved to Boston with his wife—"a godly young woman, and of special parts"—and she had lost her wits, occasioning John Winthrop to comment that she might have kept her wits if she had remained "usefully and honourably in the place God had set her.")[21] Cotton Mather, writing later in the century, actually imagines a whole library of women's works:

> Nor has even the New-English part of the American strand been without Authoresses that would Challenge a Room in such a Library: They to whom the common use of Swords is neither Decent nor Lawful, have made a most laudable use of Pens; and they that might not without Sin, lead the Life which old stories ascribe to Amazons, have with much Praise done the part of Scholars in the World."[22]

He uses these concessions, however, to call for stricter conduct on the part of women, who, he feels, should read the Bible instead of romances and maintain "a cautious Diligence never to displease" their husbands. A virtuous woman does justice, loves mercy, and walks humbly. Mather repeatedly criticizes "forwardness" as a bad trait in women, implying that women were threatening the social order by being forward.

Since women were not recognized, by and large, for their domestic / economic contributions or their religious importance, what did women do to present themselves as "builders of the Bay Colony"? Cotton Mather provides a clue: women wrote. Anne Bradstreet is the only seventeenth-century woman poet to have left us a substantial body of work. Yet other women were writing, as Winthrop's reference to Ann Hopkins indicates.[23] Urian Oakes (1631–1681) pauses in his tribute to Thomas Shephard to exorcise the ghosts of female elegy-writers:

> Away loose rein'd Careers of Poetry,
> The celebrated Sisters may be gone;
> We need no *Mourning Womens* Elegy,
> No forc'd, affected, artificial Tone. [ll. 25–28]

His reference appeals to a communal understanding of the kind of elegies mourning women wrote. John Rogers (1630–1684), whose only extant poem is a tribute to Anne Bradstreet, makes a similar reference in declaring Bradstreet superior to other *female* "poetasters":

> Then vail your bonnets, Poetasters all,
> Strike lower amain, and at these humbly fall,
> And deem your selves advanc'd to be her Pedestal. [ll. 54–56]

In the poems appended to Anne Bradstreet's first book, *The Tenth Muse*, we may find a clue to the psychology of marginalizing. *The Tenth Muse* was published in England in 1650 through the efforts of Bradstreet's brother-in-law, Benjamin Woodbridge (1622–1684) (see "Upon the Author" in Meserole, *Poetry*). Woodbridge is clearly in favor of Bradstreet's work, and even crusty old Nathaniel Ward sounds pleasantly surprised in his poem to find a woman capable of rivalling the Puritan favorite, Guillaume du Bartas. Both Woodbridge's and Ward's commendatory poems, however, reveal the spectre of male/female competition which arises as soon as a female poet must be taken seriously. Woodbridge writes in a friendly manner; he intends no disrespect. In fact, he desires to praise Bradstreet's achievement. His metaphors, however, suggest the wider cultural context in which he is writing. The orbiting, peripheral, female moon threatens to outshine the central Sun. "Mankind," synonymous with men rather than with men and women, is in jeopardy.

Nathaniel Ward, in "Mercury shew'd Apollo, Bartas Book" (in Meserole, *Poetry*), masks his sentiments by using a persona, the chilly, near-sighted Apollo. The satirist Ward frequently created mask-figures like the *naif* in *The Simple Cobbler* and Apollo here. Through them he was able to express his genuine feelings without appearing overly serious. Here Apollo, finding himself unable to decide whether du Bartas or Bradstreet is the superior poet, is appeased by being told: "The Auth'ress was a right *Du Bartas* Girle." (The "girl" was thirty-eight years old.) Harrison Meserole comments:

> Consistently adopting the satirical view of a world where appearance and reality are topsy-turvy, Ward reveals his perceptions of inversion in a

thoroughly Baroque manner. He even goes so far as to warn in his verse commending Anne Bradstreet that "Men look to't, Least Women wear the Spurrs." That, Ward satirically implies, would be the ultimate violation of proper degree and order.[24]

A commitment to "proper degree and order" lay behind many of the strategies the Puritans used to marginalize, trivialize, or tokenize female achievements. Even those who praise Anne Bradstreet's work reveal in the process an uneasiness about a woman so accomplished. "Proper degree and order" meant the subordination of females to males. Complimenting "extraordinary" women inevitably invokes this system even as it seems to question it.

However thoroughly conventions may dominate the work of a given group of writers, there are always those who choose to defy them. Furthermore, any account of a group of writers must, to be accurate, consider the defectors as well as the conformists. We began by asserting that early Puritan verse was, by and large, public and communal in its aims. We said that the prophetic vision of a certain kind of community involved depreciating women's work and male-female interdependence. Benjamin Tompson's elegy for his wife is something of an exception to the conventional elegy form used for women. However, an even greater exception is the work of John Saffin (1626–1710).

Saffin wrote many kinds of verse, but of particular interest to us are his domestic and love poems. Unlike Edward Taylor, Saffin did not use domestic life only as a source of images for spiritual works. He accorded it a legitimacy all its own. Commentators have often noted that Saffin was unusual in his time. Alyce Sands and Kathryn Derounian (in Chapter 12 of this book) have remarked on his outstanding versatility. Both Samuel Eliot Morison and Harold Jantz identify Saffin as an unusual poet because of the attention he gives to domestic life. Meserole comments: "In a period when much of the verse was of a formal, 'public' nature, Saffin's voice emerges as engagingly personal."[25]

John Saffin's poem "presenting a rare book to Madame Hull" acknowledges this woman for her "Towering fancy and Ingenious Spirit." This is unusual in itself. By far the rarest reference, however, occurs in a less well-known poem written about his wife twenty-five years after her death. In his "Revived Elegiac Lamentation" Saffin not only acknowledges his wife for her domestic virtues, he also specifically praises her for her skill in business. Martha Saffin emerges not only as a pious, submissive wife but also as a strong, capable woman.

> That with a look, a nod, in silence Beckt,
> She could comand Obedience, due Respect.
> Likewise her Husbands Merchandizes She
> when he was absent manag'd Accuratly
> was so accute therein, that none could tell
> What She did Best, She acted all so well. [ll. 33–38]

Many women served as "deputy husbands" according to Laurel Ulrich, but only John Saffin admits this fact and praises his wife for her skill in managing.

Benjamin Tompson is not as radical as John Saffin. Although his elegy for his wife contains some atypical lines, Tompson's premise is that woman's place is at home, out of the political or commercial limelight. He is a more conventional poet, therefore, and one of his poems may justly be used to indicate the way unrecognized assumptions about women's roles permeate the poems of even well-intentioned Puritans. In Tompson's "On a Fortification at Boston begun by Women" (to which the poet appended: *Dux Foemina Facti*, the leader is a woman), he commemorates a mud fortification that colonial women built in an endeavor to protect the Massachusetts Bay Colony during King Philip's War.[26] The occasion of the poem, then, is an unusual situation of role reversal, a situation that Tompson exploits in a light way to show that all is not well in the New Jerusalem. One might contend that this poem presents an unusual female activity in which women take initiative and deserve praise, as the poet tells us, even more than the men. However, if we examine the poem more carefully, we see that it reinforces the usual idea of relative status accorded males and females even as it purports to diverge from that norm.

The first clue comes in the first line where the words "grand attempt" signal an ironic tone, suggesting that Tompson has in mind a form not unlike the mock-epic so popular in the eighteenth century. The action is merely an "attempt," not a useful function. The women are called Amazonian, a tip-off in itself. (Remember Cotton Mather's words: virtuous women "might not without Sin, lead the Life which old stories ascribe to Amazons. . . .") Furthermore, these women wish to glorify their own names. He does not ascribe to them a "public and communal," therefore glorious, motive. These women are dubiously engaged in centralizing themselves by constructing their own margin, a "ruff" of mud and turf. The ruff was an article of clothing under a cloud of controversy because of its ornamental as opposed to plain and instrumental function.

Finally, we hear that the normal and worthy functions usually supplied by women have been left undone. "The wheel at home counts it an holiday, . . . " This tribe of women "forsake at home their pasty-crust and tarts." Although Tompson here seems to take an indulgent if condescending view of the women's efforts, his allusions to the work left undone at home invoke the image of a topsy-turvy world not unlike Ward's. In his elegy for his sister Sarah Tompson,[27] we find a revealing passage which may help us illuminate Tompson's attitude toward these women. Here the poet praises his sister's diligence and prudence:

> And ordering her household by an Art
> Not common: But in her Example true
> And imitable but by very few.
> An housewife mostly to be found at home
> While others from the tents doe ride and rome [ll. 34–38]

Though in the fortification poem the women provide a needed reproof to the men, who have left the community vulnerable in time of war, they are stepping out of bounds to do so; Tompson would be happier to see the topsy-turvy world righted.

In the center portion of the war poem, woman is once again set against woman. Emphasizing competition is one of the maneuvers we recall in the poems which allege that women are divided by envy. The figures, puffing and sweating, seem faintly ridiculous. The *little* wagon's weight is all they can manage, and, unlike hearty male workers, they must eschew the "sack and cakes" lest they be overtaken by fainting fits.

The most telling structural moment comes at the end, however, where this mock-epic venture draws forth "Male stronger hands." Whereas women have simply made a beginning, an attempt, men (now sufficiently chastised) take over: "These do the work, and sturdy bulwarks raise." The female workers are once again exiled to the periphery. Thus, the praise condescendingly offered in the last line is tainted by dramatic irony—irony not intended by the poet, perhaps, but available to us as informed readers. It seems as though, by their very effort to invade the center, these women have reinforced their marginal status. If they deserve praise, it is because they know when to relinquish their attempt and acknowledge themselves merely "beginners."

The Puritans would have been surprised, even more dismayed, to learn that the patriarchal order they found so inevitable and necessary strikes us as suggesting weaknesses by its very defensiveness. Their need to create an opposition between center and margin was not apparent to them in our terms. Yet this fact by no means diminishes the legitimacy of our attempt at deconstructing such an opposition. What lies at the fringes of cultural consciousness is often what determines the structure of culture itself.

NOTES

1. Here and elsewhere I follow the lead of Harold Jantz in attributing "Good News from New-England" to Edward Johnson. See Jantz, *First Century*, p. 27.

2. Bercovitch, *Puritan Origins*, p. 133.

3. In Marlene Springer, ed., *What Manner of Woman: Essays on English and American Life and Literature* (New York: New York Univ. Press, 1977), pp. 15–38.

4. All references to Puritan poetry (except those designated otherwise in footnotes) are to Meserole, *Poetry*.

5. Page Smith, *Daughters of the Promised Land* (Boston: Little, Brown, 1970); Laurel Thatcher Ulrich, *Good Wives: Image and Reality in the Lives of Women in Northern New England 1650–1750* (New York: Oxford, 1983); Lyle Koehler, *A Search for Power: The*

"Weaker Sex" in Seventeenth-Century New England (Urbana: Univ. of Illinois Press, 1980); Mary Beth Norton, *Liberty's Daughters* (Boston: Little, Brown, 1980).

6. Eugenie Andress Leonard, *The Dear-Bought Heritage* (Philadelphia: Univ. of Pennsylvania Press, 1965).

7. *Ornaments for the Daughters of Zion: Or the Character and Happiness of a Vertuous Woman* (Boston: Samuel Phillips, 1692).

8. An early discussion of female occupations occurs in Elisabeth Anthony Dexter, *Colonial Women of Affairs* (New York: Houghton Mifflin, 1931). More recent presentations draw upon this one.

9. *NEQ* 50 (Sept. 1977): 484–504. In 1979 *Signs: Journal of Women in Culture and Society* ran a review article on the important recent scholarship on women in American history. Under the colonial section the three articles mentioned which are particularly relevant for this study are Malmsheimer's, John Faragher's (noted below) and Laurel Thatcher Ulrich's " 'Vertuous Women Found': New England Ministerial Literature, 1668–1735," *AQ* 26 (1976): 19–40.

10. The text of this poem is taken from White, *Tompson*, pp. 141–142.

11. For a discussion of Puritan attitudes toward women speaking in church, see Carl Holliday, *Woman's Life in Colonial Days*, 2nd ed. (1922; rpt. New York: Frederick Ungar, 1960), p. 35.

12. *Humanities in Society* 2 (Summer, 1979): 201–21.

13. Koehler revises the position previously taken that Puritanism was a boon to American women, concluding that there is little evidence of New England support for reforms recommended by seventeenth-century English Puritans.

14. See Koehler's argument that toward the end of the century the changed realities of provincial life accentuated female deviance. According to Koehler, approximately sixty percent of those unmarried women who discovered they were pregnant did not marry during this period, a great increase over the number who remained unmarried in the founding era.

15. *Feminist Studies*, 1 (Fall, 1972), p. 86.

16. Malmsheimer says this sermon by an unknown minister was included in a book called *The House of Mourning*.

17. In his important study of Wethersfield, Connecticut, John Faragher comments on the difficulty of finding good comparative data from other communities, since the births of female children were often not recorded. "It soon became obvious from the census and family reconstitution work that the women's data were seriously under-recorded," Faragher writes in "Old Women and Old Men in Seventeenth-Century Wethersfield, Connecticut," *Women's Studies* 4 (1976): 11–31.

18. Church widows were assigned many duties, according to Faragher. "The work for widows was a variation on women's domestic work of nurture, only now in the general community rather than the family" (p. 25).

19. Textual references are to edition of P. M. Zall (Lincoln: Univ. of Nebraska Press, 1969), pp. 25–28.

20. Mather, *Ornaments*, p. 46.

21. Winthrop, *The History of New England*, ed. James Savage (Boston, 1853), II, p. 216.

22. Mather, *Ornaments*, p. 5.

23. For a full discussion of colonial women poets, see Pattie Cowell, ed., *Women Poets in Pre-Revolutionary America* (Troy, N.Y.: Whitston Publishing Co., 1981).

24. Meserole, *Poetry*, p. 366.

25. Meserole, *Poetry*, p. 195.

26. In Meserole, *Poetry*, and White, *Tompson*, pp. 98–99.

27. White, *Tompson*, p. 145.

II

INDIVIDUAL ACHIEVEMENTS:
SELECTED POETS

9 THE WOUNDS UPON BATHSHEBA: ANNE BRADSTREET'S PROPHETIC ART

ROSAMOND R. ROSENMEIER

Cotton Mather, in *Ornaments for the Daughters of Zion,* strongly affirms the propriety for women of the vocation of writer: "As one *Woman* was the Mother of Him who is the *Essential word* of God, so diverse *women* have been the *writers* of His *Declarative word.*[1] Mather's mention of several New English "Authoresses" suggests the example of his great aunt, Anne Bradstreet, author of the first volume of poetry in the New World, *The Tenth Muse Lately Sprung Up in America . . .* (1650), and of a posthumously published volume, *Several Poems . . .* (1678).[2] Women, Mather wrote, can sometimes be "scribes" of that *"Spirit, who moved Holy men, to write the most sure word of Prophecy.*[3] Mather's biblical example here is Bathsheba, the mother of Solomon, who, "after a very scandalous Fall, becomes a very eminent saint, yea, a *Prophetess* of the Lord." Bathsheba's powers of prophecy are related, Mather writes, to the fact that she reflects the typology of Eve and Mary; the historical analogue between the woman who had the "disgrace of the first transgression," and the woman who had the "glory" of bringing into the world the "second Adam," finds expression in the prophetic figure of Bathsheba. A woman may, like Bathsheba, have "many wounds upon her," but she can nevertheless assist in bringing about the Second Coming of Christ.[4] In fact, "she may *enter into the Kingdome of Heaven, before others that have not had such wounds upon them."* Bradstreet's contemporary, "N.H.," also found Bradstreet a poet of this order of power and importance; he called her a Western star, brighter than the sun, whose "divine and lucid light" not only disclosed "natures dark secret mystereyes" but had the power of birth and rebirth; it revived whatever seemed to have died.[5]

Such acclaim was doubtless the kind Charles Eliot Norton had in mind when he looked back two centuries later and observed that as "great" as Anne Bradstreet's "repute" as a poet was "in her own little circle," it "hardly stands the test of time, and it is not their poetic merit which will lead anyone at the present day to read her verse."[6] John Harvard Ellis, responsible for the 1867 edition of her work, had similarly weak praise; his adjectives are "quaint" and "curious." His edition included poems and prose the Bradstreet family had previously withheld from publication and that modern critics select as her finest. Ellis, however, concluded only that her writing "contains many beautiful and original ideas, not badly expressed." Ellis, as others have, suggests that the reader take into consideration the "peculiarly unpropitious circumstances under which they were written." For Ellis, the importance of Bradstreet's work is that it constitutes a "singular and valuable relic of the earliest literature of the country."[7] A century later, Jeannine Hensley concluded her review of the critical treatment of Bradstreet's literary achievement with a succinctly phrased summation: Bradstreet was a "genuine, if minor, poet."[8]

Yet the interest in Bradstreet's work persists. Sometimes that interest is in the woman herself, in the scant details we have about her emigration from Boston, England, to the Massachusetts "frontier"—in Newtowne (now Cambridge), then Agawam (now Ipswich), and finally Haverhill (now North Andover).[9] She is of interest as an example to students of women's roles in America.[10] To many she represents a classic case of the conflict between instinctual life and societal repression. Kenneth Murdock found in Bradstreet the "strain set up between the essential instinctive emotion and the bonds drawn tight against full expression by elements in the Puritan's way of thought."[11] Murdock's conception is still (thirty years later) the dominant view of Bradstreet's relationship to her culture. The central thesis of Ann Stanford's fine study, *Anne Bradstreet: The Worldly Puritan* (1975), is in accord with the basic outlines of Murdock's thinking. Stanford shifts the terms of the dialectic slightly when she writes that "above all Anne Bradstreet's canon represents the struggle between the visible and the invisible worlds." Stanford, further, finds Anne Bradstreet firmly in the "grasp of the earth and the things of earth." Stanford concludes that "the voice of the world was never quite overwhelmed even in her most religious poems."[12]

New knowledge about the Puritan Massachusetts of Anne Bradstreet's era has begun to provide an increasingly promising basis for understanding her world and her poetic purposes.[13]. Although modern critics have moved beyond the "almost offensive condescension" of which Samuel Eliot Morison complained,[14] they yet praise Bradstreet's work for qualities she disavowed.[15] In this essay I will suggest that in addition to their "genuineness," Bradstreet's texts are designedly suggestive; furthermore, the rich texture of her poetry reveals a consistent poetic intention, one that suggests the presence of an artist who was serious, inventive, purposeful. But her work and method now seem very far away. Our window looks back at a dim, distant landscape when we attempt to describe the first generation of immigrants to Massachusetts. Absorbing its remote features—its habits of mind and belief—is crucial for the act of literary interpretation. As readers of Bradstreet's poetry, we must be ready to entertain radically new (by being very old) ideas about the very nature of poetry itself.

Anne Bradstreet's work tells us that she felt she was living through perilous times. Not only were the Massachusetts Puritans settling a wilderness; they believed they were living through the last days of life as it had been on earth. The Bay Colony Puritans were building Zion in the wilderness; its citizens were readying themselves for the Last Judgement and the Second Coming of Christ.[16]

It is little wonder, then, that the two most frequent images in Bradstreet's work are the journey and the sun.[17] For Puritans, the two are connected. The journey is a figure for the Christian's individual life, as well as for the life of the group as it moves through history. Christian pilgrimage, both individual and tribal, was said on biblical authority to be leading to a reunion with Christ, the Sun of Righteousness. That Sun, the Puritans believed, will shine without ceasing when the Millennium comes. Bradstreet reminds her readers repeatedly that the Christian pilgrimage on earth contains the possibility of the fulfillment of God's promises to His Chosen. Yet, in the fact of its constant reiteration, this assertion can be seen to suggest anxiety over the possibility of loss. A simple Psalm-like plea, dated 1661, expresses this anxiety directly: what if that which has been continuous throughout history should prove discontinuous? On the occasion of her husband's mission to England to renegotiate the Massachusetts charter, Bradstreet prays to the Lord to remember His "folk" whom He has brought to the "wildernesse." Her greatest fear is that He will permit His "own Inheritance" to be "sold away for Nought."[18]

In 1630 the original charter had provided the settlers of Massachusetts Bay with the legal foundation for their ambitious undertaking. But almost at once, the spiritual foundation of the New English mission appeared less sure. Divisiveness within the group seemed to evidence the possibility of spiritual failure. Bradstreet observes that some of the worst trials that "storm" a "mortal creature's State," and "break" his "mind" and "body" are those arise "from friends, from dearest, near'st Relation." Bradstreet feared that such "vexation," such "troubles" might weaken her people's dedication to the vision of the future.[19] Being cut off from that assurance of direction would have meant, for her, the loss of a sense of self, and of the power to act constructively and creatively. Although she admits that some vexations come from "without," her diagnosis of her group's troubles is clear. She writes, "A sore finger may disquiet the whole body, but an ulcer within destroys it, so an enemy without may disturb a Commonwealth, but dissentions within overthrow it."[20]

One issue that provoked "dissention within" was described by Bradstreet, following the Apostle Paul, as the relationship of "Spirit" to "Flesh." The Massachusetts Puritans felt that planting the saints of God in their New English plantation must follow the paradigm of the biblical description of planting the seeds of Solomon's vineyard. Each seed was said to contain kernel and husk. The allegory was clear: kernel and husk are contraries; one is mortal, the other immortal; one is historical, the other eternal. One will be gathered at the "appointed time," and the other discarded. But, in day-by-day reality, how does one distinguish between the two? And how, as history moves towards its conclusion, does one conceive of the relationship between them? It was, in part, because this first group of settlers viewed the literal and the spiritual as already densely interwoven that the distinction between them could seem unclear.[21] This failure of distinction could at times confuse both the process and the terms of the exchange between this world and the next. A further complication was introduced by the biblical suggestion that, in the Millennium, the flesh and the spirit will be joined again. The vision of the New Jerusalem, as held out in Revelation, is a vision of the re-creation of the world, of a new Heaven *and* a new Earth.[22] Bradstreet's focus is never on a spiritual hereafter, of a future, exclusive of present and past. When she writes of her marriage, for example, she portrays an ideal quality of earthly experience as an interrelationship between this world and the next, in which the quality of this life has a direct bearing on the quality of the next. Her exhortation is "Then while we live, in love lets so persever, / That when we live no more, we may live ever."[23] There is, thus, something mysterious in the very composition of the seeds planted in Solomon's vineyard. The curious interdependence of husk and kernel of this world and the next is one of Bradstreet's chief subjects. The dread possibility that the interdependence may not hold provides the impetus to poetry, the necessity for it.

Indeed, Bradstreet found the central contrarieties of her life so akin that she portrayed them as "Sisters," even as "Twins." In her poem, "The Flesh and the Spirit,"[24] two sisters "reason" about "Things that are past and things to come"— the subject probably uppermost in the minds of those trying to forge a Puritan society. "Flesh" argues that to exchange the more than ample satisfactions of this life, such as wealth and fame, for the perhaps spurious satisfactions of the next is, in effect, a bad bargain. She counsels "industry" and "sense." She preaches what was called (and in the trial of Anne Hutchinson became a central issue) a "covenant of works."[25] Flesh's most telling point is that the things of this world are "known" and are therefore more reliable than the future and unseeable expectations her sister, Spirit, holds out. She accuses Spirit of a willingness to ransom what is sure for what is a "shadow."

Spirit responds by describing the future. She boasts that what is coming is sumptuous beyond the ability of the earth to "parallel." Of course, the jewels that bedeck her heavenly "city" are biblical ones, borrowed from the Book of Revelation. But the ornateness of Spirit's vision Bradstreet in no way disclaims, explains, or apologizes for. By spiritual life, Spirit means an abundant life of "eternal substance." Spirit expects to be "inriched." She refuses to settle for less. An edge of impatience (even anger) in Spirit's voice suggests that Bradstreet is handling a vital subject. Here she reasserts her allegiance to the biblical vision of the Millennium, including the promise that the flesh will be restored to splendor. God's folk can expect to inhabit a city as beautiful as the biblical New Jerusalem, and as pleasurable, other poems suggest, as the marriage of Solomon and Sheba. The poetic strategy here is complex; a certain "worldliness" in this Puritan's Puritanism, to use Anne Stanford's just term, is suggested largely by means of the adoption of biblical language. The infusion of the scriptural overtones serves to augment the sensuousness of Bradstreet's imagery.

Bradstreet's figurative strategy employs paradox. Her references to time suggest that the riches she is describing have a literal, if future, existence. The ornateness of "The Flesh and The Spirit" seems designed to demonstrate the *eventual* oneness of the riches of this world and the riches of the next. Bradstreet felt that she had already caught evidences in her own experience of moments of that future reality. Such glimpses are most vividly portrayed in her poems to her husband, not published until the Ellis edition in 1867. These poems are infused with the language of Canticles, suggesting that Bradstreet wants to present her marriage as having a double reality. Not only does she accept the traditional representation of Christian marriage as a reminder of Christ's marriage to His Church, but she finds her marriage already infused with that eventuality. Bradstreet calls her husband her "earthly store," suggesting that their life together is enriched by Spirit's "eternal substance." Their marriage is portrayed as increasingly warm, indeed sun-filled, with both the implications of personal happiness and the suggestion that in their marriage she finds Christ, the Sun of Righteousness, an already dawning presence.[26] Bradstreet does not simply liken her husband's love to Christ's love; she represents both as somehow ultimately one.[27]

In Bradstreet's tendency to merge this world with the next, she is typical of Massachusetts Puritanism. In addition, this tendency relates Bradstreet, more broadly, to seventeenth-century English protestant poetics. Her heavy reliance on Canticles and Revelation for a language to address her earthly experience is characteristic of a tradition which Barbara Lewalski defines as essentially biblical. Lewalski places Edward Taylor in this tradition; Taylor emphasizes "Christ of the *Escaton* rather than the Christ of the Gospel."[28] So, too, Bradstreet's work, like Taylor's, is properly described as prophetic, not mystical. The hallmark of Taylor's prophetic stance has been called his humanity.[29] Several aspects of Bradstreet's similarly human stance serve to mark her poetics as prophetic too. First, like Edward Taylor, she frequently speaks as one who is half-mute, confused, artless.[30] Second, she speaks as one who is echoing or imitating an ancient, usually male, often biblical, spokesman. And third, she speaks as one who has been, as the Puritans said, afflicted or wounded. These tendencies persist in her writing from early to late, and in both her published and her unpublished writings. By adopting such postures the poet conveys certain messages; such postures heighten certain effects, and these messages and effects are designedly prophetic. We can, thus, accept Cotton Mather's suggestion that Anne Bradstreet's method was prophetic, even though our interpretation of what that designation means may not conform to his. Furthermore, Mather's retrospective comments and Bradstreet's apparent success among her contemporaries suggest that being a "scribe" of the Holy Spirit was, in certain respects, a suitable vocation for women.[31]

Bradstreet's prophetic vocation and her identity as a Puritan woman are in fact closely related. The prophet must stand with one foot within history; must be a member of a nation, group, or family; and must feel the assaults of mortality. At the same time the prophet must glimpse, or to use Bradstreet's verb, "taste" God's gifts, gifts that the world knows not of.[32] The prophet then leads by means of a pattern we might call dialectical, advancing in the direction it has been his (or her) privilege/curse to see, and then returning to the world in order to identify with, reclaim, and encourage his or her people to go forward. In *Meditations when my Soul hath been refreshed with the Consolations which the world knowes not*,[33] Bradstreet conceives of herself as engaged in a continuous transaction. Her personal identity is defined by a relationship to God that is ever-changing. Her sense of self progresses from a subordinate relationship to God (as "servant" and "child") to a relationship as His equal (as "sister" and "wife") to a full joining with Him (as a "member of his Body"). Bradstreet describes herself as undergoing a constantly ascending development; in each stage she is related to God, but each stage soon seems "not enough." Each stage emerges from, surpasses, and yet depends on, the one before. One cannot be a "wife" before one has been a "child." When the day of resurrection comes, the Puritan man or woman can expect to become a full member of Christ's body. Bradstreet here, as she does elsewhere, suggests that she has already felt the "consolation" that comes from knowing such moments. As a regenerate wilderness wayfarer she reenacts the stages of the Christian journey, moving from dependence outward to independence. This reenactment is seen in Bradstreet's work as a pilgrimage along a path that develops, recedes, ascends, falls, and begins again. At points, her journey appears to turn to "nought." In effect, it dies, changes, and is transformed. Readers who join her in this reenactment, her language implies, will feel supported through profound changes, changes even in the sense of self.[34] Bradstreet's sense of identity is defined by the developing quality and nature of her relationship to God. Some aspects of her identity can be characterized as female; others cannot. Furthermore, within each believer lives a female self that is servant-like and earth-bound (as Eve is) as well as a female self that is redeemed and redemptive (as Mary is).

Basic to Bradstreet's sense of herself and her art is the idea that all processes, including cosmic ones, occur in stages and are marked by interdependence and mutability. Adopting the persona "Air", for example, Bradstreet writes that Air is "the breath of every living soul"; she is responsible for the portentousness of events and shows that "earth appears in heaven, O wonder great!" The spirituality of her nature, akin in its attributes to the Holy Spirit, makes Air the supreme element. Her nature's primary attribute is its ability to change. Bradstreet writes,

> My moist hot nature, is so purely thinne,
> No place so subtilly made, but I get in.
> I grow more pure and pure, as I mount higher,
> And when I'm thoroughly rarifi'd, turn fire.
> So when I am condens'd, I turne to water;
> Which may be done, by holding down my vapour.
> Thus I another body can assume,
> And in a trice, my own nature resume.[35]

Thus Bradstreet's poetic universe is dynamic, not static. In "Contemplations," for example, Bradstreet leads her reader through a series of progressive stages, beginning not with a mystical truth beyond the reader's grasp but with commonplace experience. In "Contemplations" the reader is taken from what looks like true assurance, through what looks like the loss of all assurance, to a transformed recognition of what true assurance is. Bradstreet speaks from the vantage point not of the mystic but of the Christian everyman, journeying through the afflictions of mortal history. From this vantage point her readers participate in a process all can share. "Contemplations" reveals the dialectical process which Bradstreet, among others, found to be the mark of the Holy Spirit's work in the world. As she often does, Bradstreet positions herself (and her reader) at a specific point in time—the fall of the year, one hour from night. Before the dawn comes, the world must go through its darkest coldest hours. The poet adopts the persona of an exemplary Christian embarking on a series of thoughtful stanzas in praise of God. The series is developmental. Starting with a rather child-like simplicity, with the knowledge of the senses, she finds the view "delectable." Turning (in Stanza 2) to syllogism, she affirms God's excellence by more sophisticated means—by logic. Her reasoning leads her to deduce God's glory from His works. But in Stanza 3 she focuses her attention on a single metaphor; she arrives at the figure of the "stately Oak," and there introduces the first note of doubt or questioning.

Bradstreet's readers would recall the biblical contexts to which the figure of the oak belongs and would understand her imagery as implying the biblical circumstance. In Isaiah 1:29–30 Isaiah prophesies that his people "shall be ashamed of the oaks which ye have desired . . ." and that they will be "as an oak whose leaf fadeth." The reference casts a shadow over Bradstreet's apparent admiration. Bradstreet's first generation readers would hear the echo, too, of John Cotton's farewell sermon; there he told the first settlers that, as oak trees, they could trust God's promises to His plantations. If, as Elizabeth Wade White suggests, Bradstreet was in her early fifties when she wrote "Contemplations,"[36] the reference to Cotton's sense of the imminence of the fulfillment would serve as a painful reminder of disappointment.[37] Isaiah's shameful oaks are part of a chapter devoted to the castigation of the Jews. The commentator in the Geneva Bible read that chapter as a "double prophesie—of the destruction of Jerusalem and of its restitution.[38]

Thus having suggested uncertainty and loss in Stanza 3, Bradstreet identifies the means of "Israel's" restitution in Stanzas 4 and 5. She directs her readers' eyes upward, beyond the oak to the heavenly Bridegroom, the Sun of Righteousness. These two stanzas suggest that the Millennium—at least ultimately—is assured. But the assurance is clouded. Bradstreet's image of "earth" calls to mind the images of loss, anxiety, and depression used to portray her condition during her "husband's" absences "upon public employment." The striking figure, "darksome womb of fruitful nature," connotes fertility, but not without a sense of foreboding; it resonates with the dark time and fall season mentioned in Stanza 1. Further, the sun's diving into the womb of earth suggests not only sex and birth, but rape, death, and separation. The theme of contrariety is struck. The poet realizes that God's "presence" makes it "day," but she is unnerved by the equally certain observation that His "absence" makes it "night." As the poem approaches night time, it thus approaches a time of God's absence. The distance begins to seem great between His glory and the things in the "earthly mould." She introduces doubts. Are You so great, so high, no mortal can see You? She begins to feel inconsequential, worse than "abject." She begins to account herself nought. Stanza 8 brings the poet to a moment that is crucial in the poem's development and typical of the way Bradstreet imagines the process of "restitution." She turns "silent" and "alone." Her "muse" is "mazed," her eyes "humble."

This moment of utter loss and confusion is also filled with biblical echoes. Here the echoes come from Psalm 44, the source Bradstreet used for the reference in the 1661 poem about the selling of God's inheritance. Not only does Bradstreet's little poem use the imagery of the Psalm; it also recaptures the Psalmist's voice. There the poet's fear is that God will, as the Psalmist said, "cast" His people "off." He has put them to shame, sold them for "meat, and scattered [them] among the heathens." Bradstreet's 1661 poem echoes the Psalmist's accusation that God has nearly destroyed Israel and has, furthermore, not even acted in His own best interests. "Thou sellest thy people for nought, and doest not increase *thy wealth* for their price." The commentator in the Geneva Bible found this Psalm "made by some excellent Prophet for the use of the people, when the church was in extreme miserie, either at their returne from Babylon, or under Antiochus, or in suche like affliction."[39] Bradstreet's readers would have heard her words as a warning and would have drawn a parallel between Israel's condition and the condition of the Massachussets churches.

Similarly, the Psalmist's angry and anguished outcries inform this section of "Contemplations." He is brought in Psalm 44 to a point which he describes as Bradstreet describes hers. He suddenly turns silent. His silence is a crisis that signals a turning point. His recovery from a state that feels like utter loss is then initiated when he declares that he has not "forgotten" the Lord. The Psalmist feels confused, ashamed. Bradstreet's description of her state of mind and spirit follows the same outlines. The Psalmist asks not to be the "reproach of the foolish"; Bradstreet feels her "imbicility." The design of the Psalmist's progress shines through her words; when confronted with that moment when all her powers of creativity are eclipsed, she does what the Psalmist in Psalm 44 did; she turns to the past. She does not "forget." Her ascension into solace begins with Stanza 10.[40] Turning to the past in "Contemplations" returns the poet to a condition that seems dark, not light; she recounts a sinful past, not a redeemed future. Yet in this reenactment, she finds assurance of restitution. It is by becoming "aged in conceits" that she is transformed and enabled to go forward. By imitation of and identification with spokesmen of the Holy Spirit in human history her life is sustained. She does not rely on the senses or on reason. She relies on the re-creation of a process. In Meditation LVI, she writes of such a use of history as a necessity: "The remembrance of former deliverances is a great support in present destresses . . .God is the same yesterday, to day, and for ever, we are the same that stand in need of him. . . ."[41] The fact of the speaker's identification with Solomon (Eccl. 1:9–14) in Bradstreet's Meditations serves once again to reinforce her meaning. Bradstreet writes, "There is no new thing under the sun there is nothing that can be sayd or done, but either that or something like it, hath been both done or sayd before."[42] As dynamic as she felt her universe to be, she maintained that its processes followed well-established patterns, and that those patterns provide reassurance.

Bradstreet feels herself to be the very antithesis of the "merry bird" in "Contemplations," that "fears no snares." The poet, caught on "the fatal wrack of mortal things," repeatedly contends with all the troubles and toils that the bird has escaped. The biblical overtones suggest more. In Ecclesiastes, 9:12, Solomon says, "For a man knoweth not his time: as the fishes that are taken in an evil net, and as the birds that are caught in the snare; so are the sons of men snared in an evil time, when it falleth suddenly upon them." Unlike the poet, the merry bird "reminds not what is past, nor whats to come dost fear." The bird's soul "escaped out of the snare of the fowler." The poet's soul, and the prophet's words, have not yet arrived at that point of liberation. They live in time and depend on the patterns of history to give direction to their lives.

The prophet's words demonstrate the presence and evidence of the Holy Spirit's ongoing work in history. Such, too, Bradstreet felt, was the obligation of the poet. Reiterating the words of the Psalmist and the Preacher, of Job and Isaiah, was, then, a way of demonstrating the continuity of history, despite whatever appeared to be so. Bradstreet, of course, devoted a large portion of her writing career to historical subjects. Her longest poem, "The Four Monarchies," is but one example; many of the poems in *The Tenth Muse* contain what to modern ears sound like mere restatements, recitals of history, as written by others.[43] She does not however apologize for her borrowings, her imitations. Apparently she fully intended to interweave other poetic and biblical voices with her own. Even in poems where we might not at first notice Bradstreet's adoption of a double speaker, such a speaker often emerges when we recognize the references to a biblical context. In "The Vanity of all Worldly Things," for example, we find obvious references to Ecclesiastes, but the poem begins with the assertion that the poet is saying over again what Solomon said: "As he said vanity, so vain say I." Bradstreet then concludes with "And all the rest, but Vanity we find," as if to reinforce the fact that she and the Preacher are speaking through her voice.

Some time after 1650 Bradstreet gave up history as the subject of poetry.[44] She did not, however, give up her preoccupation with the processes and stages of Christian pilgrimage. She turned, rather, to the experience of her personal life for evidence of that pilgrimage. The later work suggests, too, that just as she had been supported by parents and by the "remembrance of former deliuerances," so she increasingly intends her words to be a source of support to her posterity. Bradstreet calls her letter, "To My Dear Children," a bequest. Through it, she intends to be "dayly" in their "rembrance."[45] In this letter her children are to "find/What was yr lieving mothers mind." Following their living mother's mind will be, she suggests, regenerative; her writing will bring about another birth in them. As she bore her children into this world, she now uses writing as the means to "travail in birth again of you till Christ be formed in you." Her children's inheritance is thus to be not a text, or a set of moral dicta, but the effects of a process. The nature of the process is described by use of analogy and built in the way Bradstreet's description of personal identity was built. The second birth (of Christ) in her children is like their first birth, which, she emphasizes, took place "with great paines, weaknes, cares & feares." Bradstreet's sentence moves almost imperceptibly from a reference to actual facts of personal history (her waiting "a long while" for the birth of her first child, Samuel) to an exact quotation from Paul's Epistle to the Galatians (4:19).

This reference, in its Pauline context, would remind Bradstreet's readers of a text important in its implications for Massachusetts Puritans. The Galatians are being chastized for having turned from the "spirit" to the "flesh." They are "foolish" and "bewitched" in their too literal adherence to the "works of the law." Paul's counsel, like Bradstreet's, is that at certain stages the law may be essential. But Christian development involves moving out of the "bondage" of such dependencies. In both Ephesians and Galatians, Paul's point is that the regenerate Christian is, ultimately and most basically, a "member" of "Christ's body," and should not cling to the false security of old, familiar ways. In Old Testament times, Paul writes, the law was a necessity, but in these times, Christ "has redeemed us from the curse of the law." The Geneva Bible commentator interpreted this text to mean that the ceremonies of the law are mere "shadowes" which "must end when Christ the trueth commeth."[46] The implication for the nature of Bradstreet's poetry is clear. The text of the poem is like a husk— a means on which the Christian reader would depend in order to grow into union with Christ. But the text would become, like the law, a "mere shadow," as the spiritual condition which the poem was to engender became a reality.

Thus, too, Bradstreet's letter to her children implies that the dying mother's body is like her poetic text. It, too, is a husk. The first and actual birth of her children is analogous to Paul's description of Old Testament life under the law; it is, for Christians, a necessary stage, not an ultimate condition. Bradstreet's children's second and spiritual birth will come, not by means of the mother's body but by means of the mother's "lieving mind" at work in the text of the poem. The reference to Galatians provides a clear indication to the modern reader of the nature of Bradstreet's complex conception of poetry. Paul writes that "I through the law am dead to the law, that I might live unto God." Thus, when Bradstreet writes that her intention for writing is to "declare the Truth, not to sett forth my self, but the Glory of God," she understands that the "Truth" (another word for Christ) will not be found in the words but beyond them, in the effects which the words will help to form in her readers. Bradstreet's steadfast insistence on her works' artlessness, her denigration of their literary merits, are consistent with a conception of poetic texts as "mere" "shadows" which, like the law, "must end when Christ the trueth cometh." Poetry, too, must be lived through. In that process the poetic text, since it belongs to the riches of this world, will be *exchanged*.

Further and interesting dimensions of meaning are suggested by Bradstreet's use of Galatians; the Pauline text underscores and clarifies her definition of her roles as woman and as writer. In her mortal life Bradstreet has been daughter, wife, and mother, but as she feels herself moving into membership in "Christ's Body," the earthly sexuality of her identity is being transformed. In Galatians Paul writes that for those who are in union with Christ, there is "neither Jew nor Greek, there is neither bond nor free, there is neither male nor female; for ye are all one in Jesus Christ." As we have seen, Bradstreet's relationship to her husband has, she feels, already been transformed into a relationship that reflects a future reality, presently glimpsed, but not yet fully visible. So, too, her emergent relationship to her children, analogous to her original mothering of them, suggests a mothering beyond that of "our Grandame" Eve's, whose brutal and depressed life is the subject of Stanza 12 of "Contemplations." Bradstreet represents herself as not altogether free of that identification; nevertheless, she sees herself as moving towards what Cotton Mather called the "glory" of another kind of mothering.

Throughout history, Paul claims in Galatians 4:22–31, there have been notable examples of regenerate mothers—those who, rather than "gendereth to bondage," bore "children of the promise." He finds the distinguishing marks of the "free woman" to be her desolation and her *apparent* barrenness. She represents the "Jerusalem which is above" and "the mother of us all."[47] The figure of Bathsheba gives biblical outline and substance to the figure of the mother and the persona of the writer in Bradstreet's letter to her children. There, the poet, like Bathsheba, has been "taught" by God. Her condition is analgous to Christ's church, in that the afflictions sent by God have repeatedly set her to "searching," "studying," "observing." Thus, like Solomon's spouse, she has gained "more understanding" and has been led to use "more circumspection." She reports that she has been upheld by Christ; the Bridegroom similarly upholds the Bride in Solomon's "Song." As a writer, she resembles both mother and spouse; her poetry, she expects, will bear fruit, in the same way Solomon's "vine" is said to bear Solomon's "fruits."

Indirectly, too, Bradstreet's letter, through its reliance on the worlds of

Solomon and Paul, suggests Bradstreet's sense of Massachussets history and of her own place in that perilous adventure. Again Bradstreet's uses of the biblical analogy suggest the influence of John Cotton's theological positions on her poetic imagination. Cotton's exposition on Canticles set forth his millenarianism. Perhaps Bradstreet as a young girl would have known how, following a detailed exegesis, Cotton had come to feel that the Christian church was being led out of the darkness of her historical role into the period of a dawning nuptial life with Christ. Cotton's optimistic conclusion is that Christ's mystical body, the Church, "if it fall into decay through corruption of doctrine or worship, it may be most fitly repaired." The whole of Canticles, in Cotton's view, tells of the churches' "deliverance out of captivity."[48] In Cotton's exposition much is made of the bride's race; that she is dark, paradoxically, bodes light. The extent to which the Christian church has been marked by profaneness, schism, apostasy, rebellion, seems to suggest that it has been brought near to death but thus closer to resurrection. Bradstreet's claim that she was tempted to "Atheisme" and has been so sorely tried she did not know what to think, "since the world has been filled with Blasphemy and Sectaries," precisely reflects Cotton's depiction of the condition of the church as it nears the end of history.

Bathsheba was, for the Puritans, a figure of doubleness; taken in adultery by David, she was marked by the experience of affliction. Her afflictions were said to be related to her entry into union with Christ. In Bradstreet's letter to her children, she characterizes her experience as pain-filled. Affliction has, she writes in her meditations, prepared the way for her salvation. She has been cast into the "furnace of affliction," and thereby, like iron, become capable of being "wrought" by God. Similarly, "corn till it have past through the Mill and been ground to powder, is not fit for bread."[49]

Such burnings and grindings accompany the forming of Christ in the heart of the Christian, just as pain accompanies childbirth. Interestingly, Bradstreet complains (in a meditation written in 1657) that she had actually "not been refined in the furnace of affliction as some have been, but have rather been preserved with sugar than brine. . . ." This meditation, addressed again to her children, suggests that her poetry is not primarily a retelling of the events of her life so much as it is a re-creation of afflictions so that her children may be changed by reliving them. Bradstreet's method is deliberate. She writes,

> Thus (dear children) have yee seen the many
> sicknesses and weaknesses that I have passed
> thro: to the End that if you meet with the
> like you may have recourse to the same God
> who hath heard & delivered me, and will
> doe the like for you if you trust in him;[50]

Thus Bradstreet's posture in the letter to her children is prophetic, not only in the fact that she witnesses the Holy Spirit but in the fact that she speaks out of her own "real world" experience—out of "sinkings and droopings," "sickness and pain." The figure of Bathsheba as wife and mother stands behind these presentations of affliction, as well as the phrases, again from Canticles, that express Bradstreet's recovery from dark moments. God has, she writes, "oft given me his word" and, in an echo of Canticles, has "sett to his Seal that it shall bee well with me."[51]

In Anne Bradstreet's coupling of statements that she has sometimes tasted of that "hidden Manna" that the world "knows not of" with apparently opposing statements—of her experiences of despair and doubt—can be seen the paradigmatic prophetic figure of Bathsheba, who is, above all, a figure of the regenerate mother and a type of the perfect society, the New Jerusalem. However Bradstreet felt about her everyday life, she appears not to have separated those feelings from her eager anticipation of a world-wide transformation. She concludes "As Weary Pilgrim," one of her last poems, with an expression of that expectation. Again, in the role of Christ's bride, she writes, "Lord make me ready for that day/ then Come deare bridgrome Come away."[52] Here she is, of course, anticipating her own death, which she again imagines as a "divine translation." Her universe depended for its coherence on such conceptions. Her disappointments, losses, and fears were made bearable by being thought of as the burning effects of Christ's dawning presence. In every aspect of her life one thing was in the process of becoming another.

Thus, when Bradstreet writes of her adult children in 1659, she portrays them as birds who have flown the nest. They are air-born; not yet escaped from mortality, they are, nevertheless, "unsnared." Bradstreet recounts each one's life history; each one's marriage and vocation are significant to record. These are stages in their development. As her adult children live out their lives, the poet "sits and sings" in the "shady woods." She lives in the twilight, looking back, looking forward, into a "country beyond sight, / Where old ones, instantly grow young. . . ." From that future place where "spring lasts to eternity," she imagines she sees her children telling their children about her. Not only will she be remembered, she will "live" among them, and "dead, yet speak."[53] She concludes, "I happy am, if well with you," a deceptively simple sentence, astonishing in its condensation of her view of her existence in this world and the next.

Bradstreet, at the end of her life, seems determined to project the promise of an inheritance. But missing from her last poems are assurances that in her lifetime or in her children's lifetimes God's promises will be fulfilled. In fact, the opposite seems true. The later poems resound with bleak reminders simply of time's *passage*. Her comfort in "Contemplations" is that the one "whose name is grav'd in the white stone / Shall last and shine when all of these are gone."[54] Her later poems have affliction as their principal subject matter, and personal life, rather than world history, as the theater in which God's consolations are reenacted. As the Day of His Coming in universal history seemed to stretch ahead into the unknown, the seasons seem a surer way of imaging His "return." All of Bradstreet's modern critics agree that the later poetry is firmer and more controlled in the management of its poetic elements. It appears that Bradstreet began to believe that the seed might have to live longer in the "shadow" of its husk than she and her group had originally expected.

NOTES

1. Cotton Mather, *Ornaments for the Daughters of Zion, or the Character and Happiness of a Vertuous Woman* . . . (Cambridge, Mass.: Green, 1692), p. 5.

2. Cotton Mather was the son of Increase Mather, and grandson of John Cotton. Increase Mather's brother, Seaborn, married Dorothy Bradstreet, daughter of Anne and Simon Bradstreet.

3. Mather, *Ornaments*, p. 6.

4. *Ibid.*, p. 7. See, too: Margaret W. Masson, "The Typology of the Female as a Model for the Regenerate: Puritan Preaching, 1690–1730," *Signs: Journal of Women in Culture and Society*, 2 (1976), 304–15.

5. Bradstreet, Ellis, p. 91.

6. Bradstreet, Norton, p. x. A new complete text of Bradstreet works provides a carefully edited edition from which all Bradstreet citations will be taken in this article: Bradstreet, McElrath, and Robb.

7. Ellis, p.xiii.

8. Bradstreet, Hensley, xxxiv. See also: Ann Stanford, "Anne Bradstreet: An Annotated Checklist," *Bulletin of Bibliography*, 27 (April-June, 1970), 34–37; Ann Stanford, *Anne Bradstreet: The Worldly Puritan, An Introduction to Her Poetry* (New York: Burt Franklin, 1975); see, particularly, the "Selected Bibliography of Works by and about Anne Bradstreet," pp. 145–49; and, Josephine K. Piercy, *Anne Bradstreet* (New York: Twayne Publishers, 1965). Piercy's "Epilogue" is devoted to a review of the literature about Anne Bradstreet.

9. See especially: John Berryman, "Homage to Mistress Bradstreet (a long poem)," *Partisan Review*, XX:5 (Sept.-Oct., 1953), 489–503. Adrienne Rich, "Anne Bradstreet and Her Poetry," in Bradstreet, Hensley, pp. ix–xx. In the nineteenth century Anne Bradstreet's life was the subject of a popular fictionalized history by Helen Campbell, *Anne Bradstreet and Her Time* (Boston: D. Lothrop, 1891).

10. Conceptions of Anne Bradstreet's role as a Puritan woman vary. She is generally thought to have written in the face of popular sentiment against women writers. Some critics have noted Bradstreet's "feminism" in, for example, "In Honor of Queen Elizabeth," but have found her, nevertheless, a deeply Puritan poet. See: George Frisbie Whicher, *Alas, All's Vanity, or a Leaf from the first American Edition of Several Poems*

by Anne Bradstreet printed at Boston, anno 1678. (New York: The Spiral Press, 1942), p. 25. Few go so far as Wendy Martin, in "Anne Bradstreet's Poetry: A Study of Subversive Piety," in suggesting that Anne Bradstreet, too, "by determining her own priorities, . . . risked being branded a heretic," in Sandra M. Gilbert and Susan Gubar, eds., *Shakespeare's Sisters* (Bloomington: Indiana University Press, 1979), pp. 19–31.

11. Murdock, *Literature*, p. 151.

12. Stanford *Anne Bradstreet*, pp. i–ii.

13. New knowledge about and new approaches to the subject of American Puritanism are reviewed in Sacvan Bercovitch, ed., "Introduction," *The American Literary Imagination: Essays in Revaluation* (London: Cambridge University Press, 1974), pp. 1–16. Recent editions of documents have extended first-hand knowledge of the period. One is David D. Hall, ed., *The Antinomian Controversy, 1630–1638, A Documentary history* (Middletown: Wesleyan Univ. Press, 1968). A major reevaluation of Puritan literary method began with the publication of Ursula Brumm's *American Thought and Religious Typology*, trans. John Hoaglund (New Brunswick, N. J.: Rutgers University Press, 1970). Bercovitch, *Typology*, provides a thorough introduction to the method of typology. Lewalski, *Poetics*, expanded these findings and described a tradition of biblical poetics among Protestant poets of the seventeenth century in England and New England.

14. Samuel Eliot Morison, *Builders of the Bay Colony* (Boston: Houghton Mifflin, 1930), p. 331.

15. Albert Gelpi, for example, commends her "individuation of experience," and the "cadence, and timbre and diction of a poetic voice." *The Tenth Muse: The Psyche of the American Poet* (Cambridge, Mass.: Harvard University Press, 1975), p. 20. Adrienne Rich, as did Percy Boynton, suggests that Bradstreet was a "Romantic writing out of her time." George Whicher and Ann Stanford find a fortunate trend in Bradstreet's later poetry towards a "more direct relationship between the experience and its expression," Stanford (1974), p. 27. Bradstreet's intentions were probably closer to George Herbert's, who, in the words of Rosemond Tuve, attempted "to make of literary creation—entire—a devoted and self-forgetful religious act," *A Reading of George Herbert* (Chicago: Univ. of Chicago Press, 1952), p. 195.

16. Anne Bradstreet was raised and educated in the household of the Earl of Lincoln where the plans were laid for the emigration to Massachusetts. She was converted and probably married by John Cotton, minister of the church in Boston, England. See White's carefully detailed chapters on Anne Bradstreet's English life, pp. 3–101. In 1630, Anne Bradstreet, her husband, Simon, and her parents, Dorothy and Thomas Dudley, crossed on the mother ship *Arbella* with the initial settlers of Massachusetts Bay.

17. Rosemary Laughlin, "Anne Bradstreet: Poet in Search of Form," *AL* 42 (1970), 1–17.

18. McElrath and Robb, p. 233.

19. Ibid., p. 174.

20. Ibid., p. 198.

21. Roger Williams, for one, was particularly critical of John Cotton and the Massachusetts magistrates on this point. In his view, it was the fact that they had "made the garden of the church and the field of the world all one" that led to the possibility that they "might . . .sometimes in their zealous mistakes persecute good wheat instead of tares. . . ." Literal nations are, Williams writes, "a mixed seed." It is only the "spiritual

Israel" that is the "seed of Christ." For Williams no actual group should expect God's inheritance, which he emphasized is "spiritual." Perry Miller, *Roger Williams: His Contribution to the American Tradition* (New York: Atheneum, 1962), p. 137, 151. See also: Jesper Rosenmeier, "The Teacher and the Witness: John Cotton and Roger Williams," *WMQ*, Third Series, 12 (July, 1968), pp. 408–31.

22. For a summary of the Puritan's millenarian expectations, see: Cecelia Tichi, *New World, New Earth: Environmental Reform in American Literature from the Puritans through Whitman* (New Haven: Yale University Press, 1979).

23. McElrath and Robb, p. 180.

24. Ibid., pp. 175–177.

25. Hall, *Antinomian Controversy*, pp. 16–20.

27. Morgan, *Family*. Morgan's chapter, "Husband and Wife," suggests how representative a Puritan Bradstreet is in her portrayal of her marriage. See also Rosamond R. Rosenmeier, " 'Divine Translation': A Contribution to the Study of Anne Bradstreet's Method in the Marriage Poems," *EAL* 12 (1977), pp. 121–35.

28. Lewalski, *Poetics*, p. 129.

29. Keller, *Taylor*, p. 209. Keller writes that unlike the medieval mystics, who also used the imagery of sexual love and marriage to express divine ecstasy, Taylor's imagery is "doggedly earthy." Mysticism, Keller says, "belongs to a different tradition from the Puritan. . . ."

30. Anne Stanford writes that Bradstreet's "expression of inadequacy becomes a theme uniting the poems . . ." *Anne Bradstreet*, p. 16. That Bradstreet's artlessness is deliberate is suggested, also, in such metrically hobbled lines as "These ragged lines will do't, when they appear," surely roughed up and, thereby, capable of "clearing" her "innocence." McElrath and Robb, p. 6.

31. Mather suggests that women's writing is a reflective art; although women were not to speak in church, it was acceptable, even desirable, for them to record and reflect the minister's sermon. "B.W." (probably Benjamin Woodbridge) suggests the same aspect of the writer's role in his dedication to *The Tenth Muse*. Stanford has noted that "A Dialogue between Old and New England" has elements of the broadside and the sermon, neither one a form used by women; casting her exhortation into the dialogue form permitted her to reflect a kind of statement she otherwise avoided. Stanford, pp. 60-61. Nathaniel Ward's characterization of Bradstreet as a "right Du Bartas Girle" again suggests the idea of true reflection. McElrath and Robb, p. 526.

32. Ibid., p. 176.

33. Ibid., p. 223.

34. Puritans expected, following the biblical pattern, to go into "life" through "death." Indeed, they expected to have to "die daily," as a part of the Christian pilgrimage. One is, furthermore, empowered to change or translate one's life by the free gift of God's grace, not by the efforts of human will. By "God's inheritance" in the 1661 poem, Bradstreet means, in part, the strength to undergo that process, always accompanied by grief and a sense of loss.

35. McElrath and Robb, p. 18.

36. In her 1971 book on Bradstreet, p. 329.

37. John Cotton, "God's Promise to His Plantations" *Old South Leaflets*, General

Series, III, 53 (1894–1896), 12–13. In 1639–40, Cotton, after his arrival in New England, had tentatively set 1655 as the date for the arrival of the millennium. If Bradstreet did have hopes for that date, those hopes would have been dashed by this time. See Jesper Rosenmeier, *"Veritas:* The Sealing of the Promise," *Harvard Library Bulletin*, 16 (1968), 35.

38. *The Geneva Bible,* a facsimile of the 1560 edition (Madison: Univ. of Wisconsin Press, 1969), Isaiah 1:29–30, p. 283.

39. *Ibid.,* p. 244.

40. In Meserole, *Poetry*, and McElrath and Robb, p. 169. Ann Stanford's chapter on "Contemplations" demonstrates the intricacy of Bradstreet's poetic construction. Robert D. Richardson, Jr. analyzes the poetic argument, in "The Puritan Poetry of Anne Bradstreet," *Texas Studies in Literature and Language*, 9 (1967), 317–31. (Reprinted in Bercovitch, 1974, 99, 107–22).

41. McElrath and Robb, p. 204.

42. Ibid., p. 198.

43. The harshest criticism of Bradstreet's work is directed at her long poems in heroic couplet, and among these at her histories. Ellis demonstrates that she imitated large portions of Sir Walter Raleigh's *History of the World.* Her numerous borrowings (from Guillaume Du Bartas, Spenser and others) have been seen as "decidedly in the academic tradition," and "school exercises in verse." Whicher, *Alas*, p. 24. Josephine K. Piercy takes the opposite view when she suggests that Bradstreet was writing to "find an outlet for a pent-up rebellion" against her circumstances in the new world. Piercy, *Anne Bradstreet*, p. 33.

44. Thomas Dudley died in 1653, and thus Bradstreet may have had personal reasons for not being able to complete her "Four Monarchies." I have argued elsewhere, in an interpretation of "Verses upon the burning of her house, July 10, 1666," that she was in doubt about the direction of history in New England, and thus turned from the confident retelling of history to the psalm-like lyrics that plead for God's mercy. *EAL* 12 (1977) 131–34.

45. McElrath and Robb, pp. 215–19.

46. *Geneva Bible*, p. 88.

47. Samuel Mather's interpretation of the biblical figure of Bathsheba rests on this reference to Galatians; he, too, finds Bathsheba a type of the Church, and, as such, of the New Jerusalem. In *The Figures or Types of the Old Testament* (New York: Johnson Reprint Corporation, 1969), pp. 66 and 108.

48. John Cotton, *A Brief Exposition of the Whole Book of Canticles*, or, *Song of Solomon* (London: 1642, 1648; John Nichol, 1868), p. 49. Internal evidence suggests that the exposition was based on a series of sermons given around 1620.

49. McElrath and Robb, pp. 199, 197.

50. Ibid., p. 227. Ann Stanford has observed that the fact that Bradstreet could record in 1661 that she had gone four years with "no great fitt of sickness" suggests that she was perhaps not as sickly as has been thought. McElrath and Robb, p. 228.

51. Ibid.

52. Ibid., p. 211.

53. The Bradstreets' good friend John Norton's elegy of John Cotton was called *Abel*

Being Dead Yet Speaketh: Or the Life and Death of John Cotton (London, 1658). The echo "dead, yet speak" in Bradstreet's verse may be coincidental, but Norton's view of the regenerate writer's role was one Bradstreet shared.

54. McElrath and Robb, p. 174.

10 THE DANFORTHS: PURITAN POETS IN THE WOODS OF ARCADIA

ROBERT DALY

At a time when parts of London combined the odors of a sewer with those of a slaughterhouse, the westering Puritan, bound from Old England to New, could smell the pine forests of America when his ship was still sixty leagues, one hundred eighty nautical miles, from land. Familiar as we are with the typological significances of this wilderness, we need to remember that among Puritan writers typology operated not only at the level of trope, but also at the level of perception, and that a number of Puritans could see the forest for the trees as well as the types.[1] Among these writers deeply interested in both Nature and Grace were Samuel Danforth I and his two sons, John Danforth and Samuel Danforth II, all ministers, all poets well-known in their own day though less so in ours.

Scholars have long taken note of the Danforths, usually without analyzing their poetry in detail. Though he does not number them among his colonial verse-writers, Moses Coit Tyler does record the epitaph on the elder Samuel Danforth, who died just after he had completed his series of sermons on the Gospel of St. Luke, and his congregation had completed a new and larger meeting house:

> Our minds with gospel his rich lectures fed;
> Luke and his life at once are finished,
> Our new-built church now suffers too by this,
> Larger its *windows*, but its *lights* are less.[ll. 5–8][2]

John May affords us a genealogy of the family, Kenneth Murdock a sympathetic introduction to the elder Samuel Danforth and a fair sample of his poetry, Samuel Eliot Morison glimpses of his undergraduate career and work as a poet and astronomer. In 1943 Harold Jantz included all three Danforths in *The First Century of New England Verse* and made interesting comparisons among them. And in 1968 several scholars added considerably to our knowledge of the family. Hyatt Waggoner noted "that there are discoveries remaining to be made in Puritan verse despite the pioneering work of Murdock and Jantz. The work of John Danforth seems especially worthy of reprinting and study." That same year Thomas A. Ryan reprinted the poetry of John Danforth, ably edited and intro-duced. Harrison T. Meserole included all three Danforths in his excellent selec-tion of seventeenth-century American poetry. And Marjorie Wolfe McCune included an edition of their poems along with pertinent textual notes and bio-graphical material in her dissertation on the Danforths. Since then John E. Trimpey and Astrid Schmitt-von Mühlenfels have studied the poetry of John Danforth, particularly his experiments with verse forms in the elegy and other genres.[3]

Over the years, then, the Danforths have been ably catalogued, edited, described in general terms, and recommended to our attention. What remains to be done now is to accord them that attention, to read them in detail, not just for their evidential value as sources of historical information, but as poets, human beings making artistic choices and trying to write a particular kind of poetry. In their poetry, as scholars have noted, they employ "very homely and quaint imagery and allusions from the Bible side by side with classical allusions and references to modern science."[4] Reading them closely and in context will enable us to see this mixing of local, biblical, classical, and scientific referents neither as a curious idiosyncrasy nor as a lapse in sensibility and decorum but as part of a deliberate and coherent poetics.

The sources of that poetics are twofold. As Puritans, the Danforths kept clear some crucial distinctions regarding the use of images and metaphors. These distinctions are made explicit and precise by Samuel Mather (1626–1671), who argues concerning the biblical prohibition of graven images:

> 1. *That it is not meant of Images for Civil use, but for worship; thou shalt not bow down to them, nor serve them.* For the Civil use of Images is lawful . . . but the scope of the Command is against Images in State and use religious.
> 2. Neither yet is it meant of all Images for religious use, but *Images of their own devising*, for God doth not forbid his own institutions, but only our inventions.

Mather's distinctions are quite precise: only images used as objects of worship and religious images devised by man are anathema. About metaphorical or typological linkings between the Old and New Testaments, or in the Eusebian tradition between both Testaments and the secular history of a chosen people, or in the tradition of Puritan meditation between the natural objects of the created world and the supernatural Creator who made 'them, Mather makes a similar distinction: "It is not safe to make anything a Type merely upon our own fancies and imaginations; it is *God's* Prerogative to make *Types*."[5] Forbidden to make types out of their own fancies and imaginations, the Puritans were commanded to *see* types in nature and history. The Danforths, then, lived in a symbolic world intended by God to be read by them along with their Bible. Like Jonathan Edwards, they extended the typological method from biblical exegesis to a reading of spiritual significances of the created world. Ursula Brumm has written that Edwards saw "the natural world" (the only one accessible to human comprehension) as "the image and the key to the transcendent world of religion, which could thus be understood indirectly." The Danforths shared Edwards' belief that "the things of the world are ordered [and] designed to shadow forth spiritual things." Like Edward Taylor, they saw "the world slickt up in types/ In all Choise things chosen to typify."[6]

That Samuel Danforth II participated in this tradition is evident in his poem "Ad Librum," (in Meserole, *Poetry*) from the *New-England Almanack* for 1686. Each year a young Harvard graduate was chosen to do the calculations and ready the copy for the Cambridge almanac and was given some space of his own that he could fill with appropriate poetry or prose of his own composition. "Thus the Cambridge almanac," as Samuel Eliot Morison has noted, "became the annual poetry magazine of New England."[7]

Samuel's father had authored verses for the almanac nearly forty years before, so he was working within a familial as well as a communal tradition. Perhaps for that reason, he is quite careful to dissociate his work from the astrological tradition from which he borrows much of his vocabulary. He apologizes for using "The *Names* impos'd by old Idolatry / On Months and Planets" (ll. 31–32) and asserts that he is neither a natural astrologer, who claims to describe the actual influences of the stars and planets upon natural disasters, like storms and plagues, nor a "Judicial Astrologer" (l. 62), who claims to describe their influences on persons and nations. Sending his book out to an audience well able to appreciate such distinctions, he separates himself from the tradition of fraudulent astrologers and argues that his "*Harmless Astronomy*" (l. 65) is sanctioned by "The sacred Oracle itself" (l. 40), the Bible, in which we learn that God created the heavenly lights as signs: "And God said, Let there be lightes in the firmament of the heaven, to separate the daie from the night, & let them be for signes, . . ." (Genesis 1:14).[8] Like Chaucer, and like Spenser who was much read at Harvard, Danforth is sending out his book with a poem, "Ad Librum," "to the book," and he is sending it into a world which he also sees and enfigures as a book, a collection of intelligible signs.

In lines (42–47) destined to gladden the hearts of semioticians, Danforth focuses on God's creation of this world, a world full of signs that men must read. Both the repetitions and the punning are important. Danforth insists that the significance of these signs is external, in the world itself and seen, not created, by the poet. His poetry is made up, not of metaphoric linkings forged in his own fancy, but of metaphors made by God, necessary to all men and pointed out to them by the poet. "*If None can see*" this divine significance, the heavenly lights will be insignificant only to us. The significance immanent within them will still be there, quite real, waiting for some other poet to render a public service to his community by seeing it and articulating it for the benefit of the other members of that community. Even Danforth's punning on the word "sign" is an attempt not to make but to read the signs, since language itself is a metaphoric gift from God.

To ignore these signs "is to defie / The sacred Oracle itself, besides / Each Days Experience in *Winds* and *Tydes*" (ll. 38–41). Danforth's poem, then, is didactic in the best sense, intended less to lead the passive reader to some predetermined homilectic conclusion than to invite the reader to join the poet in the community of observers, to participate in the poet's own sense of wonder (ll. 68–76). That sense of wonder leads Danforth into a closer and closer reading of God's other book, the creation. Tracing out the meanings of these clues, pondering the action of welkin, Danforth bases his poem on a close adherence to particular observation. With a much more individual sense of metaphor, Milton could afford, at least in his poetry, to be somewhat indifferent to the Copernican revolution. For the purposes of his poem, it hardly mattered whether Satan invaded a Copernican or Ptolemaic system:

> Thither his course he bends
> Through the calm Firmament; but up or down
> By centre, or eccentric, hard to tell. [Bk. III, ll. 573–75][9]

For Danforth, however, the fact was itself metaphoric, significant, and he would have trivialized his poetry had he failed to take careful account of it. Danforth, therefore, had to choose between the cosmos of Ptolemy and that of Copernicus and Brahe. He could not simply tap the poetic power of both, or choose the more convenient. Once he had decided that the Copernican view was correct, he had to say so:

> Yet think not that I'le give my Affidavit
> Each Star shall prove as Ptolemy would have it:
> I know the contrary. (ll. 48–50)

And since there could be for Danforth no contradiction between the truths of the new science and the truths of the Bible, he could retell biblical stories with metaphors drawn from the science of his own day: "In Joshuah's *Solstice* at the Voyce of man / The *Rapid sun* became *Copernican*" (ll. 77–78). He could write a public poetry within an ancient and clearly defined tradition, a poetry that would lay open to view the harmony of God's symbolic world, in which the Bible, the Greek and Latin classics, the new science, and the history of his own community were all linked by the deft hand of the greatest Poet. Danforth could send out to his readers a book that would make clear to them some of the signs in God's book. And he could see the place of his own era in the long cycle of ages, could in his almanac lay out the year 1686 for the understanding of his readers and, as it ended, lay it out for proper burial in a winding sheet of words (ll. 94–98). For Danforth, the year of his almanac was part of a coherent procession of years from the birth of Christ to the advent of the Millenium. That procession of years was a single coherent book from which Danforth had undertaken to read a few pages for his readers. It is not that Danforth was trying to write Romantic lyric poetry of self-revelation and failing. He was writing a particular kind of public poetry, and the first major source of his poetics was, as we have seen, the Puritan view of the created world as a book, a system of metaphors wrought by God in loving accommodation to the limited faculties of men.

Like many other Puritan poets including Bradstreet and Taylor who wrote personal as well as public poetry, the Danforths could have described their poetics in the words Anne Bradstreet used in her letter to her children: "I have not studied in this you read to show my skill, but to declare the truth, not to set forth myself, but the glory of God."[10] Needless to say, Bradstreet did work to develop her skill, and we should take her words not as a conclusive description of the work itself but as her sense of the work's importance. This view of poetry as chiefly a matter of perception and articulation rather than as a product of the poet's creation is hardly limited to the Puritans. It has far more in common with the Roman notion of the poet as "*vates*," a "seer" who observes and utters a truth outside himself, than with the Greek notion of the poet as "*poeta*," a "maker" who fashions verbal artifacts finally of his own creation, however deeply he or she draws from the world for materials.

The writer who gave wide currency to the notion of the poet as *vates* was a favorite of the Danforths and the second major source of their poetics. Before Vergil's time, *vates* had referred to soothsayer and was used pejoratively. Vergil restored the term to respectability by using it to describe his attempt to articulate and preserve his own culture, by locating his complex pastoral idyll in Arcadia and by giving Arcadia the features of his own country. For Vergil, his community was a part of the vision of Arcadia, and his Arcadian landscape of the imagination is figured forth through the marshy landscape he knew, a landscape quite unlike the mountains and plains of the geographical Arcadia in the central Peloponnesus. His goal as a poet is made explicit in the third book of his "Georgics": "primus ego in patriam mecum, modo vita supersit / Aonio rediens deducam vertice Musas." ["I shall be the first, if I live, to bring back with me into my own country the Muses from the Aonian peak."][11] Vergil refers here not to his entire country but to his own familiar ground, that little part of northern Italy comprising his father's farm on the sloping banks of the Mincio just outside of Mantua. In his complex pastoral, Vergil mingles classical allusion, contemporary political events, and the scenes and history of his local community. By doing so, he includes his own community (usurped when his father's farm was confiscated to provide land for soldiers) in the flow of history, thereby taking on the public role of *vates* and performing a public service.

Samuel Danforth I arrived at Harvard "an unwholesomely pious freshman, whose shocked comments when 'reciting to his Tutor out of the Heathen Poets' are recorded with approval by Cotton Mather.[12] Then, as now, a Harvard education had a way of diminishing such shock, and by the time young Danforth came to write his verses for the Almanac of 1647, "he had clearly learned to enjoy and imitate such 'heathen' poets as Vergil."[13] Danforth's almanac verses are clearly attempts to emulate Vergil's eclogues, ambitious public poems in which the poet weaves together local, historical, and mythical referents to form an intricate pastoral. Aimed at a particularly well-defined audience who could be depended upon to share with their poetic spokesman a good deal of specific knowledge, these early poems are often puzzling to moderns who cannot recognize the local referents. For this distant audience, Danforth's poem on March must make up in energy what it lacks in intelligibility:

> A Coal-white Bird appears this spring
> That neither cares to sigh or sing.
> This when the merry Birds espy,
> They take her for some enemy.
> Why so, when as she humbly stands
> Only to shake you by your hands?

After several shrewd guesses about the meaning of "Coal-white," Kenneth Murdock concludes: "Possibly Danforth's 'Coal-white Bird' represents a book, appearing in the spring. If 'Coal-white' means simply 'white,' the bird may be conscience, or God's grace, or, perhaps, the fever common in the spring in colonial New England. . . . If by the bird Danforth means fever, then his last line 'Only to shake you by your hands' becomes a play on words, referring to the shaking caused by disease."[14] I can neither rest content with these surmises nor improve upon them and must conclude that in writing so well for his immediate audience, Danforth has excluded readers outside that local community. Writing this kind of heavily allusive public poetry is a craft that takes some learning, and several of Danforth's early attempts evince more of the effort than the achievement. But all are enlivened by energy and wit: even these first efforts benefit considerably from comparison with the academic verse of the younger Thomas Shepard, whose notion of classical allusion was to have Phoebus Apollo carried weeping to the Harvard Commencement.[15]

By the time he wrote his second almanac, Danforth had learned his art well enough to usher in the spring with a song ("Awake yee westerne Nymphs" in Meserole, *Poetry*) that we may still read with pleasure, a song in which he succeeded at last in the Vergilian task of bringing the Muse to his own country. He directs attention to the newly planted colony of New England, only twenty-some years old but already "grown unto such a comely state / That one would think't an Olive tree or Date." Transplanted "from afar" by a "skilfull Husband-man," the colony is part of a long line of His plantations, including the natural world, the Bible, the Greek and Latin classics, and all human history. For that reason, this plant is central to an almost unlimited context, and Danforth can pertinently weave New England into a fabric containing the olive trees of the Old Testament, the wilderness that in this context supports the chosen colony rather than either threatening it or serving as a symbolic alternative to it, a panoply of classical gods and goddesses who nurture the plant, several medieval hypostatized abstractions, and practically everything else he has learned at Har-vard. For all its richness and variety, the poem is neither obscure nor chaotic.

Danforth achieves his clarity and control through both prosody and narrative line. The regular meter, end rhymes, internal rhymes, and assonance all suggest order and inevitability. The single controlling metaphor of a plant raised carefully so that other stock may be grafted from it is developed in considerable complexity but never mixed with other metaphors or replaced by them. The colony trans-planted by God from the Old to the New World is so clearly chosen and protected by Him that one might well think, looking at it, of the ancient olive trees of Israel. It is cared for even by the wilderness. The mingling of dung and blessings seems oxymoronic to us, and probably to the Puritans as well. The point of it is that Danforth's view of New England history necessarily mingles such concrete details with their extraordinary spiritual significance, and the poet had, therefore, good religious reasons (as well as good poetic reasons) for observing the natural world in careful and precise detail.

After God and Nature, the classical deities are introduced. "Bright Phoebus casts his silver sparkling ray" upon the growing plant, "And with a pleasant aspect smiles upon / The tender buds and blooms that hang thereon." With such help the plant soon begins to bear fruit. Astraea waters the plant and sings to it with the result that it appropriately bears the fruit of "JUSTICE," a branch that "yearly shoots forth Lawes and Libertyes" to bring order to this new culture. The classical deities, then, serve as shorthand names for natural forces, as evidence that New England already has the learning and culture that Danforth aims to assert, exemplify, and augment in his poem, and finally as a clear indication that Danforth is casting himself as poet in the classical role of *vates*, the poet who sees and utters the truth for the good of his community. An important part of that truth is that the colony, far from being an isolated and insignificant outpost on the periphery of the world, is both old and new—carrying in itself all biblical and classical lore and making all this old wisdom new by bringing it to its culmination in the new world. For him New England *is* Israel but an Israel freed from the historical failures of the biblical Israel. New England is the culmination of both sacred and secular history central to any context: it is a huge tree linking earth and sky, past and future. The poet can see this paradoxical truth, even if others cannot. Novius, the "upstart newcomer" from the *Satires* of Horace,[16] thinks "no old thing can be new" and therefore cannot see the connections between New England, a unique plant that has no parallel, and all the old roots from which it grew. In America, of course, all people are newcomers, and they look to the poet to include them in the community of those who know the truth.

What the poet will do for the "newcomers" of New England (open their eyes, enable them to see their position in secular and salvation history), New England will do for the rest of the world. It will become, not an orphaned child cut off from the history and culture of the larger world, but the parent stock onto which the other plants in God's garden will be grafted. Beginning with the Indians, this process will continue as New England becomes ever more clearly the culmination of God's plan for history and finally ushers in the universal conversion preceding the thousand years of peace and justice of the Millenium:

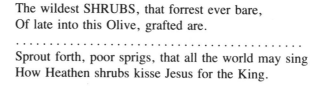

> The wildest SHRUBS, that forrest ever bare,
> Of late into this Olive, grafted are.
> ·
> Sprout forth, poor sprigs, that all the world may sing
> How Heathen shrubs kisse Jesus for the King.

This long poem, itself one of the finest fruits of New England, serves to assist in the very process it describes, the awakening of New Englanders to their place in the universal order of things. It brings together the expected biblical and classical references with local references to life in New England and with scientific references because all were divinely ordained and significant: all were coherent and harmonious for the poet with eyes to see and ears to hear. And it fulfills the poet's duty, which is neither merely to entertain nor merely to twist dogma into rhyme, but to proclaim to and for his community the truth he sees.

The comprehensiveness and the coherence of that truth are evident in Danforth's well-known prose composition, *An Astronomic Description of the late Comet or Blazing Star, with a brief Theological Application thereof*. In his description and explanation of the comet that appeared at the turn of the years 1664–1665, Danforth argues that comets "proceed from natural causes, are subject to mathematical laws, and are composed of the same stuff as the stars"—a somewhat advanced position in 1665. Having begun with this scientific explanation, he goes on with no apparent sense of contradiction to argue that comets are signs sent to us by God, carriers of divine portents, and consequently to be studied by theologians as well as by astronomers.[17] In fact, Danforth's work as an astronomer and as a poet was one with his work as a minister, to interpret the texts of the Bible and world, to serve as example and spokesman for his congregation, to make sense of his and their lives.

The duties he performed at Roxbury were performed at Taunton by his younger son, Samuel II, who served as physician, lawyer, teacher, and minister to that community, and at Dorchester by his elder son, John, who ministered to that community for nearly fifty years. Though John experimented with lyrics, almanac verse, epigrams, anagrams, epitaphs, and verse epistles dedicatory, his *forte* was the elegy, a genre in which he set out to make sense of the individual life within the rich contexts of an exceptionally well–furnished mind. Like his father and brother, he attempted to read Nature as well as the many books in his library. Aged twenty, he traveled out to Dighton Rock to record carefully the strange inscriptions carved on it, to try to make some sense of this remarkable text.

That same concern to read aright a world rich with significance is evident in his elegy on the death of Mrs. Mary Gerrish, "*Who on* Novemb. *17. 1710. the Night after Publick Thanksgiving, Entred on the Celebration of Triumphant Hallelujahs, to her Profit, and our Loss. Aged 19.* Years *and 20.* Days" (Meserole, *Poetry*). Danforth's long title establishes not only the exact time of her death, just after a day of public thanksgiving, but also her place within the local community—she was the wife of Samuel Gerrish and the daughter of Samuel Sewall. From this immediate familial and communal context she has been taken, and Danforth comforts the survivors by having his poem move out to all the larger communities in which both she and her survivors are included. He begins with the community of other women named Mary and with an allusion to George Herbert's anagram on the Virgin Mary. Herbert often played off line length against rhyme in experimenting with various verse forms, and I think that Danforth's verse form is more than merely quaint. The varying type, the staggered lines, and the varying line lengths all suggest in this context and serve as typographical correlatives for uncertainty and potential disorder, exactly the feelings effected in the community by the death of a young, virtuous, and needed woman. The rhyme and the repetitions of this single verse form reintegate that potential disorder into a larger and more complex order, even as Danforth reintegrates Mary into larger and more complex communities until he finally closes with a community to which Mary and her survivors all belong.

The anagram serves a similar purpose. At first glance the anagrammatizing of Mary as Army seems fanciful and almost willfully farfetched, seems almost an adventitious imposition of meaning where no meaning is immanent. But Danforth cites the example of Herbert and repeats (ll. 5–8) Herbert's reading of the anagram. The connection between army and Mary, then, is really there and has already been seen and explained by another poet. Danforth can therefore see a veritable army of Marys, an immortal line of mortal women descending from the Virgin Mary and including "Our beauteous *MARY* too," whose personal beauty was a metaphor for the spiritual beauty of grace. She was "Besides all other Brightnesses, / enobled most by Grace."

This theme of separation and isolation ended by inclusion into larger communities is developed coherently throughout the poem. Though Mary is separated from the local church communion,

> She has Attaind now, with Advance,
>   what she desir'd below;
> (Joyn'd to the Church in Heav'n,) She doth
>   to Full Communion go. [ll. 41–44]

The local community may then be comforted that Mary has gone "To better Friends, than any here;/and will Return anon." She is part of the community of Christ's elect and will return with Him, more beautiful than ever, at the Second Coming and resurrection of the dead. In the classical tradition, she has, of course, become a star. But Danforth both taps that tradition and transcends it by arguing that she was a star when living, a star now lost for a time to the community, who, she is confident, will make an improvement even of this suffering (ll. 65–68). They will look to God for comfort from a grief that Danforth makes no attempt to trivialize. There is no attempt to deny that "Partings are Grief", that "*A Daughter, Sister, Spouse*, is tak'n; / whom dear Relations miss" (ll. 97–98). The attempt here is to comfort them by helping them to understand the significance of her life and death and the grounds for hope. In the final lines expressing that hope, the multiple caesuras of the early lines fall away, the verse becomes more regular; even the type face becomes uniform as the poet brings together all his learning and all his skill to speak the expected and communal word of comfort: "You want her Much: SEEK HER IN CHRIST/AND YOU WILL FIND HER THERE." Out of context, of course, these final words might easily be mistaken for mere theology. As the final cadence of this complex poem, however, they are earned in human, poetic, and musical terms and are quite likely to have comforted a community able to appreciate these considerations and to make them important and inseparable parts of their theology.

Though Puritanism begins in separation, these Puritan poets aimed at inclusion, at a rich and communally useful poetry that would sing not only in but also of harmony, the harmony of a huge choir blending their individual voices into a single song that unites in rich counterpoint all the paradoxes of their learning and their lives.

NOTES

1. For information on the fragrance of America, see Richard Hofstadter, *America at 1750: A Social Portrait* (New York: Random House, 1973), p. xi. For a more detailed discussion of this aspect of Puritan typology, see Daly, *God's Altar*, pp. 40–81.

2. Tyler, *History*, p. 232. Weld's poem on Danforth is quoted from Cotton Mather, *Magnalia Christi Americana* (1702; rpt. New York: Russell and Russell, 1967), II, 62.

3.   John Joseph May, Danforth Genealogy (Boston: C. H. Pope, 1902); Murdock, Paul, Morison, Life, pp. 226–227; Jantz, First Century, Waggoner, Poets, p. 659; Thomas A. Ryan, ed., "The Poetry of John Danforth," PAAS, 78 (April 1968), 129–193; Meserole, Poetry; Marjorie Wolfe McCune, "The Danforths: Puritan Poets" (Diss. Pennsylvania State University, 1968); John E. Trimpey, "The Poetry of Four American Puritans: Edward Johnson, Peter Bulkeley II, Nicholas Noyes, and John Danforth" (Diss. Ohio University, 1968); Astrid Schmitt-von Mühlenfels, Die "Funeral Elegy" Neuenglands: Eine gattungsgeschichtliche Studie (Heidelberg: Carl Winter, 1973).

4.   Ryan, "Poetry," p. 138. Ryan is writing only of John Danforth. Meserole makes the same point about Samuel Danforth I: "Danforth's almanac verses contain topical references to current events in Massachusetts, as well as the more conventional classical and mythological allusions" (Poetry, p. 414).

5.   Samuel Mather, A Testimony from the Scripture against Idolatry & Superstition, in Dickran and Ann Tashjian, Memorials for Children of Change: The Art of Early New England Stonecarving (Middletown, Conn.: Wesleyan Univ. Press, 1974), p. 6; Samuel Mather, The Figures or Types of the Old Testament, 2nd ed. (London: Nath. Hillier, 1705; rpt. New York: Johnson Reprint Corporation, 1969), p. 55.

6.   Ursula Brumm, American Thought and Religious Typology, trans. John Hoaglund (New Brunswick, New Jersey: Rutgers University Press, 1970), p. 98; Jonathan Edwards, Images or Shadows of Divine Things, ed. Perry Miller (New Haven: Yale Univ. Press, 1948), p. 44; Edward Taylor, Meditation I, Second Series, Stanford, Taylor, 83.

7.   Morison, Life, p. 226. See also Robert Secor's chapter in this book.

8.   Genesis 1:14 is quoted from The Geneva Bible: A Facsimile of the 1560 Edition (Madison: Univ. of Wisconsin Press, 1969), p. 1. Meserole notes the biblical allusion and Danforth's word-play on "sign" (p. 486).

9.   Milton, Paradise Lost, in John Milton: Complete Poems and Major Prose, ed. Merritt Y. Hughes (New York: Odyssey Press, 1957), p. 272.

10.   Bradstreet, Hensley, p. 240.

11.   Vergil, "Georgics," Book III, lines 10–11, quoted from Virgil, ed. H. Rushton Fairclough, the Loeb Classical Library (Cambridge, Mass.: Harvard Univ. Press, 1960): I, 154. The English translation is mine.

12.   Morison, Life, p. 226.

13.   Meserole, Poetry, p. 414.

14.   Murdock, Paul, pp. 130–31.

15.   Morison, Life, p. 227.

16.   Meserole identifies this allusion in Poetry, p. 419.

17.   Morison, Life, p. 241.

11 TO KEEP IN MEMORY: THE POETRY OF EDWARD JOHNSON

JESPER ROSENMEIER

In 1650, William Bradford, governor of Plymouth, abruptly stopped the history *Of Plymouth Plantation*, he had been working on for twenty years. He had begun writing in 1630, when he feared that the rapid dispersal of settlers to nearby villages like Duxbury or Marshfield would lead to the desertion of the Plymouth church—the "ancient mother," as Bradford called it—and to the loss of Plymouth's role as the model community for the rapidly approaching millennium. By telling his audience, especially the younger generation, the story of the first planters' mutual love and affection, Bradford had hoped that the children would return to the ways of their fathers and protect and support the Plymouth mother church. In spite of the growing evidence that the bonds holding Plymouth together had unraveled, Bradford had continued to work on *Of Plymouth Plantation,* impelled by his conviction that if the church could be restored to her ancient "order, liberty, and beauty,"[1] she might yet serve a prophetic role in the imminent redemption of the world. It was that promise which had sustained Bradford and his fellow Separatists in their journey from Scrooby, England to Leyden, Holland to Plymouth, Massachusetts. They had spared no effort to insure that the light of the millennium would break over Plymouth, and from there spread eastward across England and the Continent, and westward across New England's Indian world.

However, in 1650, events in England caused Bradford to despair about Plymouth's role as the prophetic fellowship. Surprised at Cromwell's defeat of King Charles in the late 1640s, Bradford greeted the English Puritans' success with a mixture of elation and despondency. He must be joyous, he felt, at the rooting out of the episcopal hierarchy, but he also feared that all his sufferings and sacrifices had been in vain. God, Bradford felt, had turned his face from Plymouth; the New Jerusalem would likely be planted in England's green and pleasant land. "Full little did I think," he writes, "that the downfall of the Bishops, with their courts, cannons, and ceremonies, etc. had been so near when I first began these scribbled writings . . . or that I should have lived to have seen, or heard of the same. But it is the Lord's doing, and ought to be marvelous in our eyes."[2] Marvelous it might have been, but with his confidence in the promises deeply shaken, Bradford could not continue writing. What was the use of exhorting the young to imitate their fathers if the mission had gone awry? After 1650, the sad, persistent voice *Of Plymouth Plantation* went silent.

Yet the very events that caused Bradford to cease writing compelled another New England historian, Edward Johnson, to begin *A History of New England. From the English Planting in the Yeere 1628 until the Yeere 1652*, also known as *Wonder-Working Providence of Sions Savior in New England,* first published in London in 1654.[3] Unlike Bradford, Johnson proclaimed New England as heir to all the ages. He insisted that all the last great events in the history of redemption, as foretold in the Book of Revelation, would indeed take place in New England: The defeat of Antichrist, the millennium, the battle of the saints with Gog and Magog, the resurrection of the dead, the last judgment, and the descent of the New Jerusalem. In fact, so eager was Johnson to get to the very end of history that in spite of his repeatedly stated belief in a millennium to precede the coming of the New Jerusalem, he conflated the future events and wrote as if eternity would arrive not in 2651 A. D. but in 1651 when he closed his History by promising his audience that "Babylon is fallen, the God of truth hath said it; then who would not be a Souldier of Christs side, where is such a certainty of victory? Nay I can tell you a farther word of encouragement every true-hearted Souldier that falls by the sword in this fight, shall not lye dead long, but stand upon his feet again, and be made partaker of the triumph of this Victory."[4]

Johnson's assertive proclamation of final triumph should not mislead us into thinking that he felt deeply confident about himself or about events in old New England. Rather, his rhetoric, often "shrill and bombastic" in its self-assertion, reveals that he shared Bradford's anxiety about New England's future. Beneath the high-pitched voice, we hear the "psychic uncertainty,"[5] the fear that he and the other New England Puritans "were really more banished *from* England than led *to* Canaan."[6] Implicitly Johnson implores the mother country not to abandon her daughter across the seas, and explicitly he calls on the people of New England to reform before God averts His face permanently and chooses another people to lead the world into the millennium.

Nevertheless, though afraid of being abandoned and of being judged to have failed, the New England—the American—self that emerges in *Wonder-Working Providence* has severed sufficiently from its parent figures to have established its own discreet identity, however shaky and uncertain. Ironically, it is Bradford, the Separatist, who finally cannot cut his emotional ties to England, and it is Johnson, the Non-Separatist, who finds his voice and, for better or for worse, makes one of our earliest proclamations of cultural independence. As Edward Gallagher comments, *Wonder-Working Providence,* is "the most important early contribution to the body of writing concerned with our national self-identity."[7]

The distinctly American characteristic of Johnson's History is the fusion of the spiritual with the literal, of New English fact with biblical promise. Anticipating the day when all that was presently invisible would become fully visible and substantial, Johnson sought to establish that *in preparation* New England had already achieved the longed for fusion, if not as fully as it would be in the millennium and the New Jerusalem, then at least in part. Johnson's belief in the possibility of establishing the ultimate society led him to claim that the people of New England need not wait passively for the New Jerusalem to descend; they could actively help "create" it now, for "this is the place where the Lord will create a new Heaven and a new Earth . . . new Churches, and a New Commonwealth together."[8] Using the biblical imagery of the New Jerusalem as the bride of Christ, Johnson envisioned the day when Christ would marry His New England bride, and he encouraged his contemporaries not to let her out of their grasp: "Here is a people not onely praying but fighting . . . that they . . . may enjoy that glorious resurrection-day, the glorious nuptials of the Lamb; when not only the Bridegroom shall appear to his Churches both of Jews and Gentiles (which are his spouse) in a more brighter array than ever heretofore, but also his Bride shall be clothed by him, in the richest garments that ever the Sons of men put on, even the glorious graces of Christ Jesus, in such a glorius splendor to the eyes of man, that they shall see and glorifie the Father of both Bridegroom and Bride."[9]

Throughout *Wonder-Working Providence*, there are many such passages in which New England's special role in the future redemption of the world is asserted. Johnson and his contemporaries claimed that they stood alone, far in advance of all other nations in the world. So strongly did Johnson feel the need to separate from Old England that he gave New England a past as unique as her future. In fact, the sense of separation increased the need for strong and nourishing ancestors. Johnson provided New Englanders with a viable past by creating and maintaining personal bonds with the dead. He found ancestors who had died in New England between 1620 and 1651 and endowed them with the power to lead all of New England to the New Jerusalem. If he could muster an army of extraordinary heroes who had died in New England, Johnson thought that the present and future generations could take heart, for already residing in God's eternal household would be the dead saints who had been translated directly to heaven without going by way of English graveyards. Precisely because they were *New English* these dead ancestors could be held up to the living in New England as models for imitation. To achieve this end, Johnson, like other contemporary historians and preachers, wrote of the dead as having the power to "speak" to the living from beyond the grave.

It is in this context of creating ancestors that we must read the sixty-seven poems about New England's dead that are scattered throughout *Wonder-Working Providence*. As Harrison T. Meserole perceptively comments, poetry was for Johnson "a means of fixing things into permanence."[10] "Let no man be offended," Johnson wrote, "at the Authors rude Verse, penned of purpose to keepe in memory the names of such worthies as Christ made strong for himselfe, in this unwonted work of his," and a little later he again asks the reader not to "be offended that the Author quickens up his own dull affections, in telling how largely the Lord hath bestowed his Graces upon these instruments of his, although sinfull dust and ashes."[11] Johnson's great need for local ancestors and his deep sense of loss over the deaths of many of the first generation ministers and magistrates is evidenced in the following four stanzas, the most moving Johnson wrote in *Wonder-Working Providence*:

> But Lord, why dost by death withdraw thy hand
>   From us, these men and means are sever'd quite;
> Stretch forth thy might, Lord Christ do thou command,
>   Their doubled spirit on those left to light:
> Forth of their graves call ten times ten again,
> That thy dear flocks no damage may sustain.
>
> Can I forget these means that thou has used,
>   To quicken up my drowsie drooping soul?
> Lord I forget, and have the same abused,
>   Which makes me now with grief their deaths condole,
> And kiss thy rod, laid on with bowels tender,
> By death of mine, makes me their death remember.
>
> Lord, stay thy hand, thy Jacobs number's small,
>   Powre out thy wrath on Antichrists proud Thrones;
> Here [hear] thy poor flocks that on thee daily call,
>   Bottle their tears, and pity their sad groans.
> Where shall we go, Lord Christ? we turn to thee,
> Heal our back-slidings forward press shall we.
>
> Not we, but all thy Saints the world throughout
>   Shall on thee wait, thy wonders to behold;
> Thou king of Saints, the Lord in battel stout
>   Increase thy armies many thousand fold.
> Oh Nations all, his anger seek to stay,
> That doth create him armies every day.

For the memorializing of a new army of ancestors, Johnson used two major methods of Protestant figuration; typology and mnemonics.[12] In the case of *Wonder-Working Providence,* Sacvan Bercovitch and Edward Gallagher have demonstrated the central significance of typology to "Johnson's impassioned vision of New England's destiny; . . . clearly the import of that vision lies in the deliberate interrelationship of the immediate narrative with corresponding events in the Old and New Testaments."[13] Two of the most important types in *Wonder-Working Providence* are the Exodus and the Temple. Johnson sees the crossing of the Red Sea and the journey through the wilderness as prefigurations of the Puritans' Atlantic crossing. In Johnson's "characteristic fusion of direct narrative and scriptural allusion, the Puritans both participate in and surpass the miraculous biblical event; they reenact the Israelites' sea passage in a way that points forward

to their larger purposes."[14] Likewise, the New England churches fulfill the proph-
ecy Johnson believed embodied in the Temple of Israel, a prophecy of both the
Apostolic church and the eventual New Jerusalem, the two sacred Christian
communities. In his use of these and many other types, Johnson consistently
emphasizes New England as the place where the literal visible fulfillment will
take place, where the civilizing of the landscape will give evidence of the
transforming power of the Puritans' faith. While Johnson's typology focuses on
the similarities between Israel and New England, between the two societies as
corporate entities, his mnemonics leads us to see how New Englanders looked
to the Old Testament as the storehouse of memories that would ennoble particular
figures with meaning, and so endow people in New England in the 1640's and
50's with a personal past. Clearly what Johnson believed about the house of
memory, about where and how images were recollected, was of major importance
for his art. As we might expect, for Puritan poets, mnemonics must be a means
of making certain that the memory, the image, is indissolubly joined to a his-
torical, literal event or person. For Johnson, this felt necessity to anchor the
present in the biblical past was especially strong, and drew upon his training in
that aspect of rhetoric concerned with memory that he had received as a young
boy in the Canterbury grammar school. In the late sixteenth and early seventeenth
centuries Johnson and his fellow Puritan immigrants were taught to remember
in ways representing the final break with the mnemonics that had existed in
European education since antiquity.

Classical rhetoric and dialectic, as Aristotle distinguished them in the *Organon*,
are similar in their use "of logical means of persuasion" but they differ in that
"dialectic is concerned . . . with the discernment of truth from falsehood, and
with intellectual conviction. It surveys scientific and learned questions. Rhetoric
is concerned with practical questions of policy, with producing conviction in a
real audience, and with emotional effectiveness."[15] In fashioning his arguments
to "produce conviction," the classical orator depended on a quintuple process
consisting of invention, disposition, memory, elocution, and pronunciation. These
five aspects were not considered "abstract parts of an abstract art . . . , but five
activities in which an aspirant was disciplined so that he might become an orator
or public lecturer—the common ideal of all ancient liberal education. . . . As
the training which the normal educated person received, these activities today
would be called simply education, or perhaps general education."[16]
    The general information on all possible subjects that the orator turned to when
he wanted to invent or 'come upon' the arguments for his discourse had been
divided by Aristotle into commonplaces, a commonplace being defined as "a
kind of locale in the imagination . . . where one goes to seek arguments to be
used in proving cases, in persuading an audience, or in teaching. The *topos* was
the seat of the argument or, when transferred to the memory . . . it was something
like a pigeonhole in the mind."[17] When the orator had "informed" his subject,

he would "dispose" it and then commit it to memory, "the firm perception in the soul of things and words." Memory was twofold: natural and artificial, natural being "that which is engrafted in our minds, born simultaneously with thought. The artificial memory is a memory strengthened or confirmed by training." In assisting his artificial memory, a student was trained to use two sets of intellectual tools: *loci* and images. A *locus* was "a place easily grasped by the memory, such as a house," while "images are forms . . . of what we wish to remember." Images are divided further into two kinds, "one for 'things' [*res*] the other for words [*verba*.] That is to say, " 'memory for things' makes images to remind of an argument, a notion, or a 'thing'; but 'memory for words' has to find images to remind of every single word. . . . Things are thus the subject matter of the speech; words are the language in which that subject matter is clothed."[18]

Thus, when the classical orator wanted to imprint his discourse firmly on his soul, he would first build in his imagination a house, a palace, or a church—a *locus* whose layout and features (such as columns, courtyards and fountains) would assist him in recalling the proper succession of points in his arguments.

To choose the aptest images the orator was told to look to the natural world, for, as the anonymous author of the famous rhetorical text *Ad Herennium* wrote:

> Nature herself teaches us what we should do. When we see in everyday life things that are pretty, ordinary, and banal, we generally fail to remember them, because the mind is not being stirred by anything novel or marvellous. But if we see or hear something exceptionally base, dishonourable, unusual, great, unbelievable, or ridiculous, that we are likely to remember for a long time. Accordingly, things immediate to our eye or ear we commonly forget. Incidents of our childhood we often remember best. Nor could this be so for any other reason than that the ordinary things easily slip from the memory while the striking and the novel stay longer in the mind. A sunrise, the sun's course, a sunset, are marvellous to no one because they occur daily. But solar eclipses are a source of wonder because they occur seldom, and indeed are more marvellous than lunar eclipses, because they are more frequent. Thus nature shows that she is not aroused by the common ordinary event, but is moved by a new or striking occurrence. Let art, then, imitate nature.

Adopting the view that the most striking images were the most memorable, the author of *Ad Herennium* advocated using mnemonic devices of "exceptional beauty or singular ugliness; if we dress some of them with crowns or purple cloaks, for example, so that the likeness may be more distinct to us; or if we somehow disfigure them, as by introducing one stained with blood or soiled with mud or smeared with red paint, so that its form is more striking, or by assigning certain comic effects to our images, for that, too will ensure our remembering them more readily. The things we easily remember when they are real we likewise remember without difficulty when they are figments if they have been carefully delineated."[18]

In this rhetoric, the most striking images could be accepted precisely because the orator used them as a means to remember. He could use *"testes"* to recall the point in his oration when he must speak of *testi*monies. Of course, the unconscious connections among "testes" and "testimonies" did exist, but they could not be explicitly acknowledged if they were to be acceptable to the orator's audience. In this way, classical education allowed a young man an extraordinary psychological latitude. Whatever his earliest childhood memories might be, he could, through the use of places and images, resurrect them in his imagination. Embodied as men and women—even as gods and goddesses—his own deepest fears and joys could find a socially acceptable expression. And as he moved through his oration, his living voice renewed his relationship to his childhood and to bygone generations, affirming both his reliance on the dead and his separation from them. To a large extent, this rhetoric with its striking imagery rested on the assumption that the most effective imagery was the language of greatest trauma, and the language farthest removed from ordinary discourse. The permission to use these figures rested in cultural conventions whose existence required a great deal of trust between orator and audience. If the orator guided his audience to a new perception or stirred them to new action, it must be assumed that he did so in the name of virtue. By assigning a significant role to the use of arbitrary mnemonic devices, the Aristotelian orator acknowedged that, to some extent at least, his relationship to the people of the past lay beyond his conscious control. Stored in his memory were voices of terror and jubilation that would speak to and through him.

At the end of the fifteenth century, certain of the conventions shared by orator and audience began to break down. Instead of seeing testes, for example, as a mnemonic device for recalling testimony, men began to perceive the literal facts. The reasons for this shift are still not entirely clear, but in addition to the causes mentioned by Wilbur A. Howell—the rise of inductive science, the decline of the aristocracy, and the Protestant Reformation[19]—Walter Ong has shown that *memoria* disappeared from the training in classical rhetoric in part because of the spread of printed books as repositories of knowledge. Previous generations had relied heavily (though not exclusively) on an imagery designed to assist the voice and the ear in the transmission of knowledge. In the sixteenth century the central interaction came to be between reader and printed page rather than between listener and orator. And, as books became the storehouses of the past, the commonplaces that had been the means of remembering began to be perceived as containers that could be searched or "flipped through" for the speaker's or writer's arguments. In oratory these changes were soon apparent. The extreme imagery of *memoria*, often highly sensational, frequently drawn from the material of childhood fantasy, began to disappear. The orator continued to be trained in rhetoric, but in debate the laurels of victory would no longer go to the orator who could best manipulate the arbitrary, mnenomic devices but to the one who could demonstrate the plain fact of the matter.

The origin of a different instruction in memory in English grammar schools can be seen in Erasmus's writings which, as early as 1512, through his English friends, especially John Colet, the founder and dean of St. Paul's, were to influence English secondary education profoundly. Erasmus followed tradition when he wrote that "the storehouse of our reading . . . is aided by 'places' and 'images,' " but he suggests the changes to come when he states that "the best memory is based on three things above all: understanding, system, and care. For memory largely consists in having thoroughly understood something. The system sees to it that we can recall by an act of memory what we have once forgotten." Erasmus advocated that things "difficult to remember" such as "place-names in geography . . . , grammatical figures, genealogies . . . , aphorisms, proverbs" be written "on posters, engraven on rings or drinking cups," painted on doors and walls "or even in the glass of a window so that what may aid learning is constantly before the eye."[20] By modern standards, the world of memory that Erasmus constructed around the child was wonderfully rich in mnemonic devices, but the crucial difference from the classical teachings about *memoria* lay in Erasmus's use of actual visual reminders. Erasmus's emphasis constituted a shift away from reliance on pigeonholes inside the mind filled with whatever images of extraordinary ugliness or extraordinary beauty would prove useful to the orator as he attempted to recall the points he wanted to make.

Not only churchmen but English intellectuals in general felt the tension between the old and the new views of *memoria*. For example, Thomas Wilson's, *The Arte of Rhetorique*, published in 1553, preserved the five-fold structure of classical rhetoric with *memoria* in its traditional place between elocution and pronunciation, and instructed law students in the use of "places" and "images." Yet Wilson clearly felt very uncomfortable about advocating the continued use of the artificial memory. "This knowledge [of *memoria*]," he notes, "is not to be neglected, no though we do contemne it, yet we have the use of it. . . . There be some (emong whom is Erasmus) which like not the arte of Memorie, but say it rather hindereth, than helpeth a mans wit. And yet Tullie [Cicero] the greatest Oratour among the Romaynes, did wel alowe it and proved it good by a naturall reason." Wilson, a "militant Protestant" who had grown up in England before the Reformation, on the one hand, "condemned" a practice that he saw as inextricably linked to the medieval "remembrance of the saints." On the other hand, although he felt that God had forbidden the worship of images, he nevertheless longed for the power of the old pictures of the saints that had served so "gayly well."[21] For Wilson and other English poets and rhetoricians, the dilemma was resolved by finding a way to appropriate memories that would be acceptable to God and yet stirring of the affections. They sought a use of remembrance that would serve as "gayly well" as the "pictures" of old had served "idolators."

The means to such a resolution took a generation to develop, and when it did, it strongly reflected the views that Continental reformers, especially Peter Ramus, had worked out in the 1530s, 40s, and 50s in German and French universities. The transformation that the concept of memory underwent in England in the last decade of the sixteenth century can be traced to Ramus's view of the training of memory. Ramus himself wrote that he decided to attack the Aristotelean rhetoric and logic that he found at the University of Paris because he felt the context of trust between teacher and student had broken down. When at the age of twenty Ramus decided to seek "to learn to what end I could as a consequence, apply the knowledge I had acquired with so much toil and pain," he realized to his "stupefaction" and "grief" that he had learned nothing *useful* at all.[22] Ramus's first point of attack on classical rhetoric, as Walter Ong has demonstrated, came in his master's thesis, and it was directed at the arbitrariness of *memoria*. According to Ong, the title of Ramus's thesis should be translated to mean "*all the things that Aristotle had said are inconsistent because they are poorly systematized and can be called to mind only by the use of arbitrary mnemonic devices.*"[23]

In his search for a reliable past, Ramus decided to replace arbitrary Aristoteleans with Platonic idealists and Apostolic Christians: Platonists because they had, Ramus believed, direct access to divine—and invisible—reality; primitive Christians because their church served as the literal, historical image of the perfect and original fellowship. His search for *true* ancestors (rather than idols or pictures of saints) led Ramus to claim Plato as dearer than his own father and reflected his views on the Apostolic Church. Thus, Ramus wrote in a letter to the Cardinal of Lorraine that having surveyed the fifteen hundred years since the birth of Christ he had concluded that the "first was truely the 'golden age' and that in proportion as it has been departed from, all ages which have followed more vicious and corrupt. Hence having to choose between these different ages of Christianity, I attached myself to 'the golden age,' "[24] when pure Christians were alive. Elsewhere Ramus stated that he was working to bring back the "ancient light," and he exhorted his readers that to "speak the words of the Holy Scriptures, let us use the language of the Holy Spirit. For that is the truest doctor of wisdom and the most renowned orator of eloquence, and it uses words that can be understood by us—clear, significant, and suitable. For that will be to divide the truth rightly. Then let us not supplant divine wisdom and language with sophisms and folly."[25]

This view of a golden and secure past filled with pure and trustworthy ancestors who provided a reliable standard for later generations was first introduced to Cambridge in the spring of 1576 by Gabriel Harvey in a series of lectures, entitled *Ciceronianus* and delivered at Trinity Hall. It was Harvey who in 1578 would teach William Kempe, then a freshman, that *memoria* could be deleted from instruction in rhetoric, a position that Kempe adopted when he came to write *The Education of Children* a decade later. And, as T. W. Baldwin has stated, Kempe's book best exemplified the instruction in rhetoric in the last decade of the sixteenth century, the very years when as young boys the first generation of the future New England Puritans began school.[26] In *Ciceronianus*, Harvey charged that most teachers of rhetoric have been miserable failures because they have failed to show their students the intimate link between oratory and life. "Illustrious university professors" have searched "innumerable domiciles of argument"—the places of invention—and have come up with examples of rhetorical devices that are useless for the conduct of life; instead of helping their students, they have sought only to enhance their own reputations: "I name no names; but among so many interpreters of Cicero's orations How many are there to be found, outside of a very few who have a wealth of abundant talent and a glorious reputation for learning, from whom you could expect anything but that hackneyed tune of theirs: 'This is a notable repetition; this is an elegant agnomination; this is an appropriate transfer. . . .'" However, Harvey continued, when "these excellent rhetors" have to explain "the subject matter itself, a task which demands the proverbial 'marrow of persuasion' . . .you will find them dumber than the very fish." They have no desire to learn and teach about family, customs, laws, or to elucidate "the whole sweep of civilization." They have focused entirely on Cicero as an elegant stylist and have ignored the human being whom Harvey apostrophized as the "most divine" of orators. Confessing to his audiences of Cambridge freshmen (aged twelve to sixteen) that he himself had once "valued words more than content, language more than thought," and had preferred to be in "the company of Ciceronians rather than in that of the saints," Harvey told them that he became converted to the teachings of Peter Ramus, and so presumably joined the company of saints! In Harvey's extravagant praise we catch some of the tremendous excitement Ramus created when he seemingly promised to lead men through the union of image and reality to a "knot of friendship" with the dead. Again, in the manner of the Ciceronian orator, Harvey spoke as if he were addressing Ramus face to face.

By so marrying the heart and the tongue, Ramus had enabled Harvey to discover suddenly not only Cicero the accomplished orator but also the Roman citizen, the "possessor of a soul overflowing with the noblest virtues," an ancient patriarch whom Harvey could claim as his spiritual ancestor, as a saint worthy of imitation. Having thus told his students how he had arrived in "the ancient harbor of eloquent wisdom, Harvey exhorted them to study their rhetoric by Ramist principles, for only Ramus enabled men to move through the veil of words and get acquainted directly with the living orator.[27]

Kempe's *The Education of Children* (1588) completed the process that had begun almost a century earlier. In his preface Kempe began by asserting that even though "many learned men have alreadie bestowed verie exquisit and commendable labours" on the teaching of rhetoric, he had nevertheless found yet another manual "most necessarie to be urged in this secure and licentious generation." Using the metaphor of a house, Kempe wrote that he had "endevoured not only to fill up the emptie roome with such members as wanted, and to separate that which seemed superfluous; but also to new cast the whole in another mould, and to bring it to another forme, breefe, and easie: I suppose that it will seeme altogether a strange and new Booke." The chief "strange" and "new" aspect of Kempe's book lay in the omission of *memoria*, a final break with the past.

And yet, having dropped *memoria*, Kempe, as if he wanted not to leave his readers without memories, created a vast gallery of past schoolmasters who would serve as ancestors for teachers and pupils. Kempe added dozens of very brief "holie and ancient Histories" as a "necessarie exhortation for all other sort of people, setting foorth" as Ramus and Harvey had done in their writings, "the dignitie and utilitie of the matter . . . , with such plaine and sensible reasons, as may teach the unlearned with some delight, and not be tedious to those that are learned. Agayne, to satisfye in some part the expectation of the learned, we have handled the method more methodically. . . ." To make sure that these ancient patriarchs were securely anchored in a reliable past—and so could be trusted—Kempe traced their spiritual genealogy all the way back to the moment before which there was no past, to the creation of the world, or, rather, to the creation of Adam before whom there was only the eternal rock of ages, God, who was without image and without memory. Kempe thought that "dignity and utility" would be achieved by imitating the literal lives of these ancient heroes, and if such imitation was powerful enough to bring the dead to life in the soul of a sixteenth-century English child, what then the need for ram's testicles on fourth fingers?[28]

Of course such changes in rhetoric and memory cannot be dissociated from the broad and equally radical transformations that the early reformers wrought in every aspect of religious life. Changes in the interpretations of the exemplary lives of Old Testament figures during the Reformation were consonant with the emphasis placed on the study of Greek and Roman patriarchs by Ramus and his followers. In, for example, Erasmus's and Luther's early statements on the need for changing medieval interpretations of the Old Testament types, we find that the building of trust underlay their insistence on typology as the paramount figural mode. Luther spoke harshly of the "idle and unlearned Monks and the Schooledoctors" whose heavy allegorizing of Scripture had "rent the Scripture into so many and divers senses that seely poore consciences could receave no certaine doctrine of anything."[29] Similarly for Erasmus, Christian practices generally had dissipated into "easy obligations" that had "done great harm to Christian piety, even though it may be that they were first introduced as a result of pious fervor. Later on they gradually increased, and extended into myriad of distinctions . . . , I do not know what picture of Christ you could find there beyond certain cold and Judaic rites. In the practice of these they find much self-satisfaction, and by these they judge and condemn others. How much more consonant with Christ's teaching it would be to regard the entire Christian world as a single household, a single monastery as it were, and to . . . consider not where one lives but how one lives."[30] In view of Erasmus's and Luther's condemnation of Catholic observances as "cold and Judaic" we might, at first, have expected that they and other reformers would have rejected the Old Testament types as irrelevant to Christians, but the interrelationshp of the Old and New Testaments was too deeply lodged in the Western imagination to have been so easily erased. Rather than rejecting the Old Testament images, Protestants responded by *including* the Judaic patriarchs and matriarchs as early, though rudimentary, members of Christ's "single household" which had existed from the moment when God first spoke Adam and Eve into being.

This injection of Christ's presence into the most distant past is the single most important feature of Luther's reformulation of the *quadriga*. Having been "shamefulley seduced under the papacy," Luther wrote, "we knew nothing else, but that Christ had been a wrathful judge, whose displeasure we might have reconciled with our good works and with our holiness, and whose pardon we might have obtained through the merits and intercessions of the saints."[31] Throughout his works, Luther sought to change this picture of Christ and God as wrathful judges to that of loving fathers. This view, and the emotional security that flowed from it, depended on the believer's ability to re-envision the ancient images: "The ceremonies were intended to be understood as pictures or symbols, to remind those people of the promise of Christ until He came to establish the right service of worship. . . . This does not consist in external conduct or in lifeless types; instead, it lives in the heart and produces a genuinely new being."[32] In turn, to see Christ's presence in the types meant that the Christian believer, who though he lived thousands of years after the deaths of the biblical patriarchs and matriarchs, could establish loving bonds—covenants—as nourishing, immediate, and secure as those he had made with Christ. He had been given memories that, anchored in Christ, were, Luther felt, beyond human manipulation.

Such a sense of memories as covenants with ancestors characterized the thinking of the first generation of New England Puritans. Thus, in his farewell sermon, "God's Promise to his Plantations," John Cotton, vicar at St. Botolph's in Boston, Lincolnshire, assured John Winthrop's company, among them Edward Johnson, that with them into the wilderness went God's promises to David of a house, a throne, and a kingdom to be established forever. And in "A Modell of Christian Charity," Winthrop told his fellow passengers on the *Arbella* that they who had never been to America nevertheless were going there to possess the land that God had given their fathers to possess. For Cotton and Winthrop, as for other Protestants, these promises were to be understood literally, in the sense that the Puritans belonged to a single household of David and the other patriarchs, and that the events prophesied would actually take place in the history of redemption.

The basic tone of these farewell sermons is one of confidence. As God's chosen, the Puritans felt themselves secure in their adoption as God's children. The very same love He had given to David, He had given to the Puritans thousands of years later. God's "word of promise," Cotton said, would not fail them "till heaven and earth be no more."[33] This assurance of their adoption made the Puritans confident that they could cope with loss of family, friends, and country. "We are well weaned from the delicate milk of our mother country," John Robinson wrote to Edwin Sandys in 1617, "and inured to the difficulties of a strange and hard land, which yet in a great part we have by patience overcome"[34] The Puritans' confidence in their past was strengthened by their sense of having established a profound kinship with the men and women to whom God had given the biblical promises. Abraham, Sarah, Isaac, Rebecca, Moses, David, Deborah, St. Paul, and all the other great heroes and heroines came to stand as spiritual ancestors replacing those of mere flesh and blood. In fact, memories of this ancient "Company of Ages"[35] seemed more sustaining than those of grandparents or great grandparents; the regeneration that the biblical patriarchs and matriarchs had experienced was seen as identical to the Puritans' own. The personal types were not merely figures of rhetoric but historical realities. Behind the image of Abraham resided an actual person who, when his adoption was reenacted by others in later ages, was resurrected with the force of a living presence.

Yet, as the farewell sermons evince, for all their confidence in the security of their spiritual past, the Puritans also suffered from considerable anxiety about the possibility that God might withdraw His promises from them unless they were very careful to adhere strictly to his commandments and to live for the mutual benefit of all within the covenant. The choice they faced in going to America was, as it had been for Israel about to cross into Canaan, all or nothing. Just as the Puritans had to give up all other attachments to be divinely adopted, so Winthrop said, God had now set before them life *or* death, blessing *or* curse, and Cotton ended "God's Promise" with a warning, though less stark than Winthrop's, that if the departing Puritans whose "Ancestors were of a noble divine spirit," did not bring up their children right God would surely "plucke [them] up."[36]

Seen in the larger perspective of the development of the relationships among memory, typology, and poetry since the Reformation, Johnson's poems in *Wonder-Working Providence* are significant because they show us that a century after Luther, the principle of finding Christ's presence in biblical realities—the types—had now been extended to make even contemporary, historical presences into prophetic, type-like figures. Johnson was the first historian and poet in New England who sought to create a past by converting the dead among the first generation Puritans into memories that could support the living generations on their march to the New Jerusalem. As the first sustained example of American memory-making by European immigrants, *Wonder-Working Providence* holds a special place in the history of America's literary imagination.

Of the sixty-seven poems in *Wonder-Working Providence*, three were not memories. The first of these three was a celebration of Matthew Craddock, an English merchant who was instrumental in securing the charter for New England, but since he did not immigrate to Massachusetts, Johnson wrote his epitaph "by the way of thankfulnesse" and did not convert Craddock's life into a remembrance of a New England saint. Of the remaining three poems, one was on the founding of Harvard College; one was a "sad lament" intended "to stir us up to mourn for all our miscarriages much the more";[37] and one was the final poem celebrating the imminent marriage of Christ and His Churches. The distinction Johnson drew between the Craddock poem and the rest of the poetry in *Wonder-Working Providence* revealed his effort to make only those heroes who actually settled in New England into ancestors serving the generations awaiting Christ's Second Coming.[38] Johnson's chief means of stirring up the affections was the creation of a persona whose voice is simultaneously that of the dead ancestors, of the eternal Christ, and of the living poet. This multi-voiced persona often strikes the reader as hopelessly confused. Johnson seems not to have known or cared enough about the craft of poetry to have made clear who is saying what in his memory poems. Yet the reader's confusion may well have been the effect that Johnson deliberately set out to create. As Ursula Brumm has pointed out, Johnson merges past, present, and future into an eternal now in order to make the reader experience Christ's eternal decrees as present events: "for the modern secular historian, history is a dimension which is reached by turning back; its time is past time; its tense the preterit. For the Puritan historian, who is also a theological thinker, history is a territory between the present and the eternal truth of God's word. It is both a memorial of past events and a fulfillment of God's providence. . . . The most striking 'awkwardness' in the *Wonder-Working Providence* is its unusual time structure; the preterit is not the dominating tense as it customarily is in historical writings. . . . [The] use of the present tense far surpasses the allowances which in historical texts have been made for the so-called 'historic present,' and much of it is of a different kind."[39] *Wonder-Working Providence* opened in the past tense: "When New England began to decline in Religion, like lukewarm Laodicea, and instead of purging out Popery, a farther compliance was sought not only in vain Idolatrous Ceremonies . . .",[40] but Johnson soon shifted to the present tense, and in the second paragraph he had the heralds proclaim Christ's invitation in the present tense: "Therefore in the yeere 1628, he stirres up his servants as the Heralds of a King to make this proclamation for Voluntiers, as followeth. *'Oh yes! oh yes! oh yes! All you the people of Christ that are here Oppressed, Imprisoned and scurrilously derided, gather yourselves together. . . .'* " As Brumm comments, "the date of 1628 was more than twenty years in the past when Johnson wrote this account, but Christ's proclamation is ever present. . . . Thus the use of the present tense is a signal to the reader that he is going to hear something of vital importance to him. Intense participation in the events reported and the conviction that they are of eternal significance induced Johnson again and again to apply the present tense."[41]

This deliberate attempt to create the experience of eternity is also evident in Johnson's use of pronouns. In almost all the poems, the herald's voice simultaneously addresses the dead ancestor, the eternal Christ, and the living reader as "thee," "thou," or "thy." A simple example of this technique can be seen in the poem on "The Reverend Mr. Higginson, first Pastor of the Church of Christ at Salem in New England" (in Meserole, *Poetry*). In line three, "thee" refers both to Higginson and to the reader; it is not only Higginson but also the reader whose "toile to love" is being stirred up. And in line four, "him" refers to Christ and to Higginson; both do the feeding of the flocks in the wilderness.

Much more complex is Johnson's "A few lines in remembrance of Thomas Hooker" (in Meserole, *Poetry*). The voice calling on Hooker may be seen as simultaneously Christ's and the herald's, and "native soil" can refer to England or, if the reader were aware that Hooker had died in 1647, to the grave. Indeed, if the reader did not know that Hooker had already died, he might assume that Hooker was still alive in England and was being called on to emigrate. Having been summoned from England/the grave to New England/the New Jerusalem, Hooker addresses Christ as "thou." Since "thou" here seems to refer to Christ/ the herald, the subsequent "thy," "Thy Rhetorick," and "Thy Golden Tongue" also are experienced as referring to Christ. However, the "thou" in line seven makes it impossible for the reader to continue identifying only Christ with "thy" and "thou." Clearly, "thou sorry worme" refers not to Christ but to Hooker and possibly to the reader. At this point, both Hooker and the reader begin to be identified with the earlier "thou," Christ. The final effect is an experience of Christ, Hooker, the herald (Johnson), and the reader as one.

Having scattered some sixty poems throughout *Wonder-Working Providence,* Johnson pulled them all together and organized them into a coherent past, an army of memories ready to lend their strength to the great battles confronting New England in its world-wide mission. When Johnson died in 1672, it was not immediately evident that the "glorious nuptials of the Lamb" he so desperately longed for had been consummated in New England.

In *Wonder-Working Providence*, Johnson stressed New England's millennial role. Yet his History is also an intensely personal document. Beneath the fierce assertions of the solidity of eternity, we hear Johnson's personal grief over the loss of so many of the men he considered his spiritual fathers (the women, in the figure of the New Jerusalem, had not abandoned him yet), and his fear that their deaths signified God's displeasure with him, Edward Johnson. In its grief, fear, and longing, *Wonder-Working Providence* is one of many similar American stories.

Also, from the vantage point of the twentieth century, we can see that Johnson's conversion of literal facts into memories was seminal in another sense as well, for it would be but a matter of time before facts other than historical would be seen as the storehouse of memory. When figures like Edwards, Whitman, Emerson, Thoreau declared *their* independence from the Old World, they turned to nature to find their American ancestors. Almost two centuries after Johnson wrote *Wonder-Working Providence*, Emerson would see the prophetic memory of the New Jerusalem, Christ's bride, in the starlit sky over New England.

NOTES

1. William Bradford, *Of Plymouth Plantation*, ed. Samuel Eliot Morison (New York, 1952), p. 3.

2. Ibid., p. 351.

3. Johnson's *Wonder-Working Providence*, 1628–51, ed. by J. Franklin Jameson, New York, 1910 (Original Narratives of Early American History, vol. XIV).

4. Ibid., p. 271.

5. Bercovitch, *Puritan Origins*, p. 103.

6. Cecilia Tichi, *New World, New Earth* (New Haven and London: Yale Univ. Press, 1979), p. 42.

7. Edward Gallagher, "An Overview of Edward Johnson's *Wonder-Working Providence*," *EAL* 6 (1971), 47–48.

8. Johnson, *Wonder-Working Providence*, p. 25.

9. Ibid., pp. 271–72.

10. Meserole, p. 148.

11. Johnson, *Wonder-Working Providence*, p. 104.

12. See Frances Yates, *The Art of Memory* (London, 1966) and Walter J. Ong, *Ramus, Method and the Decay of Dialogue* (Cambridge, Mass.: Harvard Univ. Press, 1954). See also Wilbur S. Howell, *Logic and Rhetoric in England, 1500–1700* (Princeton: Princeton Univ. Press, 1956); Miller, *Mind*; Joan Marie Lechner, *Renaissance Concepts of the Commonplaces* (New York, 1962).

13. Bercovitch, "The Historiography of Johnson's *Wonder-Working Providence*," *Essex Historical Institute Collections*, civ (1968), 140.

14. Ibid., p. 147.

15. Lechner, *Commonplaces*, p. 13.

16. Ong, *Ramus*, p. 275.

17. Lechner, *Commonplaces*, pp. 1–2.

18. [Cicero], *Ad Herennium*, trans. Harry Caplan, Loeb Classical Library (Cambridge, Mass.: Harvard Univ. Press, 1954), pp. 219–21.

19. Howell, *Logic and Rhetoric*, pp. 10–11.

20. Desiderius Erasmus, *Collected Works*, edited by Craig R. Thompson, 6 vols. (Toronto: Univ. of Toronto Press, 1974–81), 24:671.

21. Thomas Wilson, *The Arte of Rhetorique* (London, 1553), p. 243. In 1538 John Sturm wrote to Roger Ascham that the third book in *Ad Herennium* should "be omitted, for the precepts of dialectic which the boys are memorizing will help more than these

rules." T. W. Baldwin, *William Shakespere's Small Latine and Lesse Greeke*, 2 vols. (Urbana: Univ. of Illinois Press, 1944), 1:289–90.

22. Pierre de la Rameé, *La Remonstrance . . . Faite au Conseil Prive* (Paris, 1567, p. 24, quoted in Frank P. Graves, *Peter Ramus and the Educational Reformation of the Sixteenth Century* (New York, 1912), pp. 21–22.

23. Ong, *Ramus*, pp. 46–47.

24. Pierre de la Rameé, *Collactaneae, Praefactiones, Epistolae, Orationes* (Paris, 1577), p. 257, quoted in Graves, *Ramus*, p. 74.

25. Pierre de la Rameé, *Commentariorum de Religione Christiana Libri Quattor* (Frankfurt, 1577), 1: preface, 1: 4:18, 343, quoted in Graves, *Ramus*, pp. 186–87.

26. Baldwin, *Shakespere*, 1:437.

27. Gabriel Harvey, *Ciceronianus*, ed. and trans. by Harold S. Wilson and Clarence A. Forbes, University of Nebraska Studies, Studies in the Humanities, No. 4 (Lincoln: Univ. of Nebraska Press, 1954), p. 87.

28. William Kempe, *The Education of Children* (London, 1588), "To the Gentle Reader," A3.

29. Martin Luther, *A Commentarie . . . Upon . . . Galatians*, fol. 210v, quoted in Lewalski *Poetics*, p. 117.

30. Erasmus, *Works*, 2:296–97.

31. Luther, *A very excellent and sweete exposition upon the two and twenty Psalms*, tr. Myles Coverdale (Cambridge: Cambridge Univ. Press, 1846), pp. 291–92.

32. Luther, *Works*, 55 vols. (St. Louis, 1955–75), 13:293–94.

33. John Cotton, "God's Promise to his Plantations" (London, 1630), reprinted in *Old South Leaflets*, No. 53 (Boston, 1894–96), p. 15.

34. Bradford, *Of Plymouth Plantation*, p. 33.

35. John Cotton, *A Practicall Commentary or an Exposition with Observations, Reasons, and Uses Upon the First Epistle Generall of John* (London, 1656), p. 84.

36. Cotton, "Promise," p. 14.

37. Johnson, *Wonder-Working Providence*, p. 257.

38. It is tantalizingly possible that Johnson wrote his poems as fulfillments of the prophecies contained in the following passage from Canticles 3:7, 8: "Behold his bed, which is Solomon's; threescore valiant men *are* about it, of the valiant of Israel. They all hold swords, being expert in war: every man hath his sword upon his thigh because of fear in the night."

39. "Edward Johnson's *Wonder-Working Providence* and the Puritan Concept of History," *Jahrbuch für Amerikastudien*, xiv (1969), 140–51.

40. Johnson, *Wonder-Working Providence*, p. 23.

41. Ibid., pp. 47–48.

12 "MUTUALL SWEET CONTENT": THE LOVE POETRY OF JOHN SAFFIN

KATHRYN ZABELLE DEROUNIAN

Scholarship on John Saffin (1626–1710), merchant, lawyer, judge, and poet, has advanced unevenly. In the early twentieth century, Esther Carpenter donated the notebook of her ancestor John Saffin to the Rhode Island Historical Society, where the manuscript remains.[1] In 1928, Caroline Hazard published a facsimile of Saffin's commonplace book.[2] Following Hazard's work was a lull until 1943, when Harold S. Jantz discussed Saffin's poetry in "The First Century of New England Verse." Once again, virtual silence followed until Alyce E. Sands' 1965 dissertation presented plentiful information on Saffin's career and considered his poetry in some detail. Sands' dissertation ensured Saffin's rightful place in both leading anthologies of early American poetry: Meserole's and Silverman's. Such desultory recognition is surprising, since among seventeenth-century New England poets Saffin ranks seventh or eighth in amount written. Yet, as Sands comments,

> Quantity alone does not make Saffin a significant poet. More pertinent to his poetic stature is his wide range of types of poems and subjects for poems. . . . Like so many others, Saffin wrote elegies, memorials, dedications, anagrams and acrostics, and philosophical poems. Unlike the others, with very few exceptions, he wrote love lyrics, valentines, Characters, satires, and perhaps the most substantial body of occasional or society verse that we have from that period. He was, then, both in and apart from the mainstream of seventeenth-century American poetry.[3]

Nowhere is Saffin's distinctive contribution furthest from mainstream Puritan literature than in his love poetry. Although no tradition of Puritan love poetry exists, Saffin was not, of course, the only Puritan to write love poems. A glance at Meserole's anthology reveals love poems by Anne Bradstreet (among her finest work); "[Go then, my Dove, but now no longer mine]," an elegiac love poem by Cotton Mather; "The Songe," a rather bawdy celebration of "Hymens joyes," by Thomas Morton; "A Love Letter to Elizabeth Thatcher," by Thomas Thatcher; "Nuptial Song" by Henricus Selyns; and snatches of anonymous almanac verse. However, this selection is uneven, and only Bradstreet is represented by more than one love poem. Sands emphasizes the value of Saffin's love poetry: ". . . in the extant manuscripts of the century, love poems are rare; thus, Saffin's group of seven love lyrics, including three that are elegiac, must be considered a significant addition to this small body of love poetry."[4]

Saffin was aware of his particular—and unusual—interest in love poetry, as the *Notebook's* prefatory comment shows:

> In this Manuscript is promiseously set down an Epitomy of various Readings of the Author on Divers Subjects as Divinity, Law, History, Arts and Sciences, some of them Poeticall fancies of his own written in his youth (as well as Elder years) which he found Scattered here and there, in loose papers; and as a Diversion at Leasure put them as they came to hand into this mixt medly Some of them Saytericall, against provd perversd damnded men; thô the most of them are rather Amorous, or Encomicastick lines which were more agreeable to his Genious, then the other as may appear by the Number of them &c. [*NB*: 1–2][5]

Actually, it is untrue that most of his poetry is "Amorous" (though most is certainly "Encomicastick" in one way or another). But because such content was indeed "more agreeable to his Genious," it is true that his best work lies here.

Saffin's interest in the subject of love includes quotations culled from various sources as well as his own poetry, work "which he sometimes did write: sometimes Reherse" (*NB*: 1). Throughout the commonplace book, he scatters quotations on love and marriage like Bolton's definition of marriage, "Marriage is rather a Felloship of Dearest Amity, then disordered Love meerly carnall which is as Different from Amity as the burning sick heat of a ffeaver is from the Naturall kindly heat of A Healthfull Body" (*NB*: 38). The metaphor comparing carnal and amorous love respectively to a fever and to natural body temperature is important because it suggests Saffin's emphasis on the physical side of marriage. It also, incidentally, recalls lines from another New England love poem: Anne Bradstreet's revealing pun when writing to her husband of their children, "those fruits which through thy heat I bore" ("A Letter to Her Husband, Absent upon Publick Employment," l.14).

Later, Saffin enters more "Sundry Readings Epitomiz'd" connected with love:

> Love is a prevailent Affection and kindness is the greatest Endeerment of Love.
> What can work upon an ingenious Spirit more than the Sense of kindness. And what more Naturall then that one flame should produce and kindle another
> Love is the Spring of Action and imployes all the factualltys in the Service of the person Beloved.
> Love that is Seated in the Will, all the actions that proceed from it are out of Choice and purely voluentary. [*NB*: 59]

These extracts show Saffin's preoccupation with definitions and assessments of love, especially human love.

Some pages further, he copies "BRIEF COLLECTIONS OUT OF ROBERT BOYLE'S SERAFFICK SERAPHICK LOVE TO HIS FRIENDS." This passage, which examines the relationship between secular and religious love, begins, "To love even with some Passionateness the person you would Marry, is not onely allowable but Expedient, being not allmost but altogether Necessary to the duty of fixing your Affection where you once Ingaged your ffaith." As the extract proceeds, it becomes clear that Boyle endorses a Platonic concept of love in which pursuit of and devotion to a woman mirror "a Chase of perfect Beauties." To show his agreement, Saffin includes other passages from Boyle, one of which describes female fickleness (*NB*: 67–70).

Extending the extracts from Boyle, Saffin paraphrases Dr. Goodwin on the mutuality of love between man and wife (*NB*: 72–73), a theme Saffin returns to in the love poetry on his beloved first wife, Martha. In the sections from Goodwin, the word "mutual" occurs seven times to emphasize marital unity. Quoting from Sidney's *Arcadia* toward the end of the Notebook, Saffin includes an epigram on love which well applies, once more, to his relationship with Martha, "Love is that which no likeness can make one, no Commandment Desolve, no fouleness Defile nor no Death finish," and quotes two other epigrams on love (*NB*: 150; 155–56). These scattered but consistent references to love complement his treatment of the subject in his own poetry.

Seven of Saffin's verses, as well as two anagrams, can be considered love poems to his first wife: "[Sweetly (my Dearest) I left thee asleep]"; "[Sayle gentle Pinnace Zepherus doth not faile]"; *"A Dialogue between John and Martha or Exonus and Plimothenia"*; "A LETTER TO HIS DEAR MARTHA 1660: *Joy of My Life*" (*NB*: 171–87); the two anagrams (*NB*: 11) and two epitaphs on Martha, *"An Epitaph on his truly loveing and Dearly beloved Wife . . ."* and "ANOTHER ON HIS DEAR MARTHA" (*NB*: 20–21); and *"Revived Elegiac Lamentation . . ."* (*NB*: 83–85).

Internal and external evidence provides an approximate chronology. "Sweetly (my Dearest)" is dated 1654 in a marginal note of Saffin's and was written four years before he and Martha married. From internal evidence, "A Dialogue between John and Martha" was also composed before they wed, and like the previous poem it stresses their separation. A kind of companion piece to "Sweetly (my Dearest)," "Sayle gentle Pinnace" has by its side Saffin's marginal comment "To her comeing home" and was written on one of his early trading voyages in Virginia, perhaps, as tradition has it, in 1657 to 1658 when he returned to marry Martha. "A LETTER TO HIS DEAR MARTHA 1660" obviously poses no problems of dating. Written two years after their marriage, it reflects the Saffins' contentedness and affection. From here a gap exists until the appearance of two anagrams and two love-poem epitaphs composed in 1678, when Martha died of smallpox. The last love poem is the exquisite "Revived Elegiac Lamentation":

above it, Saffin wrote "BRISTOL THE 2^D OF FEBRUARY 1703/4," which corroborates internal evidence concerning date, "But ah! alas! She's gone and I alone / These five & Twenty years left to bemone / my unrepaired Loss in Her since gone" (ll. 50–52) (*NB*: 85). Indeed, that date marked the twenty-fifth anniversary of Martha's death.

"Sweetly (my Dearest)" (in Meserole, *Poetry*) is a forty-four line love poem written mainly in heroic couplets. Its particular strengths are its sense of dramatic occasion, its line of argument, and its genuine emotional force. Saffin convincingly recreates a situation in which he has to leave Martha, who is asleep. Torn between not wishing to wake her, but wanting to say farewell, he compromises by softly kissing her: "Thus in sad Silence I alone and mute, / My lips bad thee farewell, with a Salute. / And so went from thee; turning back againe / I thought one kiss to little then Stole twaine / And then another. . ." (ll. 17–21). He then shifts from sadness to resigned content, persuading both Martha (and himself) to be patient until they can consummate their love. Saffin manages to convey the drama and tension of the situation by contrasting a lyrical tone at the beginning with a more rational tone at the end. In addition, the halting movement of the opening lines suggests his own hesitant, unwilling departure. However, in the final couplet (which is iambic tetrameter, not pentameter), Saffin reverts to a more tender tone, "Your Ever loveing friend whilest Hee / Desolved is: or Cease to bee. / J.S."

Saffin's argument clearly arises from the dramatic situation and falls into five divisions: the decision whether to wake Martha, the compromise to kiss but not speak, the request that she be "Chearfull quiet and at Rest" during his absence, the reassurance that reconciliation will follow separation, and the final tender farewell. However, the poet moves smoothly to each point and produces a unified work. Finally, this love poem succeeds because of its emotional force. The dramatic situation and the lover's reaction to it display his qualities of patience, concern, consideration, affection, and devotion. In part, he intensifies his sadness by repeating the word "farewell," as in these lines: "Yet loath to Rob the of thy present Ease, / or rather senceless payn: farewell thought I, / My Joy my Deare in whom I live or Dye / Farewell Content, farewell fare Beauty's light / And the most pleasing Object of my Sight. . ." (ll. 10–14). Despite the poem's conventional diction, the writer's honesty and emotion prevail as much now as three hundred and thirty years ago.

"*A Dialogue between John and Martha or Exonus and Plimothenia*" recalls the pastoral tradition in its use of names, here referring to where John and Martha were born (Exeter, Plymouth). The dialogue form is unusual for Puritan poetry in general and for Saffin's poetry in particular. Dialogue, of course, usually heightens contrast and drama (as it does in Bradstreet's "The Flesh and the Spirit" and "A Dialogue between Old England and New"); however, in Saffin's poem it emphasizes comparison. The form therefore reinforces the theme of love's mutuality, and Saffin does little to differentiate the two voices. Formally,

Saffin shows—as Bradstreet only tells—"If ever two were one, then surely we" ("To My Dear and Loving Husband," l. 1).

The poem is written in iambic tetrameter couplets which quicken the tempo and keep the exchanges moving. Speaking for both partners, Martha opens:

> When I consider seriously
> the Sorrowes and the misery
> we both Endur'd before that we
> united could together bee
> And till remov'd were all annoys
> that Interpos'd our mutuall Joys
> ô how I think the time ill Spent
> which Barr's us from that sweet content
> which we together mutually
> Enjoy'd in Each Sweet Company.
> and think it long, yea long till when
> Enjoy we may those Joyes agen.

The enjambement in lines one to six aptly conveys continued contentment and contrasts markedly with the seventh line's opening interjection, "ô," whose strong stress slows the pace. This first stanza identifies the whole poem's controlling emotional force: the contrast between the lovers' joy when together and their sorrow when apart.

In the second stanza, John echoes Martha's distinctly worldly argument by saying, "Those thoughts of thine, with paine, & smart / I in my Bosome, bear a part:/And deep Impression hath the sence / thereof in mine Intelligence." He agrees with her that they may soon marry, yet cautions her "But Providence, (with which I close) / Doth otherwise our lives Dispose." Reacting to John's reference to Providence, Martha continues her plea in stanza three: "But since we bought our love so Dear, / and cannot long Enjoy it here: / could we unto the years arive / of them that longest are alive / all is but Short, and therefore why / Doe we our Selves those joys deny." The poet skillfully constructs these six lines so that the first two are end-stopped and suggest the lovers' impeded wishes, while the last four flow into each other to suggest time passing. In stanza four, John reiterates Martha's impatience, but he then becomes more rational and resigned as he reminds her: "But when a thing, of great Moment, / of much Importence doth present, / On which good Issue, (or Right End) / the livelyhood of both Depend: / The Case here Differs, pleasure may, / And must, for (proffit) sometimes Stay." Stanza four is neatly balanced as John moves from agreeing that separation "is meer folly," to indicating that it may be necessary for their ultimate joy. Although the emphasis is secular here, John and Martha illustrate an otherwise typical Puritan trait—deferred gratification.

In stanza five, Martha agrees with John that discontent is pointless and that "true Comfort" can be found only in peace of mind. This forms Martha's rallying point: her tone is determined resignation conveyed by the conventional (and powerful) Puritan homily that acceptance is the only comfort in adversity. John's response in the sixth stanza ends the poem. He echoes Martha's previous lines but completes the argument by saying that acceptance not only comforts but turns "Sorrows, into Joys. . . ." The final couplet urges Martha, "So whether I am far, or Near/Contented be in Mind, my Dear." The dramatic form directly presents the couple's predicament and emotion, and Saffin's decision to use dialogue so both Martha and he speak also conveys "forcefully their mutual attraction as well as their mutual anticipation."[6] In "*A Dialogue between John and Martha*," two voices speak as one; in "Sayle gentle Pinnace," only one voice speaks.

"Sayle gentle Pinnace" poses a particular critical problem since it is based on Francis Quarles' *Argalus and Parthenia* and raises the question of canonical establishment and purity. Brom Weber shows in his article "A Puritan Poem Regenerated: John Saffin's 'Sayle gentle Pinnace'" how Samuel Eliot Morison first asserted Saffin's poem was merely a paraphrase and others perpetuated the belief. However, Weber plausibly argues that "Instead of paraphrasing, Saffin drew elements from three passages in *Argalus and Parthenia* to compose a new and powerful lyric statement of his own. An image in Book I ('Have ye beheld, when *Titans* lustfull head / Hath newly div'd into the seagreene bed / Of *Thetis*, how the bashful Horizon') was transformed into 'Thetis with her green Mantle.' From three lines in Book III . . . Saffin obtained (1) the refrain which, with slight alteration, opens and closes his own poem and (2) probably also his benevolent conception of Neptune. . . . [Last] Quarles in Book I had converted the idea of a voyage into a conceit that would have attracted a voyager like Saffin."[7] In other words, we should consider Quarles' poem the inspirational basis of Saffin's, but not deny or understate the Puritan poet's original contribution.

Part of Saffin's originality is the structural choice of the same couplet to open and close his eight-line lyric, "Sayle gentle Pinnace Zepherus doth not faile / with prosperous gales, Saile Gentle Pinnace Sayle." In fact, the poem's form stems from Saffin's repetition in four places of the key phrase "Sayle gentle Pinnace." This device aptly emphasizes Saffin's theme—his impatience to return home to Martha—while the four central lines balance Saffin's mild impatience by stressing nature's benevolence: "Proud Neptune Stoops, and freely Condescends / For's foremer Roughness, now to make amends; / Thetis with her green Mantle sweetly Glides / With smileing Dimples Singing by our Sides." The classical allusions hint at pathetic fallacy and divine (classical, not Christian) approval in speeding this traveller back.

Comparable to the understated emotion of the medieval lyric "Western wind," Saffin's poem derives intensity from its central image: the pinnace. Weber quotes

Quarles' original conceit, then adds, "With a sense of economy and a sharing of vision with Quarles, Saffin compressed the conceit into an allusion without sacrificing symbolic meaning. The pinnace in Quarles' poem has been expanded from the 'lover's mind' simile to become a metaphor of the lover-poet whose joyous song is the movement of a small ship through sympathetic waters."[8]

"A LETTER TO HIS DEAR MARTHA 1660" shows that such joy was not misplaced. Composed in heroic couplets, this long love poem splits into three sections: lines 1–52 address Martha; lines 53–74, Saffin's eldest son, John; and the final couplet, Martha again. In its opening, the poem recalls "A Dialogue between John and Martha" by restating the lovers' mutual joy; however, whereas in the earlier poem the love was unfulfilled, in the later poem it is. The first half-dozen lines expound the fairly standard belief that wealth cannot match content. Significantly, though, for this Puritan content is wholly earthly. After these introductory lines, the poem builds toward a definition of secular love ("Reciprocall, intire affection Sound") and a description of emotional deprivation. Once more, we note that for Saffin true love is reciprocal and that the two lovers merge into a single self. His lines here derive particular impact from oxymoron and paradox—"Deeming my Self, as of my Self Depriv'd/Liveing (me thinks) as one but Semi-liv'd"—and from a series of central one- or two-syllable words, like those in the line which ends this section, "My love, my Joy, my Dear, my Better part."

For the next thirty-two lines he moves from emotional assessment to intellectual analysis by constructing two elaborate metaphors bordering on conceits: The king of a very populous country cannot possibly *see* all his subjects, but he joys in their very existence; similarly, someone who has wealth tied up in land, rent, or goods is happy, even though he may not have much cash immediately available, because he can depend on what he owns. In the same way, says Saffin (recalling John Donne in "A Valediction: Forbidding Mourning"), happily married people are content even when their partner is not visible because the marriage represents a long-term investment. Such mercantile imagery is apt for Saffin— entrepeneur that he was—and he extends it skillfully.

Saffin next makes a rather forced transition into the second section: "Meanwhile my Johnny-Boy is not forgott/Him I Remember thô he heeds it not. . . ." Probably the transition lies in his all-embracing view of Martha as wife and mother. Saffin addresses his eldest son, John, then a toddler, and moves from the earlier elaborate conceits to a simple list of the child's activities, including his tantrums, illnesses, and prattling. Saffin's "Paternall Care" is especially apparent in his proud claim of his son's "promiseing perfection every way" (a claim particularly poignant in view of John's early death). In the final section, Saffin again makes a sudden transition, this time to the farewell couplet and signature addressed to Martha: "And so Adieu my Dove, Heavens grant that wee / may with out Wonted Joy, Each other see. / Thine or not his own. J.S."

To move from his "amorous, and youthfull" poems to his group of elegiac poems heightens the contrast between joy and sorrow, youth and age, innocence and experience.

When Martha died on December 11, 1678, shortly after the deaths of young Simon and John, Saffin was grief sticken, as his commonplace book entry shows: "On Wedensday about midnight the 11th Day of December My thrice Dearly Beloved Consort Departed this life after Eleven Dayes Sickness of that Deadly Disease of the Small pox all which hath tended to my allmost insuportable grief After the enjoyment of her my Sweet Martha 20 years" (*NB*: 10). The anagrams and epitaphs do not match the emotional intensity of this entry, perhaps because Saffin's "insuportable grief" hindered fluent composition. However, these poems are significant for other reasons.

On Martha's death, Saffin anagrammatized her name in two ways, then joined the anagrams and composed two different couplets:

> Martha Saffin
> Anagr: 1 In hart am Saff
>   2 Ah! firm an fast
> In hart am Saff ha firm and fast
> To my Beloved to my Last
>   or
> Am safe in heart, ah firm and fast
> To my Beloved to my Last.

Both couplets are short and obviously lack the development and intellectual intricacy of John Wilson's anagram on Claudius Gilbert ("Tis Braul I Cudgel") or John Fiske's anagram-elegies on John Cotton ("O, Honie knott") and Anne Griffin ("In Fanne: Rig"). However, they gain enormous emotive impetus from these questions: Who is the voice speaking? Who is the beloved? On a literal level, the voice is evidently Martha's as she speaks from heaven, safe with Christ the beloved. But on another level, the voice may very well be Saffin's own, as he speaks from earth, convinced of his eternal loyalty to his beloved Martha.

When he attempted extended epitaphs on Martha's death, he was not so subtle or skillful. The first, "*An Epitaph on his truly loveing and Dearly beloved Wife Martha Saffin . . . ,*" is a stiff, formal, stuttered piece. The rhythm is strained and the rhyme overly insistent (especially the unfortunate rhyming pair "fulfill it/Willett"). Furthermore, the poem is thoroughly impersonal; although this is not unusual in Puritan elegies, the most successful blend formality and convention with emotional and personal depth. "ANOTHER ON HIS DEAR MARTHA" is similarly strained, except for the single telling line "Liv'd Twenty years a Wife, belov'd Desir'd" which conveys Saffin's love and devotion.

Saffin's grief was such that he could not do poetic justice to Martha immediately after her death. But twenty-five years later, the memory of his "Hebian wife" led him to compose *"Revived Elegiac Lamentation of the Deplorable, and Irripairable Loss of his truely Loving and Dearly Beloved Consort Martha Saffin who Departed this life by that Epidemicall Desease of the Small Pox in Boston December the 11 1678."* It is a sustained tribute to Martha and encompasses her many social, religious, maternal, and above all wifely virtues. *"Revived Elegiac Lamentation"* opens as a love poem then moves to certain standard elegiac conventions like praise of virtue, loyalty, grace, and beauty. Significantly, Saffin "reverses the orthodox order of objects of love," beginning with divine love and *culminating* in earthly love.[9] He therefore emphasizes the crucial lines by building toward them, "But O unto her Husband (he knew well) / In Conjugall Affection did Excell / Cornelia, and Artemisia faire / Pandora, and Valeria (Ladys Rare) / famous for Love unto their Husbands were, / yet to my Dove they scarcly could Compare / The most of women, without Parallel. . . ." The classical references, of course, help stress that Martha was a paragon of "Conjugall Affection."

Saffin next turns to her social and maternal attributes: her domestic skill as a housewife, her ability to educate her children and instill obedience and respect in them, and (especially noteworthy to Saffin the merchant) her ability to manage his affairs when necessary. After indicating Martha's private face, Saffin considers once again her public face. The list might continue indefinitely with Saffin intertwining his first wife's personal and social attributes; however, the man suddenly (and humanly) takes over from the poet:

> My Muse doth flag, but grief doth more increase,
> Sorrow constraines my Numbers here to Cease;
> All I have Said; or can in words Comprise,
> Her true Perfections but Epitomise,
> Who Speaks her Praise, cannot Hyperbolize
> But ah! alas! She's gone and I alone
> These five & Twenty years left to bemone
> my unrepaired Loss in Her since gone.
> And Still the more I grieve, the more I may,
> Which will Continue till my Dying Day. J.S.

The first four lines, taken alone, might strike the reader as merely conventional, but set against the last five lines' intense longing, they gain enormous pathos. When the poet's inspiration fades, the man's grief fuels yet more grief. Even the last line, though it seems trite, suggests deeper meaning: twenty-five years after Martha's death, Saffin swears his grief will increase until *his* death. This poem fulfills in sadness Saffin's statements in "A LETTER TO HIS DEAR MARTHA 1660": "Deeming my Self, as of my Self Depriv'd / Liveing (me thinks) as one but Semi-Liv'd" (ll. 13–14).

The closest equivalent to Saffin's cluster of love poems are Anne Bradstreet's poems to her husband. Together these verses form a unique Puritan document of conjugal love written from male and female viewpoints. Scholarship on seventeenth-century American Puritan settlements suggests that in such a patriarchal and prescribed society a man's experience was much different from a woman's. Yet the poetry of Bradstreet and Saffin shows that such experience could be complementary, that for both sexes the ideal of wordly love (a type of spiritual love) lay in "Mutuall sweet Content."

NOTES

1. Information from Alyce E. Sands, "John Saffin: Seventeenth-Century American Citizen and Poet," Diss., The Pennsylvania State University, 1965.

2. *John Saffin His Book, 1665–1708*, (New York: Harbor Press, 1928).

3. Sands, p. 181.

4. Sands, pp. 242–43.

5. For the reader's convenience, I quote from Hazard's edition, though she does make some transcription errors. I abbreviate this edition to *NB* in the text, followed by the pagination in her edition.

6. Sands, p. 247.

7. Brom Weber, "A Puritan Poem Regenerated: John Saffin's 'Sayle gentle Pinnace,' " *EAL* 3 (1968), 65–71.

8. Weber, p. 69.

9. Sands, p. 249.

13 EDWARD TAYLOR, THE ACTING POET

KARL KELLER

The Connecticut River Valley poet Edward Taylor (1642–1729) had to be invented. There was no way of knowing that someone remotely that good would have lived at that remote time and in that remote place. We could not have guessed him from those who settled in the generation before him or from his contemporaries or from those who followed. We could not have guessed him from the articulated esthetics of the period either, nor from what we have known about the dogmatics or demographics or dynamics of the time. Except for a handful of historians who had him down only as a minister—Ezra Stiles, John H. Lockwood, William Sprague, John L. Sibley, Abiel Holmes, Josiah Holland, Harriet Beecher Stowe[1]—Taylor was lost for two whole centuries. The Taylor family had its own tradition about the old man as some kind of backwoods, backwater versifier, and libraries in New England had him catalogued,[2] but still the name collected centuries of dust. The first frontier poet of early America just disappeared.

He appeared first in the 1930s at the hands of Thomas H. Johnson,[3] and here for the first time was an accomplished artist at the heart of, and not merely at the fringes of or among the descendants of, American Puritan life. Not even Perry Miller could foresee what had been the art of Edward Taylor. The event of the discovery, which romanticizes Taylor a little for us now in the twentieth century, is best marked by the anecdote of Johnson and Miller scrambling to insert Taylor into their anthology and history *The Puritans: A Sourcebook of Their Writings* (1938)—pages 656a–n. He has brightened the pages of practically every collection of American literature since then. And more important, he has colored considerably our understanding of the esthetics possible within the Puritan sensibility.

Then the work of rationalizing his existence began. Apologists made two camps: those who thought he was the last flash of a lagging European culture on primitive shores (perhaps baroque,[4] maybe a little Catholic,[5] certainly unorthodox,[6] mainly quaint[7]) and those who thought he was just being reactionary (a devotional man writing private verse for no one to see,[8] a conservative man trying to preserve the faith within the American experiment[9]). The two camps warred genially over a body that, I fear, remained largely dead to them.

The period of expansion of the Taylor canon began in 1960 when Donald E. Stanford published an edition of over 240 poems, *The Poems of Edward Taylor*,[10] and Norman Grabo published two collections of sermons, *Christographia* (1962) and *Edward Taylor's Treatise Concerning the Lord's Supper* (1966). Johnson's edition had favored Taylor's *Gods Determinations* over his *Preparatory Meditations*, for he saw him as mainly an ecclesiastical poet. Stanford's edition favored the Meditations, for he saw him (as did Louis Martz in his important introduction to the edition) as basically devotional and meditative. Grabo's publication of Taylor's sermons set both views straight, however, for with them one could see that Taylor had been more of a fighter than a minister or a dark recluse. There were large, specific issues which lay behind his art. Norman Grabo also wrote the first full-length study of Taylor at about the same time, *Edward Taylor* (1961), and in it he stumbled upon mysticism as a way of reconciling his Old Worldliness, his private devotionalism, and his debates with the world around him—but it was a stumble. Taylor turned out to be far too earth-bound, too earthy, and too carelessly inconsistent for such characterization.

Important as it was to know how Taylor, through poetry, had been able to break out of the Puritan mold, or at least to stretch it considerably through meditation, which was the fine emphasis of Stanford, Grabo, and most students of Taylor in the first decades of his emergence, it took the work of some very careful analysts of individual Taylor poems,[11] of his intellectual milieu,[12] and of the demographics of the Connecticut River Valley[13] to show that while his spirit could often soar, he was of a time and a place—America in the late seventeenth century.

There came then the closer explications, and they showed for the most part that Taylor was more contender and clown than he was mystic and metaphysician.[14] His language, after all, was clever, idiosyncratic, erratic, egregious. He needed his words to move him to his meiotic and loving states; he felt what he wrote. And there came the closer attention to the American pressures that moved Taylor to write.[15] He wrote out of necessity, out of need, not out of flights of fancy or when possessed of the spirit. He was not a religious poet in that sense at all. He was a self-styled defender of American covenants, a local apologist of Valley orthodoxy. His muse was, perversely, Solomon Stoddard, the devil's liberal up the river from him in Northampton.[16] His references to heaven and hell were in reality his way of talking about New England and orthodoxy in the Valley.

We needed these close studies. That is, we needed to know the air Taylor breathed—the doctrines he loved, the language he knew, the issues he fought for—more than the Old World traditions he emerged from and refreshed. William Scheick wrote the cleverest essays linking Taylor's beliefs with his language: the theology did have its esthetics, Puritanism could produce art. But when these were collected into the book, *The Will and the Word: The Poetry of Edward Taylor* (1974), one saw that Taylor had once again been made out to be a profound thinker, a systematic philosopher of sorts, an early, smaller Edwards. Scheick's Emersonian assumption that high thought leads to high art skewered Taylor, as

Stanford and Grabo had done, on universals that might lead one to make Taylor important beyond his own time and place. Scheick's Taylor thinks he is a thinker.

I came to the writing of *The Example of Edward Taylor* (1975) because I felt the claims for Taylor had put him in the wrong categories, had in fact been too large, even perhaps, because of his surprise emergence, hyperbolic, hyperactive, a hype. Early American literature had needed a great poet, and the critics were determined to make this one great. I didn't intend to cut him down to proper size, but simply to find a way to measure him better, more interestingly, more relevantly: Taylor the American. Was there anything indigenously American at that early point in the making of a culture, I wanted to know, and Taylor seemed to give an affirmative answer. From his inadvertence came an art, that of a primitive. It was an eccentric point to make, but it at last caught Taylor at his art. It caught him making something for us: attractively flawed poems, "rough feet for smooth praises."

But the work of Thomas Davis has now overshadowed everything previous and substantially shifts the grounds for understanding Taylor accurately. Davis' correction of previously published Taylor works, his transcription of many unpublished works into three volumes (Boston, 1981),[17] and his (and his Kent State protégés') documentation of Taylor's activities and relationships[18] give us much more of Taylor to know but also, ironically, a much smaller Taylor to like. Taylor can no longer be romanticized into a baroque *brocailleur*, a high-flying Hooker, a man of much mind. Most of his works now seem narrowed to a single cause, a single motive, a single objective: S. Stoddard up the river. Others had seen Stoddard looking over Taylor's shoulder before Davis did. Now the two face each other off, eyeball to eyeball, in the grand debate of that New England century: admission to the American sacrament. We care little about that now, except for the intellectual history in it. Taylor has been put in his place. The artist was first an ecclesiastic, second an apologist, and only third an artist. He may have gained a place in history by this process but perhaps lost something in esthetics.

The struggle to find the art in Taylor will now be more difficult, if certainly more accurate. His redaction of Scripture into an American typology interests some.[19] His search for forms to accommodate church and ear interests others.[20] This is a challenge that has always been there, of course, but now far more demanding of precision and creative criticism: for all the debilities, what is it, precisely, that delights us in this man?

Holding all the studies of Taylor in mind, however, does not give one a defined or definitive Taylor. It has simply very smartly created The Problem of Edward Taylor: the criticism often looks better than the poet does. The problem with knowing, admiring, analyzing, and teaching Taylor is that, like many writers of early American literature, he is, against the best twentieth-century literary standards, a poor writer. He is a poor writer by almost any standard except his own, which understandably was not standard.

Biography is of little help because we still know little about the man, little about the environment that produced him, little about the cultural factors or the persons that influenced and encouraged him. And even as we learn more about these, especially in the writings of Grabo, Scheick, and Davis, the art of his art still seems anomalous. Somehow it came from a source we have not yet tapped, or it came attractively of itself from a poet who did not know what he was doing. Art is often an American accident.

Approaching Taylor through literary conventions is not very rewarding either, for, like many writers of early America, he is almost entirely predictable, his forms and structures are imitative and repetitive almost to the point of self-parody, and his experiments are handled with almost unfailing ineptitude or just get lost. In many formal ways, he is, like many writers of his time, a perfect bore. Nor boring, though, if we see what *he* found to do within the expected, the determined. He wanted to sing somehow, even when the hymns were all prescribed and proscriptive ones. He just sang them with the voice he had—screechy, anxious, improvisational, loving voice, but a voice indeed: his own. Maybe early America allowed that, encouraged that, demanded that. Maybe it always has, until we come to our time, when the non-singers write songs.

The condition of Taylor's poetry itself, as with much early American writing, also does not help very much in finding the art of his art. The best of it is largely unfinished and unfinishable. You will stumble over it if you try to read it aloud. You will find it was not written to be examined by anyone except Taylor himself and perhaps God. You dance around an antique if you use it at all. You will be a laughing stock if you take it too seriously. The mistakes may or may not be mistaken—who can know?—but certainly should not be mis*took*, for they have to be accepted as part of the art or else we have not taken the artist whole. Do I go too far to suggest that The Flawed Poet of American Literature was not a failure but God's fool? He fooled around with the toys of this fallen world, the words, thinking he had a calling to play. Rejoice that the man knew how to play, even when it turned out to be his own game, not God's at all. Thank God he got that part wrong. Thank *him* that it turns out right. It is right because in its silliness, its experimentation, its sprightliness, its corniness, its stretching for color and sound, its cragginess, its ugly lure, it simulates the condition of the world Taylor was in. Taylor did not like it either!

I do not know if I am yet suggesting some solutions to The Problem of Edward Taylor. Maybe we should simply read him as theologian and claim for him some artfulness in delivering his theology to us somewhat interestingly. There is much in New England Puritanism that we can see because of him: the helplessness of mankind, the awful state of the world, the mercy of God in the saving power of Christ, the power and joy of the regenerate saint. Much in the theology—pop-theology, then—is chewable in his images. Much of it stops grumbling in the gut when we see that *he* could digest it. Much then comes out "streams of Grace, . . . Heavens Sugar Cake." But this approach does not allow for many of the complexities of Puritan dogma at all. For one thing, it illustrates only one of the Connecticut River Valley brands in a fairly large New England storehouse. And it overlooks the probable motive behind such poetry: self-therapy. We know we get more of the man in his poetry (a man hunting for words) than we do of God (God hunting for words). It is humanistic, not theistic. It is poetry, not preaching.

Or maybe we should try to read him as a little psychoanalyst: a man after his own darkness for the fun in it. He wrote poetry, if we believe his apologetics, to ready himself for taking the Sacrament of the Lord's Supper through conscientious self-examination, knowing that that very attitude was evidence enough of his spiritual worth. If his poetry indeed moved him to a position of maximum humiliation and dependence, it is better than we have thought, better than we can experience. It is just there on the page for us to wonder at, in awe that so little could do so much to the man. If it balanced his mind between despair and hope, then its art had its effect but still escapes *us*. And so it is not really poetry anymore for us. How can we deal with the remoteness of the most intimate/ private poetry written in this country before Walt Whitman and Emily Dickinson? That kind of poetry, to be sure, gave him a means of demonstrating the talent which grace had vouchsafed him, that of writing poetry. Holding Taylor in mind as a little psychoanalyst, however, illustrates only his occult side and not all of his interests and abilities and personality. It makes Puritan practices seem darker (at least after reading him in the dark light of Hawthorne, Melville, and Emily Dickinson) than they actually were. And it does not pay much respect to the poem as an artifact, as a work of art, as an artful accomplishment. It becomes too much of an exercise to only watch his exercises.

If we honor Taylor as an amateur theologian or amateur psychoanalyst but find ourselves wanting more high verse and less thick doodling, we must jump into his poems as *belles lettres*. Let him handle his conflict, tension, climax, and denouement in his structures. Let him try dramatics in his rhythms and sounds. Let his metaphors move for meiotic and amplified effects. Let his skill with puns and other playful language devices show, even as you admit that such may come from a myopic New Critic rather than from any esthetics inherent in the poetry itself. Admit, as Taylor asks one to do, that he was far more interested in the process of writing his poetry than he ever was in any of his finished products, since they represented his fallen state. And admit that much does go wrong with verse-making in Taylor's hand. He *had* to fail at being faithful to the world's arts, for he had to *show* he needed the help of his God. Not the critic's help—God's.

When all of these approaches fail, and I think they do, wonderful as the criticism using them has become, I sell The Poet Primitive, The Village Verse-Maker, Taylor the Messy Emerson, Taylor Who Tried and Survived by Torment and Tease. None of these flip labels are accurate, of course, for in the attempt to see his natural art emerging out of unnatural acts, it is extremely difficult to name the Indigenous Inadvertence simply and clearly. Relaxed, we see how he simply and clearly wrote what he could. The resulting poems are acts of honesty, acts of love. They do not compete with the arts of the world, not even with the critics of the world, and so the temptations to snob it out and call them incompetent. But they nonetheless work in their cranky way. This anomaly, the Rev. Mr. Edward Taylor, therefore makes his place, unskewered, in the literature.

All of the above is a cop-out, however, for even when one can show that he knows the literature about Taylor well and knows the literature written by Taylor well enough as A Problem, one still must prove that the art of the man can be handled. Not manhandled, but handled in accurate celebration of an honest discovery that matters esthetically. We should, after all, try to know where Taylor is good, where Taylor is best—and what in his understanding of his faith and his art made him so. I propose—speculatively, airily—that Taylor had to act in order to be a good poet and that the resulting poems are very good acts indeed. He is the great Acting Poet (both as stand-in and as self-dramatist in a role) of early America.

In the late 1660s and early 1670s, he began by writing a set of well-conceited occasional poems imitative of features of an outdated baroque style. By 1682, however, for personal and ecclesiastical reasons, he was writing confessional poems for no other eyes but his own and in a much more inventive, personalized style. In between, at some point, he wrote his cantankerous, contentious, and crude series, *A Metrical History of Christianity*, and his ministerial, minatory series, *Gods Determinations*.

When one surveys the full range of Taylor's works, one comes to recognize just how special his one series is, the *Preparatory Meditations*. The main reason for their distinct difference from the rest of what he wrote lies in the fact that in all of his Meditations, but in very little of the rest of the verse he wrote, Taylor is acting—and acting a very good act, too. In them he plays a persona exacted by Connecticut Valley Preparationism. The Taylor of the Meditations is a Prepared Persona. We in the twentieth century, his only audience, can judge how well he played his part.

Taylor had found within his orthodox beliefs, especially in the Preparationism of which he became an ardent defender for over forty years, the license for a form of drama. He is, in his *Preparatory Meditations*, the most dramatic of all Puritan poets. In his Meditations he rivals John Bunyan as a Puritan initiator of fictive drama into literature in English.

What gave Taylor his drama in these poems was his decision at some point to play a part before God, and now before us his rediscoverers. Preparationism encouraged this technique. It gave him fuel for his natural ability to act. Probably the innovation was an inadvertent result of Preparational dramatics, but an innovation nonetheless. The persona of his meditative poems knows universal truths but not much about himself. So he doubts and hopes at the same time, creating drama. He is a voice-with-personality, a role or set of roles or range of roles being played coherently and consistently by an identifiable narrator. He has aura-presence by virtue of his ability to *make* a world. He plays with language more than with ideas. He flaunts his sins and sinfulness flamboyantly, theatrically trying to attract attention from his God in any way he can. He performs for Him.

We might wish that Taylor had made more of a distinction for us, as he worked up his little acts, his poems, between preparation for communion and preparation for grace. We can believe he knew the difference; we can believe equally that in ecstatic mini-states his poetry got him excruciatingly/exhilaratingly into, the difference faded away. Through his writing of poems, such as they are, he could act a part that led him to feel he was ready.

The persona that the grace-desperate Taylor plays the most consistently as he prepared himself to take the Sacrament of the Lord's Supper is that of a man working hard to put himself down severely in order to be lifted up radically by a savior. "Woe is mee!" he cries, and his efforts at self-humiliation throughout his 212 Meditations represent his need, which in turn represents his hoped-for grace.[21] In his assumed passivity he even shifts sometimes to the feminine in order to be "taken." And then his act becomes one of willing his will to be won at any cheap price. His role of unbidden "Guest" at the "Feast" of the Sacrament of the Lord's Supper in his poem "The Reflexion" is a good example. In his little sacramental drama, he is unworthy and so he weeps. He feels God is ashamed to look at him—and he may be right. He is full of filth and poison. He starves for some spiritual nourishment. He begs for some kind of recognition: "So much before, so little now!"

The metaphoric roles of searcher, seeker, desirer which Taylor creates in his Meditations to achieve this meiosis at the time of seeking to feel worthy to take the Sacrament are fanciful, consistent, entertaining, and dramatically convincing. "I am this Crumb of Dust," he writes in his Prologue to his First Series of Meditations, "which is design'd / To make my Pen unto thy Praise alone. . . ." But we know all the same that he has *chosen* to play this dunce for the nonce. His language made the act possible.

Taylor asks God to forgive the roles he plays as fallen human being ("Let not th'attempts breake down . . . Nor laugh thou them to scorn"), for the person-in-need, as Edwards was to argue two generations later, justifies the saving power of God. The (perhaps to us funny) self-demeaning masochism defines, by distance, the (no doubt to him phenomenal) greatness of God. Taylor therefore works to imagine himself in sorry, abject roles, even begs God's help to put him in such roles: "Let me thy Patient, thou my surgeon bee"—all for the sake of underscoring, or even creating, his dependence on God (I.4).

In his meiotic role of "Poor wretched man" with a "poore poore heart," he speaks of his "Graceless Soule," his "befogg'd Dark Phancy," his "naughty heart." He is thoroughly "Bemidnighted," he claims. "I . . . am all blot," he complains. "I'm but a Flesh and Blood bag." "I could do more but can't . . ." (I.34; II.17; I.26, 18, 44, 25, 30, 41). All for the sake of a convincing act before God. The irony of which, however, is that he knows God knows it is just an act. The judgment he must then hope for is that God will think the act (and not necessarily the man himself) a good one.

The consistency of the self-demeaning persona throughout the Meditations might lead one to believe that this is the real Edward Taylor talking. But it is not possible to believe that Taylor really thought so poorly of himself. It is an act, the act of The Poor Thing in Need of God:

> Was ever Heart like mine? Pride, Passion, fell.
>   Ath'ism, Blasphemy, pot, pipe it, dance
> Play Barlybreaks, and at last Couple in Hell. [I.40]

He says he is but "a Ball of dirt." He speaks of his "vile Heart." He is sure of his "little all." He claims that he is merely a "hide bound Soule that stands so niggardly" (I.40, 22, 46, 48). Such meiotic assertions, because so insistent and so repetitious, raise the important question whether this was a genuine conviction on Taylor's part or a genuine role he played. Surely the intensity is concocted, contrived. "I . . . have been a pest," he says, "And have done the Worst." "O bad at best! what am I then at worst?" (II.1, 17; I. 26). Can we really believe he believed this of himself? Acting, an especially degrading activity to the staunch Puritans anyway, demeans the man nicely. His pride must now play the clown, the fool, the beggar, the pitiful one. Acting—a creative, confessional choice of his—gives him, if he is good at it, need.

Taylor is especially good at acting when he works at berating his own writing. He speaks of "My Rough Voice, and my blunt Tongue" as he puts himself down. "I know not how to speak, . . ." he says (ironically, cutely) quite competently. "I am Tonguetide [,] stupid, sensless."

> What aim'st at, Lord? that I should be so Cross.
>   My minde is Leaden in thy Golden Shine.
> Though all o're Spirit, when this dirty Dross
>   Doth touch it with its smutting leaden lines.
> . . . .
>   Mine Eyes, Lord, shed no Tears but inke.
> My handy Works, are Words, and Wordiness.
>   [I.23, 27, 24]

Taylor is often redundant in the extent to which he writes about his bad writing, but there was a Preparational reason for this. Taylor plays the role of writer by writing. He plays the role of Humble One by meiotic metaphors and a primitive style. He plays the role of Insufficient One by writing deliberately insufficiently. He therefore makes the role real. His desires thereby become truth. Anyone (that is, God) should be able to see that.

Taylor's acting in such little scenes as he sets for himself to play roles in is factitious. In acting, he is trying to deceive God: that he is good at being no good. His Meditations are vehicles for him to act poor in (though not poorly in), so that he can sustain his hope of rescue. God (that is, the critic) should *love* watching the fool play the fool when he is in reality a fool and only needed to play it to see it himself. The act then becomes an act of honesty.

Taylor had the phenomenal task of making this humility—that is, this recurring act of grovelling before God—attractive. Both preparation for grace and preparation for the Sacrament required *at least* that of him. In his Meditations, therefore, Taylor did a certain amount of playing at humility, knowing it was really a form of worthiness. He apparently hoped that the playing at humility was not hypocrisy or presumptuousness, but a showing forth of one's faith-filled abilities. To put on a humble act—that is, to play the Prepared Persona—is human, natural. "The New Englanders," Sacvan Bercovitch observes in his *American Jeremiad*, "acted as if they were doomed while presuming they were saved."[22] Taylor's little act of self-abasement in his poems had to be attractively convincing to his God. And so what we get is his attempt at poetry. His fallen self, after all, had to be made interesting.

But what happens to *voice* when a poet creates a persona which acts only for God? Taylor's persona violates the assumption that a poetic role is for an audience.[23] Playing only to himself, as Taylor did in his Meditations, left him free to innovate, for there were no other judges, no other criteria, than his own desires. Since Taylor-the-persona is pretty much in the dark about himself, he is free to play any earthly role he wishes through the metaphors of his poems. This counterpoint of consistent persona and wild, brief flights with his roles, his voices, his images, represents the already determined soul free to play in and with a foolish world. The poet therefore has the advantage which Preparationism promised: that one might participate in one's salvation a little. Because his Self is as yet undefined (and will remain so until fully aware of his election, hereafter), he may try out many roles, not in search of his true Self but because he cannot know what his true Self is. His ignorance is liberating, for he is at liberty to play—and that leads him to all his fanciful, and sometimes extravagant, metaphors. Taylor the Tense Actor is then, through his writing of poetry, something of a free spirit, if only among the little toys of this world—which is all that a Puritan could expect of his liberties anyway.

This can help to explain the shifting roles, confusion of voices, and mixed metaphors in a Taylor poem: he does not know who he is—and can enjoy that fact. Though he desires an identity ("God's determinations," he calls such), he also enjoys the not knowing. Ignorance is his area of freedom. Taylor thus justifies the Puritan principle: Adam fell that mankind might be, and mankind *is* that it might have joy. The Fall meant living with the ambiguity of having freedom from knowing oneself, alongside the obligation to seek to know oneself—and there was a certain amount of joy in that. The Fall was therefore the form that God's grace takes: excrement dished up by angels' hands, as Taylor puts it in one of his more humorous, theological poems. Taylor appears to have understood the Fall, at least on the occasion of writing his Meditations preparatory to taking the Sacrament of the Lord's Supper, as not merely a burden but also as license to play, to act, to try out, to create. Out of unknowing came his poetry. And it is thus to be taken less as a Poetry of Piety than as a Poetry of Poverty. The "Poor wretched man" can at least write.

It should be obvious to anyone who reads through the *Preparatory Meditations* that the range of roles Taylor gives himself to play is not very wide. But he has an obsession to create; that is, to deplete, to enrich, to supplement ordinary human experience. Acting adds a new dimension to his life. His acting makes it possible for him to project some of his desires (as if out of some hell into which he delights putting himself) in the form of potentials, possibilities, hopes. The fairly chaotic variety of projected hopes out of his self-induced mire do not, however, make up Taylor's ideal self, merely some possibilities, for it would be presumptuous of him to think he knows what he might be. *That* he leaves to God. For the present this deferral means, of course, that his ideal self is one of the great unknowns. He plays the man trapped by existence and begging for a way out. And that is why his act has the simplest and worst emotions in it: sentimentality, severe melodramatic angles, hokey gestures, mumblings and screechings, cowering before the lights, lots of bathetic asides, a pause for the applause.

The gloomy Puritan is at play. Language made his game possible. I think Taylor has importance because he is the first American to discover language as a way out of some of the oppressiveness of the Fall, even while the way out was indigenous to the system of the Fall itself. It is to Taylor's credit that the voices of his persona in the Meditations have remained with us so well. He sticks—loathsomely, lovingly, Americanly—in the ear.

NOTES

1. Actually the first to give any recognition to Taylor as minister were Increase and Cotton Mather. They made use of some writings of his in their works, *Illustrious Providences* (1684) and *Magnalia Christi Americana* (1702), respectively, though they do not refer to him by name. (See my "Edward Taylor and the Mathers," *Moderna Språk* 72 [1978], 119–35.) The only other references to him in published works in the eighteenth century are Ezra Stiles, *The Literary Diary of Ezra Stiles*, ed. Franklin B. Dexter (New York, 1901), I, 367–8; *Extracts from the Itineraries and Other Miscellanies of Ezra*

Stiles, ed. Franklin B. Dexter (New Haven, 1916), 81–83, 103–4, 403–4; and Abiel Holmes, *The LIfe of Ezra Stiles* (Boston, 1798), pp. 379–82. In the nineteenth century, Taylor was known to only a few historians: Josiah Holland, *History of Western Massachusetts* (Springfield, 1855), I, 107–8, 115–18; II, 141–44: Harriet Beecher Stowe, *Oldtown Folks* (Boston, 1869), p. 453; John L. Sibley, *Biographical Sketches of Graduates of Harvard University* (Cambridge, 1873–85), II, 397–412; William B. Sprague, ed., *Annals of the American Pulpit* (New York, 1957–9), I, 181; and John H. Lockwood, *Westfield and Its Historic Influences, 1669–1919* (Springfield, 1922), I, 102–321 *passim*.

2. Taylor's major manuscripts can be found in the following places: Massachusetts Historical Society: "Commonplace Book." Boston Public Library: "Extracts." Redwood Library and Athenaeum: "Diary," "Harmony of the Gospels," "A Metrical History of Christianity." Westfield Athenaeum: "The Publick Records of the Church at Westfield." Yale University Library: "Commonplace Book," "Christographia," "Dispensatory," "Poetical Works," "Manuscript Notebook," and "Metallographia." University of Nebraska Library: "Commentary upon the Scriptures." Charles W. Mignon, Jr., is editing the "Commentary" for publication. Those other manuscripts not already in print will be published by Thomas M. Davis in volumes IV–VI of the G. K. Hall edition of the works of Taylor. Taylor's brief manuscript diary in the Connecticut Historical Museum has been edited by Francis Murphy, *The Diary of Edward Taylor* (Springfield, Mass., 1964). In addition, there is a good bibliography of Taylor: Constance J. Gefvert, *Edward Taylor: An Annotated Bibliography, 1668–1970* (Kent, Ohio, 1971); and an excellent concordance: Gene Russell, *A Concordance of the Poetry of Edward Taylor* (Washington, D.C., 1973).

3. *The Poetical Works of Edward Taylor* (New York, 1939), Johnson discusses his find in "The Discovery of Edward Taylor's Poetry," *Colophon*, I, No. 2 (1939), 100–6.

4. See especially: Austin Warren, "Edward Taylor's Poetry: Colonial Baroque," *Kenyon Review* 3 (1941), 355–71; "Edward Taylor," *Major Writers of America*, ed. Perry Miller, et al. (New York, 1962), I, 51–62: Wallace C. Brown, "Edward Taylor: An American 'Metaphysical,' " *AL* 16 (1944), 186–97; and Mindele Black, "Edward Taylor: Heaven's Sugar Cake," *NEQ* 29 (1956), 159–81.

5. See especially: Norman S. Grabo, "Catholic Tradition, Puritan Literature, and Edward Taylor," *Papers of the Michigan Academy of Science, Arts and Letters* 45 (1960), 395–402; "The Veiled Vision: The Role of Aesthetics in Early American Intellectual History," *WMQ* 19 (1962), 493–510; Stephen Fender, "Edward Taylor and 'The Application of Redemption,' " *Modern Language Review* 59 (1964), 331–34.

6. See especially: Murdock, *Literature*, pp. 152–71; Herbert Blau, "Heaven's Sugar Cake: Theology and Imagery in the Poetry of Edward Taylor," *NEQ* 26 (1953), 337–60; and Willie T. Weathers, "Edward Taylor and the Cambridge Platonists," *AL* 26 (1954), 1–31.

7. Three who have pictured him thus are: Roy Harvey Pearce, "Edward Taylor: The Poet as Puritan," *NEQ* 23 (1950), 31–46; Charles W. Mignon, Jr., "The American Puritan and Private Qualities of Edward Taylor, the Poet," unpub. diss., University of Connecticut, 1963; and Karl Keller, "The Example of Edward Taylor," *EAL* 4 (1969–70), 5–26.

8. On the issue of the essential privacy of Taylor's act of writing see: Francis Murphy, "Edward Taylor's Attitude Toward Publication: A Question Concerning Authority," *AL* 39 (1962), 393–94; Emmy Shepherd, "Edward Taylor's Injunction Against Publication,"

AL 38 (1962), 512–13; and Norman S. Grabo, "Colonial American Theology: Holiness and the Lyric Impulse," in Joseph Waldmeir, ed., *Essays in Honor of Russell B. Nye* (East Lansing, Michigan, 1978). pp. 74–91.

9. For discussions of Taylor as defender of the faith see Donald E. Stanford, *Edward Taylor* (Minneapolis, 1965); Norman S. Grabo, "Edward Taylor on the Lord's Supper," *Boston Public Library Quarterly* 12 (1960), 22–36; and Michael J. Colacurcio, "Gods Determinations Touching Half-Way Membership: Occasion and Audience in Edward Taylor," *AL* 39 (1967), 298–314.

10. Stanford, *Taylor*. Stanford also transcribed and made available a long work of Taylor's from the Redwood Athenaeum and named it *The Metrical History of Christianity* (Baton Rouge, 1963).

11. Those who have best shown Taylor as an artist in individual series and individual poems are Clark Griffith, "Edward Taylor and the Momentum of Metaphor," *English Literary History* 23 (1966), 448–60; Peter Thorpe, "Edward Taylor as Poet," *NEQ* 39 (1966), 356–72; E. F. Carlisle, "The Puritan Structure of Edward Taylor's Poetry," *AQ* 20 (1968), 147–63; Charles W. Mignon, Jr., "Edward Taylor's *Preparatory Meditations*: A Decorum of Imperfection," *PMLA* 83 (1968), 1423–28; John F. Lynen, "Literary Form and the Design of Puritan Experience," *The Design of the Present: Essays on Time and Form in American Literature* (New Haven, 1969), 61–70; Donald Junkins, "Edward Taylor's Creative Process," *EAL* 4 (1969–70), 67–78; John J. Gatta, Jr., "The Comic Design of *Gods Determinations*," *EAL* 10 (1975), 121–43.

12. It took a long time for Taylor scholars to realize the intellectual milieu in which he wrote. Some works to consult on this are Norman Pettit, *The Heart Prepared: Grace and Conversion in Puritan Spiritual Life* (New Haven, 1966); Thomas M. Davis, "Edward Taylor and the Traditions of Puritan Typology," *EAL* 4 (1969–70), 27–47; and Lewalski, *Poetics*.

13. Paul R. Lucas, "Valley of Discord: The Struggle for Power in the Puritan Churches of the Connecticut Valley, 1636–1720," unpub. diss., University of Minnesota, 1970; Stephen Foster, *Their Solitary Way: The Puritan Social Ethic in the First Century of Settlement in New England* (New Haven, 1971); James W. Jones, *The Shattered Synthesis: New England Puritanism before the Great Awakening* (New Haven, 1973); and John Gatta, Jr., "Edward Taylor and Thomas Hooker: Two Physicians of the Poore Doubting Soul," *Notre Dame English Journal* 12 (1979), 1–13.

14. Donald Junkins, "'Should Stars Wooe Lobster Claws?': A Study of Edward Taylor's Poetic Practice and Theory," *EAL* 3 (1968), 88–117; Karl Keller, "'The World Slickt up in Types': Edward Taylor as a Version of Emerson," *EAL* 5 (1970), 124–40; John J. Gatta, Jr., "Dogma and Wit in the Poetry of Edward Taylor," unpub. diss., Cornell University, 1973; William J. Scheick, "The Jawbones Schema of Edward Taylor's *Gods Determinations*," in Emory Elliott, ed., *Puritan Influences in American Literature* (Urbana, Illinois, 1979), pp. 38–54.

15. Thomas M. Davis summarizes these pressures best in his introduction to his three-volume edition of Taylor's writings (Boston, 1981).

16. From the outset, students of Taylor have seen Stoddard's presence in the Taylor canon, but this has increased now to show the serious obsession that Taylor had with the man and his heresy. On the conflict between the two and the resulting esthetics, see especially Norman S. Grabo, "Edward Taylor on the Lord's Supper," *Boston Public Library Quarterly* 12 (1960), 22–36; "The Poet to the Pope: Edward Taylor to Solomon

Stoddard," *AL* 32 (1960), 197–201; James P. Walsh, "Solomon Stoddard's Open Communion: A Re-examination," *NEQ* 43 (1970), 97–114; Dean Hall and Thomas M. Davis, "The Two Versions of Edward Taylor's Foundation Day Sermon," *Resources for American Literary Study* 5 (1975), 199–216; and David L. Parker, "Edward Taylor's Preparationism: A New Perspective on the Taylor-Stoddard Controversy," *EAL* 11 (1976–77), 259–78.

17. Until Davis' work, more than half of the manuscripts of Taylor remained unpublished. Volume One of Davis' edition, *Edward Taylor's Church Records and Related Sermons*, includes the continuous record of Taylor's pastoral activities for nearly fifty years and three sermons related to major issues in those records. Volume Two, *Edward Taylor versus Solomon Stoddard: The Nature of the Lord's Supper*, includes key manuscripts written before the published works of the Stoddard-Increase Mather controversy. Volume Three is *Edward Taylor's Minor Poetry*. Three more volumes are to follow, made up of Taylor's *The Harmony of the Gospels*.

18. Davis' students have produced some of the most original research on Taylor. Of note: Burley Gene Smith, "Edward Taylor and the Lord's Supper: The Controversy with Solomon Stoddard," unpub. diss., Kent State, 1975; Dean Hall, "Edward Taylor: The Evolution of a Poet," unpub. diss., Kent State, 1977; and Walter L. Powell, "Edward Taylor of Westfield: An Edition of the Westfield Town Records," unpub. diss., Kent State, 1981.

19. Many scholars have been attracted to Taylor's uses of typology in his poetry. Most important are: Ursula Brumm, *American Thought and Religious Typology* (New Brunswick, N. J., 1970); Karen Rowe, "Puritan Typology and Allegory as Metaphor and Conceit in Edward Taylor's *Preparatory Meditations*," unpub. diss., Indiana University, 1971; Lowance, *Canaan*; and see the essays on Taylor in Bercovitch, *Typology*.

20. Herein lies the greatest need: to relate Taylor's religion to his art. Valuable attempts to do so are Kathleen Blake, "Edward Taylor's Protestant Poetic: Nontransubstantiating Metaphor," *AL* 43 (1970), 1–24; Steven Goldstein, "The Act of Vision in Edward Taylor's *Preparatory Meditations*," unpub. diss., Tufts University, 1972; Gary A. Wood, "The 'Festival Frame': The Influence of the Tradition of Right Receiving on the *Preparatory Meditations*," unpub. diss., University of Pittsburgh, 1972; Michael D. Reed, "Edward Taylor's Poetry: Puritan Structure and Form," *AL* 46 (1973), 304–12; Daly, *God's Altar;* Michael North, "Edward Taylor's Metaphors of Promise," *AL* 51 (1979), 1–16; William J. Scheick, "Edward Taylor's Herbalism in *Preparatory Meditations*," *American Poetry* 1 (Fall 1983), 64–72; and Catherine Rainwater, "Edward Taylor's Reluctant Revolution: The New Astonomy in the *Preparatory Meditations*," *American Poetry* 1 (Winter 1984), 4–17.

21. All quotations from the Meditations are from Stanford, *Taylor*. The poems are designated by Series I or Series II and by Taylor's own numbers or titles within each series. Here, I.3.

22. P. 51

23. A thoughtful study is Caroline C. Zilboorg, "The Speaking Self in American Puritan Literature: A Study in Genre and Rhetorical Continuities," unpub. diss., University of Wisconsin, 1976. See also Paul Sorrentino, "The Metaphor of the Earth as a Theater: The Early American Actor on the Stage of Life," unpub. diss., Pennsylvania State University, 1978.

14 CANNIBALS AND TURKS: BENJAMIN TOMPSON'S IMAGE OF THE NATIVE AMERICAN

PETER WHITE

In 1965, Alden T. Vaughan published *The New England Frontier: Puritans and Indians, 1620–1675*. In his preface, Vaughan revealed his conviction that "the New England Puritans followed a remarkably humane, considerate, and just policy in their dealings with the Indians. In matters of commerce, religious conversion, and judicial procedure, the Puritans had surprisingly high regard for the interests of a people who were less powerful, less civilized, less sophisticated, and—in the eyes of the New England colonists—less godly.[1] Exactly ten years after Vaughan's study, Francis Jennings, past president of the American Society of Ethnohistory, published *The Invasion of America: Indians, Colonialism and the Cant of Conquest*. Jennings radically disagrees with traditional New England historians, from William Hubbard (c. 1621–1704) to Vaughan.

Jennings accuses the Puritans of "pervasive calculated deception of the official records," and he portrays our god-fearing ancestors as "neither more nor less than human," motivated by a rapacious desire for land, wealth, and power. The Lord's chosen, and especially their leaders like John Winthrop, Sr., "rewrote the substance of the Indian treaties to meet the Puritans' political and ideological needs, and then he (Winthrop) or a devoted descendant destroyed the originals." To Vaughan's statement that the Puritans "had no reason to conceal their attitudes or actions toward the Indians," Jennings replied that he had "found plenty of reason."[2]

It is hardly surprising that two competent historians could arrive at such divergent conclusions. From the beginning of the eighteenth century, when Cotton Mather set out to "Write the Wonders of the Christian Religion" and report with "all conscience of Truth" how God's "Divine Providence hath irradiated an Indian Wilderness,"[3] scholars have suspended themselves in a state of perpetual revision. What is shocking, though, is that Jennings and Vaughan either ignored or dismissed the vast amount of poetry written by New Englanders about the American natives. This, too, in the face of Norman S. Grabo's well-known 1962 article, "The Veiled Vision: the role of aesthetics in early American intellectual history." Arguing from the premise that ideas representing major aspects of human experience are expressed in symbolic forms of art and not merely in discursive communication, Grabo challenges contemporary intellectual historians to consider colonial "belles-lettres" as "symbolic expressions, often involuntary, of the artist's emotional framework of ideas." The pursuit of such information, Grabo believes, is "not only useful, but essential to understanding the Puritan mind."[4]

Richard Slotkin, in *Regeneration Through Violence: The Mythology of the American Frontier, 1600–1800*, met Grabo's challenge so successfully that his work will remain the classic study for decades. Slotkin magnificently probes the collective psyche of the European as he first encounters the forbidding wilderness and shapes a mythology to justify his presence, to undermine his enemies, to relieve his psychological anxieties about the terror and the attractiveness of primitivism, and to find a way to deal with his separation from the mother country. "In accounts of the Indian wars," says Slotkin, "the cultural anxieties and aspirations of the colonists found their most dramatic and symbolic portrayal. . . . It was within this genre (the captivity narrative) . . . that the first American mythology took shape—a mythology in which the hero was the captive or the victim of devilish American savages."[5] But Slotkins's study, so great in its sweep and so compelling in its theory, still leaves room for others to trace as precisely as possible the ways in which the colonial writers, particularly the poets, constructed the prototypical American myths from their emotional framework of ideas.

Specifically, Benjamin Tompson's *New Englands Crisis* (1676) is one poem which deserves closer attention. This mock-epic, verse captivity narrative, a poem in which all new England is held hostage by riotous demons who serve as the instruments of a disappointed, even avenging, God, perhaps stands as the quintessential expression of the Puritan's collective fear that they may be "consumed out of the good land," as John Winthrop warned fifty years before. *New Englands Crisis*, or its British editions called *New Englands Tears* and *Sad and Deplorable Newes*, is a fascinating and telling manifestation of the Puritans' compulsion to interpret their world symbolically, to impose analytic and dramatic structures upon experience, regardless of what we might call fact or reality. What interests me most about Tompson's poem, particularly a sub-section called "Marlburyes Fate," is the way Tompson seems to have taken some of the most exotic, even surrealistic, images from continental travel narratives and the visual arts, particularly engraving, and welded that material to mythic and classical elements, local imagery, and lore. He then imbedded all this within generic forms which had just begun to achieve popularity in England. I must admit my thesis is partly speculative and my information is spotty. In my defense, however, I will simply say that investigation into the backgrounds of seventeenth-century thought is always a risky business where texts, journals, diaries, and wills are incomplete or missing, as in the case of Benjamin Tompson.[6]

In 1676, in the middle of King Philip's devastating war with the Puritans, Benjamin Tompson was an unemployed school teacher who walked the streets of Charlestown, Massachusetts, bitterly frustrated by his unsuccessful attempts to achieve the financial rewards and the colonial prestige that he, a victim of the errand into the wilderness, thought he deserved. Since his graduation from

Harvard College in 1662, Tompson had tried his hand at poetry, taught school, studied medicine and the arcane science of alchemy, but mainly he appears to have been very unsettled, moving from town to town in an effort to find a place suitable to his temperament and a non-clerical position appropriate to his station in society. His poetry, to this point, was composed chiefly to memorialize the sacrifices of his patriarchal father, a first-generation "Boanerges" who had been driven literally insane by his encounter with the darker forces in New England. The records indicate that Benjamin was a brilliant but contentious individual who, by 1676, had grown tired of pressing one legal suit after another and had wearied of writing obsequious letters to the Mathers and other influential colonists. With the outbreak of the war, Tompson decided to declare himself spokesman, apologist, critic, war correspondent, and colonial myth-maker for New England. Perhaps through the vehicle of public poetry he might thrust himself into the limelight, thereby proving to the world that he was in fact a member of the intelligentsia and thus entitled to the land and the recognition consequent to aristocracy. He would show Massachusetts Bay that his father had not died in vain and that members of the second generation could also make significant contributions to the great Protestant cause. The glory of the settlement of the New World, with all the high drama of providential rewards and punishments, had not ceased with the ebbing of the Great Migration in 1640. When Metacomet, dubbed "King Philip" by the Puritans, whipped up his "Tawny Bands" in allied revolt against oppression, Tompson immediately perceived the mythic richness of the war between the holy Protestant crusaders and the barbaric infidels. King Philip's war would provide Benjamin Tompson with the means of self-regeneration through a violence of imagery, metaphor, and pictorial description just as the colony at large would rejuvenate itself through a baptism in blood and a confirmation (or tempering) in fire. Because he knew the English hungered for the sensational news of the apocalypse in America, Tompson believed that he could rise to fame at the literary expense of the natives and his reprobate neighbors.

Composed of about twelve separate sections and extending for 614 lines, *New Englands Crisis* covers the events in the war from 10 February to 23 April, 1676, in Plymouth Colony, Connecticut, Massachusetts Bay, and Rhode Island. The poem is a rather haphazard combination of serious elegiac tribute, caustic denunciation of English greed, witty and urbane panegyric, and brutal belittlement of the Indian character. The title page clearly announces the poet's epic intention to trace the ultimate cause of New England's lamentable condition to the "unheard of *Crueltyes* practiced upon the *Persons* and *Estates* of its united *Colonyes*, without respect of *Sex, Age* or *Quality* of *Persons* by the Barbarous *Heathen* thereof."[7] In the Golden Age, Tompson begins, the first colonists were, like the original Indians, emblems of innocence, pastoral shepherds subsisting on the plain but hardy fruits of the virgin land, all united in affection and free in their judgment. But, whether through some clandestine plot of a "Romish

Agent," or through a mysterious astrological catastrophe, or through some fever-
ish pagan heat, the planets were thrown out of their fixed course and Philip, as
all "Indian spirits," commenced the war because he needs "No grounds but lust
to make a Christian bleed" (l. 102). In the next scene, in imitation of the epic
set-speech, Tompson describes the Wampanoag Chief King Philip, whom he
calls "this greazy *Lout*," as he assembles, or "Kennel(s) together" his warriors.
So as not to mix his metaphors too badly, Tompson has Philip cast "some bacon-
rine-like looks" about his "throne / Of rotten stump" as he gives instructions in
pidgin English to swarms of his fellow demons on how to "drink [wine] out of
[English] Captains throats," or on how to "have their silken wives" in exchange
for squaws, so that in the end the hypocritical and greedy English may be "whipt
by virtue of [Indian] laws" (ll. 103–30).

In the remaining five hundred lines of the poem, Tompson deemphasizes the
shortcomings of the English to concentrate more fully on the savagery of the
Indian. In so doing, he uses many of the techniques that one might expect from
a writer of heroic or mock-heroic verse of the Restoration. He uses epic similes,
epithets, catalogues of weapons, set scenes, and decorative allusion from classical
Latin literature or Greek mythology. Thus he instructs that the Indians be pictured
as "*Vulcans* anvilling New-Englands brains" (l. 436) while Englishmen post
"daily on their *Pegasean* Steeds / [to] Bring sad reports of worse than *Nero's*
deeds" (ll. 243–44). Next, Tompson employs the standard methods of the earlier
New England historians and pseudo-anthropologists who pretended to have some
accurate information regarding the natives' origin, their laws, customs, military
strategies, or language. For example, Tompson loves to titillate his English
audience with references to such exotic words or notions as "Pawawa" "Sachem"
"Squaw" "Sagamore" "Wigwam" "matchit" or "wunnegin," the language prac-
ticed by these "Canibals" (l. 343) of "Ethiopick" (l. 345) hue. Like William
Wood, John Josselyn, or Roger Williams, among many others, Benjamin Tomp-
son delights in fascinating the foreign reader with his dubious knowledge of
Indian domestic or ceremonial life, as when he refers to "That phansie which
so stifly they maintain / That such on hunting go who hence are slain" (*NET*,
ll. 378–80).

But what I find most interesting about Tompson's imagery of the Indian is
that, except for scattered bits of local lore or common stereotype, Tompson's
New England primitives bear little resemblance to his immediate reality. Indeed,
the Wampanoags, Narragansetts, and other tribes of the Algonkian Confederation
share the visage and traits of remote and exotic natives described and portrayed
in 150-year-old travel narratives illustrated by Theodore de Bry, the Flemish
goldsmith and engraver, who, at the end of the sixteenth century, published a
fourteen-volume history of the New World called *Historia Americae*. Principally,
de Bry worked from the Floridian sketches of French Huguenot Jacques le
Moyne, from the watercolors John White made in Virginia, and from woodcuts

by Hans Staden, who was held captive by the cannibals of Brazil. De Bry's fourteen folio volumes contain the narratives of thirty-five explorations over a period of 150 years.[8] It took de Bry and his family forty-eight years to put together the 250 engravings and the various texts which were written in Latin, German, English, and French. As noted art historians have pointed out, "it was quite natural and even inevitable that the artist and the engraver should translate this new wealth of information into pre-existent patterns of thought and vision."[9] The watercolors and the engravings "serve as a perfect index to the range of European interests imposed upon the facts of native life in foreign lands."[10] For example, "fully one-third of the forty-two illustrations in de Bry's *Brevis Narratio eorum quae in Florida* deal with the major theme of war and death."[11] Similarly, it appears that the emotional framework of ideas most attractive to Tompson, New England's public voice, consisted of century-old European notions of multi-continental barbarism or cannibalism, of vast, naked swarms of idol-worshipping, butchering, infanticidal monsters.

Tompson's Indians are metamorphized animals who attack unsuspecting Christians paralyzed by the nightmarish fear of captivity, sexual assalt, and cannibalism. These "Monsters shapt and fac'd like men" (1.319) vanish as "inchanted Castles," (1. 269) or they "like the stremes along the thickets glide" (1. 362) only to reappear in another elfin or demonic form to strip, bind, "ravish, flea and roast," (1. 160) or to make sacrifice for "aiery spirits," or to the "*Molech* of their hellish guts, / Which craves the flesh in gross, their ale in butts" (ll. 371–72). The natives live in gloomy forests, mirey bogs, on cragg'd rocks, or they crawl "from a thousand holes / . . . with brands and fired poles" (ll. 457–59). Serpentlike, they dance in an avious, or twisted, path, while warriors read the white man's doom from "Vellome Rolls, flead off his right hand man / Which they send home for Sagamores to tan / With Scalpes" (NET, ll. 314–16).

"Marlburyes Fate," the most interesting sub-section of Tompson's epic, not only shows Tompson's reliance upon visual and mythological imagery, but provides demonstrative evidence that Tompson himself had at least a passing interest in the arts of the oil painter, or limner, as he was called especially in New England. Beginning with line 423, Tompson adopts the newly developed generic form of the "Advice-to-a-Painter" poem to more graphically depict the horrors of native savagery.[12] I believe that Tompson had no particular painting or engraving in mind when he wrote "Marlburyes Fate," nor do I think that Tompson actually intended for any painter to follow his instructions for visual composition. This poem, however, in both content and form, shows a sophistication and a familiarity with European visual and literary sources far beyond our traditional expectations for supposedly isolated, iconoclastic, and provincial Puritans.

Tompson begins by instructing the painter to "overtrack," that is, figuratively to trace, his literary description of the Indians. He tells the painter to mix an olive color to "trim" these elves, or "child snatchers," as Tompson would have understood that meaning of the world "elf" from Teutonic myth. Perhaps, too, his instructions to mix pigments may reveal some familiarity with the numerous recipe books available in Boston at this time.[13] He further instructs that this same hue be employed to draw "many thousand theives" like scarecrows, possibly in imitation of the engravings which show Indians with drawn bows and outstretched arms, sometimes formed into ranks across the fields surrounding their villages, almost as if they were marching in Roman columns.[14] Traditionally the engravers covered the natives' "privy parts," as they said, with the local flora; here Tompson advises that oak leaves, of course appropriate to New England, will do. Then, in a very nice mirror image within the poem, Tompson wants the painter to draw devils upon the Indians' cheeks as the Indians themselves have done with grease and mud from the swamps. Despite the fact that Tompson lived among the Indians, he represents them as having long, curly hair and beards, "Whose locks Medusaes Snakes, do ropes resemble." As a teacher of the classics, Tompson is well aware of Hesiod's portrayal of the Gorgons, often depicted as monstrous creatures with serpents in their hair, claws, and huge teeth. But Tompson is also referring to engravings such as those published with Vespucci's letters, showing natives with hip length, curly hair.[15]

At this point, Tompson conjures up the most horrible images of cannibalism mixed with surrealistic deviltry, remarkably similar to the images in Hans Staden[16] and in one particular anonymous Portuguese painting.[17] He tells the painter to "Limm them besmear'd with Christian blood and oiled With fat out of white human bodies boiled." Again, continuing the mixture of classical myth and sixteenth-century engraving, he describes "clubs, like mauls and full of stains." Possibly Tompson is including a bit of realism here, too, because King Philip made a habit of proudly displaying his ornamental warrior's club. At any rate, Tompson's Indians in the next lines appear to live in a landscape which closely resembles certain Spanish views of the West Indies or Latin America.[18] In fantastic, sometimes idyllic or pastoral settings, the Indians often retreat to the mountains to hide from invading conquistadores, to mine for silver or gold, or to engage in ceremonial dances or worship, usually around a campfire or within a fixed pole design. Once more, beginning on line 445, Tompson returns to myth with an allusion to Cupid, but as always his point is essentially comparative: these Indians shoot arrows which "drill our hearts" causing emotional or physical injury, not love. Engravings from almost every part of the world show the natives armed with bows and arrows and sheaves, but John White's watercolors frequently emphasize such armament, especially in his full length studies of chieftains. One portrait renders an Indian from behind, clearly showing the quiver, while various kinds and lengths of arrows are illustrated on the painting's border.[19] Starting at line 451, Tompson radically shifts the perspective by describing the conflicts on earth as they might be seen by an entourage of heavenly theatre patrons. I believe there is a possibility that Tompson may have been familiar with European books, such as those containing the work of Jacques Callot, in which there were engraved illustrations of massive set designs for spectacular productions. These books, like the recipe books for painters, showed aspiring directors how to stage allegorical scenes, armies on the move, kings and queens in full splendor and majestic pomp, and so forth.

As Tompson moves through the remaining fifty lines of "Marlburyes Fate," he continues to juxtapose classical literary figures with the grotesque, melodramatic, and sensational imagery of engraving. We see subterranean fiends set fire to whole colonial settlements, sleeping Puritans brutalized by pagan rapists, priests and soldiers denied access to their weapons, gluttons frying in their own, greasy fat, mothers forced to witness the immolation of their infants, and even priests "muttering ore their apish" rosary beads. Over all this, the allegorical figure of Attaxie, that is confusion, the opposite of syntax, which originally meant the order and arrangement of troops on a battlefield, arbitrarily dooms some to one or another kind of horrible death.

Whether Tompson took these ideas directly from first-hand inspection of de Bry and others, or whether he independently transformed the purely literary into the visual, I cannot say for certain. But one year after the publication of *New Englands Crisis*, Tompson wrote an introductory poem for William Hubbard's *A Narrative of the Troubles with the Indians in New England* in which he compares Hubbard's account of the Indians in the New World to the great travel narratives of Samuel Purchase, Richard Hakluyt, John Smith, John de Laet, Peter Martyre, Jose de Acosta; and he specifically mentions geographers Joseph and James Moxon, Spanish grammarian John Minsheu, military historians William Barrife, Nicholas Boone, and Richard Elton, explorers Sir Francis Drake and Christopher Columbus, and Roger Williams, translator and linguist of New England. In all probability, according to knowledgeable art historians, the educated seventeenth century Puritan had access to these travel narratives illustrated by de Bry, some from de Bry's press and some from pirated and imitated copies.

But I have a further reason for believing that Tompson had direct access to the works of de Bry. Just one year before the publication of *New Englands Crisis,* John Foster, America's first engraver, a professional limner, Harvard graduate, physician, mathematician, and former school teacher, moved from Dorchester to Boston to open a printing shop to compete with Samuel Green's in Cambridge. Foster appears to have been an immensely gifted and creative individual whose interests seemed to coincide perfectly with Tompson's. It was no wonder then that Tompson commissioned Foster to print *New Englands Crisis*: Foster had already made a woodcut to illustrate two books, the *Indian ABC* and *Indian Dialogues*; he had done another woodcut which became the official seal of Massachusetts Bay, showing an Indian in the mannerist mode of de Bry; and he was currently at work on Hubbard's White Hills (or Wine Hills) map for Hubbard's *Narrative of the Troubles with the Indians*.[20] Both Tompson and Foster were innovative and eclectic individuals with complementary interests in geography, science, art, literature, and Indians. Both were close friends of the Mathers, and they were practically neighbors in Boston. Is it unreasonable to infer that Tompson's "Advice-to-a-Painter" poem is in fact an Advice to a Painting Printer, John Foster? Is it farfetched to speculate that an engraver showed European engravings to a poet familiar with European travel narratives, while both were working on contributions to William Hubbard's history of King Philip's War?

While such questions may always remain unanswered, I can more confidently identify the precise literary model for Tompson's "Marlburyes Fate" in Thomas Higgons' translation of Italian Gian Francesco Busenello's poem, *A Prospective of the Naval Triumph of the Venetians over the Turks* (1685), and in Edmund Waller's English adaptation of Busenello, called "Instructions to a Painter," on how to portray the Duke of York's battle with the Dutch Navy in 1665.[21] From Higgons' translation of Busenello, Tompson took the spirit of the Christian crusade against the infidels, and from Waller's poem he took the learned and decorative use of classical allusion, the cosmic setting, and, in a few cases, phrases within the heroic couplets.

Near the Dardenelles on 25 June, 1656, in the eleventh year of a twenty-five-year war, the Venetian Navy defeated the Turkish Navy. A special committee of the Venetian senate awarded a commission to Pietro Liberi to paint a commemorative portrait of the victory. Either to help Liberi secure the commission or to celebrate Liberi's appointment, Gian Busenello published his "Advice-to-a-Painter" poem, the first in Europe to move beyond the pastoral and lyric restrictions of this genre as it was first practiced by the Greeks and the Romans. Thomas Higgons, a minor poet and statesman living in Venice, translated and published the poem in London in 1658, with a special poetic recommendation by Edmund Waller. In June 1664, when the Duke of York scored a minor victory over the Dutch in what is now called the Second Dutch War, Waller returned to the Italian literary model that he had recommended six years before. Waller's effusive praise for the Duke and his war, which rapidly turned into fiasco, was then satirized in at least five other "Advice-to-a-Painter" poems, two or three most certainly by Andrew Marvell.[22] This means that Benjamin Tompson was well aware of the most recent literary events in England and that he somehow secured, before 1676, copies of Higgons' and Waller's works, which he ultimately adapted to perfect use in *New Englands Crisis*.

Not surprisingly, it was Busenello's description of the horrible visage of the Turk which appealed most to Benjamin Tompson. He saw, in lines like these from the English version of the Italian prototype, a perfect similitude with New England's tragedy:

> The shocks, assaults, and cries so loud and shrill,
> Did Grecian woods, and Asian vallies fill,
> Which ecchoes from dark caves, and hollow ground
> In sad & mournful accents did resound.[23]

To Busenello, the Turks were the "barbarous Enemy" (l. 144), the "hatefull monsters" (l. 164), or the Pagan "Infidells" (l. 150). They were whipped into this frenzy, says Busenello,

> When Mars grown jealous for his native place,
> Arm'd all his Furies to defend his Thrace,
> ·
> The Heavens and Seas for thee the Zodiaks are,
> When God incites, and rowses thee to war. [ll. 121–22 and 127–28]

As in *New Englands Crisis*, the Gods, the Stars, the Heavenly Monarch, and even the barbaric chieftain, here the Turk, have a hand in this outbreak of war and cosmic chaos. The Turkish king, "upon whose aged chin did grow / A beard, which thence unto his waste did flow" (ll. 189–90), incites his pagan swarms to attack; "From cruell Bowes with force and malice bent, / Slaughters, and many feather'd deaths were sent" (ll. 113–14). So massive was the carnage, the poet claims "The blewer forehead of the Sea was dy'd / With streaks of blood, which did her face divide" (ll. 117–18). Tompson retained the same image in his description of the Puritan attempts to civilize the New England wilderness. He says that Hubbard's narrative ought best be called "New-Englands Travels through the bloudy Sea."

As the fighting goes on, Busenello advises Liberi to paint the picture of "Death and amazement, hatred, cries, and fear, / Together mixt make one confusion here" (ll. 223–24). Tompson used the allegorical figure of Attaxie to characterize the confusion and horror of combat, as in the battle about Chelmsford: "Here's midnight shrieks, and Soul-amazing moanes, . . . / Confusive outcryes every where resounds" (ll. 573, 576). Both Busenello and Tompson try to give the reader a larger perspective on the war by surveying the piteous condition of the victims. Busenello comments on the Venetian forces: "Some wring their hands, some stamp their feet, some tear / Their hair, and all are pale with rage or fear" (ll. 231–32). Using the same repetitive and sweeping structure, Tompson says that confusion and arbitrary death command:

> Some counsels she to fry and some to freeze,
> These to the garison, those to the road,
> Some to run empty, some to take their load:
> Thus while confusion most mens hearts divide
> Fire doth their small exchecquer soon decide. [ll. 494–98]

Common to both the Italian poem and the Americanized version are certain sentimentalized and melodramatic scenes, in particular those domestic tragedies that were sure to inflame the passions of the already outraged reader. Busenello traces the figure of the weeping Turkish mother who "on the shoar was sate, / With her small children, waiting upon Fate" (ll. 319–20). Upon discovering the defeat of the Turks and the death of her husband, "She dash'd the childrens brains against the ground" (l. 324). This is one of the classically barbaric acts of the savage as seen by the American or European writer. In *New Englands Crisis*, as in almost every other captivity narrative or account of the various Indian wars, the natives are invariably accused of dashing out the brains of innocent Puritan children while their mothers (here recast for sympathy) stand Rachel-like over the bodies and weep for this tragic and most gruesome loss. For Busenello as for Tompson, the ultimate fear was captivity and all the subsequent belittlement and degradation. Upon the triumphant return of the Venetians, we are presented with a picture of the more unfortunate "afflicted Poor, / Who chains about their necks and ankles wore" (ll. 263–64). These were the distressed Venetian believers, the Christian captives,

> . . . whom the Turks had caught,
> And various Fates into the Gallies brought,
> Who deform'd slavery did with patience take,
> Though us'd like beasts, for their Redeemers sake. [ll. 265–70]

While many more parallels could be drawn between the Italian model and the American epic, it is clear that in general and in many particulars Busenello and Tompson used the same emotional framework of ideas to glorify their struggles and to disparage the heathen enemy. The colonial poet borrowed or adapted the Italian verbal imagery, just as he did the European visual imagery, because he knew that his audience would respond consciously and unconsciously to the symbolic and the mythic, that they would be horrified by the prospects of slaughter, rape, cannibalism, and captivity. Both poets imagined a contest between the forces of light and dark; both wanted to probe into the shadowy and nightmarish world of the heathen warrior—to show this animalistic creature at his worst. The savage's color, his weapons, his cruel practices and strange rituals were the stuff of colonial or Renaissance ghoulish surrealism. In this world turned upside-down, the enemy is so fearsome that words alone do not suffice; the "Advice-to-a-Painter" poem carries the obligation for the poet to present dramatic recreations, action captured, drawn, colored, and frozen for the moment as in a photograph so that the artist, most sensitive of all observers, can improve upon the merely literary attempt. Thus, the writer achieves a kind of modest immediacy: his humble words have the impact of the eyewitness report. What is most important here, however, is the attempt to visualize myth, obviously at the expense of realism.

To see the power of the Puritan myth, one should consider, for example, this historical example of their firm conviction that the natives were different, sub-human in almost every way, even physically. Despite the presence of the most obvious physical evidence, the emotional and mythic framework predominates. On 22 September, 1676, during King Philip's War, Benjamin Tompson went to the home of Samuel Sewall at nine in the morning with five other colonial physicians to dissect, according to Sewall's Diary, "the middlemost of the Indian executed the day before." One Mr. [Dr.] Hooper took the Indian's heart " in his hand, affirmed it to be the stomack." The diary notation closes with this remark: "I spent 18s., 6d in Medera Wine, and 6d I gave to the maid."[24] On this social occasion, Dr. Hooper, and probably some of his associates, persisted in seeing anatomical differences—despite the fact that he held the heart in his hand, Dr. Hooper had to declare it the stomach in order to cling to the myth that the seat of the savage's passion is in his gut, normally the locale of the appetite, the sensual, craving, and instinctual part of man. It is no wonder then that the Puritans gave back to the Europeans the same images the Europeans had earlier disseminated from Frankfurt, Lisbon, or London. Nor is it farfetched to say that Colonial Protestants found a type in the Italian crusaders' holy war with the tawny infidels. The final poetic prayer from Tompson's *New Englands Crisis* summarizes his desperate attempt to cling to the myth:

> Let this dear Lord the sad Conclusion be
> of poor New-Englands dismal tragedy.
> Let not the glory of thy former work
> Blasphemed be by pagan Jew or Turk. . . . [ll. 583–86]

NOTES

1. (Boston: Little, Brown Co., 1965), vi–vii.

2. (Chapel Hill: University of North Carolina Press, 1975; rpt. New York: W. W. Norton Co., 1976), pp. 180–82.

3. Cotton Mather, *Magnalia Christi Americana*, ed. Kenneth B. Murdock, Books I and II (Cambridge, Mass.: The Belknap Press, Harvard University Press, 1977), p. 89.

4. *WMQ*, 19 (1962), 493–510; rpt. in Sacvan Bercovitch, ed., *The American Puritan Imagination* (London: Cambridge University Press, 1974), p. 29.

5. (Middletown, Conn.: Wesleyan University Press, 1973), p. 21.

6. For more on biographical information about some colonial figures, see White, *Tompson*, ch. 2.

7. Benjamin Tompson, *New Englands Crisis* (Boston, 1676) in White, *Tompson*. All subsequent references to Tompson's poetry are from this edition.

8. Michael Alexander, ed., *Discovering the New World* (New York: Harper and Row, 1976), p. 11.

9. Ellwood Parry, *The Image of the Indian and the Black Man in American Art, 1590–1900* (New York: George Braziller, 1974), p. 2.

10. Parry, p. 2. See also, W. P. Cumming, et al. *The Exploration of North America, 1630–1776* (London, Paul Elek, 1974); Hugh Honour, *The New Golden Land: European*

Images of American from the Discovery to the Present Time (New York: Pantheon Books, 1975); and Hugh Honour, *The European Vision of America* (Cleveland, Ohio: The Cleveland Museum of Art, 1975).

11. Parry, p. 2.

12. Mary Tom Osborne, *Advice-to-a-Painter Poems, 1633–1856: An Annotated Finding List* (Austin: University of Texas Press, 1949).

13. For information about the visual arts in colonial New England, I am deeply indebted to my colleague Professor Douglas George of the College of Fine Arts, University of New Mexico. I have also drawn information from several published sources, including John D. Morse, ed., *Prints in and of America to 1850* (Charlottesville: University Press of Virginia, 1970), and Ian M. G. Quimby, ed., *American Painting to 1776: A Reappraisal* (Charlottesville: University Press of Virginia, 1971).

14. See Theodore de Bry's engravings in Alexander, for example those on pp. 29, 30, 48, 53, 66, 87, 99.

15. See Honour, *New Golden Land*, pp. 10–11.

16. See de Bry's engravings in Alexander, especially ch. 3, "Hans Staden among the Cannibals of Brazil," pp. 90–121.

17. Honour, *New Golden Land*, pp. 54–55.

18. Honour, *New Golden Land*, pp. 22–23 provides a full color plate of Jan Mostaert's *A West Indian Scene*, c. 1540–50; see also, Alexander, p. 158.

19. Honour, p. 70, and Alexander, pp. 66, 87, for example.

20. Richard B. Holman, "Seventeenth-Century American Prints," in Morse, pp. 23–52, provides excellent information about Foster's career.

21. Osborne provides a full account of the literary and artistic background for Busenello's poem, Higgons' translation, Liberi's painting, and Waller's literary adaptation of Busenello/Higgons, pp. 14–17.

22. See George deF. Lord, ed. *Poems on Affairs of State: Augustan Satirical Verse, 1660–1714* (New Haven: Yale University Press, 1963), I, ch. 1; and H. M. Margoliouth, ed., *The Poems and Letters of Andrew Marvell*, 3rd edition (Oxford: The Clarendon Press, 1971), I.

23. Gian Francesco Busenello, *A Prospective of the Naval Triumph of the Venetians over the Turk. To Signor Pietro Liberi That Renowned, and famous Painter*, translated by Thomas Higgons and recommended by Edmund Waller (London, 1658), ll. 153–156. Subsequent references to this poem are cited by line number in the text.

24. Sewall, *Diary*, I, 23.

15 PETRUS RAMUS AND MICHAEL WIGGLESWORTH: THE LOGIC OF POETIC STRUCTURE

ALAN H. POPE

No other Puritan poet has suffered more negative criticism and disrespect than Michael Wigglesworth, author of America's first best-seller, *The Day of Doom*. To many, Wigglesworth, as a caricature of the grim, high-hatted Puritan, sacrificed the fine art of poetry to the sterile dogmatics of religion. Typically, Wigglesworth is portrayed as a humorless man writing galloping fourteeners and doggerel ballads. This negative view of the critics has developed partly from their failure to appreciate, or even understand, the dialectical nature of Wigglesworth's poetry. Both *The Day of Doom* and *Meat Out of the Eater* contain structural patterns that parallel the logical system presented in the *Dialectic* of Petrus Ramus.

While a student and tutor at Harvard, Wigglesworth studied Ramus' *Dialectic*, and his *Diary* specifically records his study of Ramus and his use of logic, especially syllogistic reasoning, to resolve questions of religion. In *The Day of Doom*, Wigglesworth uses syllogisms to organize the individual stanzas and the entire debate between the sinners and Christ. *Meat Out of the Eater,* a distinctly Ramean poem, contains logical patterns taken from "Invention," the first part of Ramus' *Dialectic*.

The earliest criticism of Wigglesworth's poetry is the most sympathetic. The fifth edition of *The Day of Doom*, printed in 1701, four years before Wigglesworth's death, includes the poem "On the following Work, And It's Author," written by Jonathan Mitchell. The opening lines of the poem offer an appreciation for the craftsmanship of the verse that later critics do not share: "A verse may find him who a sermon flies, / Saith Herbert well. Great truths to dress in Meter / Becomes a Preacher, who men's Souls doth prize, / That truth in Sugar roll'd may taste the sweeter."[1] In July, 1705, Cotton Mather published "A Faithful Man," which includes the funeral oration he gave for Wigglesworth, a brief biography, and excerpts from his papers. Mather makes this comment on the poetry: "And that yet he might more *Faithfully* set himself to do Good, when he could not *Preach* he *Wrote* several Composures, wherein he proposed the edification of such Readers as are for Plain Truths, dressed up in a *Plain Meeter*."[2] Both Mitchell and Mather appreciate the synthesis of poetry and religion. Wigglesworth's contemporaries viewed the preacher's truths and the poet's art as one, but later critics found the poetry merely an inartistic medium for preaching.

By 1863, in John Ward Dean's *Sketch of the Life of Rev. Michael Wigglesworth*, the religion and poetry are no longer perceived as artistically compatible. The poetry becomes a clumsy vehicle for the teaching of an outdated doctrine: "The roughness of his verses was surely not owing to carelessness or indolence, for neither of these were characteristic of the man. The true explanation may be that he sacrificed his poetical taste to this theology, and that for the sake of inculcating sound doctrine he was willing to write in halting numbers."[3]

Moses Coit Tyler's *History* praises Wigglesworth's poetic attempts in an unpoetic time, but finds little real art in his poetry: "His verse is quite lacking in art; its ordinary form being a crude, swinging ballad-measure, with a sort of cheap melody, a shrill reverberating clatter, that would instantly catch and please the popular ear, at that time deaf to daintier and more subtle effects in poetry." Tyler does not believe, however, that the poetry is completely without merit, for he finds "an irresistible sincerity, a reality, a vividness, reminding one of similar qualities in the prose of John Bunyan." In his discussion of *The Day of Doom*, Tyler notes the "truly precocious logical acumen" of the sinners in their debate with Christ, but he does not elaborate upon this comment.[4]

In a brief, general article published in 1928, F. O. Matthiessen comments on Wigglesworth's "strange imagination," and he also finds little artistic skill in the poetry. Matthiessen notes the logical quality of *The Day of Doom*: "But the tone of the whole is not sulphurous, but logical; the work is full of the homespun logic of a methodical mind."[5] He, too, fails to elaborate upon the nature or structure of this "homespun" logic.

The only book-length study of Wigglesworth's life and poetry is Richard Crowder's excellent, analytical biography, *No Featherbed to Heaven*. This thorough and readable work places Wigglesworth's life and writings in the context of Puritan ideas. Crowder notes Wigglesworth's study of Ramean logic, but he does not examine the use of the logic in the poetry. Instead, he finds the organization of *Meat Out of the Eater* to be musical: "To borrow a phrase from music, the book is structured like a theme and variations."[6] More recently in "*The Day of Doom* as Chronomorph," Crowder explores the use of time in the poem and analyzes the juxtaposition of past and present verb tenses to create dramatic effects.[7]

In 1978 Robert Daly published the first book-length study of American Puritan poetry, *God's Altar*. Revising some of the common generalizations about Puritan poetry, Daly's examination of the individual poets and poems is insightful. Daly assesses *The Day of Doom* as a failure and tells why: "One reason for its failure, and one difference between Wigglesworth and most other Puritan poets, is Wigglesworth's dismissal of the natural world, his inability to perceive, and hence to use, metaphor." But to describe the poem as a failure because it lacks metaphor is a narrow approach to *The Day of Doom*. If it does not rely on imagery from the sensible world, which Daly believes a criterium for a good poem, the reason is that the central focus of the poem is a careful and logical development of the religious debate between the sinners and Christ. Metaphor is replaced by logical comparisons and syllogistic debate.

Daly discusses the general influence of Petrus Ramus on Puritan aesthetics. Relying on Walter Ong's opinions, Daly argues that Ramus was studied only by children, and concludes that too much "intelligence and sophistication" have been brought to the study of Ramus. Daly contends that Ramus had little influence on Puritan writers.[8] Two flaws underlie Daly's analysis. First, like many other critics of Ramus, Daly relies on secondary sources. Second, Daly approaches Ramus primarily as a rhetorician. By neglecting the dialectic of Ramus, Daly ignores one practical use of Ramus for Puritan writers and the logical system that serves them as a foundation for poetic form. Ramus' influence on Wigglesworth is not rhetorical, but logical.

This short summary of Wigglesworth criticism outlines the main points discussed by the critics. While some critics briefly comment upon the logical quality of *The Day of Doom* and *Meat Out of the Eater*, they do not describe the links between Wigglesworth's poetry and Ramus' logic. Despite the work of Perry Miller and Samuel Morison on the importance of Ramus for Puritan thought and education, no critic has examined any American Puritan poet from the perspective of Ramean logic.[9] (In chapter 11, Jesper Rosenmeier considers the impact of Ramean rhetoric on the poetry of Edward Johnson.)

At Harvard, in the seventeenth century, the understanding of logic, particularly Ramean logic, prepared the student for the study of all other disciplines. The study of Ramus, as Perry Miller wrote, was a central influence on the New England mind: "The fundamental fact concerning the intellectual life of New Englanders is that they ranged themselves definitely under the banner of the Ramists. The Peripatetic system was indeed read at Harvard, but the Ramist was believed, and it exercised the decisive role in shaping New England thought."[10] Letters, speeches, and Harvard theses reveal the pervasive influence of Ramus at Harvard College. Besides the Latin texts of Ramus' *Dialectic*, the primary text for the study of Ramean logic was Alexander Richardson's *The Logicians School-Master: Or, a Comment upon Ramus Logicke*. But this commentary necessitated Ramus' own text, for Richardson often cites only part of a definition or quotation and refers the reader to the Latin Ramus. Ramus' primary contribution to the history of logic was the reorganization and presentation of classical logic into an easy-to-learn schematic and diagrammatic form.[11]

Dialectic, the art of disputing or reasoning well, is divided into two parts, Invention and Disposition (or Judgment). Invention, in the sense of coming upon or finding, declares the separate parts of which all thought is composed and presents the various kinds of arguments. Disposition explains the ways of judging or arranging these arguments.

The arguments of Invention are divided into two species, artificial and inartificial. Artificial arguments create belief by their own nature, in contrast to inartificial arguments, which are human or divine testimony that depend on the credibility of the witness rather than upon their own intrinsic logic. Wigglesworth

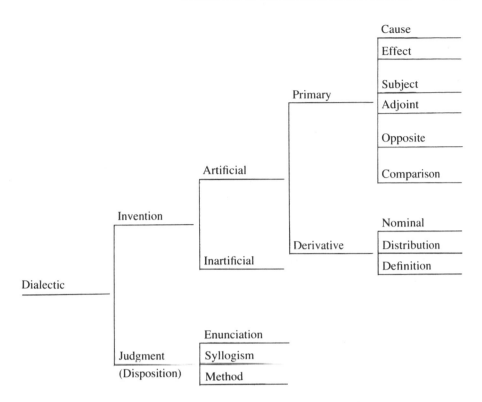

uses this distinction between artificial and inartificial arguments in *Meat Out of the Eater* by presenting artificial arguments in the ten Meditatons, and then offering personal testimony to convince the reader in the concluding hortatory. Artificial arguments are divided into primary and derivative. The primary arguments, which are simple and not derived from any others, have four species: cause and effect, subject and adjoint, opposite, and comparison.

The discussion of cause is one of the most interesting sections in Ramus. He presents a precise definition of the four classical causes—final, formal, efficient, and material—with a lengthy analysis and division of the efficient cause. Ramus concludes this section by saying that the causes of a thing should be considered before any other argument. Wigglesworth follows this advice in *The Day of Doom*, where in the prefatory poems he explains the efficient and final cause of the poem:

> Thou, Christ, art he to whom I pray,
> Thy Glory fain I would display.
> Oh! guide me by thy sacred Sprite
> So to indite, and so to write,
> That I thine holy Name may praise,
> And teach the Sons of men thy wayes. [p. ix]

Effect, treated briefly by Ramus, is defined as anything which is issued from causes.

The next primary arguments are subject and adjoint. The subject is that to which something is adjoined, as the soul is the subject of science, ignorance, virtue, and vice. The adjoint is the thing adjoined to the subject, as good and bad are adjoints of the body and the soul. In *Meat Out of the Eater* Christians are the subject, and suffering, both to the body and the soul, is the adjoint.

Opposites are contrary or repugnant. The contraries, which differ one to one, are divided into affirmative, either relative or adverse, and negative, either depriving or contradicting. For example, Wigglesworth's poetry contains many adverse contraries whose essence is separated, such as good and bad, or black and white.

The last primary argument, comparison, has two species, quantity and quality. Things compared in terms of quantity are either equal or unequal; if unequal, one is more or less than the other. Things compared in terms of quality are either like or unlike each other.

The second part of logic, Judgment or Disposition, shows the way to arrange the invented arguments. Disposition has three divisions: enunciation, syllogism, and method. If any enunciation is not clear or if the truth of a statement is doubtful or uncertain, then it is necessary, Ramus says, to convert it into a question and by syllogistic reasoning determine the truth or falsity of the statement. After defining the parts of the syllogism—proposition (major premise), assumption (minor premise), and conclusion—Ramus presents the various types with examples. The simple syllogism has twenty types, and the compound syllogism is divided into the conditional and the disjunctive. Ramus has a great deal of respect for the ability of the syllogism to resolve difficult questions—he calls it an image of the divine in the human mind. Ramus emphasizes that in literature the three parts of the syllogism are not always given, or are put in a scrambled order, thus obliging the reader to fill in the missing parts and arrange them in the proper order: "The use of the entire syllogism is very rare, for often, and nearly always in the poets, orators, philosophers, and all authors following natural usage, although they may treat of syllogistic questions, nevertheless some part of the syllogism is neglected. . . ."[12] Because the complete syllogism is not always given in *The Day of Doom*, readers have failed to see the role of syllogistic reasoning in the poet's debates and in the larger structure of the poem.

Method, the third division of Judgment, exercised strong influence on later writers and sparked frequent debate and criticism. For Ramus, method proceeds from the most general and most known to the most particular and least known. The natural method may not be suitable for certain audiences, so poets and orators often arrange the material in a prudential order, a scrambling of the natural method. Even Socrates, Ramus says, uses the prudential order in his dialogues. Throughout the *Dialectic*, Ramus also presents examples from the Latin poets to illustrate the parts of logic. The literary examples emphasize that logic is natural to everyone and is especially useful to writers.

Several features of Richardson's *The Logicians School-Master* are suggestive in the analysis of Wigglesworth's poetry. Richardson offers a lengthy discussion of comparison of quantity, which explains one thing by comparing it with another. Wigglesworth employs many such comparisons in *The Day of Doom*. Although Richardson assigns less significance to method than Ramus, his brief commentary may have had special meaning for Wigglesworth, for here he would have learned about *Crypticis methodi*, the secret method of poets: "If a man be to deliver an Art, hee must exactly observe this method in every point; but many times it falls out in discourses that disorder must be used, not for the doctrines sake, but because of the perversity of the hearers, for they often goe out of their way by reason of their weakness."[13] Richardson explains how poets can disguise the order of their arguments. Such secret disordering often makes it difficult to discover Ramean patterns and to reconstruct the argument in the natural order.

Richardson frequently argues that Ramus' logic can be applied to the study of religion. Ramus, adhering to a strict division of theology and logic, does not mention religion, but Richardson, like many others after Ramus, quotes the Bible to illustrate the logic. In addition, Richardson explains how the difficult parts of logic can be used to discuss and to debate Christian doctrine. For him, the purpose of logic is to "direct man to see the wisedom of God."[14] Besides the detailed commentary of Ramus' logic, Richardson's text described to the future poet, Michael Wigglesworth, how logic can be used in religious debate and in the organization of poetry.

Graduating at the top of his class in 1651, Wigglesworth returned to Harvard a year later and served as a tutor for two years while taking his master's degree. Two entries from the *Diary* which Wigglesworth kept while a tutor attest to his detailed study of Ramus. In the first entry, Wigglesworth says, "I disputed for Ramus in the Distribution of the 2d part of Logick against Richardson. My arguments found such acceptation with the seniours (though contrary to their former apprehensions) that pride prevailed." The second entry shows that Wigglesworth made a complete study of Ramus: "Yet for all this trouble god hath bin with me in my personal studys; for this day I began and finished all that part of my synopsis which treats about method."[15] Since method is the last topic in Ramus' logic, Wigglesworth is rejoicing in the completion of his synoptical study. The "synopsis" was a requirement for a master's degree, as described in *New Englands First Fruits*, the 1643 London publication about the new world and the recently founded Harvard College: "Every Schollar that giveth up in writing a *System*, or *Synopsis*, or summe of *Logick*, Naturall and Morall phylosophy, *arithmetick, Geometry,* and *Astronomy* . . . is fit to be dignified with his 2d Degree."[16] As an undergraduate, Wigglesworth was introduced to Ramus' logic, and as a tutor, he made Ramus a central focus of his studies and the subject of his master's synopsis.

The *Diary* records the effect of Ramus' logic on Wigglesworth's constant questions about his faith. In one passage he uses three different syllogisms to prove the existence of God, concluding with this final proof: "3ly My prayers have been answered from time to time, ergo there is a God who hath heard me. If there was no God, how should my prayers have been heard?" Here, the assumption is first, the conclusion second, and the proposition last. Placed in the correct order we have this syllogism:

> If there were no God, my prayers could not be answered.
> My prayers have been answered.
> Ergo, there is a God.

This syllogism is an example of the frequently used second manner conditional. Wigglesworth also attempts to prove the existence of God by a disjunctive syllogism: "Once I was blind, but now I see, once dead but now alive, once loving sin and hating holiness; who made this change? Not self; for to me believing was impossible. Not men, for then why are not others converted sooner (whilest it was easier). Nor Sathan; he is not such a fool to destroy his own kingdom; therefore it was God; ergo God is."[17] There are multiple terms in the proposition, but Ramus says, "The parts of the disjunctive proposition may be more than two, and nevertheless the art of concluding and judging will be the same."[18] Expressed as a syllogism:

> Either self or men or satan or God made this change.
> Self, men, or satan did not make this change.
> Therefore, God made this change.

This syllogism is an example of the second manner conditional, which contradicts one term of the proposition and concludes the other.

Another example from the *Diary* later appears in Wigglesworth's poetry: "If I regard not iniquity in my heart god will hear me in what I ask aco. to him: but I regard not iniquity, for els god would not once and again have heard my crys, and showed me a signe for good."[19] This passage illustrates Ramus' statement that the syllogism is useful for resolving a doubtful or uncertain proposition. Wigglesworth wonders if he regards iniquity. The entry begins with the proposition but reverses the assumption and the conclusion. Thus, we have this conditional syllogism:

> If I regard not iniquity, God will hear me in what I ask.
> God has heard my cries.
> Therefore, I regard not iniquity.

In this syllogism, a fourth manner conditional in Ramus, the consequent part of the proposition—God will hear me in what I ask—is restated in the assumption. The conclusion restates the antecedent part of the proposition. In the *Diary*

Wigglesworth offers proof for the assumption by recording the prayers that God has answered.

A similar syllogism is found in the "Riddles Unriddled" section of *Meat Out of the Eater*. In "A Dialogue between the Flesh and Spirit" the Flesh asks, "If God reject my Prayer / I fear he me rejects; / For how can he despize their Prayer / Whose person he respects?" The Spirit responds: "Be thou displeas'd with sin, / And he'll be pleased with thee, / He'll turn to thee his face, / If thou turn from iniquity."[20] Here the prayers remain unanswered, but both passages are resolved by the same conditional syllogism.

Although these syllogisms may not display the subtlest levels of logic, such examples reveal Wigglesworth's use of the syllogism in questions of faith and religion. Not surprisingly, then, *The Day of Doom*, published only eight years after Wigglesworth left Harvard, contains many syllogisms (complete poem in Mcserole, *Poetry*). To reconstruct the basic syllogism in *The Day of Doom* is not difficult because the sinners are always reasoning toward the conclusion that they should be saved. Further, and this is the significant structural element of the poem, the stanzas are elaborations of the different parts of the syllogism. Wigglesworth first formed the argument or syllogism and then composed verses to develop and illustrate the ensuing debates.

On Judgment Day all people—Goats and Sheep—are summoned before the throne of Christ. First, the Sheep are divided into groups, and then in stanzas 27–37 the Goats are introduced and distinguished according to their sin. In stanzas 38–50, Chrit returns to the Sheep and explains "the ground and reason why / These men do stand at my right hand and look so chearfully." In stanza 51, "the wicked are brought to the Bar." Their sins are outlined in general, and then "Christ asks a reason" for their sinful nature. The debates between Christ and the sinners take place from stanza 68 to stanza 182. The sinners, pleading to be allowed to enter Heaven, present their arguments before the throne of Christ. Christ refutes the sinners by disproving the proposition or assumption of their syllogistic argument. Wigglesworth provides marginal notes to guide the reader in the development of the eleven debates.

In stanzas 92–95, "Civil honest men" who "lov'd true dealing, and hate stealing" make their plea before Christ. They claim to be righteous men and argue, "We hated vice, and set great price, by vertuous conversation; / And by the same we got a name, and no small commendation." The second part of stanza 94 becomes the proposition of the syllogism they use to reason with Christ: "God's Laws express that righteousness, is that which he doth prize; / And to obey, as he doth say, is more than sacrifice." Thus, the proposition is that God prizes the righteous. In the next stanza the sinners offer the assumption that they have been righteous, and they pray for the conclusion that they will be saved: "Thus to obey, hath been our way, let our good deeds, we pray, / Find some regard and some reward with thee, O Lord, this day." Stanzas 92–93, detailing the sinners' good deeds, are poetic support for the assumption. The complete argument by which the sinners hope to convince Christ is contained in this simple syllogism:

> God prizes the righteous.
> We have been righteous.
> God prizes us (and will save us).

Christ's refutation, an attack against the assumption of the sinners' syllogism, comes in two steps. First, he offers the definition and proposition that a righteous person must be wholly righteous: "Justice demands at all your hands perfect obedience: / If but in part you have come short, that is just offense" (St. 96). Christ illustrates this by asking if twenty pence should recompence a thousand pound debt. Then, by the argument of final cause, Christ claims that the sinners are not perfectly obedient, for God looks at the *end* for which men do their deeds (St. 99). In stanzas 100–101 Christ argues that not from true faith and love have the civil honest men been obedient; they worked for their own advancement, not God's. Their own "haughty pride" is proof that they are not perfectly obedient. Since they are not completely righteous, God concludes that they shall not be saved. The righteousness that the sinners thought would save them, in fact condemns them: "Your Gold is brass, your silver dross, your righteousness is sin; / And think you by such honesty eternal life to win?" (St. 106).

The argument that immediately follows illustrates the interlocking, dialectical structure of the disputation between Christ and the sinners. In the previous debate, Christ has said that it is "by the end which they intend" that men will be judged. Here, the sinners say that they intended to repent but a lack of time prevented them from doing so: "We did intend, Lord, to amend, and to reform our way: / Our true intent was to repent, and make our peace with thee; / But sudden death stopping our breath, left us no libertie" (St. 107). In stanza 108 they further explain that they had no time to repent: "Short was our time. . . ." Their argument can be expressed thus:

> Those who intend to repent will be saved.
> We did intend to repent.
> Therefore, we will be saved.

Christ first attacks the idea that the sinners did not have enough time to repent: "One day, one week, wherein to seek God's face with all your hearts . . . You had a season, what was your reason such precious hours to waste?" (St. 110). Christ then turns directly to the sinners' argument and denies their assumption that they intended to repent: "Had your intent been to repent, and had you it desir'd, / There would have been endeavours seen, before your time expir'd" (St. 113). The intentions of the sinners were only "idle purposes." Christ does not deny the proposition that intentions are sufficient for salvation, but he invalidates the sinners' argument by claiming that they did not intend to repent.

In a debate concerning the nature of communion, "hypocrites" argue that they should be saved because they have taken part in communion. In stanza 74 the proposition and assumption are explicitly stated. The hypocrites quote God, "as thou thy self dost say," for the proposition that those who take communion will be saved. In the poem the assumption—we have taken communion—is placed first: "Did we not eat thy Flesh for meat, and feed on heavenly Cheer?" Stanza 75 supports the assumption, for the hypocrites say that they have "oft partaken" of the "Wine and Bread." The sinners hope the Judge will render the obvious conclusion that they will be saved. Christ accepts the proposition, but he denies the truth of the assumption; he never saw any of these sinners at communion (St. 76). Christ explains what he means by distinguishing the fancy from the heart: "Your fancies fed on heavenly Bread, your hearts fed on some Lust: / You lov'd the Creature more than the Creator, your souls clave to the dust" (St. 79). In stanzas 77–78 Christ continues his argument that the sinners were never at communion with a repentant heart. Having rejected the sinners' assumption, Christ has invalidated their conclusion. The hypocrites, concludes Christ, are very foolish to think that by such "cloaked wickedness" they would enter into heaven.

Stanzas 144–156 contain the central debate of the poem, the meaning of election and the nature of man's free-will. The sinners argue that by "Law unalterable" they are condemned, and not even true repentance and new obedience will save someone who is not among the elect (St. 145). The pleaders ask how they can save themselves if God has already rejected them, for "Who can convert or change his heart, if God with hold the same?" (St. 146).

Initially, Christ sidesteps the issue of election and declares that the sinners are damned because they have broken his laws: "I damn you not because / You are rejected, or not elected, but you have broke my Laws" (St. 147). Settling the question that the sinners are indeed condemned, Christ turns to the nature of man's free-will. Even if God has chosen the elect, man still has his own will to act good or ill: "High God's Decree, as it is free, so doth it none compel / Against their will to good or ill, it forceth none to Hell" (St. 149). Christ says the sinners, who might have been among the elect, should not have rejected God.

Realizing the complexity of the problem, Christ continues his refutation by restating the argument of the sinners: "You argue then: But abject men, whom God resolves to spill, / Cannot repent, nor their hearts rent; ne can they change their will" (St. 153). Christ replies, in the second part of stanza 153, that not because you *could* not repent, but because you *would* not repent you are condemned: "Not for his *Can* is any man adjudged unto Hell: / But for his *Will* to do what's ill, and nilling to do well." God has not rejected the sinners, but the opposite is true: "But you vile Race, rejected Grace, when Grace was freely proffer'd: / No changed heart, no heaven'ly part would you, when it was offer'd" (St. 154).

The next stanza, 155, explains the responsibility of the will and stresses that not God but the sinners themselves are the cause of their own damnation. These eight lines contain all three parts of a syllogism; the proposition is in the first four lines, while the assumption and the conclusion are in reverse order:

> Who wilfully the Remedy,
>   and means of life contemned,
> Cause have the same themselves to blame,
>   if now they are condemned.
> You have your selves, you and none else,
>   your selves have done to dy.
> You chose the way to your decay,
>   and perisht wilfully.

The word "wilfully," symmetrically beginning and ending the stanza, and the six repetitions of "you" and "your" emphasize whose will is to blame for the sinners' fate. In stanza 154, an elaboration of the assumption, God details the ways that the sinners have contemned life. For the question of whom to blame, Christ places the responsibility on the sinners because they wilfully rejected God's offer of grace. Out–reasoned again by the dialectical Jesus, the sinners stand silent: "These words appall and daunt them all; dismai'd, and all amort, / Like stocks they stand at Christ's left-hand, and dare no more retort" (St. 156).

In each debate Wigglesworth portrays the ways of God as logical and rational. Christ is a lawyer and logician debating the sinners and justifying the logic of God to weak-reasoning men. In *The Day of Doom* syllogisms clarify religious questions and assist the author in the organization and structure of the poem. Wigglesworth's achievement is the logical examination of religious dogma and complex theological tenets in a poetic form. Whether *The Day of Doom* becomes a better poem when the reader realizes the underlying structure depends on one's esthetic preferences. Showing that the poem is logical does not necessarily make it good, any more than saying that because the poem does not make use of the natural world for metaphor it is bad poetry. I have attempted to define and describe the structure of *The Day of Doom* so that we may evaluate it from the context within which it was written.

In 1669 Wigglesworth published *Meat Out of the Eater: Or Meditations Concerning the Necessity, End, and Usefulness of Afflictions unto God's Children, All Tending to Prepare them for, and Comfort them Under the Cross.*[21] Occasionally, Wigglesworth uses the syllogism to structure part of this poem, but *Meat Out of the Eater* depends upon the major divisions of Ramus' "Invention." The poem has two parts. The first is the title poem, "Meat Out of the Eater," and the second is "Riddles Unriddled, Or, Christian Paradoxes." Following proper Ramean method, the first poem discusses "in generall about Afflictions," and the second treats of "particular Ailes." "Meat out of the Eater" contains ten Meditations and a Concluding Hortatory organized in a Ramean pattern, each structured around a particular logical argument from "Invention."

Meditation I begins with the epitaph, "All Christians must be sufferers, / That would be Christ his Followers." The first stanza restates this thought: "All that resolve to be / Christ's faithful followers, / Must be contented in this world / To be great Sufferers." *Meat Out of the Eater* poetically examines the axiom, *Christians suffer*. Later, in Meditation IX, the poet divides the subject, Christians, into two groups: those who can find out the cause of their suffering and those who cannot. The "Business" of every Christian is to find out what sin has offended God, and "having once found out," the Christian "amends it" and "unto the cleansing Blood / Of Jesus Christ he flies." But some Christians never find out the cause and so continue to suffer. Such a Christian must "kiss the sharpest Rod," and "taketh up his Cross."

If we follow Ramus' logic, we should first examine the causes of affliction, beginning with final cause. In *The Logicians School-Master*, Richardson says "the finall cause is said to be the happiness of the thing; so that a thing is not to be accounted happy till it be serviceable to that end for which it was made."[22] The fifth Meditation presents a discussion of the happiness of the final rest awaiting those who suffer: "The Fifth perswades to Patience / From this Rich future Recompence; / Minding us of Our Heavenly Rest, / Which should revive us when distrest." The final cause is the end for which a thing is made, and the narrator comforts the Christian by reminding him that his light affliction will end in glorious happiness: "For this short Grief of ours, / And our Affliction light / Shall work of glorious Happiness / A far more lasting weight." In the middle stanzas, comparisons illustrate this sense of affliction ending in happiness. The farmer must break ground in order to reap a crop, and a soldier must engage in difficult battle in order to triumph. The reward of all the suffering is to be united with God, and at the end of the Meditation the soul pleads for his final reward:

> O Christ make haste, from bands,
> Of Sin and Death me free,
> And to those Heavenly Mansions
> Be pleas'd to carry me.
> Where glorified Saints
> For ever are possest
> of God in Christ their chiefest Good,
> And from all troubles Rest. [St. 10]

The final cause, or the happiness for which the Christian suffers, is to gain entrance into the "Heavenly Mansions."

The efficient cause, the cause by which a thing is made, has three divisions in Ramus. One division distinguishes the efficient which acts alone from the efficient which acts in company with others: "Alone is that which produces by itself its effect, as fire produces heat. The efficient in company with others is principal or minister and aide, as in a ship the captain is chief of navigation, the sailors are ministers and aides."[23] Richardson says of the efficient with others, "that it is, as it were, a minister and an instrument."[24] Using this same logical terminology, the poet begins Meditation IX with a consideration of the question of efficient cause:

> He sees a hand of God
> In his Afflictions all,
> And owns it for to be his Rod
> Whatever cross befall.
> For whosoever be
> Th' immediate Instrument
> He knows right well that God himself
> Was the Efficient. [St. 1]

God, the principal efficient cause, works through his instruments to bring affliction upon the Christian. The second stanza in Meditation IX presents two other aspects of the efficient cause discussed in Ramus, efficient by nature and by counsel. The efficient by nature is the cause by which all natural things are engendered, such as the wind. Efficient by counsel is that done from counsel or reason. Wigglesworth writes: "And that Afflictions / Rise not out of the Dust / Nor are they order'd by the wit / Of Man, or Devils lust."

After cause, Ramus discusses effect, that which is issued from the cause. The effect and the final cause are often confused because we sometimes use the word *end* to mean both. Richardson carefully differentiates the two: "This is the difference between the end and the effect; A house is made to dwell in, though it never be dwelt in: so for a garment, to be worne is one thing, and to be fit to weare another. So if I goe forth to speak with one, and he be gone, yet I obtaine my end: they commonly say he was frustrate of his end, but not frustrate of *finis, quatenus finis* [as end], but *quatenus effectum* [as effect]." The effect and final cause have a close relationship, for "the final cause is that that graceth the effect, and thence hath the thing his commendation."[25]

Meditation III contains both senses of the end: "The third doth further hint at th' Ends / For which the Lord Affliction sends." First, the poet expresses the end, *quatenus finis*: "God doth chastize his own / In Love their souls to save." This, as we have seen, is the subject of the fifth Meditation. Then, the definition of affliction is given in terms of the end, *quatenus effectum*: "Affliction is Christ's School / Wherein he teacheth His / To know and do their duty, / To mend what is amiss." The effect that God seeks from affliction, that the sinner find out and amend what is amiss, is also expressed in Meditation IX. God (efficient cause) creates affliction so that the sinner will leave his sins (effect) and be able to gain entrance into heaven (final cause). The final cause, heavenly rest, "graces," as Richardson says, the effect.

Meditation VI is organized by a Ramean comparison of quantity. In the epigraph the reader is asked to compare his sufferings to Christ's: "Christ's Sufferings are our Copy Book / Whereon we often ought to look." The first stanza introduces the comparison: "Let every Suffering Saint / Consider Jesus Christ / What Sufferings great he underwent / Who is our Blest High Priest." When the sinner is overcome by grief, he should compare himself to Christ: "When thou art apt to say, / No grief was ere like mine, / Then think of Christ, and sure thou'lt say, / His far exceeded thine." The entire Meditation is structured around this comparison of unequal quantity; the suffering of Christ is greater than that of the sinful sons of men.

The most common logical pattern in *Meat Out of the Eater* is the adverse contrary, one of the subdivisions of the opposites. Adverses are those whose essence is separated, such as virtue and vice. After the first two stanzas stating the subject of the poem, Meditation I is organized around two adverse paths that confront the Christian: "Our way to heavenly Rest, / Is all against the Stream; / We must not sail with Wind and Tide / As too many dream." The Christian must choose between the path "up the Hill / Which mounteth to the Skies," or the "low and down hill" path that leads "to Death and Hell." The strait and narrow path leads to life, but the broad path leads to destruction. Confronted by these two adverse contraries, the narrator chooses the narrow path:

> Let others take their Choice,
> and run what way they please;
> Let them enjoy their Lusts, and take
> Their fill of Carnal Ease:
> Chuse thou the narrow path,
> My Soul, and walk therein,
> Thou, know'st this is the only Way,
> Eternal Life to win. [St. 8]

Meditation II is also organized by adverse contraries, expressed in the epigraph: "God doth in Mercy scourge his own / In Wrath he other lets alone." Paradoxically, God in his mercy scourges and afflicts his own, but wrathfully lets the sinner alone. Like the first Meditation, the second ends with the Soul contemplating the correct opposite:

> This is a fearful case
> To be thus left of GOD:
> Great mercy 'tis to be subdu'd
> By scourging with the Rod.
> My soul be thankful then
> That God thee thus corrects,
> Who might have let thee head long run
> With those whom he rejects. [St. 7]

Meditation VII and VIII, together, present another pair of adverse contraries, the wicked man and the saint. In Meditation VII "the wordly man's prosperity" is depicted. Stanzas three through eighteen portray the worldy men who "flow in wordly wealth," or "Flourish like a tree." But on Judgment Day the wicked are summoned before the Lord and receive their final pay. Meditation VIII offers a saint to contrast with the sinner: "We have the wicked view'd, / And seen his estate . . . Now let us take a Saint . . . And view him at his worst." Although he suffers from sickness and poverty, the saint is happy: "Yet God is present with him still: / He is a happy man."

All these artificial arguments form the logical substructure upon which *Meat Out of the Eater* is organized. Meditation I is structured around the adverse contraries, narrow and broad path. Meditation II contrasts two adverse contraries, merciful scourging and wrathful neglect. Meditation III presents the definition of affliction and describes the effect of it. Meditation IV summarizes the first three. Meditation V treats final cause. The structure of Meditation VI is comparison of quantity; Christ's suffering exceeds that of men. Meditation VII and VIII contrast the saint and sinner, adverse contraries. Meditation IX discusses efficient cause and effect, and makes a division of the subject, Christians. Meditation X contrasts the internal and external form of affliction: "Although Affliction tanne the Skin, / Such Saints are Beautiful Within." Wigglesworth may have had in mind another division of cause, the formal cause, which distinguishes one thing from another. With these various artificial arguments, Wigglesworth hopes to convince the reader of the necessity to raise the cross and to suffer affliction if he wishes to enter heaven.

Just as Ramus separates artificial arguments from inartificial arguments or testimony, so too Wigglesworth offers his own personal testimony after the artificial arguments in the ten Meditations. The inartificial argument or testimony may be either human or divine: "The oracles and prophets are examples of divine testimony. The sentences of poets and distinguished persons are human testimony."[26] The validity of the inartificial argument depends on the credibility or veracity of the witness. In the Concluding Hortatory, Wigglesworth offers the most reliable human testimony, his own, to persuade the reader: "I have not told thee tales / Of things unseen, unfelt, / But speak them from experience / Believe it how thou wilt." And if the reader is still not convinced of the sincerity of his testimony, the narrator adds: "Yet I shall tell the truth, / And nothing from thee keep, / Before I wrote this sentence out / I sat down twice to weep." The narrator concludes by once again urging the reader to choose the narrow path of suffering and to raise up the cross of Christ.

In *The Day of Doom*, the sinners challenge Christ with syllogistic arguments. He, in turn, refutes them by decisive, carefully structured syllogisms. Poetic structure and religious debate are fused by the logical form of the syllogism. The poetic organization of *Meat Out of the Eater* parallels the structure of Ramus' *Dialectic*; Wigglesworth uses the major divisions of "Invention" to organize the poem. These two logical substructures emphasize the difference between the poems. In *The Day of Doom*, Christ is a stern and omnipotent judge, dividing the sheep from the goats. Christ's logic is firm, unyielding, syllogistic. He forms propositions and assumptions that lead to irrefutable conclusions. In *Meat Out of the Eater*, a gentler narrator addresses the reader, and the syllogistic debates have been replaced by the logical arguments of "Invention." These examine and explain to the Christian the nature and necessity of suffering. In both poems the logical form is an integral part of the religious teaching and the poetic structure.

Wigglesworth's poetry suggests the wide range of Ramus' influence in Protestant countries and reveals how Ramus' logic was a practical, useful tool for religious and poetic discourse. Ramus' *Dialectic* became the primary logic of Puritan thought because it was a pragmatic and schematic logic easily applied to the examination of religious problems. This practical quality of Ramus' logic may have been its most important and subtle influence upon the development of American Puritanism.

NOTES

1. Fifth edition (Boston: B. Green and J. Allen, 1701).
2. *A Faithful Man, Described and Rewarded* (Boston, 1705), p. 24.
3. (Albany: J. Munsell, 1863), p. 10.
4. P. 277, 285.
5. "Michael Wigglesworth, A Puritan Artist," *NEQ* I (October 1928), 499–500.
6. (Michigan State University Press, 1962), p. 133.
7. *Journal of Popular Culture*, IX: 4 (1976), 948–59.
8. Pp. 132, 52.
9. Leon Howard wrote several articles about Ramistic patterns in Shakespeare and Milton. Most convincing of these is "In Justifying the Ways of God to Men: The Invention of Milton's Great Argument," *The Huntington Library Quarterly*, IX (February 1946), 149–73.
10. Miller, *Mind*, p. 126.
11. My summary is based on the Latin and French editions of Ramus' *Dialectic*. The 1555 French text is an analogue of the Latin text of 1554. Later Latin editions have minor changes.
12. Pierre de la Ramée, *Dialectique* (Paris: André Wechel, 1555), pp. 114–15. Translations are my own. This text is available in a recent edition: Michel Dassonville, ed., *Dialectique* (Geneva: Librairie Droz, 1964).
13. Alexander Richardson, *The Logicians School-Master: Or, A Comment upon Ramus Logicke* (London: John Bellamie, 1629), p. 339.
14. Ibid., p. 72.
15. *Michael Wigglesworth, Diary*, Edmund Morgan, ed. (New York: Harper and Row, 1965), pp. 62, 69.

16. Quoted in Miller and Johnson, *Puritans*, II, 704.
17. *Diary*, p. 94.
18. Ramée, *Dialectique*, p. 113.
19. *Diary*, p. 19.
20. Fifth Edition (Boston, 1717), pp. 49–50.
21. Citations are made in the text by Meditation number.
22. Richardson, *The Logicians School-Master*, p. 112.
23. Ramée, *Dialectique*, pp. 11–12.
24. Richardson, *The Logicians School-Master*, p. 85.
25. Ibid., pp. 113, 112.
26. Ramée, *Dialectique*, p. 62.

III
GENRES: SELECTED POETIC FORMS

16 SEVENTEENTH-CENTURY ALMANAC VERSE

ROBERT SECOR

The RAM for clothing is the Lamb of God:
Thine OX, enmuzled that thy Corne out-trod:
Thy TWINS, the Loving Saints Communion is:
Thy CRABBS, thy turning back from whats amisse:
Thy LYON eke, thy fortitude and Faith:
Thy VIRGIN undefiled worship hath:
Thy BALLANCE Justice is, the wicked's terrour:
Thine ARCHER to the last end's aiming right:
Thy HORNED GOATES against the World to Fight:
Thy WATERMAN Sobriety would breed:
Thy FISH with Temperance thy selfe should feed.
    Nathaniel Chauncy, "New England Zodiake" (1662)

If Stars do rule the world, strange fate I wis
By direful aspects that portended is:
The prudent soul yet mounts above the sky,
And antidates celestial destiny.
    Zechariah Brigden (1659)

Astra regunt mundum, sed astra regit Deus.
    Joseph Browne (1669)

If seventeenth-century almanac verse is late in receiving our attention, the reason may be that until recently we did not expect much from it. Colonial almanac-makers themselves were apologetic about their verses. Perhaps the best of it appeared in the eighteenth-century almanacs of Nathaniel Ames, who neverthe-less in 1729 asked his readers to take his verses "as some men take their wives, for better or worse." In 1737 Franklin had Poor Richard say that an almanac-maker "should not be a finished Poet, but a Piece of one, and qualify'd to write what we vulgarly call Doggerel." This did not prevent Poor Richard from claim-ing that Titan Leeds must indeed be dead because the verse published in Leeds' almanac of 1734 was so bad that only a dead man could have written it. Nineteenth-century scholars did not improve the reputation of colonial almanac verse. In 1887 John Bach McMaster asserted that the usual almanac contained "verses destitute of feet and sense." The best Annie Marble could say was that "the crude stanzas of early philomaths formed models for improvement and expansion." In the general revaluation of colonial poetry in our time, however, almanac verse has not been so quickly dismissed, and some of it has been anthologized. Kenneth Silverman suggested that only in almanac verse are we likely to see the Puritans making the connection between natural occurrences and sensation. Robert Daly went further, arguing that almanac verse best illustrates his contention that early Americans did not reject but rather delighted in the beauties of the sensible world. Daly's chapter on the Danforths in this book pursues that theme.[1]

There is less of this verse than we have been led to expect. Samuel Eliot Morison called the Cambridge almanacs "the annual poetry magazine of Harvard College," and his statement was accepted and quoted by Miller and Johnson and, more recently, by Marion Stowall in the fullest account of early almanacs to date. Harold Jantz claimed that compilers customarily filled their blank pages with verse; according to Stowall, "verse, indifferent, bad, and sometimes good, was perennial in the American almanac." In fact, of the thirty-six extant almanacs published in Cambridge in the seventeenth century, only twenty had verse. After 1675, almanacs began to appear outside of Cambridge, but the number with verse remains only slightly over half; of the seventy-two extant almanacs published in the colonies before 1700, only thirty-eight have poetry. Moreover, instead of "usual philomath verse on the calendar pages," only one out of four extant seventeenth-century almanacs have calendar verses. The almanacs themselves were usually no more than eight leaves, or sixteen pages, and measured about six by four inches. Twelve of these pages were calendars, the remaining ones usually devoted to astronomical discussion. Where there was no calendar verse, there simply was not a great deal of empty space to be filled by aspiring poets.[2]

In content, the early almanacs were of course similar to those in England, giving information about eclipses, the sun's rising and setting, the turning of the tides, the place of the moon in the zodiac, and similar calculations useful to sailors and farmers. The colonial almanac-makers, however, were in important ways very different from their English counterparts. The English almanac-makers of the early seventeenth century, such as Booker, Gadbury, Wharton, and Hodges, were not highly educated. Almanacs, known in manuscript in Europe centuries before printing was invented, were astrological from the start, and these English compilers usually made a pedantic show of their astrological learning, their success often depending on their reputation as prognosticators. Sagendorph tells of two English almanac-makers who were "hanged on the suspicion they had started the Great Fire of 1666 just to make sure their predictions did come true."[3] Swift was protesting the silliness of astrological prognostication in 1708 when he manufactured a death-bed repentence for Partridge: "I am a poor ignorant Fellow bred to a mean Trade; yet I have Sense enough that all Pretences of foretelling by Astrology are Deceits." Despite Swift's satire, however, astrology continued to be a significant aspect of the English almanac into the nineteenth century.

The first colonial almanac-makers were a different breed. Until 1675 almanacs were produced at Cambridge on the only printing press in the colonies. Unlike the self-proclaimed astrologists in England, the compilers at Cambridge were educated men from the best colonial families. By Charles Nichols' count, of forty-four extant almanacs dated before 1687, forty-one are by twenty-six Harvard graduates: "These almanacs were published, in nearly every case, during the three years of post-graduate study for the degree of Master of Arts and the calculations in them may have been a portion of the preparation for that end."[4] When they gave their names on the title page, these compilers would append, not "licenc'd physician and student in astrology," as did Francis More in England, but "philomathemat," or "astrophil," true lovers of mathematics and the stars. Although it is difficult to divorce any almanac from the assumptions of astrology, the Cambridge philomaths clearly preferred to see their subject as astronomy and were disturbed when almanacs began to surface catering to the popular taste for prognostication in the last quarter of the century. To some extent the almanac-makers waged this battle in their verse.

Our first extant almanac is for 1646, and there is no poetry in it. Although missing the title page, it is generally assumed to have been compiled by Samuel Danforth, who was responsible for the almanacs of the next three years. In 1646 Danforth was completing his master's degree and serving as a tutor in the college, where he remained through 1649. He left for a position as minister at Roxbury in 1650, but retained his interest in astronomy and in 1665 wrote "an Astronomical Description of the Late Comet as it Appeared in New England." Cotton Mather commended the essay in his *Magnalia* not only for its science but also because "he improves the opinion of a comet's being portentious, endeavoring as it became a devout preacher, to awaken mankind by the portent, out of a sinful security."[5] The purposes of the philomaths as they studied nature were thus religious as well as scientific; by explaining the heavens they would explain God's ways to man. As the motto on Joseph Browne's 1669 almanac says, *Astra regunt mundum, sed astra regit Deus.*

Danforth's 1647 almanac is the first known to contain verse, six lines of iambic tetrameter in couplets, at the bottom of each calendar page (in Meserole, *Poetry*). In his next two almanacs, Danforth extended his lines to pentameters, and almanac poets chose one of the two lines for the rest of the century. The calendar pages begin with March, the legal beginning of the year in England and her colonies until 1752 when the Gregorian calendar was adopted. Only in the colonies, however, did the calendars (until Tulley's for 1687) begin with March. By beginning their calendar poems with the month of the vernal equinox and closing with the hint of rebirth from the deep sleep of winter in February, the almanac poets were able to give their verse dramatic shape. The natural cycle had of course religious significance for the Puritan. As Anne Bradstreet wrote in "Meditations Divine and Moral," "The spring is a lively emblem of the resurection . . . when the sun of righteousness shall appear; those dry bones shall arise in far more glory than that which they lost at their creation, and in this transcends the spring that their leaf shall never fail or their sap decline."[6]

So Danforth greets awakening nature with the image of a "Coal-white Bird" (probably the frock-coated almanac-maker himself—or his book),[7] who startles the "merry Birds" of spring. Following months evoke the New England landscape and topical affairs. Danforth celebrates the two great natural resources of the region—the forests, in October, and the sea, in July—casting the supply ships entering Boston harbor as "wooden Birds" "whose wings are white." Verses for September and May deal with local politics, August introduces a recurring joke in American almanacs—punning on "ears" of corn: "Many this month I doe fore-see / Together by the eares will bee." The observation is a mock prediction, as is the verse for November. The winter "shall be milde, let such be told. / If that it be not over cold. / Nor over cold shall they it see, / If very temperate it bee." The English colonists were still in awe of New England winters. Like Emerson, Danforth was impressed by winter's architectural abilities, so in January he conveys the loveliness of the freeze which holds the lakes and streams: "Great bridges shall be made alone / Without ax, timber, earth or stone, / Of chrystall metall, like to glasse." The lines anticipate those published the following year in Edward Johnson's *Good News from New England:* "The large tempestuous surges are bound in with frozen band, / Where ship did anker, men do walke, and cars as on the land." The last verse for the year, February, offers the moral of the fable of the grasshopper and the ant: those colonists who were not ruled by Dame Idleness and were industrious will survive the winter.

Behind all the verses of 1647, however, is the question raised in June: "Who dig'd this spring of Gardens here, / Whose mudded streames at last run cleare?" The garden in the new Eden was prepared by Him who watches His plants grow. "Yet know, one God, one Faith profest / To be New-Englands interest." Puritans commonly saw New England as a type of Eden, the garden God planted in the virgin American soil. "Hayle holy-land wherein our holy lord / Hath planted his most true and holy word," Thomas Tillam joyously wrote in the first poetic response to the new world in 1638. The fullest treatment of the metaphor in poetry, however, is in Danforth's calendar verse for 1648.[8]

Although Danforth's 1648 poem is divided into twelve stanzas to fit each of the calendar pages, it is seasonal only insofar as it begins in March by calling upon the "westerne Nymphs" to welcome returning spring (in Meserole, *Poetry*). In a coherent and extended metaphor, the rest of the poem tells what the nymphs will behold: an unparalleled plant transplanted from England, nurtured by "a skilfull Husband-man" with the help of "Bright Phoebus," who smiles upon it, and Astraea, who waters its roots. The attempt of early Americans to see life in neo-classical terms often led to ludicrous art—George Washington in a toga.

Danforth draws on poetic conventions, however, to give his allegory the sug-
gestion of myth. Moreover, as Daly observes in Chapter 10, Danforth's classical
deities are stripped of all connotations of godliness and function simply as natural
spirits helping to do God's work.

The poem is as patriotic as it is religious. The trunk of God's "matchles plant"
is Justice, "Which yearly shoots forth Lawcs & Libcrtycs." Its chicf fruit, as
Danforth explains in his homeliest image, is Peace: "Which over all house-tops,
townes, fields doth spread, / And stuffes the pillow for each weary head." God's
plenty, from wheat and pork to such New England products as masts and pipe-
staves, grows upon the tree, supplying the needs of the colonists and fetching
in trade "Wines, Cloth, Sweets & good Tobacc- / O be contented then, you
cannot lack." Below the roots are natural resources, iron and lead, worth more
than the gold found by the Spaniards in Peru and Mexico: "Which cannot weapon
us against our foes, / Nor make us howes, nor siths, nor plough-shares mend: /
Without which tools mens honest lives would end." With similar pragmatism,
Danforth's Puritans created Harvard, a nursery for tender sprigs: "Whence timely
may arise a good supply / In room of sage & aged ones that dye." The last verse
for the year reasserts the religious significance of the colonial experience, as it
promises the "wildest SHRUBS" of the forest, the savage Natives, that they will
be grafted onto the tree.

Danforth's 1649 calendar poem[9] changes the metaphor for the colonist, now
cast as a fairy-tale orphan, once secure in England's arms, but destined by its
merciless step-mother (Murdock suggests the Church of England) to be sent into
the wilderness to perish. Happily, this is one orphan with a Father to protect it,
as it undergoes a variety of trials, including "stout hounds" (hostile Indians),
storms, plagues, and even "Opinion" which would "mistress" the house alone,
breaking it into fractions. The outcome of this last trial was recorded in Danforth's
"Memorable Occurrences" the previous year, in the entry for 1638: "Mrs. Hutch-
inson & her errors banished." All of these trials are seen as occasions for God's
providence, testing the orphan's faith and proving God's grace, so that "The
worthless Orphan may sit still and blesse, / That yet it sleeps in peace and
quietnes."

The next extant almanac verse is by Thomas Shepard II in his 1656 almanac.
His eight–line calendar poems are divided and rhymed as quatrains, but unlike
Danforth, he alows himself an occasional half-rhyme (majesty / livery, brings /
begins) and eye-rhyme (stage / pilgrimage). An able craftsman, Shepard can
make the sound "seem an Echo to the sense," as Pope was to advise, altering
his rhythms and making good use of cacophony as Titan escapes Cancer for Leo
in July. When winter sets in, Shepard shows his pictorial abilities by dramatizing
its effects upon the river elf in January, at the sign of the Waterman. The only
topical allusion is for February, where dangerous opinion again appears, not in
the shape of Antinomians as in Danforth, but in the guise of Quakers. Shepard's

lines have been called "the first examples of secular verse in our literature."[10] In his final stanza, however, Shepard replaces Danforth's image of the flourishing tree with that of the ruined garden, evoking the Puritan's eternal theme that in their degeneracy the New England colonists have recapitulated Adam's fall.

Anne Bradstreet said her son was skilled at making verses, and Samuel Bradstreet did not disgrace here in his almanac for 1657, in which he tells the story of the reawakening earth through the familiar narrative of Apollo's successful wooing of the earth deity, Tellus. Samuel's mother of course also wrote seasonal verse, particularly "The Four Seasons of the Year," in which she follows the sun through the twelve houses of the zodiac. The image of the life-giving power of the sun as it revives the frozen earth recurs in her poetry in unexpected forms, from her eulogy on du Bartas where she says his poetry "dazzled sight" and unthawed her "frozen hearts ingratitude," to her "Letter to Her Husband," where she sees herself as the mourning earth and Simon in his absence as her sun far removed in the zodiac. As Daly notes, "Sun God bridegroom husband and Christ, and Spring health reunion and confidence of election—these image clusters were linked in the poet's perception of the created universe."[11] These image clusters help explain what is behind the imagery of much of the century's calendar verse; they may also suggest where Samuel received some of his inspiration.

Samuel's poem is not on the calendar pages, but on the second page of his almanac. Its six stanzas, each rhyming ababcc with the final couplet stating the essential action of the stanza, thus do not attempt to create an allegory for all the months of the year. Rather, they tell the story of awakening spring. Apollo comes to cure "slumbering Tellus" of her "lethargee" as the morning bells call "the dead to rise from silent tombes / Whilst yet they were lockt up in darker Cells." Behind the pagan imagery, Tellus is thus a type of both the resurrected Christ and the meek members of the resurrection, with Apollo promising the coming of the divine Bridegroom. As the quoted lines reveal, the verse depends heavily on alliteration and assonance, used by Bradstreet to contrast Tellus and Apollo. Thus, with the help of the welkin, Tellus "decks her self by christall glass aloft." The euphonious line contrasts with the description of Apollo's forces in the subsequent stanza, "fleet-fire-foming-steeds from farre appear," where the coming of the hard breathing horses is suggested by the alliterated "f"s and the developing vowel sounds. With his arrival, Apollo gives Tellus a garland to wear from which "Baybes" will arise. Commenting on some of Anne Bradstreet's lines in "Contemplations," Daly says "her description of the sun and earth in spring centered on marriage and impregnation."[12] In Samuel Bradstreet's case, poetic tradition began at home.

In science, however, Harvard undergraduates were being taught to break with tradition. The school was quick to adopt as a text the first book to popularize Copernicus, Wing's *Astronomie Instaurata*, which was published in 1656. It was studied by Zechariah Brigden, who graduated in 1657 and used the almanac of 1659 to spread word of the new theory outside the walls of Harvard. Rev.

John Davenport was not convinced, saying of Brigden: "let him injoy his opinion, and I shall rest in what I have learned, til more cogent arguments be produced." Confronting the Bible's account of creation, Brigden argued that literal adherence to scripture "fitted well to the capacity of the rudest mechanic," but that "the proper literal sense is always subservient to the casting vote of reason."[13] The Copernican system made it all the more difficult to take astrology seriously, based as it is on a Ptolemaic universe. The philomaths would not believe without qualification that *Astra regunt mundum*. Thus Bridgen says in the only poem in his almanac, the quatrain beginning "If Stars do rule the world," the Soul "anti-dates celestial destiny."

The almanacs for 1660 and 1661, prepared by Samuel Cheever, return to monthly calendar verse. Saying that Cheever treats in these poems "the same Tellurian theme with more originality and less clarity than had Bradstreet," Jantz judges them "quite passable."[14] Cheever gives us the first verse extant which combines Bradstreet's Tellurian theme with the imagery of the zodiac as used by Shepard. At the same time, the elaborate allegories that evolve are meant to reflect the expectations of each season. As the allegory for 1660 develops, Phoebe, jealous of Sol's interest in Tellus, enlists the help of Mars and some banished "impes" (the stars of the night sky) to avenge her. By June, Tellus recognizes the threat and "Resolves to leave her lover for a while, / Although how loth to part, her tear-torn-eye / And Slowly pace to all men testify." Cheever thus suggests the summer solstice at the sign of the crab, when the sun turns retrograde. The allegory reflects the lengthening days of June and seems to anticipate a cool, wet spell. By the end of September, Phoebe's armies, the stars of the night sky in spring and summer, fade in the day sky of autumn, the "upstart *lights*" eclipsed by Sol "in this our Hemisphear." *Tempus fugit*, however, and by December Tellus is stripped of her glory as she lies "Shivering with cold, and pittyed by none" until the skies "Send down white woolen robes." Phoebe is after all victorious, as she gloats in February among the constellations, who are unconcerned about the fate of the earth below: "Thus whilst starres their dayes in glee bestow, / The fainting earth lyes gasping here below." Luckily, the earth is only fainting, not dying; its rejuvenation in the new year is implicit even as it gasps.

The almanacs for 1662 through 1664 were prepared by two of the sons of Charles Chauncy, professor of Hebrew and Greek at Trinity College, Cambridge, before he came to America and later served as president of Harvard. Charles Chauncy himself contributed an elaborate verse satire to John Richardson's almanac of 1670, and Jantz says that the brothers followed their "father's incli-nation toward small sets of occasional verses" in "contributing their share of collegiate almanac verse." We have extant for the Chauncy brothers only the three short poems in Nathaniel's 1662 almanac, "The Phaethontick," signed "Incerti Authoris," and presumably two original contributions: "Upon the Eclipse of the Moon" and "New England Zodiake." Nathaniel was probably nurtured in the ideas of his father, who "believed the divine will was to be achieved by a rationalistic conformity with the divine 'plan' of the universe." "New England Zodiake," quoted in full as an epigraph to this chapter, thus intends to illustrate neither the power of the stars nor God's arbitrary will, but to show how the symbols of the zodiac reveal the ways God uses his power in the interests of man. He provides for man by supplying the lamb, protects him by muzzling the ox, proves His love through the image of the twins, teaches him to resist temptation by the backwards moving crab, and so on through the remaining signs. The moral meaning of each sign makes this a truly New England zodiac.[15]

Alexander Nowell's 1665 almanac contained no verse, but it did contribute to the discussion of who rules the world in an essay, "The Sun's Prerogative Vindicated," in which Nowell argued that there was no reason comets could not be portents from God while at the same time subject to natural laws. In contrast, Josiah Flint, who prepared the 1666 almanac, had no interest whatever in either the New England zodiac or the impact of the new science. Flint, later to serve as a minister in Braintree and Dorchester, found all he needed to know in scripture. Where others offered a scientific explanation for astronomical phenomena, Flint printed an essay titled,"The World's Eternity is an Impossibility." In his zeal, Flint refused to use the pagan names for the months, but gave their Hebrew names next to his calendar verse.[16] Flint would have agreed with Wigglesworth, who in his prefatory poem to *The Day of Doom* refused to engage in the "Heathenish Impiety" of invoking the muses. For the heathenish calendar verse of other almanacs, Flint substituted the monthly versification of scripture, telling the history of the Jews as appropriate to the month. Since "the image of Christian Israel underlies all Puritan expectations for the new world,"[17] Flint found it more appropriate to tell of the exodus of the Jews out of Egypt than of Apollo's wooing of Tellus. Other philomaths saw the awakening Tellus as a type of the resurrected Christ; Flint found his types in scripture: "Emanuel in's Holy beauty came / To dwell with men, to solemnize his Name."[18] However, there is little to recommend Flint's versified scripture as poetry. Presumably, Flint did not think God's altar needed his polishing.

The better verse in Flint's 1666 almanac took most of the last page. It was contributed by Nicholas Noyes and was titled, "A Short Discourse about 66." Nehemiah Hobart referred to the "practical genius" for which Noyes was "so remarkable, when a student at Camebridge," but most of Noyes' early poems are lost and Flint's almanac preserves the only extant representation of his collegiate verse. Jantz writes briefly about this poem:

> A large part of the intellectual world of the day was stirred with anticipation about the coming of the prophetically ominous year 1666 ("The mark of the beast," etc.). His attitude is the cautiously skeptical one (shared by many another interested New Englander) that even though the Papacy might not fall nor the Millenium begin in that year, yet the

succession of years was tending inevitably toward that goal. . . . Though
the theme is rather far from our present interests, and the allusions at
first seem obscure, it is at once clear that both theme and verse are
competently handled.[19]

Jantz, however, takes the poem too seriously as a prognostication. Rather it
belongs in the tradition of the mock prognostication, a satiric rejection of astrol-
ogists which goes back at least as far as Rabelais' ridicule of "crazy astrologers"
in his *Pantegrueline Prognostications*. An almanac poem on the prophetic year
would seem to call for a prognostication, and so Noyes begins with a mock
apology for attempting what is generally repellent to judicial men, who do not
like to appear to be losing (or lessening) their sense of balance and proportion:

> Here, *Reader*, mind not a Prophetick strain,
> Nor doubtful guesses, or conjectures here:
> Wise men in counting love a judicious brain,
> Or else the *Ballance* will to *Less* appear.
>> Mistake me not in what I undertake,
>> And of my thoughts a short account I'le make.

The account Noyes makes immediately afterward, however, is of what he will
not undertake. He will not "treat of *killing of the beast*" or "speak of *Fates of
Kings and States*"; he will prognosticate neither about affairs of heaven nor of
earth. What he will prognosticate is that anyone with his wits will be able to
tell in 1666 which of the things predicted for it have been fulfilled and which
have not:

> But I shall briefly something else relate,
> That will fall out by *Sixty sixes* date.
> What Prodigy's foretold, the false and true,
> What Prophesies that were of Hells invention:
> What Dreams and Visions, were they old or new,
> Of *Sixty six* foretold, and their intention:
>> Of the false Glosses on this holy Writ,
>> Will much appear to him that hath his Wit.

As prophecy, the lines are as ironically self-evident as the weather prediction
of Danforth in 1647. Noyes is not a serious prognosticator, but he is a serious
Puritan, so he ends his poem with a couplet which, as Jantz says, indicates his
acceptance of the biblical promise of the eventual millenium: "The Lord a *Fur-
nace* is preparing ready / To *Cast the heavens and Earth anew*, and speedy."
    "Although Samuel Brackenbury's almanac for 1667 lacked the usual philomath
verse on the calendar pages, a rhyme appeared on the page with the eclipses."[20]

So writes Marion Stowall, although in 1667 the colonist would not have thought calendar verse "usual" since in the previous five years only Flint's 1666 calendar had it. Moreover, only one of the next eleven philomath almanacs would carry calendar verse. With a couple of exceptions, the almanac-makers over this period showed little of the serious interest in verse exhibited by Danforth, Shepard, and Bradstreet. Samuel Brackenbury, physician, preacher, and son-in-law of Michael Wigglesworth, suggests in his fourteen-line "rhyme" that the muse of astronomy, Urania, is the philomath's true muse. Poetic harmony is to be found in the stars and explored in prose: "My Friends, you look for Verse, be pleas'd to know / You'l miss, *Urania* would have it so: / Here's how the Sun his course in's Circle goe's: / I write Celestial harmonie in prose." If Noyes' poem was in the tradition of the mock prognostication, Brackenbury's is in that of the mock apology. Not only does Brackenbury's verse apologize for having no verse, but it goes on to apologize for any errors: "If such there be, it is by oversight, / Believe me, I'd as leve it should be right."

There is little verse in the almanacs of the following two years. In 1668 Joseph Dudley, who would rise to become governor of Massachusetts, allowed himself only an inconsequential eight-line poem in couplets, "Upon the Suns Eclipse," in which "That glittering Sol by Phebe thus is curb'd." The next significant philomath verse is in John Richardson's almanac for 1670. Each almanac indicated on its title page the longitude and elevation for which the astronomical data was calculated. Charles Chauncy, "perhaps the most learned man to settle in Plymouth Colony," contributed to Richardson's almanac a poem which parodied the data in its title: "A Perpetual Calendar, fitted for the Meridian of Babylon, where the Pope is elevated 42 degrees." Jantz says of the poem: "It is one of the sharpest anti-Catholic satires of early New England, lacking the smoothness and amenities of the classical school, but intellectually brilliant, packed with double meanings and triple connotations, so that it would require an elaborate commentary for a present-day reader who is less well versed in church history, though at the time its implications were no doubt quickly perceived and enormously relished."[21]

Whether or not the implications of the poem were "quickly perceived" by all readers, the poem is an intellectual tour de force before which some readers must have felt inadequate. If there was from the start a pedantic strain in the way the Harvard graduates paraded their knowledge, it is no wonder that in the other poem of the 1670 almanac, Richardson patronized some of his readers as rustics and plough-men. Stowall calls the poem the "first humorous satire" in almanac verse, "directed against astrology."[22] It can also be seen as another mock prognostication, with its satire extended from the belief in astrology to the rustic believer. In his *New England Almanac* of 1703, Samuel Clough gives his reason for including the astrological illustration of the Man of Signs: "For Country-men regard the Sign / As though it were Oracle Divine." Richardson's poem similarly suggests that while the intellectual philomaths at Harvard know better, the country bumpkins require astrology.

If *Stars do Rule the World*, then never fancy
What's told from them is wrought by *Nigromancy*.
Th'admiring *Rusticks* faith will shrink perhaps,
Hearing the Tidings of such After–claps.
Who marvels not? The sun shall once *stand still*,
Whilst that the Earth shall round him *dance his fil*,
Signes in the Sky shall now be seen; for there,
A *fiery Dog* will *Chace* a *skittish Hare*;
Which *nimble Elf*, at last, do what he can,
Runs 'tween the *Legs* of a *fierce Armed Man*. [ll. 1–10]

The question is once again whether stars rule the world. The naive rustics who
so believe understandably quake at what the stars foretell. The homely verse in
which Richardson describes the constellations captures the limitations of the
anthropomorphizing imagination of the rustic star-gazers.

Later in the poem Richardson makes mock predictions of what country bump-
kins will find when they visit their city cousins: on winter days trees walking
with roots towards the sky, or if the skies are clear perhaps men with swine's
heads, city men wearing either three-cornered hats or wigs of animal hair. The
gullible rustics may believe the moon is inhabitable, but the true measure of
their gullibility is signalled by the horned quarter moon. Similarly, in predicting
a conjunction of male and female planets, Richardson suggests rustics coupling
below. The result is the prediction of a crawling baby at the end of the poem—
or is it rather the reduction of rational man to four-footed ignorant animal if he
believes the claims of the astrologers that stars rule the world?

We should not be surprised if some "plough-men" took offense. One who did
was a farmer from Little Compton, who was moved to reply in verse. Have
aged fathers sent their sons to Harvard to learn how to mock them as ignorant
peasants, asked Samuel Bailey in a poem he sent to the town clerk of Provi-
dence:[23] "Most learned academicks, have your gownes, / and college taught
you to abuse the clownes / In empty rimes trussd to an Almanack." Bailey con-
cludes his poem, our first record of the collision between town and gown, by
charging

These are grave sophisters, that are in schooles
Soe wise they thinke ther aged fathers fooles
That plough and cart and such they seeme Indeed
Or els they would not worke soe hard to breed
Their boyes to flout them; but I cannot stay
foddering of asses thus I must away
and give my sheepe their breakfast who I feare
Wait at the stack while I make verses heere.

Daniel Russell's almanac of 1671 marks a return to calendar verse. With the exception of Flint's anomalous versification of Jewish history in 1666, there had been none since Cheever's almanacs of 1660 and 1661, and Russell's verse returns to Tellurian themes. In poetry more controlled than Cheever's, Russell tells how in March the "Starry Monarch" comes "marching" (in almanac verse all puns are intended) up to his "full careere," and then woos Tellus as he awakens the cold, dead earth and metamorphizes our "Frigid Zone" to a temperate one. The spring months depict the rebirth of nature, as in May: "And now the croaking Crew, late *All-a-Mort*, / By their Nightchantings, their new life report." Such lines support claims that in their almanac verse at least the Puritans were not, as Hyatt Waggoner insists, "thoroughly world-denying."[24] Similarly in June, Russell evokes the sights and tastes of strawberries and cherries: "The smiling Fields, attired in their Suits / Of Taste-delighting, and Eye-pleasing Fruits; / Their Strawb'ry Mantles now begin to wear, / And many orchards Cherry-cheekt appear."

The lines for July introduce a punning allusion to battle, as "Fierce Hus-bandmen with crooked Cutlash" defeat the "Armies of Tall Blades," Ceres' offspring, and "together th'Blades are bound, / Transported home, and soundly thresh'd on th'ground." Once introduced, military imagery ties together the rest of the months. An exception may be September, with its lush, sensual imagery of a nature so painfully ripe it needs to be delivered of its load, although even here the suggestion of rape evokes one of the traditional horrors of war:

> The *Indian* Stalks, now richly fraught with store
> Of golden-colour'd Ears, seem to impore
> By humble bowing of their lofty Head,
> From this their load to be delivered.
> *Pomona's* Daughters now at age, and dight
> With pleasing Beauty, Lovers do invite
> In multitudes: it's well if they escape
> From each of these, without a cruel Rape.

In the poem's developing allegory, "the *Aeolian* Lords" meet to appoint "blustring *Boreas*" as general in an attempt to overthrow Tellus's Kingdom, and the fol-lowing months tell of winter's successful offensive as it strips the earth of fruits and flowers in November, drives men to "th'Fortress of a well-made Fire" and Phoebus from sight in December, and captures Tellus and Neptune in January. February suggests the completion of the circle and the continual wheeling of the seasons: "Natures Law commands / That fiery *Phoebus* Charriot never stands, / Without a Miracle; but that it be, / Still termed *Certus: semper Mobile.*"

There is again no calendar verse for Jeremiah Shepard's 1672 almanac, only an eighteen-line verse on the page giving information about eclipses for the year. Shepard begins with the familiar pose of the almanac-compiler who apologizes for invoking the muse at all: "Here grant me leave to rouse the *Thespian* train /

(Those noble *Genii* of a Poets Brain) / And sure I may attempt, since Pearls may dwell / In Rocks, and Riches in an Oister-shell." The poem as a whole, however, like Dudley's for 1668, is in the tradition of the eclipse poem, as Shepard laments the time when "The horned Queen damps Phoebus Golden Beams, / To mask our roving sight, with duskish steames." The temporary masking of the sun, "heavens most glorious eye," is not as tragic as it seems, for it offers us in compensation the greater appreciation of the light when it reappears: "But 'tis in providence, this tragick sight / Will adde a lustre to next rising light. / Let *Phoebus* rouse and *Phoebe* shall be hid. / The great the lesser ever will out bid."

When the Massachusetts colonists opened their Cambridge almanac in 1679, they were probably surprised to find poetry in it, for there had been none at all by the philomaths for the previous half-dozen years, since Shepard's eclipse poem of 1672. Moreover, they had a choice that year of almanac verse. John Foster, who had published the 1675 Cambridge almanac, was operating a press and issuing a yearly almanac out of Boston since 1676. Five of his six Boston almanacs are extant, and four of those carried calendar verse, most of it not very good. Perhaps to compete, the Cambridge people chose a Danforth to compile their almanac for 1679: Samuel Danforth's son John, who would become a serious and prolific poet.

In John Danforth's calendar poem, the sun once again comes as a royal lover to awaken earth from its darkness. We recall Phoebe's jealousy when Apollo wooed Tellus in Cheever's 1660 poem. Luckily for her now, Danforth predicts an eclipse of the sun for the last day of March. The "Queen of heaven" manages to put horns on the "Prince of Light" as she causes him to lose face, and the month is called "Equal" both because it marks the vernal equinox and because in it Phoebe gets back her own. The war of the sexes is not carried further, and Danforth's other verses are sometimes closer to those of his father's 1647 almanac than those of later years. For May of 1647, for example, Samuel's verse made topical allusions. Similarly, using paradox and the rhetorical device of polyptoton, John treats May's political elections: "Now Freemen in their Liberty rejoyce / of Choicest men to make a Worthy choice; / The which, who e're are wise or otherwise / This moneth agree with joy to Solemnize." July recalls Samuel's image of the supply ships entering the harbor like "wooden Birds" with white wings and full bellies:

> The noble ships, which the vast Ocean try,
> And nothing neer them see, but Sea and Sky,
> Now homeward with their Wings advance apace,
> And having periodiz'd their restless race:
>> The Merchants house will fill with plenteous Store,
>> But Silver Angels only ope' the dore:
>> The Sun from th'Lyon now will make retreat
>> In truth 'twould joy a blind man much to se it.

Danforth's allusion to the guiding stars as silver angels opening the door is lovely. The last line, however, is strained, and the final rhyme is John Danforth's own.

The next extant Cambridge almanac, for 1682, was also compiled by a member of a famous family, William Brattle. The Brattles, however, were scientists, not poets. William's brother, Thomas, "the most famous of the Harvard scientists,"[25] had no verse in the almanacs he compiled at Cambridge in 1678 and at Boston in 1694. William, whose *Compendium Logicae* became a long–used text at Harvard, did not distinguish himself by his calendar verse. The puns are tired and flat, as plants "Spring up and thrive" in March and men "lose their Ears" in September. As in Shepard's verse, the heavens are anthropomorphized to reflect the toil of the farmers below, but the verse is less felicitous. There are some original subjects, such as the "*Apes*" (bees) in May and Harvard commencement in August, but the verse is crude throughout, as Brattle pads out lines and distorts syntax for rhyme. One example, from November, should suffice: "But they that dread this time will much Rejoice / When that they hear of the next month the voice."

In the next three years we have five almanacs extant from Cambridge and Boston, but there is no verse until "Ad Librum," in the 1686 almanac of Samuel Danforth II, John's younger brother. "*Judicial astrologer* I am not," claims Samuel: "That *Art* falsly so call'd I loath, I hate, / Both *Name* and *Thing* I much abominate." Marble suggests that Danforth is reacting against Tulley's astrological almanacs,[26] but Tulley did not begin his Boston series until the following year. If Danforth's poem is a reaction, it is against the almanacs of John Foster, who ended the first Boston almanac in 1676 with "Prognosticks of unhealthy seasons," and two years later introduced the traditional astrological figure of the Man of Signs." The figure shows how the zodiac governs parts of the body, and underneath is a twelve–line explanatory poem: e.g., "The *Head* and *Face* the *Ram* doth crave, / The *Neck* and *Throat* the Bull will have." The tone is humorous, but the New England zodiac has gone over to the astrologers. The Cambridge philomaths tried to hold their own against the inroads of popular astrology. As we have seen, their serious concern was to explore natural phenomena without denying the will of God. Thus in the 1685 almanac, William Williams' essay "Concerning a Rainbow" gives the natural explanation of the rainbow and then tries to reconcile it with the passage in Genesis where God offers the rainbow as a sign to Noah. Williams' conclusion is that, while the rainbow always existed as a natural event, only after the flood did God choose it to be a token of His covenant with man. Danforth's poem of the following year, the last extant verse from the Cambridge philomaths, similarly takes the findings of science seriously while affirming the will of God and the verity of scripture.

In an implicit attack on the presumption of the astrologers, Danforth sugggests in "Ad Librum" (in Meserole, *Poetry*) that to define the influence of the stars "Infallibly is far beyond the Line / Of finite skill." Nevertheless, God has given us the sensible universe as signs to interpret: "*If None can see what 'tis that these signs shew us / They'l be but insignificant unto us.*" The almanac-maker and poet thus serves the high function of God's interpreter. It will wait for Emerson to claim the role of seer who shows man how to see rightly by revealing the spiritual significance of the natural universe, but for Danforth as well as for Emerson, the natural universe first had to be rightly observed. Brigden did not settle anything when he came out on the side of Copernicus in 1659, and in 1686 John Davenport may still have been waiting for more cogent arguments to be convinced. So Danforth makes Brigden's choice anew, suggesting that the Ptolemaic epithets are useful conventions of "former Ages-Sages," but "I know the contrary." He knows it not only by observation of "the Divine Decree / To Nature given," but from scripture: "In Joshuah's *Solstice* at the Voyce of man / The *Rapid Sun* became *Copernican.*" Thus once again, as in Williams' rainbow, natural science and scripture are reconciled. The poem's final apocalyptic vision evokes some of the images of Sol the charioteer and his Queen that have recurred in previous almanac verse. Once again, however, there is no question that it is neither Apollo nor Phoebe but the Christian God who rules the stars: "*Light* was before the Sun; / Most Radiant Light shall be when *Sol* hath done."

"*Oh Eighty Six; thou'rt quickly come about! / This Sheet that brought thee in shall lay thee out.*" Similarly, Samuel Danforth has bought us into a discussion of philomath verse, and Samuel Danforth II has brought us out. We have not, however, completed a survey of seventeenth-century almanac verse. Since 1676, almanacs coeval with those of the philomaths at Cambridge were being issued at Boston. We have noted the verse in Foster's Boston almanacs, which ran to 1681. From then to the end of the century, almanacs were issued in Boston by a number of different men, most notably John Tulley, but also Cotton and Nathaniel Mather, Gillam, Newman, Harris, Lodowick, and Thomas Brattle. Except for Tulley's famous series, the only poem in any of these was a short tribute to William and Mary by Benjamin Harris in 1692. Harris, printer and bookseller, was probably also responsible for most of the verse in Tulley's almanacs (1687–1702).[27] Tulley himself was not interested in poetry, and there is no verse on the calendar pages of any of his sixteen almanacs. Of his thirteen seventeenth-century almanacs, there is verse in only five, none of which he seems to have written. We can identify the two poems in 1698 as largely borrowed from the earlier almanacs of Brackenbury and Brigden. Tulley himself disowned a poem of 1694 when Christian Lodowick attacked its astrological assumptions in his rival *The New England Almanac* (1695). Lodowick argued that the effect of the "sinful love of that Soul-bewitching Vanity of Star-Prophecy, commonly called Astrology," is to "withdraw Persons from a holy Reliance in God's will & Providence," just what the philomaths had worried would happen. Tulley explained the following year: "As for the French King's Nativity, it was acted and put into my late almanac by the Printer unknown to me."

Harris was probably also responsible for the best poem in Tulley's almanacs, observations on the various months following the calendar pages (which Tulley began in January) for 1688.[28] The verse for January 1688 illustrates the new tone in Tulley's almanacs: "The best defence against the Cold, / Which our Fore-Fathers good did hold, / Was early a full Pot of Ale." The irreverent tone is carried in part by cant words, like "Drab (slut) in June, where we have an analogy for the sun entering the crab different in kind from those of the philomaths: "The Sun is entred now into the *Crab*, / And days are hot, therefore be aware a Drab; / With French diseases, they'l thy body fill, / Being such as bring *Grist* to the Surgeons Mill." Similarly, where the philomaths punned on ears, this poem puns on lads and lasses making hay and tumbling on cocks: "Now wanton Lads and Lasses do make Hay, / Which unto lewd temptation makes great way. / With tumbling on the cocks, which acted duly, / Doth cause much mischief in this month of *July*." Meserole clearly has this poem in mind when he speaks of the "broad humor of almanac verses in which lads and lasses were as likely to roll in the hay as sit primly at meeting."[29] In the philomath almanacs they did neither, and the broad humor of this poem is hardly representative of the more sober (although sometimes witty) verse in the Cambridge almanacs.

From outside New England copies are extant of Samuel Atkin's *Kalendarium Pennsilvaniense* for 1685 and 1686, with no verse, and John Clapp's New York almanac for 1697, with long unpoetic calendar poems. Much more poetic was Daniel Leeds, whose major almanac series began on the Philadelphia press of William Bradford in 1687 and continued on Bradford's press in New York. For one thing, Leeds moves away from the abstract moralizing of the philomaths toward the practical moral aphorisms of Poor Richard: "No man is born unto himself alone, / Who lives unto himself he lives to none" (1687); "Now Food that's warm is best to eat / And let's be moderate in Drink and Meat" (1693). Even when he looks to God, Leeds carries the tone of eighteenth-century common sense, as when he tries to reconcile man to death in 1697: "In sleep we know not whether our clos'd Eyes / Shall ever wake. From Death we are sure to rise. / Ay, but tis long first. O is that our fears? / Dare we trust God for Nights, and not for years?" Leeds wears a very different mask from that of the philomath. In a 1706 verse he satirizes the lawyer whose "Pen's his Plough, the Parchment is his Soil." "I dread to touch at State affairs," he says in a 1693 verse, "for fear / Lest that Apollo pull me by the Ear. / I'm safe while moving in my proper Sphere. / In Plowing, Planting, there's no treason there." Rejecting the snobbery of Richardson's "The Country-Mans Apocrypha" (1670), Leeds echoes Samuel Bailey's sharp response. In fact, Leeds identifies himself on the title pages of his early almanacs as a "Student of Agriculture." Like Foster and Tulley of Boston, Leeds was not a "Harvardine," showing academic prowess by drawing on classical and scientific learning. Instead, knowing the needs and interests of the American colonists as they approached the eighteenth century, these almanac-makers used their pages to tell farmers when to plant and when to bleed, while offering some common-sense morality and earthy humor. The mask they wore was not that of the learned man patronizing the superstitions of the country bumpkin; it was rather that of the bumpkin himself who moves in his "proper

Sphere." In truth, of course, this bumpkin believes himself superior to the learned professional men who make their pens their plows.

NOTES

1. John Bach McMaster, *Benjamin Franklin as a Man of Letters* (Boston: Houghton, Mifflin and Co., 1887), p. 101. Annie Marble, "Early New England Almanacs," *New England Magazine*, 19 (Jan. 1899), p. 557. Silverman, *Poetry*, p. 36. Daly, *God's Altar*, p. 9. Almanac verse of Samuel Danforth for 1647–1649 was published by Murdock in *Paul*; poems from the almanacs of Samuel Bradstreet (1657) and Daniel Russell (1671) were reprinted by Miller and Johnson in *Puritans*. Roy Harvey Pearce's *Colonial American Writing* (New York: Holt, Rinehart & Winston, 1950), Silverman's *Poetry*, and Meserole's *Poetry* all included almanac verse. However, the same poems were usually reprinted so that the total number of different poems in Murdock, Miller and Johnson, Pearce, Silverman, and Meserole is just seven.

2. Samuel Eliot Morison, *Harvard College in the Seventeenth Century* (Cambridge: Harvard Univ. Press, 1936), I, 133; Miller and Johnson, *Puritans*, p. 551; Marion Stowall, *Early American Almanacs* (New York: Burt Franklin, 1977), pp. 236, 278, 45. Jantz, *First Century*, p. 49.

3. Robb Sagendorph, *The Old Farmer's Sampler* (New York: Ives Washburn, 1957), p. 6.

4. Charles L. Nichols, "Notes on the Almanacs of Massachusetts," *PAAS*, NS 22 (April 10, 1912), p. 18.

5. Cited by Marble, p. 550.

6. *Bradstreet*, Hensley, p. 279.

7. See chapter 10 and Murdock's notes in *Paul* for other possibilities.

8. Danforth also used this metaphor in his 1647 "Chronological Table of Some Memorable Things which happened since the first planting of Massachusetts." Similarly, Joseph Browne's "Table of Some Memorable Occurences" in 1669 lists 1620, "Plymouth colony planted," and 1628, "Massachusetts Colony planted."

9. Since it takes only eleven months to tell, the orphan's tale ends before February, which Danforth fills in with a mock "Prognostication."

10. Marble, "Early . . . Almanacs," p. 550. Shepard's skill as a humorist is discussed in chapter 10 of the present book.

11. Daly, *God's Altar*, p. 95. (I cannot explain Nichols' claim that "this almanac contains all the explanations in verse in place of the usual prose" [p. 26]. An examination of the copy in the AAS, given by Nichols in his check-list, shows only the narrative poem on p. 2 and a few wry lines of poetry at the bottom of the February calendar page.)

12. Ibid., p. 93.

13. Morison, *Harvard*, I, p. 216.

14. Jantz, *First Century*, p. 66.

15. Ibid., p. 66. Max Savelle, *Seeds of Liberty* (New York: Alfred A. Knopf, 1948), p. 34.

16. Nichols is thus in error in saying Flint "omitted all the months' names, heathen and scripture alike" (p. 23).

17. Silverman, *Poetry*, p. 37.

18. Isaiah 7:14; Matthew 1:23.

19. Jantz, *First Century*, p. 90. The coming of the beast marked 1666 is prophesied in Revelation 13:11.

20. Stowall, *Early . . . Almanacs*, p. 45.

21. Both quotations in this paragraph are from Jantz, *First Century*, p. 17.

22. Stowall, *Early . . . Almanacs,* p. 46.

23. See *NEHGR* (October 1855), p. 356.

24. Waggoneer, *Poets*, p. 15.

25. Stowall, *Early . . . Almanacs,* p. 49.

26. Marble, "Early . . . Almanacs," p. 552.

27. Tulley's almanacs for 1691 and 1692 were issued from Cambridge (and carried no verse); the others were all printed by Harris in Boston.

28. Titled "A Prognostication for 1688," the verses were attached only to those almanacs sold directly by Harris. In Meserole, *Poetry*.

29. Meserole, *Poetry*, p. xxx.

17 ANAGRAMS AND ACROSTICS; PURITAN POETIC WIT

JEFFREY WALKER

> The Acrostick was probably invented about the same time with the Anagram, though it is impossible to decide whether the Inventor of the one or the other were the greater Blockhead.—Addison, *The Spectator*, No. 60

Once caricatured as a humorless and colorless primitive, the American Puritan has in recent years escaped this exaggerated and inaccurate historical stereotype. With the growth of early American textual scholarship, modern readers also have discovered with delight the range of seventeenth-century American poetry. Thought by many to be the province of the austere minister writing to a wrathful God, Puritan poetry has emerged as verse penned by men and women of all ages and occupations. It is in effect a diary of the period, providing readers with a sampler of everyday life and depicting a people concerned with all elements of this world and the next. But Puritan poetry also reveals an engagingly personal side of seventeenth-century Americans, and it does so in a manner that is often witty and humorous.

While Puritans did little to elicit belly laughs, they did relish exercising their poetic wit, especially in the anagram and the acrostic, two forms that required the poet to use the letters of a person's name to create words or epigrams that revealed aspects of that individual's character. Because many Puritans believed that nothing in their world was haphazard and that all indications of God's attitude toward them were highly important, some writers of anagrams and acrostics found great providential significance in the rearrangement of the letters in a subject's name. But whether the Puritan reverence for God is reflected in their philosophy of poetic composition is a matter of conjecture. To be sure, their poetry tends to demonstrate the Puritan obsession with order, in life as well as in poetry. And while there are many examples of anagrams and acrostics that do demonstrate an apparent connection between God's ability to predestine events and the linguistic skill with which these colonial poetasters manipulated their language, to assume that all Puritan poetry was ordered in this fashion, or to fail to acknowledge the level of etymological tomfoolery in the seventeenth century, is a mistake. As Roy Harvey Pearce has observed, seventeenth-century American poetry reflects the poet's delight in "exercising his ability not only to discover meaning but to express it: in effect, to discover himself as a poet."[1]

Viewed from this perspective, the Puritan anagram and acrostic represent with few exceptions a form of Puritan gaudiness, a conscious attempt on the poets' part to show off, not only for their fellow New Englanders, but also for their God.

That Puritan poets achieved celebrity status through the creation of anagrams and acrostics is indicated by the diversity and number of occasions on which they were called to compose them. For example, one of the most common occasions in the seventeenth century for the poet to exercise his ability to discover meaning through language and express it was the death of a fellow Puritan. No other form of poetry seemed so natural to the Puritans as the elegy: "Because death tested the conduct of a man's whole life, and because the passing of great men showed God's disposition toward the community, the elegy could stake as its province theological doctrine, social theory, and personal grief, while elaborating the ideals of conduct Puritans valued. . . ."[2] And for the anagrammatist, who selected his theme from the epigram or motto he formed from the letters of the subject's name, death provided the basis for investigating whether there was some significance in nomenclature. In submitting to the very disciplines of meter, rhyme, and structure, however forced, the anagrammatist placed himself in the position of demonstrating not only the order that existed in both poetry and life, but also his poetic wit.

Certainly one of the finest elegies of its kind, "O, Honie knott," John Fiske's anagrammatic exercise on the death of John Cotton (in Meserole, *Poetry*), incorporates intricate metaphysical conceits into the poem as a vehicle for expressing this order in death. On one level, Fiske celebrates Cotton's death as an explanation of the complexity of all things. Through the gnarled syntax and complex imagery of his anagram, Fiske mirrors life's perplexity, but he also shows how everything in life fits into a pattern, how meaning arises when order prevails. At one point in the poem, Fiske notes that while "The knott sometimes seems a deformity / It's a mistake," for "The knott it is the Joynt, the strength of parts."[3] In the search for meaning, it is the form through which that search is carried out that provides order.

On the one hand, Fiske's poem is a social gesture, designed as a vehicle to celebrate and to suggest epic stature for the dead Cotton, but Fiske makes clear that it is not merely the social gesture that interests him but also the opportunity to extol Puritan dogma and describe a saintly life and character through poetic means.[4] The Cotton elegy is an intricately woven and carefully developed poem written to show Cotton's eminence as a minister and his ability to unravel God's mysteries. Despite this, it is still Fiske who consciously weaves a series of elaborate metaphors together into a pattern to provide the reader not only with a doctrinal statement but also with a word puzzle to solve. While Fiske's elegy is more than a collection of random linguistic tricks used to display his verbal adroitness and wit, it is nonetheless a tour de force of the genre at its best, indulged in for its own sake too.

Fiske brilliantly displays at every turn the seemingly disparate parts of Cotton's nature by describing him as a "gurdeon knot of sweetest graces as / He who set fast to Truths so closely knitt / As loosen him could ne're the keenest wit." For the Puritan audience, Cotton "the knotts of Truth, of Mysteries / Sacred, most cleerely did ope 'fore our eyes." And life for the Puritans was sometimes knotty. It was for John Cotton, the man of great intellect and compassion, to interpret and reflect those Puritan dogmas, to provide a sense of order in a disordered world. He was a "knott exemplary" who was a master of "knotty Learning," and, therefore,

> When knotty theames and paynes some meet with then
> As knotty and uncouth their tongue and pen
> So 'twas not heere, he caus'd us understand
> And tast the sweetness of the knott in hand.
> When knotty querks and quiddities broacht were
> By witt of man he sweetly Breathed there. [ll. 51–56]

To understand, through his devices of metaphor and pun, the uses of "honie" and "knott" is to recognize the roots of Fiske's showmanship. In his punning on "bee" ("Even hee who such a one, is ceas'd to be," "Which crabbed anggry tough unpleasing bee / But wc as in a honi-comb"); "honie" ("O knott of Hony most delightfull when / Thou livd'st," "This knott thereof so surfetted we see / By hony surfetted we know som bee"); and "knott" ("I guess why knotty Learning downe does goe / 'Twould not, if as in him 'twere sweetened soe," "When knotty theames and paynes some meet with then / As knotty and uncouth their tongue and pen / So 'twas not heere, he caus'd us understand," "Woe to that knotty pride hee ne're subdude"), Fiske has compiled a fugue of meanings from a pair of words. By searching out and by using every nuance of these words, Fiske fits them all into a cogent argument for a proper celebration of death and, therefore, life.

Three years later, Fiske returned to the anagrammatic form in a poem on the death of Anne Griffin, wife of Richard Griffin of Concord (in Meserole, *Poetry*). Here the anagram is "In Fanne: Rig," and Fiske dazzles the reader by exploiting to the fullest the images of nautical rigging and the threshing of grain. Throughout the poem, Fiske compares Anne Griffin "to the wheate, Thy wheate appeare that't may / As twere in Fanne" and her journey to a "long home" with the ship that will carry that wheat as it prepares for sailing to a "hoped safe Port." By suggesting that her journey will be hard from "seas [not] calm," and by emphasizing that "Time calls . . . / Longer abroad tis not for Thee to be," Fiske celebrates Mrs. Griffin's certain success and warns his audience that it is time for "us to Rig, for us acquaint / Will God with Tryalls such, And lay us low / Yea lay us low, and humble us Hee will."

Fiske's anagrams on Cotton and Griffin are probably his best although certainly not his only attempts at creating aesthetically delightful word puzzles. Others include his anagrams, often composed in Latin, on John Wilson ("W'on Sion-hil"), Thomas Parker[us] ("*Charus es, promat*"), Thomas Hooker ("A Rest; oh com'! oh"), William Snelling ("All mine will sing"), Margaret Snelling ("Grant mee all: Sr, I am willing" and "Sr, Grant me all: I am willing"), Samuel Sharp[ias] ("*pura samis; selah*"), Samuel Sharpe ("Us! Ample-share"), Ezechiel Rogers[ius] ("*Reus zeli, hoc eriges*"), and Nathaniel Rogers ("He in a larg Rest. / No").[5] The Puritan anagrammatist became, therefore, not only a maker of word puzzles, but more significantly a decoder of them. His art suggests the lengths to which the anagrammatist went to carve out his niche in the Puritan social order.

To assume, then, that Puritan society was made up entirely of Bible-toting and grimly-scowling citizens is to misunderstand what everyday life was like in colonial New England. In fact, the seventeenth-century American was a man who was "fond of his world—of beer and wine, of household amenities, of fashionable clothing in rich color, of music. . .who enjoyed the company of his friends. . .[and] went about his business very much in the world and with delight in his natural environs."[6] It is understandable, too, that these Americans were fond of displaying their cleverness and earthy humor whenever the occasion arose. While the label *Puritan* might imply a tone of solemnity to modern audiences, we can also associate the terms *wit* and *humor* with the Puritans, for "the surface paradox begins to fade when we remember that many of the earliest New Englanders were university-trained and were the inheritors of a well-established Renaissance tradition of wit."[7] For the Puritans, this Renaissance wit is best illustrated in their propensity for word games, among which the anagram and acrostic stood in high favor.

On one occasion, a Puritan's sense of humor overcame his sense of decorum when he sent his elegy to Anne Bradstreet's father, Governor Thomas Dudley, who in 1645 was still very much alive. The anagram of Dudley's name is "ah! old must dye," and the anonymous poem (in Meserole, *Poetry*) twists and turns on the various nuances of those key words and sparkles in its rhythmic movement from image to image. While this anagram might suggest to some Puritans that the meaning in such a fortuitous twist of a name is directly related to God's design, it more clearly indicates the ingenuity and verbal facility of its author. A careful reading of the third, fifth, and seventh lines makes this clear: "you neede not one to mind you, you must dye, / . . . Younge men may dye, but old men, these dye must, / . . . Before you turne to dust! ah! must! old! dye!" This skillful rearrangement of the letters of Dudley's name and the message read in the lines from the poem is a semantic exercise, one that is an important part of the Puritan use of language, a commitment to words that Larzer Ziff has discussed:

> Deep within the culture's overwhelming commitment to the certainty of
> words over commitment to ambiguous images, to the dominance of the

pulpit over the altar, was a folk belief in the animism of language. The meaning of words on this level was not arbitrary but organically connected with the essence of the thing signified by the word. . . .

Pun as well as anagram therefore flourished in New England writing:. . .Wit, so severely confined in other areas of life, was indulged in verse and other shapings of language. Here reason and pattern were called upon because such were the proper tools in the psychological conquest of nature.[8]

Just as Puritan ministers and historiographers used the sermon and the history to create a dazzling system of typology to provide order and meaning for their readers, so, too, did the writers of anagrams use these ingenious displays of verbal fireworks to create a place for themselves in the intellectual order of seventeenth-century New England.

We recognize, of course, that for some the anagram was taken as a serious element of a Puritan *ars poetica,* that the temporal order was closely associated with and foreshadowed the eternal. John Saffin, the Puritan merchant and poet, wrote that verse should be "Significant, plaine, yet Ellegant,"[9] and in practice most poets worked with whatever ornaments and conceits attracted them. Many undoubtedly saw anagrams as a way to sharpen their sense of imagery or to polish their style for the more important moments when they might be called upon to perform. While most poets usually associated their own plain style with truth and an ornate style with fraud, it was Cotton Mather, whose *Magnalia Christi Americana* was somewhat ironically peppered with puns and anagrams, who observed a biblical precedent for the use of such word play:

> Yea, 'tis possible that they who affect such *grammatical curiosities,* will be willing to plead a *prescription* of much higher and elder antiquity for them; even the *temurah,* or *mutation,* with which the Jews do criticise upon the oracles of the Old Testament: "There," they say, "you'll find the anagram of our *first father's* name *Haadam,* to express *Adamah,* the name of the *earth,* whence he had his original." An anagram of *good* signification, they'll show you [Gen. vi. 8,] and of a *bad* one [Gen. xxxviii. 7,] in those glorious oracles; and they will endeavour to perswade you, that *Maleachi* in Edodus is anagrammatically expounded *Michael,* in Daniel.[10]

Yet it is clear that not even this precedent was considered definitive, for as Robert Daly has argued, "No American Puritan has left us an *ars poetica.*" Daly explains that it is almost impossible to recognize a "pattern of explicit poetics emerging from their scattered comments (always made in passing in works devoted to other subjects) on the nature and function of poetry."[11] Hyatt Waggoner makes a similar point regarding the Puritans and their philosophy of poetry: "They would not have understood an art for art's sake doctrine, not because they had contempt for art but because for them life was all of a piece and lower values should properly be subordinated to higher ones. The use of poetry was to help one to live well—and die well. For this purpose even the simplest poetic memorial of the humblest versifier might serve."[12] The vast majority of Puritan poetry demonstrates that while some might have seen the rearrangement of the letters of a man's name as prophetic, most viewed the anagram as a flash of poetic wit.

John Wilson, probably the most prolific of Puritan anagrammatists, demonstrates the sport of witty verse at its best. In "Tis Braul I Cudgel," an anagram on his friend Claudius T. Gilbert (in Meserole, *Poetry*), pastor of Limerick, Ireland, and author of a number of tracts attacking Quakerism, Wilson denounces the Quakers and their "Brauling Questions [that] whosoever reades / May soone perceive, These are their proper heades." "What Better Cudgels," Wilson asks, "then Gods holy word / (For Brauls so cursed) and the Civil Sword?" As "God Abhorreth, as he doth the Devils," so puns Wilson, "Lett these blessed Cudgels knocke them downe." Wilson's reputation as anagrammatist was widely known. Cotton Mather wrote of him: "I believe that never was a man who made so *many*, or so *nimbly*, as our Mr. Wilson; who together with his quick turns, upon the names of his friends, would ordinarily *fetch*, and rather than *lose*, would even *force*, devout instructions out of his anagrams." Mather's remarks on the use of anagrams, set forth in "Memoria Wilsonia, the Life of Mr. John Wilson" in Book III of the *Magnalia*, indicate that Mather himself found a "certain little sport of wit, in anagrammatizing the names of men." As one who would never have been accused of being jovial, Mather did have a sense of humor and appreciated the anagrammatist who made "this *poetical* and *peculiar* disposition of his ingenuity a subject whereon he grafted *thoughts* far more solid, and solemn, and useful, than the *stock* it self."[13] Nathaniel Ward's assessment of Wilson's abilities as anagrammatist (in Meserole, *Poetry*) is far more famous:

> We poor Agawams
> are so stiff in the hams
> that we cannot make Anagrams,
> But Mr. John Wilson
> the great Epigrammatist
> Can let out an Anagram
> even as he list.

If Wilson, according to Ward, "Can let out an Anagram / even as he list," then the spiritual authority given to such examples of Puritan verbal dexterity cannot be taken too seriously.

Even less serious is the Puritans' attitude toward the acrostic. Unlike the anagram, the acrostic used the letters of the subject's name as the first letter of the opening word, or the last letter of the closing word, in the lines of a poem. In some poems, the letters were used to open or close a word in the middle of lines. Read downward, these spelled the name of the subject of the poem. Because the acrostic relied very heavily upon a visual pattern, its form was less flexible than that of the anagram. This rigidity of form not only restricted the poet's freedom to compose; it also tended to portray verbal wit as mere verbal artifact. If we believe that most poets composed their verse because of what they felt they saw in the fortuitous rearrangement of a person's name, the acrostic is in some ways a misrepresentation of what they as poets intended. Instead of seeing the theme of the poem surfacing organically as from the anagram (making the invisible visible), the writer of the acrostic tended to impose a theme on the poem resulting from its visible structure.

John Saffin's acrostic on Elizabeth Hull (in Meserole, *Poetry*), for example, reveals a light-hearted glimpse of Puritan life, but does not display the verbal flourishes found in the anagram. The result, then, is a poem that is forced, albeit ingenious. Using the letters in the name of Elizabeth Hull to begin the first word in each line, Saffin displays his verbal dexterity as well as the more salient features of this "Beautious-Sweet-Smileing and Heart-moveing Creature." For Elizabeth Hull to be granted such "fair and comely feature[s]," she certainly must have deserved God's grace. And for Saffin to be able to compose a poem using the letters of her name suggests that she must, at least in the Puritan view, prosper. There is little spiritual authority in the poem, of course, but then Saffin was probably more concerned with revealing the beauties of a woman—a true subject for verse—and the linguistic and numerological tricks he was capable of creating within the poem than unveiling a providential design for which he might be held accountable.[14]

In another acrostic, Saffin worked his word magic on Mrs. Winifret Griffin (in Meserole, *Poetry*).

As in his acrostic on Elizabeth Hull, Saffin's poem fails as anything more than clever word play, although the poem does achieve some social significance in its presentation of theme. Saffin no doubt felt that to delight as well as to instruct was an important function of Puritan verse. Thus, his image of Mrs. Griffin as the possesor of the "merits of A Noble mind" and as a repository of "Witt, and Beauty" serves to revise our image of all Puritan females as wives laboring solely in the daily routine of caring for their families in isolated frontier villages or as young girls educated only in simple household skills and in lessons of submission. To recognize that women in general, and Mrs. Griffin in particular, are "Rare Master-piece[s] of Natures Excellence," and that admirers believed them deserving of "Fresh new Supplys of riches, Honour, Pleasure," is to establish the point that some Puritans at least felt that women should and could enter into the affairs of daily living with the same vigor and pleasure as men.

The fact that many acrostics were written for or about women is not surprising, for beauty was a prime topic for verse of all kinds. Certainly one poem that displays a remarkable control both over its visual pattern and its use of words is Edward Taylor's acrostic love poem to his wife, Elizabeth Fitch.[15] Taylor's visual scheme is complexly organized to present a circle inside a triangle, the circumference of that circle touching each of the triangle's three sides. Positioned around the sides of the triangle are letters of the alphabet that, if read carefully, reveal the message of the poem: "The ring of love my pleasant heart must truely be confind within the trinitie." Likewise, a second message is in place around the circumference of the circle, utilizing in addition those letters positioned at the three points of the circle that touch the triangle's sides. This message reads: "Lovs ring I send that hath no end." This poem, like Taylor's elegies on Charles Chauncy and Francis Willoughby, are examples of the visual and verbal fireworks Taylor set off when he composed some of his poems. However, more often than not, they are more admirable for their ingenuity than for their succinctness or power as poetry.[16]

Years later Taylor rejects the acrostic form when he expresses his sense of loss in "A Funerall Poem Upon the Death of my ever Endeared and Tender Wife Mrs. Elizabeth Taylor":

> What shall my Preface to our True Love Knot
> Frisk in Acrostick Rhimes? And may I not
> Now at our parting, with Poetick knocks
> Break a salt teare to pieces as it drops?
> Did Davids bitter Sorrow at the Dusts
> Of Jonathan raise such Poetick gusts?
> Do Emperours interr'd in Verses lie?
> And mayn't such Feet run from my Weeping Eye?[17]

There is no acrostic "frisking" in this poem, however, for as Taylor laments, "Impute it not a Crime then if I weep / A Weeping Poem on thy Winding Sheet" (ll. 55–56). Taylor felt the acrostic appropriate for displaying his poetic wit, his sense of word play and love play, but inappropriate for a "Weeping Poem" to announce his grief or as a way of understanding the relationship between this world and the next. Taylor's elegy cannot reach his wife unless "Some Angell may my Poem sing/To thee in Glory, or relate the thing" (ll. 57–58), and there is no reason to amuse in this poem, but only to grieve. As the subject of the poem grows more serious, so, too, does Taylor's imagery. Whatever artificiality Taylor may have seen operating in acrostics is not present in his expression of grief.

Robert Daly makes a similar point in his discussion of Benjamin Tompson's elegy on Elizabeth Tompson.[18] While Tompson begins his elegy with an appropriately religious anagram (o i am blest on top) and develops this imagery throughout the first half of the poem, he abandons the verbal tricks of the anagram in the middle and instead concentrates on writing an apostrophe which more sincerely expresses his sorrow:

> A lovely Cluster on a vine i saw,
> So faire it did my admiracion draw,
> Climbing the sun side of an house of prayer,
> And solaceing it selfe in heavenly aire
> Yet sudenly upon an eastward blast
> The beuty of his boughs was over cast
> The fairest grapes were pickt off one by one.
> The Dresser looking like one half undone. . . .[19]

The rest of the poem is equally moving, suggesting that Tompson was more concerned with writing serious poetry to express his sorrow over the death of his niece than with exploring the linguistic possibilities of the anagrammatic form.

In fact, for most Puritan poets, the anagram and the acrostic were simply vehicles for demonstrating their wit. In very few cases do we find poets using either form for serious poetry, despite whatever biblical authority or precedent they might have cited. They were not convinced that the anagram or the acrostic were poetic effusions inspired by God, or that their ability to compose them was a providential sign of their election. For Mather, Ward, Tompson, and Taylor, as the century came to a close, poetic wit tended to reflect the creative process itself. In "Some OFFERS to Embalm the MEMORY of the Truly Reverend and Renowned JOHN WILSON," a poem attributed to Benjamin Tompson, this function of the anagram is most fully articulated:

> By *Words, Works, Prayers, Psalms, Alms*, and ANAGRAMS:
> Those *Anagrams*, in which he made to Start
> Out of meer *Nothings*, by *Creating Art*,
> Whole *Worlds* of Counsil; did to *Motes* Unfold
> *Names*, till they Lessons gave Richer than *Gold*,
> And Every *Angle* so Exactly say,
> It should out-shine the brightest *Solar Ray*.
> Sacred his *Verse*, Writ with a *Cherubs* Quill;
> But those Wing'd Choristers of *Zion*-Hill,
> Pleas'd with the *Notes*, call'd him a part to bear,
> With *Them*, where he his *Anagram* did hear,
> I Pray Come in, Heartily Welcome; Sir.[20]

As Tompson suggests, creating anagrams "Out of meer *Nothings*," is like "*Creating Art*." Even more important, Tompson argues that these verses are more valuable for teaching moral lessons "Richer than *Gold*" than for use in serious attempts to understand the definitive connection between this world and the next. There was little perceived prophetic value in anagrams and acrostics for most seventeenth-century American poets, although their accepted value as popular indications of God-given talent makes them important elements of the Puritan culture.

For Cotton Mather, Nathaniel Ward, John Saffin, John Fiske, John Wilson, and other writers of anagrams and acrostics in seventeenth-century New England, the final line from Benjamin Tompson's elegy on Edmund Davie ("Ad DeumVeni") might bespeak their feeling for poetic wit: "Heres an Eternal feast of Love: fall to it."[21] Sometimes used in the name of social criticism, sometimes written to commemorate the dead, sometimes penned to display verbal neat-handedness, sometimes created to praise the salient virtues of a beautiful woman, the anagram and the acrostic were used alongside hymns, sermons, and ballads to provide some sense of order in the Puritan world, but more frequently to enliven and enrich the sights and sounds, the rigors and hardships, the routine and often bleak circumstances of everyday life. There is little question that the New England mind was a lively one, that the literary heritage of seventeenth-century America was a rich tradition filled with wit and earthy humor, and that Puritan poetasters were individuals who despite their sex or social position had an obsession with cementing their niches in the world. They were a gaudy crew, a group of people whose number included far more John Wilsons than either they or we would be likely to acknowledge.

NOTES

1. Pearce, *Continuity*, p. 30.
2. Silverman, *Poetry*, p. 121.
3. Meserole, *Poetry*, p. 188, ll. 37–39.
4. Astrid Schmitt-von Mühlenfels, "John Fiske's Funeral Elegy on John Cotton," *EAL* 12 (Spring 1977), p. 50.
5. Poems in Jantz, *First Century*, pp. 118–30.
6. Meserole, *Poetry*, p. xxv.
7. Meserole, " 'A Kind of Burr': Colonial New England's Heritage of Wit," in *American Literature: The New England Heritage*, ed. James Nagel and Richard Astro (New York and London: Garland, 1981), p. 12.
8. Larzer Ziff, *Puritanism in America: New Culture in a New World* (New York: Viking, 1973), p. 119.
9. *John Saffin: His Book (1665–1708)*, ed. Caroline Hazard (New York, 1928), p. 2.
10. Cotton Mather, *Magnalia Christi Americana* (1702; rpt. New York: Russell and Russell, 1967), I: 318.
11. *God's Altar*, p. 40.

12. Waggoner, *Poets*.

13. *Magnalia*, I: 318.

14. Meserole, in " 'A Kind of Burr,' " p. 14, cites a number of subtleties that make Saffin's acrostic even more dazzling than it first appears.

15. *Edward Taylor's Minor Poetry: Volume 3 of The Unpublished Writings of Edward Taylor*, ed. Thomas M. and Virginia L. Davis (Boston: Twayne, 1981), pp. 37–41.

16. "An Elogy upon the Death of the Reverend & Learned Man of God Mr. Charles Chauncey President of Harvard Colledg in N. Englend Who Departed this Life 20th 12m 1671/2 And of This age 80" (*Minor Poetry*, pp. 32–35) contains a double acrostic on Chauncey's name, a quadruple acrostic whose treble is an anagram (Charles Chauncey, A Call in Churches), and an acrostic chronogram (where Taylor uses Roman numerals as the first letter of the first word of each line to total the year of Chauncey's death); "An Elegie upon the Death of the Worshipfull Fran[cis] Willoughby Esq., Deputy Governour of the Masach[usetts] Colony in N: E: who departed at Charlestown 3rd [2m 1671]" (*Minor Poetry*, pp. 22–24) is an acrostic in which Taylor uses the letters of Willoughby's name as the first letter of the first word, the last letter of the last word, and as a letter in one of the words in the middle of each line in the poem.

17. "A Funerall Poem Upon the Death of my ever Endeared, and Tender Wife Mrs. Elizabeth Taylor, Who fell asleep in Christ the 7th day of July at night about two hours after Sun setting 1689 and in the 39 yeare of her Life," in Stanford, *Taylor*, p. 473, ll. 41–48.

18. Daly, *God's Altar*, p. 151.

19. "The Amiable virgin memorized Elizabeth Tompson who deceased in Boston at Mr. Leggs august 22, 1712," in White, *Tompson*, p. 179.

20. "Some OFFERS to Embalm the MEMORY of the Truly Reverend and Renowned JOHN WILSON; The First Pastor of Boston, in New England; Interr'd (and a Great Part of his Countries *Glory* with him) August. 11. 1667. Aged, 79.," in White, *Tompson*, p. 187.

21. "EDMUND DAVIE 1682 anagram Ad Deum Veni," in White, *Tompson*, p. 147.

18 BAROQUE FREE VERSE IN NEW ENGLAND AND PENNSYLVANIA

HAROLD JANTZ

European free verse, at least one type of it, seems first to have developed out of a form that was not verse at all: the Roman monumental inscription, more specifically the memorial or commemorative inscription, whether on a tomb, a public building, or the base of a statue. When the inscription went beyond a sober recounting of basic facts to a laudation, a balanced and measured rhetoric of high dignity could result. And when in such a tribute the balance was made visual in lines equally distributed to left and right of an invisible middle axis, then intimations of a new literary form become manifest. Such a disposition of lines of different length arranged symmetrically around a middle axis did occur occasionally in antiquity, but the instances are relatively rare and are usually confined to brief votive dedications. One such I happened to reproduce in 1969 in *The Mothers in Faust: the Myth of Time and Creativity.*[1] Throughout Roman times it was possible to distinguish between metrical inscriptions that were clearly verse and the non-metrical that were simply prose, even though the latter did occasionally incorporate elements of rhythm and sound that made them literarily noteworthy.

Building upon this somewhat casual and adventitious basis, the humanists of the early Renaissance prepared non-metrical inscriptions of their own, at first usually written as prose, then gradually, beginning with the very brief ones, balanced around a middle axis, until this middle-axis form became the usual and accepted one even for longer inscriptions. After the transfer was made from chisel and stone to pen and paper, then to printed page, at first in collections of old inscriptions, the next step was the crucial one: the creation of new inscriptions in these lighter and easier media. As is to be expected, this greater ease soon tempted men of letters to develop inscriptions to a length that would have made any ancient stonemason quail. Therewith, a new literary genre arose in the Renaissance and more amply in the Baroque, leaving its point of origin far behind and developing poetic potentialities of which the old Romans never dreamed. In this new expressive form, this technique of balanced and incremental phrasing, the poets found an attractive alternative to the old traditional form of metric regularity and equivalent length of line. Furthermore, the new form lent itself to quite new purposes, for instance to the writing of lengthy satires, as we shall see.

Ultimately, however, it was the transfer of this Latin form to the vernacular that established it as a poetic genre, now largely liberated from its merely inscriptional origins. From early and mid-seventeenth century onward, leading poets began to experiment with the new form, and soon masterly compositions in this "lapidary style" began to appear in various languages. Indeed, by 1725 it was possible to issue an anthology of German inscriptions of well over 450 pages, with a second edition appearing in 1732. The editor, Friedrich Andreas Hallbauer, citing numerous predecessors, wrote a lengthy introduction with both historical and theoretical reflections on this expressive new poetic variant.[2] For a proper and informed understanding of parallel American developments, it is important to note at this point that even though most of the middle-axis compositions in this anthology are unrhymed, some of them do have the element of rhyme, thus establishing one more bridge from inscription to poetic composition. Naturally, many an ancient monumental inscription, whether sepulchral or dedicatory, included a metrical epitaph or epigram as an integral part of the whole. However, the even more intimate fusion of the inscriptional and the poetic that took place in the Baroque is a decisive step in a new direction. Modern handbooks and encyclopaedias seem to have lost sight of this further development, and so has the generality of historians and critics of literature. Indeed a vast amnesic silence would have spread over this whole area if it had not been for one of the boldly intuitive modernist poets of the turn of the century who discovered that this middle-axis inscriptional form offered him the almost ideal medium for expressing his cosmic vision in an eloquent and memorable manner. It was Arno Holz with his *Phantasus* of 1898, successively revised and expanded until 1925 and gradually becoming recognized as one of the classics of the new experimental poetry.

Anyone who has read extensively in the neo-Latin and vernacular literature of the Baroque would inevitably have come upon numerous examples of the new inscriptional genre, shorter or longer, closer to the ancient or departing farther from it. Thus, in my young years when I set about writing *The First Century of New England Verse*, I saw no problem when I came upon the several examples of middle-axis inscriptions, Latin and English, that I found in the course of my search. I merely took it for granted that the Baroque inscription was a variant poetic form and I simply included examples of it in my bibliography along with the other poetic efforts, according to the well-established European precedents. Just then I had no particular interest in the matter, and it was only later in the mid-1950s, at the time of my guest professorships for American studies at the Universities of Hamburg and Vienna, that I came upon the Hallbauer and the preceding treatises on poetics that usually contained a chapter on the middle-axis inscription as a poetic form. My growing Baroque collection already contained several books largely or entirely composed in inscriptional form, such as the Jesuit Nicolaus Avancini's splendid laudation of the Roman German emperors,

1658, and in the next decade the quite different political satires using this form, these issued by Balthasar Venator in seven parts of between forty-eight and seventy-two pages. Thus I became mildly interested, then decidedly more so when I encountered great difficulty in acquiring a copy of Emmanuele Tesauro's *Il Cannocchiale Aristotelico*, first issued at Venice in 1655. Finally in Florence I found the title listed in the well-thumbed card catalogue of an antiquarian bookseller. I asked him about it, and he told me sorrowfully that the book had been lost or misplaced years ago. I pleaded with him to try to find it for me, that I urgently needed it. He descended into the vaults of his *maggazini* and finally emerged with a quarto volume that he triumphantly laid before me. It was the *Aristotelian Spyglass* in the edition of 1685, and there in Chapter XIII is the "Trattato Delle Inscrittioni Argvte." All the examples are in Latin; the last one is the only long one: forty-four lines, although in his collected *Inscriptiones* of 1666 there are much longer ones. The trans-Alpine practitioners and theoreticians were deeply indebted to him, but they did in various ways also go beyond him. The *Cannocchiale* remains a fascinating book for other reasons also and opens up many an avenue into the widespread realm of the Baroque.

When Leo M. Kaiser undertook his basic and indispensable critical work on the neo-Latin verse of New England, he raised objections to my inclusion of inscriptions in a survey of early New England verse. I regarded this as a normal difference of opinion, as for instance when the "ancients" look critically at the opinions of the "moderns" with all their deviation from classical norms and standards. In this case I felt that seventeenth-century standards are appropriate to seventeenth-century literary products. I only began to give new consideration to the problem when an article by Kaiser appeared in *Early American Literature*, Winter issue of 1979/80, entitled "On the Epitaph of Thomas Shepard II and a Corrigendum in Jantz."[3] Here he attributes an anonymous epitaph on Thomas Shepard II to Urian Oakes, for cogent reasons, and I intend in the new edition of the *First Century* to transfer the work to its probable, indeed certain author.

Yet this is not what Professor Kaiser would want me to do; he believes that I should remove the epitaph entirely from the bibliography of verse, since it is an inscription, therefore prose and not poetry. He also lists seven other non-metric inscriptions that he feels I should remove. Clearly, one can no longer take it for granted that these can be regarded as poetic pieces; one must reexamine them carefully to see whether they continue to conform to the manner and dimensions of the classic Roman inscription or whether they have made the transition to the more poetic diction and broader expanse that caused the progressive critics of the day to make room for them as a valid albeit different form of poetry. Moreover, I felt I should no longer rely solely upon my own judgment and interpretation in this matter. Therefore, after I had written the first draft of this chapter I paused to search out whether there might be some newer work on the subject and whether the author's conclusions and perspectives would differ significantly from my own. As good fortune had it, there is an isolated, excellent work in the field, John Sparrow's *Visible Words: A Study of Inscriptions in and as Books and Works of Art.*[4] As he states in the Preface: "the interest I had taken over many years in the history since the Renaissance of the inscription, both as a form of art and as the subject or the matter of published books, had led me to become acquainted with the works of Emmanuele Tesauro and his followers, and the effusion of 'lapidary' books by these composers all over Europe in the seventeenth century seemed to be an episode in the history of literature and of book production interesting and unfamiliar enough to provide a topic suitable for the occasion [the Sandars Lectures]." Clearly he had looked into the matter far more thoroughly than I had. On the central point he came to much the same conclusion as mine: the Baroque inscription was indeed a new poetic form, as he demonstrates especially in his final chapter: "The Inscription as a Literary Form."

Let just a few quotations from Sparrow's book suffice here. First under 'Inscriptiones Argutae': "Another factor that affected the development of the inscription wás the fashion of witty writing, or *argutezza*. Even before the beginning of the sixteenth century, composers had begun to infuse into their imitations of classical inscriptions unclassical strains of feeling and turns of expression. The epitaphs of Pontano in his chapel in Naples in the 1490s are among the earliest examples of the effects of this new spirit" (p. 103). Earlier in the book, after converting these epitaphs from their original linear form into middle-axis form, he remarks: "It would be hard to find anything quite like these inscriptions on any gravestone of classical Rome, still more on any mediaeval or fifteenth-century sepulchral monument. They are prose poems, in which the composer's emotions are expressed in words which presuppose that the text is to be inscribed on a memorial" (p. 23). Sparrow calls Christian Weise's *De Poesi Hodiernorum Politicorum Sive De Argutis Inscriptionibus Libri II* of 1678 "the classic guide-book to the new epigraphy" and goes on to observe: "Weise treats his subject as a kind of poetry: 'modern political poetry', as he puts it. He explains in his Address to the Reader why he calls his book 'De Poesi Hodiernorum Politicorum'; this is not, he says, because he wishes to suggest that all who concern themselves with politics should take up this kind of writing, but because nowadays notable judgments on affairs of state are commonly cast in this form. Anyone, he says, who keeps his eyes open must have seen inscriptions which deal, in the way either of satire or of panegyric, with the issues of peace and war. And such productions, Weise continues, are none the less poetry for not being metrical; meter is the clothing, not the body, of poetry" (p. 106).

There is, however, an unresolved paradox in Sparrow's book between two general observations he makes earlier and one specific instance he offers just before the Epilogue. The one remark, when he is sketching the historical backgrounds, reads: "While this activity was taking place on the Continent, England was lagging about a century behind, both in the production of inscriptions and in the production of books about them" (p. 32). And again: "By the beginning of the seventeenth century the inscription had come into its own; elaborate sculptured monuments were still of course produced (in Britain, always a century behind the times in such matters, the monumental art flourished then as never before), but in most memorials the inscription was the dominant feature" (p. 102). And yet, almost as an afterthought, he adds as a final paragraph before the Epilogue: "The most remarkable lapidary work in English that I have come across is Francis Quarles's *Memorials upon the Death of Sir Robert Quarles*, 1639, a little book consisting of an elegy of 253 lines upon the death of the poet's brother. In reprinting this work [in Quarles's *Complete Works*, Chertsey Worthies Library, III (1881), 27] Grosart obscures the fact that, though continuous, it consists of fourteen *elogia* of equal length (save that one, anomalously, is nineteen lines long), each of which occupies, in the original edition, a single page. So far as I know, this is the only *carmen lapidarium* on such a scale attempted by Quarles or any of his contemporaries in English" (p. 131). What is particularly noteworthy is that these inscriptions by Quarles are indeed in English, not in Latin, and that 1639 is, up to this time, the earliest known date for a poetically conceived middle-axis inscription in the vernacular. Actually, it comes well before the decisive classical handbooks or collections by Jacob Masenius (1649), Emmanuele Tesauro (1655, 1666), and Christian Weise (1678). Sparrow mentions nothing of earlier date in Italian or any other modern European language. I also knew of no earlier example in German than mid-century. Quarles has no known predecessor, nor is there any known succession in English—until we come a bit later to the recently settled New England colonies. How did it happen that amid the observed "cultural lag" in England there should be one isolated individual who in one work apparently outstripped everyone on the Continent in the vernacular development of this new poetic form?

The writers on Quarles, to my knowledge, are silent and unseeing about the innovative quality of the *Memorials*. The modern literary handbooks, English and Continental, single or multivolume, seem to have forgotten that there ever was such a literary form as the inscription. The most compendious of the encyclopaedias, the Spanish and the Italian, do tell briefly and inadequately about Renaissance continuities in Latin; the latter even claims that the first inscriptions in Italian did not come until the nineteenth century. Then there are the English, the French, and the German encyclopaedias in descending order of inadequacy. Indeed, one must go back to the eighteenth century, for instance to Zedler's encyclopaedia in sixty-eight volumes, 1732–54, for any mention of the inscription in the vernacular; here Quirinus Pegeus' (i.e., Georg Philipp Harsdörffer's) *Ars Apophthegmatica . . . Kunstquellen denkwürdiger Lehrsprüche* of 1655–56 is said to contain the first German inscriptions. This was as far as my own casually gathered knowledge had gone until I found John Sparrow's startling news about Francis Quarles.

This poet's close relationship to the New England colonists is well known. Time and again poems of his occur in the commonplace books of early colonists, and John Saffin, for instance, takes one of Quarles' poems as a point of departure for one of his own ("Sayle gentle Pinnace"). John Josselyn, himself a poet of few lines but great originality, in 1638 brought over to John Winthrop and John Cotton Quarles' verse translations of six psalms. These have apparently been lost; certainly the *Bay Psalm Book* at these six places contains translations more like those that surround them than like anything that Quarles ever wrote. If a copy of his *Memorials* reached New England at the time, as is likely, there is no clearly visible sequel there. Till now we also know of no antecedents. Where can they be?

The beginning of an answer comes with the biographical observation that Francis Quarles, in the retinue of the Earl of Arundell, accompanied the Princess Elizabeth in 1613 to Heidelberg after her marriage to the Palatine Elector Frederick V, and apparently, at least in passing, held the ceremonial office of cup-bearer to her. Frederick, like his father, Frederick IV, and preceding ancestors, was a great and knowledgeable patron of the arts and learning. Impressive palace structures already stood on the heights above the city, and young Frederick continued with further splendid structures as well as with the fabled Palatine gardens. Later all were reduced to ruins during the French invasion of 1689. Add to this patronage that the men of letters of Heidelberg and adjoining regions, well before Opitz, were striving to develop the German language to a new classical elegance and that the best models from antiquity and the Renaissance were at their command in the magnificent library. At this time the library was still in place, though in the next decade, early in the Thirty Years War, the imperial forces after the conquest of Heidelberg had it transported to Rome, where at the Vatican the words "Codex Palatinus" could refer to the unique copy of the Greek Anthology or to many another manuscript nearly as illustrious. Taking all these factors together, it becomes almost inevitable that the splendid architecture being erected, the pageants and festivals being celebrated, should be accompanied by a wealth of inscriptions, most of them in Latin of course, some of them, however, already being fashioned in German.

To this point the transition from Latin to German is only an inferrence, a likelihood considering the Heidelberg constellation at the time. But where is the solid evidence? At first I found none, either among the prominent men of letters around Georg Michael Lingelsheim or among the remarkable group of young men just then rising to literary fame: Janus Gebhard, Balthasar Venator, Julius Wilhelm Zincgref, Caspar Barth, who a few years later were joined by the even younger Martin Opitz and became his close friends. However, a volume about Heidelberg castle by Fritz Sauer seems to indicate that the evidence may be found in a less probable place, in a book by Heberer with the unpromising title, *Ægyptiaca Servitvs, das ist, Warhafte beschreibung einer dreyjährigen Dienstbarkeit*, Heidelberg, 1610.[5] One of the most remarkable men in Heidelberg at the time was the registrar in the Electoral chancery, Johann Michael Heberer. After his studies in Heidelberg he set out to visit the French and Italian universities, but he had to flee Paris in 1585 for religious reasons and unfortunately at Marseilles embarked on a Maltese ship that was captured by the Turks. During his three years of slavery that took him from Alexandria to Constantinople, he mastered the Arabic language. After the French ambassador secured his release, he went on to further travels in Bohemia, Poland, Sweden, Denmark, and adjoining regions, studied at Padua, and finally in 1592 returned to Heidelberg. In his lengthy memoirs, in an early passage about Heidelberg and the castle, he records what clearly seems to be a German inscription commemorating the palatial structure erected by Frederick IV. I have not yet been able to consult more than the direct quotation in Sauer, and still need to learn whether there was such an inscription in a place of prominence on this still newest addition to the castle, or whether Quarles could only have known it from Heberer's book with its attractive array of portraits, maps, and plans. Here possibly was Quarles's precedent, perhaps the earliest classic middle-axis inscription in a modern language. In the present state of knowledge one must concede that earlier examples may come to light.

The specimen in Heberer is nobly phrased with a real care for rhythmic harmony and balance. The Quarles memorial inscription, however, surpasses it not only in length and carefully calculated articulation but also in poetic quality. What is more, there is no readily discernible sign of an influence from the earlier work, aside from the unusual and courageous act of employing a modern language in this new genre. Equally, there is no readily discernible sign of an influence from the Quarles *Memorials* upon the few and brief examples of the inscription in English produced in the American colonies. Thus Quarles may well have reinvented the vernacular inscription on his own, and so also the New England colonists may have done. In the Latin language, however, the Americans clearly remain in the mainstream of the new European tradition. Let us first examine briefly with what validity one may continue to include their inscriptions in a bibliography of early New England poetry. Then let us turn to the few and brief but highly original English inscriptions that maintain a poetic level—alongside one that definitely does not. Thereupon let us look at the best known of all early American inscriptions, one from Pennsylvania, and observe how a famous nineteenth-century American poet with sure artisitc instinct turned it from a Latin into an English poem.

For the two Latin examples of New England inscriptions that I examine, the texts are readily available.[6] They are both by Cotton Mather. The first is the forty-four-line epitaph that he appends to his 209-line elegy on his school teacher, Ezekiel Cheever, who died at Boston, August 21, 1708, at the age of ninety-three. It begins in dactyllic rhythm with name and profession,

> Ezekiel Cheeverus:
> Ludimagister;

continues with his four places of residence in the balanced sequence of Primo . . . Deinde . . . Postea . . . Postremo . . . , then after a "cujus" (whose), the first of the very short lines that serve to articulate the sequence, comes a laudation of his achievements, in ascending order, first the literary from Grammaticus through Rhetoricus to Poeta, and then transcending these via Lucerna to Theologus, before the pious ritual words of entombment, together with the biographical numerals of the elapsed years.

After reading the whole forty-four-line composition aloud and listening to the rhythm (an essential element of which is the major pause of line division), it becomes clear that we cannot reduce it to an unarticulated, continuous prose paragraph without doing violence to its intent and indeed to its meaning. Nor would it, on the other hand, be possible to believe that Cotton Mather ever seriously intended all forty-four lines to be chiseled into marble, let alone into New England granite, and placed over the venerable schoolmaster's grave. No, here was simply an innovative Baroque literary form, already well established in Europe in this fusion of inscription and poetry, that Mather used in his own way with genuine poetic flair and effectiveness.

The whole matter becomes even clearer when we turn to the Latin epitaph that Cotton Mather composed and appended to his sermon at the funeral of Wait Winthrop, 1717. To erect a monumental inscription of over seventy lines above the tomb of a pope, emperor, or king might have occurred to the mind of one of the more extravagant Baroque memorialists on the Continent, but it could hardly have been contemplated in New England, even for such a distinguished person as the grandson of the founding governor of Massachusetts, and the son and intellectual heir of the founding governor of Connecticut. The origins in the classic Roman inscription are plainly manifest in the very first lines:

> Sta, Viator,
> Tumulumque mirare.

But so throughout, outwardly and inwardly, are the rhythmic poetic elements that bring about its transcendence into the realm of poetry, as for instance in the early laudation of his public service as a light and a pillar, "Lumen et Columen" and the close of the final laudation of his services as a devoted physician:

> Qui jam sub hoc saxo dormit mortuus,
> Vivit in Cordibus multorum, imo millium,
> quorum vitas prolongavit,
> Winthropi merita cum Winthropo,
> non Funerabit Oblivio.

When we examine the Baroque inscription entering into New England vernacular verse, we can observe further interesting phenomena in this process of amalgamation. Before we turn to the certain instances, let us look at a quite uncertain but most fascinating instance, where Vergilian poetic inspiration combines with Anglo-Saxon rhythmic and alliterative pattern, and (I now believe I see) some of the strong rhythm and end-line pauses of the "lapidary style"— all this encompassed in lines that correspond to no regular metric scheme and yet are arranged in rhymed couplets. It is the description of a storm at sea that John Josselyn, friend of Quarles, incorporates in *An Account of two Voyages to New-England*, published much later, after the second voyage, in 1674. I quote here only these few lines, readily fitted into an inscriptional pattern:

> no star shown;
> Blind night in darkness, tempests,
> and her own Dread terrours lost.

From this possibility we come to certainty when we look at the two vernacular epitaphs that Joshua Moody composed for Thomas Bailey in 1689 and for his sister-in-law Lydia two year later. The first consists of 12 unrhymed lines in a series of balanced epithets, the second, and poetically more remarkable one, consists of three double lines unrhymed in a series of contrasting epithets:

> Good betimes   Best at last
> Lived by faith   Died in grace
> Went off singing   Left us weeping.

Here is indubitable free verse, with its inscriptional origin quite manifest.

An inscriptional sequel of similarly contrasting epithets, after a conventional rhymed epitaph, is to be found in John Danforth's tribute inscribed on the gravestone of Hopestill Clap, 1719. Six uninspired lines in rhymed couplets are followed by the dignified and quitely eloquent concluding lines:

> Present Useful,   Absent Wanted,
> Liv'd Desired,   Died Lamented.

By contrast, the inscription on the tomb of Henry Sewall, 1700, is clearly in prose, despite its genuinely inscriptional syntax. Only the concluding lines on his wife, who died the following January, rise gently on the wings of the Psalmist. The probable author was the son, Samuel Sewall. I did not include it in the bibliography appended to *The First Century*:

> Henry Sewall, sent by his father, Henry Sewall, in the ship Elizabeth and Dorcas, arrived at Boston 1634, wintered at Ipswich, helped begin this planation 1635, furnished English servants, neat cattle, and provisions. Married Mrs. Jane Dummer March 25, 1646, and died May 16, 1700. His fruitful vine, being thus disjoined, fell to the ground January following. Ps. 27:10.[7]

The free verse that developed in New England from 1689, apparently, to 1719 was followed slightly more than a decade later by quite another kind. By a strange twist of historical fate, just as New England verse was becoming more conformist, more dependent upon English fashions early in the eighteenth century, it developed, for political, satirical, parodistic purposes, a free verse for which there is no precedent in the old country. J. A. Leo Lemay was the first to call attention to this further American innovation when he examined the verse in the early American periodicals.[8] In his introduction he observes: "So far as I know, these American poems are the earliest examples of satiric free verse in English poetry. The travesties of public speeches became common during the Revolutionary Period. . . . Evidently Joseph Green created this genre with a series of burlesques of the speeches of Governor Jonathan Belcher in the early 1730s. None of these were published at the time, but manuscript copies of several of Green's free verse parodies (which seem to have circulated widely) survive." A decade or so later a congenial follower was to arise in Benjamin Franklin when he wrote a wickedly comic travesty, in free but rhymed verse, on the speech of Sir William Gooch, Lieutenant Governor of Virginia, delivered on the 30th of March, 1747, after the burning of the Capitol at Williamsburg. Franklin (1706–1790) had left Boston for Philadelphia as early as 1723, too late to make the acquaintance of Francis Daniel Pastorius (1651–1719), though not too late to hear about him from friends and acquaintances of his, such as James Logan (1674–1751).

For present purposes two manuscripts of Pastorius are of special importance. There is his extensive folio commonplace book, generally called *The Beehive*, a vast gathering of everything that he had found interesting and worthwhile and wished to pass on to his descendants. He included his own collected verse (largely still unedited), most of it in English, much also in German and Latin, some in Greek as well as in Dutch, Italian, and French. As is proper in a commonplace book, there is also the anthologized verse from other writers, rarely identified as such, as well as his small group of translations to and from English. On his grand tour through Europe, before he came to America, Pastorius had made a large collection of inscriptions, both metric and non-metric. These he recorded systematically in his *Beehive*, and it is likely that he was the best authority on this literary form in the American colonies.

However, his own finest effort in the middle-axis inscription occurs at the beginning of another manuscript, the *Grund- und Lager-Buch*, containing the fundamental documents and details of the newly founded Germantown settlement from 1683 onward. It is in the form of a poetic address to the future inhabitants of the town he had founded:

Salve Posteritas!
Posteritas Germanopolitana!
et ex argumento inseqventis paginae
primitus observa,

Parentes ac Majores Tuos
ALEMANIAM,
dulce Solum, quod eos genuerat, alueratq' diu,
voluntario exilio
deseruisse;
[seventeen lines omitted]
Et sic te faciant aliena pericula Cautam.
Vale Posteritas!
Vale Germanitas!
Æternum Vale!

The Vergilian echoes are of course calculated and integral. There can hardly be any question about poetic intent and achievement. There certainly was none in the mind of John Greenleaf Whittier when he translated this address into English, retaining its inscriptional form and rhythm but otherwise exercising his poetic freedom, most conspiciously in the addition of rhyme, leaving no doubt as to where, in his judgment, it belonged:

Hail to Posterity!
Hail future men of Germanopolis!
Let the young generations yet to be
Look kindly upon this.
Think how your fathers left their native land,—
Dear German land! O sacred hearths and homes!—
And where the wild beast roams
In patience planned
New forest homes beyond the mighty sea,
There undisturbed and free
To live as brothers of one family,
What pains and cares befell,
What trials and what fears,
Remember, and wherein we have done well
Follow our footsteps, men of coming years!
Where we have failed to do
Aright, or wisely live,
Be warned by us, the better way pursue,
And knowing we were human, even as you,
Pity us and forgive!
Farewell, Posterity!
Farewell, dear Germany!
Forevermore farewell!

German predecessors, nearly two centuries before Whittier's *The Pennsylvania Pilgrim* of 1872, had also occasionally added rhymes to their inscriptions, under the same silent assumption that the poetic inscription adapted to the vernacular could be either rhymed or rhymeless as the author desired.

It is a pity that this new poetic form, so promising in its future possibilities, particularly for our poetically experimental century, was lost sight of in the meantime, largely because our native Baroque traditions were kept carefully out of sight by the genteel literary historians who esteemed only the derivative works that conformed to Old World standards. But there is an ironic consolation: the German literary historians, on the whole, did no better with the middle-axis poetry of Arno Holz. The German literary historians and critics also had their genteel tradition which put nearly everything Baroque beyond the pale, and only in recent decades are they exploring the field more intensively.

What requires closer scrutiny is the unresolved paradox that occurs in John Sparrow's book when, seemingly as an afterthought or belated discovery, he added the notice about Francis Quarles' *Memorials* of 1639 after having earlier remarked twice about Britain being "always a century behind the times in such matters." And yet his history of the new poetic inscription makes the European vogue emanate primarily from Tesauro's work of 1654 to 1666. To be sure, Tesauro's earliest such inscriptions date from 1619 and 1620, but these and the ones that come in the following decades are local and occasional, not likely to have had a wider international circulation, except by the hands of a traveller who chanced to witness some ceremonial occasion or pageant for which they were prepared or who brought home with him the often splendidly illustrated works memorializing the occasion. There were two earlier Italian collections of inscriptions, published 1638 and 1641. North of the Alps the earliest volumes supposedly date from 1654 and 1658. How did it happen that Heberer could already record a vernacular specimen in 1610 and Quarles create a far more developed one in 1639, not to forget the remote New Englanders who seem to have come next, far more modestly but no less independently? How justifiable is the general acceptance of "insular lag" for Britain and of "colonial lag" for New England, especially the latter, as though colonial lag were an established and verified historical law? What are the real facts of the case, first of all for New England and then in general literary history?

As for New England, the simple facts are that the first truly good epic dactyls in the English language were produced in the frontier settlement of Woburn, Massachusetts, by Edward Johnson about 1650. Even more surprising, the apparently quite new form of contrapuntal verse was developed about the same time in the frontier towns of Wenham and Chelmsford, Massachusetts, by another, somewhat younger man, John Fiske. Colonial lag? Nonsense. It took another two hundred years before equally good epic dactyls were produced in the British Isles. In the matter of the inscription we may also have some rethinking to do, if not decisively so in the seventeenth century, then certainly in the eighteenth century when the Boston wits reinvented the free-verse political satire.

Let us therefore take a straight look at this whole theory of colonial lag and the gullibility with which our intellectuals have accepted it as an established historical doctrine when they substituted logic and reason for feeling and factuality. In early American literature Moses Coit Tyler, for instance, gave eloquently vituperative expression to his belief in colonial retardation and imitation when he wrote of Nicholas Noyes: "even in his old age, he continued to write the sort of poetry that, in his youth, had been the fashion, both in England and in America—the degenerate euphuism of Donne, of Wither, of Quarles, of George Herbert. To this appalling type of poetry, Nicholas Noyes faithfully adhered, even to the end of his days, unseduced by the rhythmical heresies, the classic innovations, of John Dryden and Alexander Pope."[9] If Edward Taylor's poems had come out of hiding in Tyler's time, the critic would no doubt have adjudged him far superior to Noyes in every feature he found loathsome.

As irony would have it, it was precisely Edward Taylor to whom the clichés of colonial lag were most elaborately attached, and this decades later when evidence and critical insights to the contrary had been adequately established. This was not done by his first discoverer and selective editor, Thomas H. Johnson (who, to be sure, did at one time speak of him as a "belated conceittist") nor by the editor of the complete Yale manuscript, Donald E. Stanford, but by a professor of English, Louis L. Martz, by way of a long foreword to the poems from English perspectives little modified by the relevant American perspectives. Writing about the English literary traditions that accompanied Edward Taylor into the wilderness, he observes: "They will suggest too, Taylor's place in literary history as the last heir of the great tradition of English meditative poetry that arose in the latter part of the sixteenth century . . . and, so far as England was concerned, died at the death of Thomas Traherne in 1674, with both his prose meditations and their companionate poems unpublished." When he tries to assess the specifically American, he finds only such local allusions as rattlesnake and canoe, plus a frontier crudity, the language a "peculiar mixture of the learned and the rude, the abstract and the earthy, the polite and the vulgar; for such distinctions do not exist in the wilderness," the result being that out of "deficiencies" he created "a work of rugged and original integrity."[10] If Martz had only had the opportunity for making a broad comparative study of the other prose and verse of Taylor's time and place, he might have seen not simply the ruinous fragments of an old but the creative coming together of a new diction unheard of in old England.

To be sure, there are in history striking examples of colonial lag, of peoples cut off from the homeland, also of people isolated in remote mountain fastnesses or on sparsely settled heaths where the "heathen" continued their "pagan" ways long after the populated areas had been Christianized. Here is where the fascinating survivals of old folk literature and art could be found together with old costumes, customs, manners, and rituals. In colonial and federal America, too, there were remarkable survivals in the more isolated regions. Samuel Kercheval's *History of the Valley of Virginia*, 1833, with its description of community life in the Shenandoah Valley, is a fascinating early classic in the field. As for colonial dependence, there is the sadly amusing story of dwellings constructed in New Zealand on the English model, quite disregarding the different orientation required in the Southern Hemisphere.

And yet, with many further specific examples added of colonial retardation and imitation, we have come nowhere near the establishment of a historical law. For the precise opposite can also be found in any more careful study of history and its instances. On the first great flowering of lyric poetry in seventh and sixth-century Greece, from which regions did the great poets come? Most of them, most of the best of them, came from the peripheries; only a few came from the heartland, even though most of the great ritual and ceremonial centers were there. This is so striking a case that we can well speak of homeland retardation and colonial leadership. Only after the heartland had assimilated all these literary innovations, could it enter into its own classical period of the fifth century. At first the great poets were on the eastern periphery, the coast of Asia Minor and the adjoining islands: Alcaeus and Sappho and Arion of Lesbos and Anacreon of Teos. Then they arose in the remote western colonies of Sicily and across the straits in southern Italy, notably Stesichorus from far-away Heimera and Ibycus of Regium. In the Greek heartland there was only Alcman from Sparta, and from a nearby island there came Simonides of Ceos—and even he went west.

Let us take another instance from a millennium and a half later. Around 1100 A.D. where were the best European prose narratives arising, narratives that remain living literature to this day? These prose narratives, bold new experiments, were created not in Italy or Germany or Spain or France, but on the remotest island far out in the Western Ocean, created by Scandinavian colonials not long settled in Iceland (a land, by the way, that also had the first effective literacy laws for all children, followed much later by the German lands and then by New England, long before Old England). Why should this be? Why are there some colonials who remain utterly dependent and imitative, particularly during their first century or two, and only gradually develop their own distinct individuality? And why are there other colonials who at once assert their individuality, actually assume leadership, and only later lapse into a somewhat greater cultural dependence on the homeland, as did the Greek periphery and Iceland—and also New England?

Part of the answer comes easily when we look at the political situation, where New England was also in the vanguard. Here again a word of caution: the literary quality of a period often runs contrary to its political quality. If tradition reports truly, Oliver Cromwell himself had wanted to leave for New England and through one of the saddest mishaps for the royal party was prevented from doing so. Later when he came to power, he recalled or tried to recall some of the leading New Englanders who by then had far more experience in the governing of a commonwealth. Hugh Peter and Sir Henry Vane are only the best known of those who did return. In sum, when it is the most vigorous, most enterprising, best endowed, most restive, even rebellious who venture forth, then the colonial enterprise is likely to develop more in accordance with the Greek and Scandinavian patterns. If and when it does, then it is likely that there will be innovations, new departures in literature also. Two such innovations have already been noticed: the writing of truly good epic dactyls in the English language and also the contrapuntal verse of John Fiske, especially the remarkable poem on John Cotton together with his most perfect as well as briefest poem, the one on Thomas Dudley. In a much more qualified way the inscription also led to a first modest development of English free verse, though it was the paradodistic offshoot of another rhetorical form, the oration, that somewhat later led to a larger development of free verse.

Furthermore, it would seem that the individual genius in letters and the arts can arise in the most unlikely places and times, and also can fail to arise when the circumstances are most favorable: great Roman literature arising during the terrible civil wars and failing to arise under the benign rule of such an understanding patron as Emperor Hadrian. The first triumphs of Elizabethan literature coincided with the naval triumph over the Spanish Armada, but the Golden Age of Spanish literature also coincided with this disastrous defeat. And so we could go on. But why should we? Sophocles said it all in one memorable sentence: "The wonders of this world are many, but the greatest wonder of all is man." If we can preserve our sense of wonder, unmitigated by pretentious and presumptuous theory, the continuing reception of new insights is bound to confirm this openness as the more enjoyable as well as reliable and profound approach to literature and the arts.

NOTES

1. Baltimore: Johns Hopkins Univ. Press, 1969, p. 79.

2. *Sammlung Teutscher auserlesener sinnreicher Inscriptionen* (Jena: 1725, 1732).

3. See also his "A Census of American Latin Verse, 1625–1825," *PAAS*, 91 (1981), 197–299.

4. Cambridge & New York: 1969.

5. Fritz Sauer, *Das Heidelberger Schloss im Spiegel der Literatur* . . . (Heidelberg: 1910), pp. 5 and 73.

6. In *IV. Early American Poetry: Elegies and Epitaphs 1677–1717* (Boston: The Club of Odd Volumes, 1896) final pp. 33–34, 43–46.

7. Joshua Coffin, *A Sketch of the History of Newbury, Newburyport, and West Newbury from 1635 to 1845* (Boston: 1845), p. 13; see also Sewall, *Diary*, I, 455 (Bible reference only), 1074 (omits grandfather's name).

8. *A Calendar of American Poetry in the Colonial Newspapers and Magazines and in the Major English Magazines through 1765* (Charlottesville: Univ. Press of Virginia for American Antiquarian Soc., 1972); orig. pub. in *PAAS*, 1969–70.

9. Tyler, *History*, II, 39.

10. Stanford, *Taylor*, pp. xxxv–vi.

19 WIT, HUMOR, AND SATIRE IN SEVENTEENTH-CENTURY AMERICAN POETRY

ROBERT D. ARNER

Among the remnants of seventeenth-century American poetry there is wit in abundance but precious little humor—and even less of that rare commodity in the poetry of the Puritans. The distinction is a perilous one, to be sure, since humor may feature wit as a major stylistic element and since wit may aspire to and even occasionally achieve true humor (it does not always aim at humor, of course). But if we take as our definition of humor literature written with the primary purpose of entertainment rather than instruction, explanation, justification, or self-examination, we easily see the sort of lines that can be drawn between John Fiske's "Upon the decease of Mris Anne Griffin,"[1] wit without any intention of being humorous, and Nathaniel Ward's editorially entitled "Mr. Ward of Anagrams thus" (p. 368), humor that depends upon wit to no apparent extra-poetical purpose except the gentle mockery of an acrobatic literary form, the verse anagram, and and a good-natured joke about a respected New England neighbor with an unfortunate weakness for bizarre verse forms. It may be argued that both of these thematic elements suggest Ward's little poem might better be designated satire than humor, but satire is generally considered to be broader in scope, more substantial in subject matter—the making of anagrams, after all, is only an amusing New England foible as Ward presents it here, not a vice to be castigated—and less genial in tone than Ward's seven-line effort.

Some early New England poems are, it is true, satire pure and simple. Such, for example, are the verses Thomas Morton affixed to his fabled maypole at Merrymount, inviting all sad Separatists to try to expound his riddle. Morton, an Anglican, composed in "The Poem: Rise Oedipeus" a frankly phallic "proclamation that the first of May, / At Ma-re Mount shall be kept hollyday" (p. 372) reminding us of the primitive origins of satire in classical Greek comedy and sexual festival.[2] The maypole itself stands as the symbolic center of the *New English Canaan*, as the allusion in the title makes clear, for Morton not only means to extend and to make a jest upon the Puritans' own favorite metaphor for America of the New Canaan or the Promised Land but also to recall the Biblical story of the dispossession of a tree-worshiping people, the Canaanites, by the ancient Israelites.[3] Rather than another version of the Puritan trope, his allusion offers a counter-myth of America in which he and his revelers become identified with the Indians and the story he unfolds becomes a tragic chronicle of displacement.

As satire, "Rise Oedipeus" aims to cast out the evil spirits represented by the Pilgrims and Puritans, who have brought a blight upon the land, while in other ways the verses seem related to riddling rhymes, again in at least semi-serious recollection of the magical function of such verses. Similarly, Morton derives his poetic persona from Thomas Scogan, the fifteenth-century English poet who authored *Scoggins Jests*,[4] and, more mythically and inclusively, from the legendary lord of Misrule who presided over Saturnalia and the medieval Feast of Fools, among other celebrations of the world turned temporarily upside down. The phallic humor displayed in "Rise Oedipeus" finds its counterpart in the hymenal humor of "The Songe"—"Let all your delight be in Hymens joyes" (p. 373)—and establishes Morton as an important celebrant of the fresh, green breast of the New World which he saw turning into a valley of ashes, another Golgotha, as a result of Puritan policies. Nevertheless, even Morton could not entirely avoid the negative implications of European invasion for the innocence of this new Arcadia, although he cast his vision of inevitable westerly expansion in erotic images of mutual desire rather than in the images of aggression he reserved for portraits of the Puritans. In his mind's eye, New England and the American continent stretch away to the storied Lake Champlain "Like a faire virgin, longing to be sped, / And meete her lover in a Nuptiall bed. . ." (p. 370). The mythic greenness of the American Arcadia and the emphasis on sexuality impart to the pastoral sections of *New English Canaan* a pervasive comic tone reminiscent of late Renaissance comedy as in *Midsummer Night's Dream*.

Morton also displayed considerable talent in writing mock elegies and mock heroic verses, as "Carmen Elegiacum" and "The Poem: I Sing th' Adventures of Nine Worthy Wights" (pp. 371–72 and 374–77, respectively), will testify.[5] Unfortunately, the first of these becomes so tangled in classical allusion—employed to mask contemporary references—that it is virtually impossible to follow in its entirety. It appears, however, that Morton intends to satirize not only the overblown elegy itself but also Miles Standish's ineffectual pursuit of an Indian squaw, the widow of Nanepashemet whom Morton refers to as the "Barren Doe of Virginia," for alleged sexual indiscretions.[6] In this poem, Miles Standish is characterized as a "beare" who "oft hath bayted ben, / By many a Satyres whelpe" (p. 372, ll. 19–20). In "I Sing th' Adventures of Nine Worthy Wights," Morton himself becomes just such a "Satyres whelpe" by lampooning Standish, along with Bradford and John Endicott, among the leaders he satirizes as "Minos, Eacus, and Radamand" (p. 375, l. 49), judges of the Underworld.

As poetry, "Nine Worthy Wights" is more successful than "Carmen Elegiacum," in part because its purposes and meanings are clearer, in part because in it Morton occasionally achieves a level of compression and irony rarely encountered in his other verses. The second line of the poem, for instance, declares that it is a pity Morton cannot call his adversaries "Knights," a reference that sustains the mock-epic and mock-romantic tone introduced by the opening "I sing th' adventures." It is also a reference that takes on a second meaning in the context of Morton's own sympathies for English aristocracy over Puritans or "Roundheads" and his hope that the plans and polity of Sir Fernando Gorges will Triumph in New England. Throughout *New English Canaan*, Morton shows himself thoroughly familiar with classical legend and literature, and "Nine Worthy Wights" is no exception, bringing allusions to the portentous birth of heroes, Jason's quest for the Land of Colchis and the Golden Fleece, the epic scales of justice, and the hero's obligatory descent into the Underworld to bear upon antagonists who are, after all, only "Squires of low degree" (p. 374, 1. 5). The comic technique is similar to that employed by Washington Irving in his *History of New York* (1809) and is certainly one reason why the story of the maypole of Merrymount has so readily entered into American romance.[7] Morton's verses unabashedly promote the mythic role that Governor Bradford assigned to him as the Lord of Misrule and are primarily responsible for our continuing to see him through the mists of history, whether we entirely approve of him or not, as a comic character of his own creation who also predicted his own demise and the demise of the festive spirit in America, the prototype of all antic humorists we continue to do our best to suppress: "And for his crest with froth there does appear, / Dextra Paw Elevant a Jugg of Beare" (p. 377, ll. 9–10).

Far different from Morton's mythic and pastoral vision of New England is the one poetically propounded by Captain Edward Johnson in "New Englands's annoyances."[8] In this poem, possibly penned before Morton's enthusiastic encomia, New England appears as "a wilderness wood, / Where grass is much wanting that's fruitful and good" and where "From the end of November till three months are gone, / The ground is all frozen as hard as a stone" (p. 503). In the winter, "the northwest wind with violence blows," in the summer worms destroy the crop, and in the autumn marauding squirrels, raccoons, and deer make off with the little harvest that remains. The difference between this account of New England's soil and climate and Morton's poetic raptures is in part explained by the different rhetorical purposes, for while Morton unashamedly wished to lure more Anglican settlers to America and thus wrest control of New England from the Puritans, Johnson with equal fervor wished to keep such undesirables away. His poem is addressed, finally, only to those "whom the Lord intends hither to bring" (p. 505), an ecclesiastical and political exhortation that in some measure undercuts the comic efforts of the opening dozen or so stanzas. Even so, his flaunting of "New England's annoyances" in the face of English audiences as a way of simultaneously establishing the superiority of the saints (who stay) and of discouraging unwanted immigration links the poem to comic folk traditions also found in "The Arkansaw Traveler" (who "grew so thin as sassafras tea" he could "hide behind a straw" and "never knew what misery was" until he "struck old Arkansaw").

Despite the deliberate narrowing of audience at the end, "New England's annoyances" is a poem that, stylistically at least, is addressed to the common man. The problems encountered in the poem are those that agricultural and laboring people could well understand, presented in a folksy, homely idiom that perhaps explains why Nathaniel Ward's Simple Cobbler later became so endur-ingly popular in New England:[9] despite his classical antecedents, the Cobbler was a leather-apron artisan of a type already established in the City on the Hill and in surrounding rural areas. Like the Cobbler, Johnson's persona reveals an admirable ability to compress into one memorable and earthy proverb the problem of premature defections versus the ultimate promose of God to His plantations: "Whilst liquor is boiling, it must have a scumming" (p. 505). With another proverb, the speaker dismisses all those who precipitously flee and honor those who remain: "birds of a feather / Are choosing their fellows by flocking together" (p. 505). In "New England's annoyances," Johnson has produced the first poe-ticized list of absent things—no food, no liquor, no money, no clothes—in American literature (though both William Bradford and Captain John Smith beat him to it in prose).[10] In so doing, he distantly anticipates Henry James, who in his famous study of Nathaniel Hawthorne identified the extraordinary blankness of America, the distance between expectation and emptiness, as the *locus classicus* of the great American joke. If this seems far-fetched, one reason might be that Johnson deliberately truncates his joke at the end, employing instead the gesture of William Bradford, in turning his eyes upward toward the heavens for evidence of the things not seen, the invisible Almighty working His mysterious will through the wild and savage hues of the country and through all that appalling emptiness: "no friends to welcome them nor inns to entertain or refresh their weatherbeaten bodies; no houses or much less towns to repair to, to seek for succour."[11]

Within a very short time after Bradford and his colleagues came ashore into the vacancy of America, the Puritans arrived in great numbers and set about the task of erecting their holy commonwealth. The establishment of Harvard College, followed quickly by the first printing press in America, soon gave evidence of the desire and determination of the newest wave of immigrants, and, indirectly at least, also led to one of the earliest American comic verses of which we have record. The occasion was the decision to translate the whole Book of Psalms into English meter, which prompted Thomas Shepard's rhymed advice and met-rical joke to his colleagues from Roxbury and Dorchester:

> You Roxborough Poets take this in Time
> See that you make very good Rhythme
> And eke of Dorchester when you the verses lengthen
> See that you them with the words of the text do strengthen.[12]

Cotton Mather, who first detected the joke, made it still clearer in the version he provided in the *Magnalia*:

> You Roxb'ry *Poets, keep clear of the Crime*
> *Of missing to give us very good Rhime.*
> *And you* of Dorchester, *your Verses lengthen,*
> *But with the Texts own Words, you will them strengthen.*[13]

Shepard's verses, or rather the circumstances in which they arose, signal a transition in the cultural situation of New England and, not surprisingly, a transition in the subject matter of comic poetry. In Samuel Danforth I's almanac verses of 1647, for example, the cultivation of the soil and the vagaries of the climate are still very much topics of continuing comic interest, but politics, social relationships, and social definitions of the self also begin to assume some measure of comic importance. One stanza in "New England's annoyances," it is true, had referred in passing to the social structure of New England, apparently complaining in the voice of a typical malcontent who does not understand the fine points of Puritan theology. This voice, which seems to dominate the first thirteen stanzas of the poem, the litany of hardships, in a sort of antiphonal structure with the proverbial voice of the final three stanzas, declares that in New England "some are rejected and others made saints, / Of those that are equal in virtues and wants" (p. 505, ll. 51–52), but the theme of internal dissensions is not developed to any significant degree. In Danforth's lines, however, we catch amusing glimpses of New England's ministers as "Coal-white" birds (p. 414, l. 1) who stand outside of church doors shaking parishioners' hands while "merry Birds" (like Thomas Morton?) try hard to avoid them. Ships from England arrive as "wooden Birds . . . / Whose mawes are fill'd with hose and shooes, / With wine, cloth, sugar, salt and newes" ("July," p. 415), and Puritan leaders meet in September to pass regulations governing commerce in fishing ("How hony m[a]y be brought to these [i.e., the "little Bees" or industrious citizens of the Commonwealth] / By making fish to dance on trees" ("September," p. 416). The approach of spring is celebrated in "April"—"That which hath neither tongue nor wings / This month how merrily it sings" (p. 414)—and the arrival of winter foretold in January: "Great bridges shall be made alone / Without ax, timber, earth or stone . . ." (p. 417). Such verses achieve their comic quality more by the domination of images of singing and dancing and by the playful manipulation of metaphors and paradoxes as the oppositional elements in a series of riddles than by their subject matter and content, though there is no question that one of them, "May," speaks in its own veiled way of controversies then raging in the English Parliament:

> White Coates! who choose you! whom you list:
> Some Ana-tolleratorist:
> Wolves, lambs, hens, foxes to agree
> By setting all opinion-free:
> If Blew-coates doe not this prevent,
> Hobgoblins will be insolent. [p. 415]

Reading these lines, we are reminded that in certain historically repressive societies or at certain critical times in the history of all nations both riddles and humor may surface as less dangerous ways of advancing minority political opinions, and it is clear that the New England way, a position staunchly against religious toleration of any kind, was in the minority in Parliament and would not win the approval of Oliver Cromwell. Nonetheless, Danforth was not the only New Englander to attempt to sway the course of history, in however limited a way almanac verse may provide, for in the same year that those verses were printed in New England, 1647, there appeared in London a work entitled *The Simple Cobler of Aggawam in America*, Nathaniel Ward's immensely popular contribution to the Puritan's cause and a work long regarded as one of the most entertaining and readable books written by an American Puritan. Ward's wit, alas, is to be found almost exclusively in his prose, which is replete with multiple puns, humorous internal rhymes, and alliterative devices but which lies beyond the scope of this chapter; the merely verbal circularity of

> *The world is full of care, much like unto a bubble;*
> *Women and care, and care and women, and women and care and trouble*[14]

is not a fair sample of his ability to play with words. Nevertheless, though poetry and not prose is my present subject, I cannot forbear remarking that, in deliberately calling attention to the American as well as to the European antecedents of his persona, that is, in emphasizing his American origins and using the Indian "Aggawam" instead of the English "Ipswich," Ward establishes an American voice which enables him to perpetrate one of the earliest successful tall tales about America. He plays artfully upon the Englishman's ignorance of American geography ("the West pole"), upon English preconceptions of the loquacious Yankee ("we know not how to conclude"), and upon a tradition of promotional literature that had long made extravagant claims for New England's weather ("the fault is in the Climate") to fashion a complex exercise in comic deconstruction in the "*Errata at Non Corrigenda*" section of *The Simple Cobler*:

> 6. For, *tediousnesse*, read, *I am sorry for it*—we have a storng weaknesse in N. E. that when wee are speaking, we know not how to conclude: wee make many ends, before we make an end: the fault is in the Climate; we cannot helpe it though we can, which is the Arch infirmity in all morality: We are so near the West pole, that our Longitudes are as long, as any wise man would wish, and somewhat longer. I scarce know any Adage more grateful: than *Grata brevitas*. [p. 76]

Perhaps the most successful comic verse in *The Simple Cobler* comes at the end of the volume, a pastiche of bilingual and homophonic puns that invites all those dissatisfied with the course of church polity in England to embark for New England (whither the Cobbler himself intends to sail) and that concludes with a mock valedictory in which, as William J. Scheick has demonstrated,[15] through

intentional mis-hyphenation a simple shoemaker becomes a "shoem-aker," that
is, a wiseacre:

> *And farewell simple world*
> *If thou' lt thy Cranium mend*
> *There is my Last and All,*
> And a Shoem-Akers
> END. [p. 77]

Ward's best comic poem, however, is not to be found in *The Simple Cobler*
but is transcribed into Thomas Weld III's commonplace book, where all who
read must wonder what other unpublished gems from Ward's pen have either
eluded our research thus far or been lost to literary history altogether. In this
brief work, referred to elsewhere in this essay as "Mr. Ward of Anagrams thus,"
Ward sharply contrasts the natural and the artificial, the instinctive and the
intellectual through a series of scatological metaphors that portray his own con-
stipation when faced with the task of "making" an anagram (not exactly like
Alexander Pope's poor poet who "strains from hardbound brains eight lines a-
year,"[16] but close) as compared with the ease with which "Mr. John Wilson /
the great Epigrammatist" (Meserole, *Poetry*, p. 368) relieves himself of his own
anagrammatic urges.

Ward's best known poem, his dedicatory verses to Anne Bradstreet's *Tenth
Muse* (1650), may serve as sufficient reminder that the war between men and
women has long been one of the mainstays of comedy and humor and will, I
think, not be legislated out of existence by any Federal enactments or laid to
rest by all the affirmative actions in the world. It is certain, at any rate, that
Ward did not pen the couplet, "It half revives my chil frost-bitten blood, / To
see a woman once do, ought, that's good" (p. 367) merely to incense modern
feminists, though such is the historical myopia often brought to bear on literary
texts from other eras that one would think, sometimes, anti-feminist insult was
some poor benighted ancient author's sole reason for writing. Note also that
Ward extends the sexual themes of this preface to include more than a hint of
Mercury's loss of masculine vigor (and, by extension, his own loss of the
"Spurrs" which symbolize masculine poetic preëminence), another comic rever-
sal of what the seventeenth century considered the natural order of things.
Throughout the poem, in fact, Mercury is a consistently ludicrous, ineffectual
figure, unable to solve the problem of authorship the goddess Minerva propounds,
which ought to be enough to demonstrate to any reader but those unwilling to
see it that Ward's humor is distributed rather evenhandedly (even his famous—
or infamous—misogynist attack on women and their fashions in *The Simple
Cobler* occupies only a few highly wrought pages, while his criticism of the
King and Parliament is sustained throughout the tract).[17]

In contrast to the dance of sex, which in its wide-ranging manifestations from ribald amorousness to open animosity seems to be one of the universal themes of humor, an indigenous theme arising in the New World was the difference between Europeans and Indians. While Captain John Smith's *Generall Historie of Virginia* (1624) abounds in such comic miniatures, most of them added editorially as he reworked material from various sources, humorous references to the Indian are rare in seventeenth-century American poetry (and, of course, are subject equally with jokes about women to modern misreadings). Amidst his catalogues of America's plenty, however, William Wood in *New Englands Prospect* (1634) offers the following portrait of the dismal lives led by Indian squaws, who

> to the flats daunce many a winters Jigge,
> To dive for Cocles, and to digge for Clamms,
> Whereby her lazie husbands guts shee cramms. [p. 402]

No Puritan or even Puritan sympathizer (despite his legendary role in transporting Francis Quarles' translations of several psalms for inclusion in the *Bay Psalm Book*),[18] John Josselyn sees Indian women differently, erotically evoking their naked perfection that "neither wind nor sun-shine fears" and serio-comically portraying them as viands well prepared for the table: "Nor can ought so please the tast / As what's brown and lovely drest" (pp. 403–404). But it was the outburst of hostilities between settlers and savages in King Philip's War (1675) that inspired the most extended quasi-comic portrait of the Indians in seventeenth-century American poetry, a picture of Philip himself as conjured up by the imaginative vision of Benjamin Tompson—with the unacknowledged assistance of John Milton's *Paradise Lost*—in *New Englands Crisis* (1676) (p. 228). There follows Philip's speech, which exploits whatever humor Tompson can milk out of the "animalistic" sounds of the Narragansett language and emphasizes envy, love of alcohol, miscegenation, and rape as the Indians' motivations for their devastating uprising. Assuredly, it is an unsympathetic portrait, to say the least, and yet, like Ward's unfavorable images of women, these lines must be seen in their historical context to be fairly understood. So, too, Tompson's amusement at the efforts of women to build on Boston neck a fortification against the Indians, an amusement conveyed by his employment of domestic imagery to describe their work and by the fact that "Male stronger hands" eventually must come to the rescue and "do the work, and sturdy bulwarks raise" (p. 236), is entirely good natured, the proper stuff of comedy. Tompson reserves praise for the women's valiant spirit while registering his humorous appreciation of the sight of women aping traditional male roles.[19]

In the seventeenth-century South, meanwhile, the only writer to compare with Morton, Ward, and, to a lesser degree, Johnson and Tompson was the indentured servant George Alsop of Maryland, although all New England humorists before

Benjamin Franklin would shortly be surpassed by Ebenezer Cooke and his bril-
liant *Sot-Weed Factor* (1708). Alsop, indeed, unwittingly appears to have sup-
plied some of Cooke's raw material, particularly the type of glowing promotion
tract which Cooke deflated.[20] But Alsop was also a skillful writer of satire and
comic verse in his own right, as a glance at "The Author to his Book," which
begins as sexual humor before turning its attention to the castigation of critics,
will show. In addition to spoofing a metaphoric equation between books and
children already hackneyed by 1666 and the equally conventional equation between
impregnation and poetic inspiration, Alsop directs his satire against the English
Puritans, alluding to the "Small-beer Col'nel *Pride*" (p. 447, 1. 24) and mounting
a full-scale satiric attack on the treachery of Oliver Cromwell whose successful
revolution, we must surmise, drove Alsop into exile in the New World.

Perhaps the most delightful discovery in early American poetry for connois-
seurs of the cosmic is John Tulley's *Almanack* (1687), which contains monthly
verses and occasional prose observations revolving around the themes of court-
ship, sex, and marriage: "The Weather is very cold; but where Jealousie is hot,
that house is Hell, and the woman the Master Devil thereof" (p. 512). Richly
folkloric, these almanac poems feature surprising (for New England) references
to St. Valentine's Day and the Christmas holidays along with information about
New England folkways—the presentation of scarves, ribbons, and gloves during
courtship, for example—and a number of bawdy poems whose humor depends
largely upon agriculturally oriented *double entendres*:

> Now wanton Lads and Lasses do make Hay,
> Which unto lewd temptation makes great way,
> With tumbling on the cocks, which acted duly,
> Doth cause much mischief in this month of July. [p. 514]

The tone is mock moralistic, for we are constantly kept aware of clucking
admonitions, to say nothing of thundering denunciations from the pulpit, which
were once the price such sexual transgressors could expect to pay in New Eng-
land. But, as the almanac Poet says in another verse ("April") that also sounds
preachy but in reality represents an attempt to describe the physical sensation
of sexual intercourse, "Love is made of different mettle":

> Of Joy, and Pain; in Dock out Nettle.
> A painful pleasure pleasing pain,
> A gainful Loss, a loosing Gain, . . . [p. 513]

What emerges from the verses of Tulley's almanac is a portrait of our Puritan
ancestors enjoying life to the fullest, snugly sheltered against the winter with
pots of ale, great loaves of bread, and roaring fires ("January," p. 512), a far

cry from the hapless immigrants exposed to the ravages of the northwest wind in Johnson's "New England's annoyances." Wives prepare Christmas pies, "roast beef, mince-pies, pudding and plum porridge" (p. 515), duties already familiar to the colonial dames of Tompson's verses of 1676, who left their Christmas baking to begin work on the fortification. Prostitutes and other loose women, those who "bring Grist to the Surgeons mill" (a wonderful folkloristic metaphor that unites crime and punishment in a single stroke), seem common in Boston, as also in the days of Benjamin Franklin's youth (see "Do-good No. XIII") or in the Charleston of the South Carolina "Meddler."[21] Above all else, the colonists enjoy a tumble in the hay, a romp in the fields and forests, an almost casual intimacy in bundling. Tulley's rendering of both urban and rural customs in old New England may owe as much to English almanac traditions and English folkways as to the realities of late seventeenth-century Boston, but many entries in Samuel Sewall's diary for approximately the same period demonstrate that Tulley's emphasis on the good life in Old Boston, the pleasure of the senses, was not altogether the production of his own fancy.

Tulley's almanac serves as a useful introduction to the *Journal* of Sarah Kemble Knight, whose comic verses form a fitting capstone to this chapter. The world through which Madam Knight journeys between October, 1704 and March, 1705 is both rural and urban, both agricultural and commercial. It is is a world that minds the main chance but that still can recall and recite the formulae of piety. As in Tulley's almanac verses, Hell is no longer a realm of everlasting flames where sinners suffer eternal torment but a New England household inhabited by termagant wives and drunken husbands or a country hostelry run by an inhospitable landlord named, appropripately, "Mr. Devill" (p. 483). So far as American humor is concerned, the increasing availability of the vocabulary of religion and professed piety for the purpose of jests and jokes is a crucial development, as demonstrated by Johnson Jones Hooper's account of Captain Simon Suggs at a camp meeting, Mark Twain's tale (based on Hooper's story) of the Duke and the Dauphin at another camp meeting in *Huckleberry Finn*, and—better than both of these—George Washington's Harris' "Parson John Bullen's Lizards." Madam Knight's humor does not reach these heights, yet it points the way that later American humor would go. Indeed, Knight's journal represents in some ways the culmination of nearly all the comic themes and character types we have been considering: courtship, cultural deprivation, the American Indian, the talkative and taciturn Yankee, the shrewd Yankee trickster, the bumpkin; nearly all the stylistic techniques: mock epic language, surprising and unusual metaphors— "His shade on his Hors[e] resembled a Globe on a Gate post"[22]—comic colloquialisms, and—an important new dimension—the interplay among sophisticated Bostonian dialect, backwoods speech, and the pidgin English of the Indian. There is folklore (a child's finger game) in the verse editorially entitled "Pleasent Delusion of a Sumpteous Citty"—

> Here stood a Lofty church—there is a steeple,
> And there the Grand Parade—O see the people! [p. 484]—

and withal the special poignancy of the longing of the lost American, wandering through the tangled wilderness, for the symbols and splendors of civilization and culture. In short, both in its prose and its poetry, Madam Knight's *Journal* is a vastly underrated contribution to American comic traditions, an unfortunate neglect it shares with many another minor (or, perhaps, even major) comic masterpiece of the period: Morton's *New English Canaan* and Ebenezer Cooke's *Sot-Weed Factor* come most readily to mind, or, for the middle of the eighteenth century, Dr. Alexander Hamilton's *Itinerarium*. This survey could not do justice either to the quantity or to the quality of early American comic literature, most of it to be discovered in prose rather than in poetry, but I hope I suggested some of the reasons and rewards for reading seventeenth-century comic poets with more appreciation than we have in the past.

NOTES

1. The poem appears on pp. 190–91 of Meserole's *Poetry*. Unless otherwise indicated, all texts cited in this chapter are in this anthology and will be annotated in the text by page and, where appropriate, line numbers only.

2. See Francis M. Cornford, *The Origins of Attic Comedy* (London: E. Arnold, 1914), especially pp. 35–52, and Robert C. Elliot, *The Power of Satire: Magic, Ritual, Art* (Princeton: Princeton Univ. Press, 1960), pp. 261–62. See also my "Mythology and the Maypole of Merry Mount: Some Notes on Thomas Morton's 'Rise Oedipus,'" *EAL* 6 (1971), 156–64, and my "Pastoral Celebration and Satire in Thomas Morton's *New English Canaan*," *Criticism: A Quarterly for Literature and the Arts*, 16 (1974), 217–31.

3. On the worship in Canaan, see W. Robertson Smith, *The Religion of the Semites: The Fundamental Institutions* (New York: Meridian Books, 1956), pp. 185–94.

4. For Scogan's continuing popularity in the seventeenth century, see John Ashton's *Humour, Wit and Satire of the Seventeenth Century* (New York: Dover, 1968), pp. 361–62.

5. "Nine" rather than Meserole's "Mine" in the first line seems a more likely reading since the poem treats the invasion of Merrymount by Miles Standish and eight others from Salem and Plymouth. "Mine" also seems uncharacteristic of the type of irony Morton employs when speaking of the Separatists, with whom he clearly wishes to disclaim all kinship, even of an ironic nature.

6. *New English Canaan* (Amsterdam: Jacob Frederick Stam, 1637); repr. as *New English Canaan of Thomas Morton*, ed. Charles Francis Adams, Jr. (Boston: The Prince Society, 1883). The episodes concerning the "Barren Doe" appear in Chapters 9 and 13.

7. Quick overviews and useful bibliographies of Merry Mount as romance may be

found in Richard Clark Sterne, "Puritans at Merry Mount: Variations on a Theme," *AQ*, 22 (1970), 846–58, and Robert J. Gangemere, "Thomas Morton: Character and Symbol in a Minor American Epic," Israel, *Discoveries*, pp. 189–203.

8. Though unidentified in Meserole's anthology, the author of these verses is identified as Johnson by Jantz, *First Century*, p. 29.

9. See, for example, Neil T. Eckstein, "The Pastoral and the Primitive in Benjamin Tompson's 'Address to Lord Bellamont,' " *EAL* 8 (1973), 111–16, and Hawthorne's "Main Street."

10. Captain John Smith's more hopeful recitation appears in *A Description of New England* (London, 1616): "And here are no hard landlords to racke us with high rents, or extorted fines to consume us; no tedious pleas in law to consume us with their many years disputation for Justice: no multitudes to occasion such impediments to good orders, as in popular States," in *Travels and Works of Captain John Smith*, 2 vols., ed. Edward Arber; re-ed. A. G. Bradley (Edinburgh: John Grant, 1910), I, 195–96.

11. William Bradford, *Of Plymouth Plantation*, ed. Samuel Eliot Morison (New York: The Modern Library, 1967), p. 61.

12. Jantz, *First Century*, p. 21.

13. Cotton Mather, *Magnalia Christi Americana* (London: Thomas Parkhurst, 1702); facsimile repr. New York: Arno Press, 1972, Book III, p. 100.

14. *The Simple Cobler of Aggawam in America*, ed. P. M. Zall (Lincoln: Univ. of Nebraska Press, 1969), p. 27. Further references to this text will be made by page number only.

15. "Nathaniel Ward's Cobbler as 'Shoem-Aker," *English Language Notes*, 9 (1971), 100–102.

16. Alexander Pope, "Epistle to Dr. Arbuthnot," *The Poems of Alexander Pope*, ed. John Butt (New Haven: Yale Univ. Press, 1963), p. 604, 1. 182.

17. For those who doubt that scolding wives, lascivious women, and women's fashions were as commonplace in English humor of the seventeenth century as the figure of the cobbler himself, a glance at Ashton's *Humour, Wit and Satire* (see note 4) should set the historical record straight.

18. The story of Josselyn's supposed involvement with the *Bay Psalm Book* is told in Zoltan Haraszti, *The Engima of the Bay Psalm Book* (Chicago: Univ. of Chicago Press, 1956), pp. 17, 55.

19. Other perspectives on Tompson's attitudes toward Indians and women are given in chapters 14 and 8 of this book. Tompson also appears to have appreciated somewhat slyer spoofs if his tribute to Cotton Mather as a "Necromancer" may be taken as evidence. See White, *Tompson* and *Magnalia Christi Americana, Books I and II*, ed. Kenneth B. Murdock (Cambridge, Mass. and London: The Belknap Press of Harvard Univ. Press, 1977), p. 80.

20. See Robert D. Arner, "The Blackness of Darkness: Satire, Romance, and Ebenezer Cooke's *The Sot-Weed Factor*," *Tennessee Studies in Literature*, 21 (1976), 1–3.

21. For a full consideration of almanac verse see chapter 16 of this book. Also see "The Meddlers Club Papers," in *The South Carolina Gazette*, August 30, 1935; a convenient text is in *Colonial and Federalist American Writing*, ed. George F. Horner and Robert A. Bain (New York: The Odyssey Press, Inc., 1966), pp. 293–95.

22. "The Journal of Madam Knight," Miller and Johnson, *Puritans*, II, 426. See also chapters 2 and 8 of this book.

20 TOMBLESS VIRTUE AND HIDDEN TEXT: NEW ENGLAND PURITAN FUNERAL ELEGIES

WILLIAM J. SCHEICK

A wide-ranging genre referred to by a variety of names, the elegy participates in a long heritage extending from the classical age, through the seventeenth, eighteenth and nineteenth centuries, to the modern period. Such a work as Edgar Lee Masters' *Spoon River Anthology* (1915), for example, adapts the manner of the first-person variety of the seventeenth-century funeral elegy. In Masters' work, the humor intermingled with the more traditional sobriety originates principally from Enlightenment modes of and reactions to the funeral elegy of the preceding century. These modes and reactions are exemplified by the mocking or ironic patterns characteristic of eighteenth-century American southern elegies.[1] But even a century earlier the elegy proved vulnerable to distortion. John Donne indicates his use of the genre to cultivate "Satyreque thornes" and "Love-song weeds,"[2] and Thomas Morton embedded a mock elegy in his *New English Canaan* (1637). Generally, however, the elegy conveyed a more serious disposition during the seventeenth century.

For poets during the English Renaissance the term *elegy* referred to an occasional poem concerned either with death or, if more aligned to classical models, with a gravely reflective subject often expressed in lines of dactylic hexameter alternating with lines of dactylic pentameter. Seventeenth-century English poetics augmented classical authority for the elegiac tradition by including scriptural commentary disclosing the presence of the genre in the Psalms and the Lamentations of Jeremiah, the latter regarded as an elegy mourning the decease of Josiah and adumbrating the Babylonian Captivity.[3] Some poets distinguished between the funeral elegy of Jeremiah and the pastoral elegy of David. Although both varieties express grief over the death of someone, the pastoral elegy (e.g., Milton's *Lycidas*) evinces greater self-consciousness in the employment of allegory, pastoral imagery, and the eclogue—the latter two features influenced by the tradition emanating from Theocritus' *Idylls*".[4] Oddly, the more contrived pastoral elegy appears to be closer to the lyric than is the funeral variety. The funeral elegy, which inclines towards the lyric more than does the seventeenth-century philosophical poem and verse letter, emphasizes communal rather than individual significance; it utilizes a public rhetoric potentially oratorical and it addresses the reader directly as a participant in a ritual occurring during a communally relevant moment.[5] Such traits characterize the seventeenth-century funeral elegy in both England and New England.

These preliminary observations expose at least two dubious critical notions pertaining to New England Puritan funeral elegies. One assumption lurks within a distinction between how authors in England and those in New England managed the didactic purpose of the funeral elegy, obliquely suggesting that this "emphasis on instruction, however qualified, suggests that to the Puritan the elegy was not a personal cry but a communal exercise."[6] What is implied in this comment is transcribed by another critic to read: "the colonial elegy differs from its European antecedent, as Kenneth Silverman has noted, because it speaks of regional rather than of personal matters"; "in accordance with the technique of inversion, the [New England] elegists translate private loss into an affirmation not (primarily) of immortality but of political continuity."[7] Funeral elegies are indeed principally didactic and communal, though not exclusively or even chiefly in New England. A second assumption, equally erroneous but more embarrassing, surfaces in the remark that "to remember that while Puritan Milton was writing 'Lycidas,' his American coreligionists were composing acrostic elegies is to recall how provincial American Puritans quickly became."[8] A poetic genius beyond national identity, Milton was of peculiar Puritan persuasion. Moreover, *Lycidas* is a pastoral rather than a funeral elegy, and, as the most cursory glance through John W. Draper's *A Century of Broadside Elegies* (1928) reveals, Milton's English contemporaries wrote countless acrostic funeral elegies.

One apparently reliable observation on the subject appeared in 1929 and stressed continuity rather than difference: that in New England the funeral elegy "retained its most archaic characteristics longer than did the parent stock."[9] As recent historians of the American colonial period have been busy to demonstrate, New England settlers remained English citizens who transplanted the parent culture in the New World. Not that no changes eventually occurred; they did, but even these mutations manifest an evident genetic relation to English origins and hardly appear during the first two decades of settlement. First generation colonists, many of whom planned to return to England when the time became propitious, were necessarily conservative in preserving their cultural heritage. And, as has been argued concerning the specific matter of funeral practices, the New England ritual of burial followed the English model very closely, not significantly departing from that example until the end of the seventeenth century.[10] Such facts not only underscore the unreliability of the two critical assumptions noted above but also vex any attempt to differentiate between funeral elegies composed in early colonial New England and those written in early seventeenth-century England.

Moreover, efforts to discern intrinsic patterns within the New England funeral elegy as a literary mode prove similarly problematic. One reason for this difficulty readily emerges: funeral elegies vary in accordance with whether the author knew the deceased personally as a relative or close friend; whether he knew the deceased only publicly as an acquaintance or as a social figure; whether he perceived his immediate audience as the family, town, or nation of the deceased; whether he was familiar with a limited number or a wide variety of previous examples of the genre; and whether he was inclined to be imitative or inventive in responding to these antecedents. In short, authorial context discourages treating New England Puritan elegies collectively.

A second contravening factor surfaces in the inclusion in the genre of at least two typological traditions. In the funeral elegies of both England and New England, each nation is respectively imaged as an Israel and its leaders are likened to Old Testament figures. In "Upon the Tomb of the Most Reverend Mr. John Cotton" (1652), for example, Benjamin Woodbridge refers to a deceased eminent New England divine as Moses, and in "A Mournfull Epitaph upon the Death of . . . John Rogers" (1636) J. L. (John Long?) similarly describes a deceased revered English divine as "Our faithfull Moses."[11] In New England funeral elegies *generally* the typological manner tends to be somewhat more historical than allegorical—that is, they evince a preference for the view of the literal-spiritual continuity between the two Testaments of Scripture and the national endeavor, in opposition to a view of that effort as only spiritually parallel to biblical types fully completed in the New Testament. In fact both views prevail in both countries, as the controversy between John Cotton and Roger Williams reminds us,[12] and the funeral elegies written in these two countries during the early seventeenth century reflect both systems, thereby preventing easy distinctions of elegiac design on the basis of typology.

A third hindrance in detecting constitutional patterns within the funeral elegy includes such extrinsic factors as the intermingling of pastoral and funeral modes of the genre, the possible influence of other poetic forms, and the effect of national historical developments. The typological problem comprises a large subject worthy of a separate essay, whereas the problem of extrinsic factors, albeit also sizeable, can be briefly approached here, especially since it has been investigated by scholars and exposes other questionable conclusions about the New England Puritan funeral elegy. In England the funeral elegy underwent several transformations during the early Renaissance, through the Protectorate and Commonwealth, to the Restoration.[13] Such implied cultural pluralism in England is, recent scholarship has argued in reaction to Perry Miller, equally characteristic of New England; and such an observation, in conjunction with the fact that colonial funeral elegies retained the most archaic features of the genre longer than did their English source, makes these works more difficult to categorize than has been suggested by critics.

A recent attempt, for example, to locate an intrinsic pattern in the New England funeral elegy claims that the primary influence upon the genre originates from the funeral sermon, particularly from the portrait-exhortation technique of the application sections of these sermons.[14] This approach not only denies the genre any integrity as a form in itself, but it also fails to take account of precedent English elegies and the development of the funeral sermon in England and New England. Until about the turn of the century New Englanders followed the English custom of delivering a funeral sermon some days after the interment of the deceased, and only late in the century did eulogizing become prevalent in the funeral sermon.[15] Similarly another critic concludes, without elaboration, "After 1660, poets more and more identified the death of leaders with the fall of Wilderness Zion,"[16] and then includes in his selection of funeral elegies Benjamin Woodbridge's previously mentioned "Upon the Tomb of the Most Reverend Mr. John Cotton," published as a broadside in 1652 and 1666–67[17] and later in Nathaniel Morton's *New Englands Memoriall* (1669). Woodbridge's work concludes:

> But let his Mourning Flock be comforted,
> Though Moses be, yet Joshua is not dead:
> I mean Renowned Norton, worthy hee
> Successor to our Moses is to bee,
> O happy Israel in America,
> In such a Moses such a Joshua.[18]

Woodbridge's instance of New England's still immanent arrival into the promised land of fulfilled destiny is no anomaly. Nor is the paradoxically complementary and contrapuntal theme of this and other funeral elegies, the threat of divine disapproval as symbolized in the death of a minister, unique to New England. Among abundant evidence, one might readily cite the passage noted above from the English funeral elegy on John Rogers (1636) and the following lines (echoing the image of Moses in the earlier passage) from George Harrison's "An Elegie on the Death of . . . Robert Blake" (1657): "Our Sins a war on us shall bring agen, / Who then shall stand i'th Gap His Noble Arme?"[19]

Doubtless the 1660s comprised a time of change for New England Puritans. Though insufficiently noted in literary scholarship, the restoration of Charles II must have had a profound effect on New England Puritans' sense of themselves and subsequently on their literature. Increase Mather returned to New England promptly, for instance, and Massachusetts Bay's charter of 1629 suffered incursions by royal commissioners who sought power in the colony superior to that supported by the charter. This obstacle was finally removed by the Crown in 1684 and was followed by direct English political intrusion in Boston in the form of services conducted according to the Book of Common Prayer. Furthermore, 1662, the date of the institutional (if not general parishional) endorsement of the Halfway Covenant and the commencement of a generation of debate on the nature of baptism, might have been, as one student of colonial intellectual history has observed, the turning point in the American jeremiad tradition.[20] There were other changes, less certain in significance, such as the appearance in the late 1660s of the first symbolic designs on New England tombstones[21] and the publication of Nathaniel Morton's *New Englands Memoriall* (1669).

Another historian traces somewhat earlier cultural modifications to the colonial Puritans' perception of excessive religious toleration in England during the Commonwealth and to the decline of their belief in an imminent Second Advent. Seeming to be on their own, colonial Puritans apparently experienced during the 1660s a cultural instability manifested, for instance, in the replacement of a previous absence of ceremony and a restraint of emotion at funerals with a ritual of elaborate funeral practices, including elegies whose jeremiad tendencies sometimes become somewhat more emphatic than their English prototypes.[22]

With the onset of the apparent colonial cultural instability following the restoration of Charles II in 1660, the New England colonists' tendency to turn inward upon themselves as individuals and as a community increased as a consequence of their renewed sense of religious mission. It was a renewal since the first generation similarly had experienced isolation and an internal orientation in every aspect of its emigration and settlement. Herein lies a key to the emergence of filio-piety among the articulate of the second generation,[23] for in facing the failure of the Puritan Commonwealth in England, the second generation in New England found itself, like the preceding generation, cut off from the homeland and on its own (presumably still with divine favor) in achieving identity and purpose. Indeed, the second generation might have experienced this sense of themselves even more intensely than did the first; for, unlike its predecessors, the second generation could not dream of expanding the New Jerusalem beyond the Atlantic and eventually returning victorious to the homeland. This re-emergent colonial self-image of permanent isolation doubtless was nurtured by the increment of worldly possessions, especially land, in the New World—assets which the second generation inherited from their parents and which they increased and multiplied. These material goods did not resolve the second generation's psychological insecurity, their search for identity and for reaffirmation or redefinition of purpose, any more than they ever can. Indeed, in a culture nominally weaned from a trust in the things of this world, these possessions covertly intensified the colonial Puritans' post-Restoration sense of their religio-political isolation and of the permanence of their settlement in the New World.

Within this context, several New England Puritan funeral elegies of the post-1660 period highlighted those earlier features of the genre that emphasize turning inwardly upon the isolated colonial community as a whole, an inward focus upon the collective self. Just as the Puritans' diaries and sermons probe the lonely individual self, some of their funeral elegies, especially those with distinctive jeremiad tendencies, plumb the depths of the collective self. Puritan elegy writers found scant evidence of a secure social structure in their colonial world, certainly nothing similar to the comforting authority, tradition, and patterns of social delineation typical of life in England. New England colonists clung to English models, but extrinsic conditions differed in the New World. Most specifically the physical environment was less serene than the English landscape. A clearing in the wilderness had to be made, and herein the Puritans discovered an apt metaphor for the ministerial effort to effect a clearing in the soul of a potential saint. And, given the lack of cultural firmness in the settlements, this metaphor refunded its charge to the community as a whole, so that the clearing in the wilderness constituting Puritan society came to be imaged in terms of the ideal saintly self. Thus, recent critics have expanded Edmund S. Morgan's observations about Puritan tribalism to demonstrate how Puritan historians and biographers created an image of society as if it were a collective individual.[24] Just as Puritans believed the human self to be comprised of head (reason), heart (will), affections, and body, they viewed society as a collective self in which ministers represented the soul (reason and will) ideally guiding the New World laity or corporation (corpus/body), as if the prelapsarian Adamic experience of an harmonious hierarchy between spirit and flesh might be rejoined within the New Israelites collectively. This image of a collective self, isolated in the world and lonely before God, informs several New England Puritan funeral elegies, early and late, albeit somewhat more emphatically after the Restoration. This mannerism of depicting their society as if it evinced faculties equivalent to those of the human self is evident only in certain elegies on ministers and comprises but one thematic strand in a genre as polymorphous and resistant to critical synthesis as the cultural influences impinging upon it. But the presence of this strand, however cautiously regarded, distinguishes these particular works from similar extant seventeenth-century English funeral elegies, even those written during the Protectorate and the Commonwealth.

Extant English funeral elegies do not depict society as a collective self. Nor do they generally turn inward upon the community, and in those rare instances when they somewhat incline in this latter way, as in Harrison's elegy on Robert Blake, the imagery requires solely biblical and political analogues, never alludes to the faculties of the human self, and is conveyed in a manner measurably less intense than the New England variety. A sense of community is indeed present, not as vital center but as comforting frame for the English funeral elegist. In the English funeral elegy this sense of community, perhaps an outgrowth of the *ars moriendi* tradition stressing a sustaining Christian solidarity at the time of death,[25] provides a large circumference within which can be found consolation for the loss of the deceased. In "Tears for the Death of the Most Gracious Prince Lodouicke" (1624), for instance, the anonymous poet fashions several assuaging conceits derived from a communal context: "Wee see in losse, this alwayes still remaines, / Some evermore to gather up the gaines";

> Death shall not bring thy praises to the grave;
> For after-ages that are yet unborne,
> Shall with their hearts thy memorie adorne.[26]

A similar note during the English civil wars is sounded in John Leicester's "An Elegiacall Epitaph upon the Deplored Death of . . . John Hampden" (1643); Jeremiah Rich's "An Elegie on the Death of . . . John Warner" (1648), which concludes, "Thy fame that cannot die, shall be / A Monument in the worlds memory"; and Josiah Ricraft's "A Funerall Elegy upon . . . Robert Deveraux Earl of Essex" (1946), which opens,

> No, he is only vanisht from our sight,
> And made a star; to give these Isles more light
> To see the way to peace.[27]

Such imagery readily contrasts with the prevalent pattern of New England funeral elegies in which the death of a minister is depicted as an occasion when "these Lights extinct, dark is our Hemisphere" (J [ohn?] N [orton?], "A Funeral Elegy upon the Death of . . . John Cotton," 1652) and when "doth the Sun retire into his bed" (Benjamin Woodbridge, "Upon the Tomb of . . . John Cotton," 1652). Even more notable, a year after the appearance of Ricraft's poem, colonist P. B. laments the demise of Thomas Hooker as evidence of how "Gospels light which shineth from on high, / Should clouded be, and darkened in our skie."[28] P. B.'s imagery specifically reverses that of Ricraft. Ricraft's communal content, moreover, includes overt political dimensions, which in fact inform numerous early seventeenth-century English funeral elegies. In such poems grief is in effect deflected away from self and diffused within the communal framework, where tradition and history provide consolation. Sometimes this movement is accompanied by solace offered through analogies drawn from nature, another broad frame, like society, mitigating grief in the English funeral elegy. In "An Elegie upon the Most Pious . . . John Hewitt" (1658), the poet consolingly explains that "Nature and Reason both plainly show, / After an Ebb we must expect a Flow"; and in "An Elogy upon the Death of Mr. Luke Fawne Junior" (1650), Robert Tutchein concludes: "Whoever saw a loaded ear of Corn/Not earth-wards tend? the empty upwards born."[29]

New England contemporaries also read nature emblematically, as the Second Book, an at once majestic and (especially in the New World) terrifying art work of the Logos. However beautiful and indicative of the promise of salvation for the elect, nature, like Scripture, also indicts humanity for its depravity, hence providing no security or consolation for the spiritual pilgrim, least of all concerning death. On two separate elegiac occasions (1652 and 1655), for instance, John Fiske spoke of the bereaved's ongoing experience of "surviving [the] worlds ocean" and of "Tossings heere in wildernes."[30] This image of the world as a tempestuous sea appears as well on the tombstone of Edward Taylor, whose elegies, one critic has cogently observed, commence "with a metaphor taken from the physical world and presumably placed there by God to offer comfort in the face of death" but is finally strained or torn apart because it proves inadequate.[31] Little wonder, then, that in responding to his grief over the demise of his wife Elizabeth Fitch, in 1689, Taylor interiorizes the focus of his attention (in imagery and sentiment remarkably similar to Benjamin Tompson's "A Short Memoriall," 1679):

> Some deem Death doth the True Love Knot unty;
> But I do finde it harder tide thereby
> My heart is in't and will be Squeezd therefore
> To pieces if thou draw the Ends much more. [ll. 7–10][32]

The failure of nature, in spite of its loveliness, to answer the postlapsarian human self's quest for identity, context, or solace is also apparent in Anne Bradstreet's "Contemplations," in which, in contrast to nineteenth-century Romantic poetry, the poet discovers indictment rather than comfort in the cycles of nature. The inadequacy of nature in this regard is somewhat differently, but nonetheless pertinently, suggested in an elegy on Samuel Stone by E [dward?] B [ulkeley?]:

> Last Spring this Summer may be Autumn styl'd,
> Sad withering Fall our Beauties which despoyl'd
> Two choicest Plants, our Norton and our Stone,
> Your Justs threw down. [ll. 1–4][33]

What nature failed to provide the New England Puritan by way of consolation was not redressed by colonial society. New England colonists tended their transplanted English heritage conservatively, especially since many planned to return to the homeland and perceived the New World as culturally void. Yet, their desire to purify English religion went hand in hand with the need to purify English social traditions and rituals, for colonial Congregationalists and Presbyterians held a theocratic ideal. This quest for reform and concomitant sense of isolation, underscored by the realities of frontier settlement, denied New England Puritan authors a secure exterior social framework of the sort available to their English contemporaries. The earliest Puritan writers turned inward as a consequence of their theology and their circumstances. Even Anne Bradstreet, who began her literary career as a public poet highly influenced by her English heritage, attained a distinctive voice only when she abandoned this public attitude and turned within to focus on personal matters; and her "Contemplations," written approximately fifteen years after the appearance of *The Tenth Muse* (1650), reads nature as an "emblem true" of the poet's psychic terrain, Bradstreet's self: "O could I lead my rivulets to rest."[34] If nature provided Puritans with images for projecting the human self, that self, particularly as delineated by faculty psychology, provided these colonists with images for depicting the collective self of their society. This latter pattern is especially pronounced in elegies on departed clergy, in which the consoling communal frame of the English variety of the genre collapses in upon itself, even as the Puritan saint assails his self; and this subsequently indicted collective self becomes the focus. The funeral elegy of colonial New England is as communal as its English prototype, but sometimes merges this social feature with a configuration of the private self and in the process transforms any movement toward extrinsic mitigating frame, such as nature and society, into an inward indictment of an intrinsically vulnerable collective identity.

By way of illustration, Urian Oakes's "An Elegie upon . . . Thomas Shepard" (1677) provides a useful instance. No anomaly, this poem is firmly rooted in English elegiac tradition; even its depiction of Shepard as a Leonidas at Thermopylae, as "the man that stood i'th' gap, to keep the pass,"[35] has nearly identical imagery with lines in the previously cited English elegies on John Rogers and Robert Blake. Divergent from the English pattern is Oakes's personal identification with the collective prophetic voice of the Puritan ministry and his representation of the Puritan community as a collective self. Through his elegy Oakes seeks to "set . . . eyes abroach, dissolve a stone." As exemplified by an elegiac tribute, thirty years earlier, remarking how Thomas Hooker "The stoutest Hearts . . . filled full of fears, / He clave the Rocks, they melted into tears,"[36] Oakes's clichéd imagery refers not only to weeping eyes and mourning hearts, but also to the unenlightened eye of reason and the stony heart, or will. In a manner resembling how Puritan ministers oriented their sermons, Oakes focuses on the two chief stages of the conversion process, the awakening of the reason and the turning of the heart of the audience. Unlike the sermon, Oakes's elegy emphasizes the community as a whole, as a collective self possessing an impaired rational eye and a resistant or stony heart.

In the poem Shepard is represented as comprising the reason and will of New England; and his demise is attributed to the insubordination of the laity, "a lifeless Corporation," whose behavior mirrors the rebellion of the postlapsarian body (*corpus*/corporation) against the weakened soul (reason and will). Since he comprised the "very Soul" of his parish, Shepard's death "sorely wounds both Head and Heart." In this manner Oakes develops and finely tunes elegiac imagery to suggest the role of the deceased as the soul of a collective self. A year earlier, Joshua Moody called John Reiner "A precious Soul," superior to others "As Souls than Bodies more excelling are," and with whose death the "sight of our eyes / Is gone." In 1663, E.B. spoke of Samuel Stone as a "Whet-Stone, that Edgefi' a th'obtusest Mende: / Load-Stone, that drew the Iron Heart unkinde"; and a decade earlier Edward Johnson, in *The Wonder-Working Providence of Sions Saviour in New England* (1653), wrote similarly of Shepard's father:

> . . . thy lips Christ hath made
>   Thy hearers eyes oft water springing blade.
> With pierced hearts they cry aloud and say,
>   Shew us sweet Shepheard our salvations way.[ll. 11–14]

Still earlier, in 1647, a poet, who signed himself P.B., equates Thomas Hooker's demise to the disappearance of the sun, the source of life, and then refers to the death as a "soul-destroying Plague," for in typical Puritan thought the soul is like a little sun animating the body.[37]

Moreover, by identifying with Shepard's prophetic role—it was commonplace in colonial elegies to speak of the ministry as "New Englands Prophets"[38]— Oakes presents himself as a soul-principle in the act of trying to resuscitate the communal body, "a lifeless Corporation" unless animated by a sunlike soul evincing the image of God. In Shepard's stead Oakes asks a series of questions pertaining to the possibility of the subsequent demise of New England:

> What! must we with our God, and Glory part?
> Lord is thy Treaty with New-England come
> Thus to an end? And is War in thy Heart? [ll. 109–11]

Implying no dire forecast, these questions are designed to enliven the corporation by goading it to consent to a proper government by the ministerial collective soul. Furthermore, the questions are left unanswered, and in this sense Oakes's poem remains unfinished. What completion can it attain? It cannot prognosticate, and it does not exist for itself or as a permanent monument to the memory of Shepard, whose death merely provides an occasion to address matters concerning the collective self. In short, Oakes's poem dissolves as an artifact as it points away from itself and even from its subject to its audience. This dissolution of the elegy's "self" coincides with the coalescence of Oakes's and Shepard's identities; and it coincides with his refusal to proffer any sense of consolation akin to that of contemporary English funeral elegies. Through his elegy Oakes imitates Shepard as a soul-principle and hence strives to resuscitate the "corporate" audience, lifeless without a ministerial soul; if he succeeds he will also keep alive the ideal of a collective self and he will have awakened his audience's collective rational eye and turned its heart, set its "eyes abrooch, dissolve[d] a stone."

Other New England elegies on deceased ministers similarly ask questions for which, in contrast to their English prototypes, no answers are discovered in the processes of nature, society, or art. In "An Elegy upon the Death of . . . Sam[uel] Hooker" (1697), to cite another instance, Edward Taylor inquires:

> Lord art thou angry with the Flock, that thou
> Dost slay their Shephard? Or dost disallow
> The Fold, and lay it Common that thou smite
> Down dost the shory that upheld it right?
> Shall angling cease? and no more fish be took? [ll. 225–29]

This passage represents a typical interlude in a long poem replete with such unanswered queries. As in Oakes's poem, Taylor's elegy suggests that in the quest for answers to such dire questions the audience of the elegy must look to

itself as a collective self. Like Oakes's, Taylor's elegy points away from itself
as an artifact and from the deceased as its focus; it emphasizes the need for the
Puritan community "To Stay thy Head, & heart from ill recover," to look within
its collective self where it will be able to scrutinize itself as if it were looking
into a mirror:

> To see thy Freckled Face in Gospell Glass:
> To feele thy Pulse, and finde thy Spleen's not well:
> Whose Vapors raise thy Pericordium t'swell:
> Do suffocate, & Cramp thee and grow worse
> By Hypochondrick Passions of the purse
> Affect thy Brains toucht with the Turn. [ll. 146–151][39]

This focus on the collective self in elegies on ministers is reinforced by the
tendency of colonial elegists in general to diffuse specificity of details pertaining
to the deceased, the nominal subject. Concerning this characteristic, one critic's
lament that "the first century of New England verse . . . tells us almost nothing
of the concrete, existential experience of people, places, or things"[40] is somewhat
accurate and unwittingly to the heart of the matter. Like Puritan biographies and
histories, colonial funeral elegies eschew specific details in preference for broad
saintly configurations. Disregarding the deceased's quirks of selfhood and par-
ticularity of external behavior, these works emphasize exhibited virtues to be
imitated by others. Imitation thematically informs the elegies of both New Eng-
land and England, but the New England variety specifically presents these virtues
in terms of an ideal or saintly collective self. In New England the deceased is
limned entirely in terms of these virtues, so that in elegy after elegy the nominal
subjects coalesce in a broad configuration, the ideal collective self against which
the audience is to measure itself and in terms of which it is to imitate the virtues
of the deceased. Saintly virtue, the manifestation of the collective self, is not
entombed; the broad configuration of saintliness is the true monument celebrating
the deceased. Consequently, colonial funeral elegies seek no lasting identity for
themselves as monuments to the deceased or as permanent artifacts; as an expres-
sion of "no good poetry / Yet certainly good will," as no "Pompous monuments
of . . . Funeral[s],"[41] they point away from themselves as a source of answers
or of consolation, directing their audience to turn within even as they have
interiorized the deceased in terms of the collective self.

In other words, the New England funeral elegy, particularly when treating a
deceased minister, transfers its text to the soul, the reason and will, of each
member of its audience. Its final emphasis, then, falls upon this text of the self,
this tombstone or elegy to be read within each person. For the dead need no
such memorials; they are presumably among the living in heaven, whereas the
bereaved—according to a typical explanation by Samuel Torrey in "Upon the
Death of Mr. William Tompson" (1666)—have not been "By Death deliverd
from [the] liveing grave" and are "the lively portrature of Death, A walking

tomb, a living sepulcher." Each heart is a sepulcher, according to Benjamin Woodbridge, on which the text of a name is engraved; and like John Cotton, Woodbridge continues, every name should be "a Title Page" and every "Life a Commentary on the Text" of Scripture. Similarly, in "To the Memory of . . . Jonathan Mitchell" (1668), F.D. instructs his audience: "reade Rev'rend Mitchel's Life," "Reade his Tear-delug'd Grave," and learn that "The Scripture with a Commentary bound/(Like a lost C[h]alice) in his Heart was found"; this Scriptural text in his heart, life, or grave is implicit in his name, to be read on his tombstone, and "He that speaks Mitchell, gives the Schools the Lie." Or, as another elegist anonymously wrote in 1645:

> A death's head on your hand you neede not weare.
> A dying head you on your shoulders beare.
> You neede not one to mind you, you must dye,
> You in your name may spell mortalitye.

One's very name is the definitive elegy or epitaph comprising the enigmatic text of the self, the text to which the non-consoling funeral elegy yields up its own text and which is to be deciphered (as much as it can be in this world) in terms of Scripture and the collective self informing the pattern of internalization evident in certain colonial funeral elegies on ministers.[42]

In the Puritan view, the true name of something reveals its essence. Adam, they believed, knew the names of the animals in Eden not by means of his senses (*scientia*) alone but principally by means of his divinely inspired intuition (*sapientia*). He could read the text of nature because of a divine illumination infusing his faculties. After the Fall, the Book of Nature became cryptic to the human mind, which was henceforth dependent upon *scientia* for knowledge and, after Christ's sacrifice, upon whatever vestiges of *sapientia* might be restored through special grace. In lieu of the Book of Nature, Scripture was to aid postlapsarian humanity, but benefiting from the Bible requires faith (a gift of special grace, according to conservative Puritans) and, as Bunyan's *Pilgrim's Progress* (1678) indicates, also requires expertise in reading the text of the self. Hence the Puritan fascination with the anagram, which unlike the acrostic apparently rarely appeared in the seventeenth-century English funeral elegy. A name provides one text of the self, especially a *memento mori* or elegiac text of the self, since "You in your name may spell mortalitye." The anagram represents a mode of the New England Puritans' elegaic-emphasis on the collective self, modelled on their concept of the individual self and designed to bring that self into conformity with the ideal. Each anagram conveys, as it were, an epitaph pertaining to virtues or traits characteristic of the collective self; it transcends the specific identity of the deceased by attributing identity only in terms of a collective configuration. Like other modes of the Puritan elegy, the funeral anagram transfers its text to the more significant text found in each self. Within each person, anagrams imply, lies a hidden text, one clue to which can be found in his or her name.

To some degree elegiac anagrams evince "devout ingenuity," as one critic has suggested, and, as another has observed, they "put into some sort of order as much as possible of events and ideas connected with the person to be celebrated," thereby "exhibit[ing] a latent concern with the self and sensibility of the poet."[43] *Latent* is the key word, for the explicit and most of the implicit emphasis of the colonial Puritan funeral elegy, particularly when written on ministers, falls upon the selflessness of the deceased (the nominal subject), the ideal selflessness of the audience (the actual subject), the selflessness of the poet (the prophetic voice), and the selflessness of the poem (the text)—all integrated in the concept of the collective self. Not only do these funeral elegies inherently point away from the deceased, the author, and themselves as texts, in evocation of a similar emptying of sinful selfhood by their audience, they were items to be literally discarded. Printed on broadsides, elegies were attached to the hearse, thrown into the grave, or at best distributed among the mourners to be read on the occasion. Extrinsically or intrinsically, they were not designed to survive this occasion, and that they did not is evident from their scarcity today.[44] Just as the nominal subject was interred, just as the actual subject (the audience) was instructed to imitate the deceased by burying perverse selfhood in the idealized tombless virtues objectified in the collective self, the elegy was funerated. Neither lasting monuments to the deceased nor expressions of art for art's sake, New England minsterial funeral elegies were designed to be consumed as their texts yielded specific identity to the hidden text buried within the sepulcher of each human heart (will). For Puritans this inmost text commands: discard self and identify with the selfless virtues of all deceased saints, whose virtues comprise a communal collective self. In other words, the elegist's assumption of a collective prophetic voice implicitly points to two related questions which underlie all the unresolved explicit questions in elegies on ministers and are potentially answerable only in terms of the text hidden within each person's self: have you deciphered the elegiac text buried in the tomb of your heart and has that text been immolated, that is, self-consumed or made selfless?

Generally these two implicit questions are directed at the laity, but in one epitaph at least they were aimed at the clergy. In this epitaph (1666), a remarkable and somewhat cryptic poem, Benjamin Tompson employs all of the previously discussed fundamental patterns in elegaic tribute to his deceased father, Reverend William Tompson, but uses the ideal of the collective self to indict clerical malfeasance:

> Judicious Zeale: New-Englands Boanerges
> Lies Tombless: not to Spare the Churches Charges
> But that the world may know he lacks no Tomb
> Who in Ten thousand hearts commanded room.
> While thus the thundring Text man hidden lies
> Some Virgins slumber: Others wantonize.[45]

Initially this poem recalls "A Mournfull Epitaph upon the Death of. . .John Rogers" (1636, 1642), in which the deceased is spoken of as a "blessed sonne of thunder" and "In zeale. . .a flaming fire, / yet humble and discreet."[46] But whatever its debt to antecedent elegies, Tompson's poem is quite distinctive, not only an instance of how "in his hands, the elegy continued a noble and dignified instrument for the promotion of community ethical awareness,"[47] but also at once an eccentric variation and an epitome of certain colonial New England elegiac patterns. Addressed to "New-Englands Boanerges"—that is, to her sons of thunder or vociferous preachers—the poem advocates "Judicious Zeale" as an ideal virtue[48] which neither lessens "the Churches Charges"—that is, her cannonfire, responsibilities, authority, or number of parishioners—nor produces so much noise that "the thundring Text" of Scripture is lost in the overly zealous delivery of the biblical message by the sons of thunder. As presumably exemplified by Tompson's father and as a trait of the collective ministerial identity, the fact that judicious zeal "Lies Tombless" reflects an evident virtue derived *imitatio Christi*; for just as the resurrected Christ abandoned his tomb, so should everyone forsake the tomb of the heart or self if he or she wishes to follow Christ, "Who in Ten thousand hearts commanded room." Ministers who do not strive to open the tomblike hearts of their parishioners are slumbering virgins (cf. Matt. 25), non-zealous preachers permitting their "Charges" to slumber with unpenetrated, perversely virginal selves. Ministers who over-zealously, extravagantly execute their "Charges" or responsibilities are perversely non-virginal and violate or "wantonize" their "Charges," their parishioners, by, as it were, raping or blasting, as if by cannonfire, the closed tombs of the laitys' selves. The true task of the sons of thunder is to echo, not ignore or surpass, the thundering text of Scripture.

The thundering text, an image alluding as well to the day of doom when all of the graves will open and the dead assemble for the last judgment, to a large extent *to* "man hidden lies,"[49] in the sense that it requires prophetic or ministerial interpretation. The thundering text also *in* "man hidden lies," in the sense that the biblical message applies to the human self and confirms what is imprinted there as the image of God in man. Hence ministers should not sleep through their duty to interpret the Bible and thereby permit their parishioners to relax from reading the text of the self; nor should ministers roar louder than Scripture, vest themselves in powers greater than they actually possess, and thereby encourage their parishioners to read the text of their apparently blasted selves too easily and mistakenly. A virtue typical of the collective ministerial self, as modelled after the example of Christ's manner of preaching and undramatic resurrection from the dead, judicious zeal characterizes how ministers are to proceed in executing their charges and how those parishional charges are to proceed both in reading the text on the sepulcher of the heart and in rising from the tomb of mortal selfhood.

In short, Tompson's epitaph emphasizes selflessness: the nominal subject,

William Tompson, is never mentioned directly; the audience, the actual subject, is directed away from the extremes of virginal self–ishness and wanton self–fulness towards identification with an ideal virtue. The poet, who represses explicit reference to the specific occasion, submerges his personal voice—indeed the poetic persona may well be the deceased—into the collective prophetic voice predominant in colonial funeral elegies on ministers; and the poem, however imagistically ingenious, points away from itself as an epitaph memorializing William Tompson and transfers the burden of its message to its audience, ministers who are implicitly instructed to read the hidden text in their own hearts concerning how well they have discharged their duties in instructing each of their parishioners in reading his or her respective elegiac text of self. In this way Tompson's elegy eschews selfhood as a lasting artifact; in its extra-referentiality, in its need to be finished in the self of its audience, it is consumed and, as it were, funerated. In these terms, Tompsons' epitaph emerges as a remarkable poem, a wonderful epitome of colonial New England funeral elegies generally and most particularly of those treating deceased ministers.

NOTES

1. See Richard Beale Davis, *Intellectual Life in the Colonial South, 1585-1763* (Knoxville: Univ. of Tennessee Press, 1978), 3:1401–19.

2. Louis L. Martz, *The Poem of the Mind: Essays on Poetry / English and American* (New York: Oxford Univ. Press, 1966), pp. 7–12.

3. Lewalski, *Poetics*, pp. 50–51, 69.

4. Ruth Wallerstein, *Studies in Seventeenth-Century Poetic* (Madison and Milwaukee: Univ. of Wisconsin Press, 1950), p. 67.

5. Norman K. Farmer, Jr., "A Theory of Genre for Seventeenth-Century Poetry." *Genre*, 3 (1970), 293–317.

6. Silverman, *Poetry*, p. 127. See also Edwin S. Fussell, "Benjamin Tompson, Public Poet," *NEQ* 26 (1953), 504.

7. Bercovitch, *Puritan Origins*, p. 121.

8. Waggoner, *Poets*, p. 13.

9. John W. Draper, *The Funeral Elegy and the Rise of English Romanticism* (New York: New York Univ. Press, 1929), p. 176.

10. David E. Stannard, *The Puritan Way of Death: A Study in Religion, Culture, and Social Change* (New York: Oxford Univ. Press, 1977), pp. 109–10.

11. Meserole, *Poetry*, p. 410; Silverman, *Poetry*, p. 135; Draper, *A Century* of Broadside Elegies (London: Ingpen and Grant, 1928), p. 21. Dates given for the elegies are those of first publication; see also notes 18 and 28.

12. See Sacvan Bercovitch, "Typology in Puritan New England: The Williams-Cotton Controversy Reassessed," *AQ*, 19 (1967), 166–91, and W. Clark Gilpin, *The Millenarian Piety of Roger Williams* (Chicago: Univ. of Chicago Press, 1979), pp. 108–11.

13. See Draper, *Funeral Elegy*, pp. 24–154; Wallerstein, *Studies*, p. 143.

14. Robert Henson, "Form and Content of the Puritan Funeral Elegy," *AL* 32 (1960), 11–27.

15. Stannard, *Puritan Way*, pp. 115–16.

16. Silverman, *Poetry*, p. 128. Cf. Henson, p. 24.

17. Harold S. Jantz, "Unrecorded Verse Broadsides of Seventeenth-century New England," *Papers of the Bibliographical Society of America*, 39 (1945), 1–19.

18. Meserole, *Poetry*, p. 410; Silverman, *Poetry*, p. 135.

19. Draper, *Century of Broadside Elegies*, p. 73. See also A. L. Bennett, "The Principal Rhetorical Conventions in the Renaissance Personal Elegy," *Studies in Philology*, 51 (1954), 119–20.

20. Bercovitch, *Jeremiad*, pp. 62–73.

21. Allan I. Ludwig, *Graven Images: New England Stonecarving and Its Symbols, 1650–1815* (Middletown, Conn.: Wesleyan Univ. Press, 1966), pp. 358, 453; also chapter 6 of this book.

22. Stannard, pp. 122–25.

23. See, for instance, Robert Middlekauff, *The Mathers: Three Generations of Puritan Intellectuals, 1596–1728* (New York: Oxford Univ. Press, 1971).

24. Morgan, *Family*, p. 168; Cecelia Tichi, "Spiritual Biography and the 'Lords Remembrancers,' " *WMQ* 28 (1971), 69.

25. See Bettie Anne Doebler, " 'Rooted Sorrow': Verbal and Visual Survivals of an *Ars* Commonplace (1590–1620)," *Texas Studies in Literature and Language*, 22 (1980), pp. 358–68.

26. Draper, *Century of Broadside Elegies*, p. 7.

27. Ibid., pp. 23, 51, 39.

28. Nathaniel Morton, *New Englands Memoriall* (Cambridge: Green and Johnson, 1669), p. 136; Silverman, *Poetry*, p. 133; Meserole, *Poetry*, p. 410. See also "Upon the Death of . . . Samuel Arnold" (1687), in Ola Elizabeth Winslow, *American Broadside Verse* (New Haven: Yale Univ. Press, 1930), p. 15; Morton, p. 127. Dates given for the elegies are those of first publication.

29. Draper, *Century of Broadside Elegies*, pp. 77, 63.

30. Silverman, *Poetry*, pp. 136, 138; Meserole, *Poetry*, p. 188.

31. Daly, *God's Altar*, p. 175.

32. Thomas H. Johnson (ed.), "The Topical Verses of Edward Taylor," *Publications of the Colonial Society of Massachusetts*, 34 (1943), 535. For Tompson's lines see White, *Tompson*, pp. 141–43.

33. Silverman, *Poetry*, p. 142.

34. *Bradstreet*, Hensley, p. 211.

35. Meserole, *Poetry*, p. 209. My remarks here comprise a revision of one concern taken up in my "Standing in the Gap: Urian Oakes's Elegy on Thomas Shepard," *EAL*, 9 (1975) 301–6.

36. Morton, *New England's Memoriall*, p. 128.

37. Jantz, *First Century*, pp. 151–54; Silverman, p. 143; Meserole, p. 151; Morton, p. 129.

38. T. S., "Upon the Death of . . . John Wilson" (1667), in Morton, p. 188. See also Morton, pp. 136, 166.

39. Johnson, "Topical Verses of Edward Taylor," p. 538–46.

40. Waggoner, *Poets*, p. 14.

41. Percival Lowell, "A Funeral Elgie (Written Many Years Since) on the Death of . . . John Winthrope" (date uncertain), in Winslow, p. 3; Morton, pp. 117–18.

42. The passages cited in this paragraph are from, respectively, Silverman, pp. 143–44, 134–35; Morton, pp. 193–96; and Meserole, p. 505.

43. Austin Warren, "The Puritan Poets," *New England Saints* (Ann Arbor: Univ. of Michigan Press, 1956), p. 15; Pearce, *Continuity*, pp. 28, 39. Pearce is echoed in Waggoner, *Poets*, p. 14.

44. This scarcity is evident, for example, in Worthington Chauncey Ford's *Broadsides, Ballads, Etc. Printed in Massachusetts, 1639–1800*, volume 75 (1922) in MHS Collections.

45. White, *Tompson*, p. 77. I have revised White's version to reflect Joseph Tompson's reading of "Text man" rather than Edward Tompson's reading of "Textman." In general Edward Tompson's copies are more reliable than Joseph's, but in this instance, as explained in note 49, the former is preferable.

46. Draper, *Century of Broadside Elegies*, p. 21.

47. Fussell, "Benjamin Tompson . . . ," p. 504.

48. In "The Harangue of King Philip in *New-Englands Crisis* (1676)" (*AL*, 51 [1980], 536–40), Wayne Franklin, apparently echoing Edwin Fussell, remarks Tompson's alleged sympathy for Roger Williams. Such a conclusion may be vexed by Tompson's emphasis on judicious zeal in the epitaph under discussion.

49. The line reading "While thus the thundring Text man hidden lies" is difficult. The line may refer to the fact that William is buried and cannot be seen; but more satisfying, in my opinion, is a recognition of Tompson's metrical constraints in the line in conjunction with his extensive scholarship in the classics that permit us to perceive *man* as an indirect object, reading in effect *to man*. Moreover, the ambiguity nicely permits the possibility of *in man*.

21 *VOCES CLAMANTIUM IN DESERTO:* LATIN VERSE OF THE PURITANS

LAWRENCE ROSENWALD

For the subject of Puritan Latin verse, apart from Harold Jantz's remarkable bibliography and Leo Kaiser's expert editions,[1] the field is pretty much bare, and there is no tradition of interpretation in which to take a position. This chapter is accordingly intended as a suggestive introduction. It is both an inventory of individual poems and an assessment of the *corpus*. In making this assessment, I have found two questions critical. The first is: What evidence does the Puritans' Latin verse offer for ascertaining the place of humanism in Puritan culture? The second is: What was the function of the Puritans' Latin verse for those who wrote it? Normally the latter question is not in the domain of a literary historian but of a literary anthropologist, so to speak. In the present state of research, answers to these questions can be only tentative.

I shall begin with the inventory, proceeding from dross to gold. The purest dross, sadly, is the one exclusively Latin genre, the *quaestio*-verse. A *quaestio* is a proposition in philosophy or theology;[2] candidates for the M.A. at Harvard were asked to support or refute a *quaestio* at commencement, and from 1658 to 1669, when candidates were few, some wrote poems on the *quaestiones* assigned them. All of these are in elegiac couplets,[3] and most are mediocre; some, however, exhibit a learned and playful wit uncommon in Puritan verse. Gershom Bulkeley's is a good example—it is a denial of the proposition that the will always follows the dictates of the practical understanding.

> Nullus Daemon erat qui non fuit ante δαήμων;
>   Nec sine peccato mentibus error inest.
> Impulit in vitium ergo imperiosa voluntas,
>   Quod bene mens dictat, Non, ait illa, Placet.
> Stat contra Ratio: Stat pro ratione Voluntas,
>   Noluntas potius nonne vocanda tibi?[4]

> No devil but was once devilishly smart;
>   not without sin do minds entertain error.
> It was, therefore, the imperious will that pressed toward vice;
>   and to the good advice the mind decrees, No, says will.
> Reason is opposed, but Will is in reason's place;
>   or shouldn't you rather be called Won't?

In the first line, δαήμων, *daêmôn*, means "knowing," "experienced," "clever"; it looks like (but is in fact unrelated to) Latin *Daemon*, "devil," and the similarity gives Bulkeley the opportunity for a false but beguiling *lusus etymologicus*.

Once past the *quaestio*-verse, we find several poems of uneven quality and great diversity, which, if they can be said to belong to any genre at all, must be assigned to the expansive and hospitable genres of epigram and occasional verse. I shall discuss them in roughly chronological order. Grim Richard Mather left a brief inscription, almost charming in its stiffness, in his son Samuel's Hebrew psalter.[5] Peter Bulkeley, the pastor of Concord, left epigrams on an illness, a birthday, and an earthquake. Bulkeley had a certain literary reputation; Cotton Mather, whose life of Bulkeley in the *Magnalia Christi Americana* is the source of the Latin poems we have, singles his subject out as having had "a competently good stroke at *Latin* poetry."[6] But the poems Mather transcribes are flat and repetitious; when Bulkeley gets hold of a conceit—as that his birthday, the *first* day of his life and of each of his years, is also the *last* day of May— he worries it to death. An agreeable contrast is the distichs exchanged in 1681 by Increase Mather and the surveyor John Foster, then on his death-bed. These allude adroitly to Foster's occupation, and are worth quoting:

> Mather:
> Astra colis vivens, moriens, super aethera Foster
> scande, precor; coelum metiri disce supremum.
> Foster:
> Metior, atque meum est: emit mihi dives Iesus:
> Nec teneor quicquam, nisi grates solvere. Vale.[7]

> Mather:
> Even while alive you cultivate the stars; now, Foster, climb in death above the skies; learn to survey the highest heaven.
> Foster:
> I survey it, and find it mine; rich-man Jesus bought it for me; nor am I held to anything but to give thanks. Goodbye.

I have supplied *Vale* ("Good-bye") where Foster's tombstone (the source of these lines) offers a blank, to fill up the meter of the hexameter.

The *Magnalia* also preserves Benjamin Tompson's brief Latin tribute to Mather, which is less good than his own free English version of it, and Nicholas Noyes's two eight-line anagrams on Mather's name, which are distinguished by the same dense arraying of conceits that unjustifiably provoked Moses Coit Taylor to refer to him as "the last, the most vigorous, and, therefore, the most disagreeable representative of the Fantastic school in literature."[8] Nehemiah Hobart, the pastor of Newton, wrote one of the few Latin broadsides, a rambling, pedantically learned exhortation to Judge Samuel Sewall about to ride off on the circuit for 1712. [9] Sewall himself left more Latin poems than any other Puritan, and on a greater variety of subjects—his stillborn son, the burning of the Quebec cross, Father Rasle, a local wedding—but most are brief and few are very interesting. [10] (It is striking that his free English versions of them are often superior—like Tompson, Sewall is a better ipso-translator than Latin poet.) Benjamin Colman, on the other hand, left only one Latin poem, but that one of great merit, an impeccably classical epitaph; and the graceful translation with which he accompanied it does not overshadow it. The Latin verses begin, "Laetum Rus genuit, Cultos Academia Mores, / Ingenuasque Artes dedit. . . ."

> The *farm-house* boasts his Birth with humble pride;
> Manners and arts the Liberal *Schools* provide:
> The *Seas* invade, and claim with angry strife
> His flying days, and toss his careful life:
> A *sore Disease* then called an hasty Death;
> We strove, but calmly he resignd his Breath.
> A neibouring Isle retains his dust: his Mind
> Washed in *Christs* blood, and by his grace refind,
> The *Heavens* embrace, with *soft* Endearments kind.
> Stay *Reader*, Bathe with tears this lonesome *Tomb*,
> A prosp'rous Course of Virtue learn, and hasten home. [11]

The Latin poems of John Wilson deserve separate notice. They include neatly paired epigrams on the Spanish Armada and the Gunpowder Plot, written while Wilson was still in England and furnished with Wilson's own translations—ipso-translating evidently being something of a Puritan habit—and three anagrams, on John Harvard, Thomas Shepard, and John Norton. The epigrams are the deft work of an English writer on English subjects; the anagrams are of more interest here. The three we have are ingenious, and their elaborations in the poems exhibit the virtues one might call rhetorical, the virtues of good prose: balance, shapeliness, economy. The anagram on Harvard[12] is set apart by Wilson's speaking in Harvard's *persona*—while pointedly alluding to Ovid's *Metamorphoses*. I give the first five of his eleven lines in Latin.

> Johannes Harvardus
> Anagram: Si non (ah!) surda aure.
> En, mihi fert animus, patroni nomine vestri
>   (*Si non, (ah!) surda* spernitur *aure*) loqui.
>   Sic ait. . . .

> John Harvard
> Anagram: If not (ah!) by a deaf ear.
> Look: I feel an urge to speak (*if not (ah!)*
>   spurned *by a deaf ear*) in the name of your patron.
> He speaks as follows. . .
> Me (though unworthy) the grace of Christ singled out
>   to found a pious dwelling for pious learning.
> Not that at my death I lacked a dear wife,
>   or that I had no other heir besides;
> but I was led to leave you my heirs,
>   as far as half my lot, by God himself.

Two of Wilson's lines artfully echo Ovid. One might note also the vivid touch of Harvard's indignantly denying that he willed his books to the college *faute de mieux*. But Wilson's virtues are still more evident in his anagram on Shepard:

> Thomas Shepardius
> Anagram: Paradisus hostem?
> Heu! *Paradisus* alit Sanctis infantibus *hostem*?
>   Quos Baptizari praecipit ipse Deus?
> Quos Deus ambabus, clemens, amplectitur ulnis,
>   Non sinet in gremio Tingier Ille suo?
> Annon pro Sanctis Ecclesia (mater) habebit,
>   Quos sancti Sanctos vox ait esse Dei?

> Thomas Shepard
> Anagram: Paradise an enemy?
> Alas! does *Paradise* nurture *an enemy* to those holy infants
>   whom God himself teaches should be baptized?
> Whom God mercifully embraces in his arms,
>   will he not permit them to be washed in his bosom?
> Shall the church (their mother) not hold them holy
>   who are called holy by the voice of holy God?

Here one should note the forceful repetitions of *quos*, dignified in handbooks of rhetoric by the name of anaphora; the symmetry of *ambabus amplectitur ulnis* ("embraces in his arms") and *gremio tingier suo* ("washes in his bosom"), two corresponding phrases made to correspond more closely by similarity in word order and metrical position; the fantasia of forms of *sanctus*, another device from the handbooks, called polyptoton; the leonine in the sixth line; the recurrently end-stopped lines; and the general air of order and neatness. Wilson is no visionary, but he is surely a craftsman.

It is probably no accident that the best Latin poems the Puritans wrote belong to the lofty and popular genre of the funeral elegy. In a century in which distinctions and conventions of genre are less obediently attended to, we forget how fruitful it may be, especially for minor poets, to write a poem according to rules. Obedience does not guarantee success, of course, and of the extant Latin elegies some, including the Indian prodigy Eleazar's on Thomas Thatcher and the fragment preserved of Peter Bulkeley's on John Cotton, are undistinguished; but the overall quality is high.

The first of those I would single out is also the earliest, Elijah Corlet's elegy for Thomas Hooker.[14] Following are the first eight lines in Latin and a full translation:

Si mea cum vestris valuissent vota, Nov–Angli,
　　Hookerus tardo viserat astra gradu.
Te, reverende senex, sic te dileximus omnes,
　　ipsa invisa forent ut tibi jura poli.
Morte tua infandum cogor renovare dolorem,
　　quippe tua videat terra Nov-Angla suam.
Dignus eras, aquilae similis, renovasse juventam
　　et fato in terris candidiore frui.

Had my prayers and yours prevailed, O New-Englanders,
　　Hooker would have gone to see the stars at a slower pace.
We loved you so, venerable old man,
　　that you would have found distasteful even the sentence of heaven.
By your death I am compelled to renew an unspeakable sorrow—
　　for by your death New England may see her own.
You were worthy to renew your youth as eagles do,
　　and to enjoy on earth a happier destiny.
Emmanuel College, eminent sister of Cambridge, mother
　　of a thousand prophets: you shall be a witness for me.
You also I summon, Chelmsford, who once were near
　　to heaven—for your preacher lifted you up.
This Chalcas could not bear, priest of Phoebus on the citadel;
　　he sees his rites spurned by the people,
and he saw the seer prophesy war to the people
　　from his pulpit; for it was a people wholly in rebellion for Christ.
This seer a fierce bishop exiled; a bitter fever, though a lesser enemy,
　　afflicts him among the Dutch.
Shaken after various dangers, God's branch-bearing dove
　　at last comes to you, New England.
There he adorns your assemblies and feeds the faithful,
　　and by countless praises given him wins praise for you.
He was a gentle friend, a notable pastor, and eminent
　　in mind, in eloquence, in virtue, in wit.

Shame, that we are alive to see him taken! and did not
     lay snares for his departing soul—
snares of ceaseless prayers and tears, by which
     the heavenly road might have been blocked.
But in vain do I muse so—
for sixty years Hooker was a wayfarer;
     now he comes into possession of his celestial homeland.

Corlet's first line echoes Ovid *Metamorphoses* XIII 128: "si mea cum vestris valuissent vota, Pelasgi," and his fifth line echoes Vergil, *Aeneid* II 3: "infandum, regina, iubes, renovare dolorem." His reference to Chalchas (actually Calchas) recalls Homer's *Iliad*. By his allusions to Homer, Vergil, and Ovid, Corlet plays variations on the theme of Hooker as Aeneas. Another of his themes is that Hooker's death might have been averted had New England's tears and prayers for him been more fervent. The two themes together make for an intricately contrapuntal organization. The formal conventions of the funeral elegy require only an initial lament, a recapitulation of the subject's life, and a final exhortation; sometimes elegies ramble, or seem mechanically assembled. But Corlet has interwoven, with this given and general order, principles of organization specific to this elegy, and thereby animated and disciplined its form. He has also skillfully exploited that combination of biblical and classical allusion which is one of the principal resources and pleasures of Christian Latin verse. Lines 19–20 offer good example. The first three words evoke Vergil's Aeneas; the remainder, the biblical account of the flood. The associations interanimate one another; the mind's eye is directed not only to Hooker, like Aeneas making his long, troubled voyage to bring his gods to new soil, but also and simultaneously to the colonists, awaiting, like Noah, God's promise of peace to the sole repository of virtue in all the wicked world. The condensation of the two notions in the single image endows them with great intensity.

Corlet's other elegy, on John Hull, is distinguished by equally organic coherence and also by one moving passage on Hull the merchant, patron to Corlet the poor scholar:

> . . . cum mihi per quasi ter duo lustra fuisset
> dulcis amicus et hinc rerum tutela mearum,
> quique bonos alios mihi conciliavit amicos;
> vestibus et nummis animum relevavit egentis,
> sic cymbam prohibens tenuem mihi mergier undis.
>
> . . . since for twenty-four years he was
> my dear friend and also the guardian of my affairs,
> and found me other good friends;
> when I was in need he cheered me with money and clothing,
> keeping my skiff from sinking in the water.

Charles Chauncy's brief joint elegy for Hooker and John Winthrop, who died within two years of one another, is remarkable for its typological richness— Moses, Aaron, Joshua, Zarubbabel, Naomi, Pandora, the Lernaean Hydra, and the Trojan Horse are all incorporated into its twelve lines— and for the haunting resonance of its first couplet and the grave punning of its last, which is reproduced in the translation.

> Heu, me nunc caecam quis ducet filius, orbam
>   luminibus binis quae mihi nuper erant?
> . . . .
> Vere independens iam nunc Neo-Anglia dicor:
>   non est spes terris pendeat unde mea.

> Alas, what son will lead me now,
>   who am blind, bereft of my two eyes?
> . . . .
> Truly now I, New England, may be called independent;
>   there is no one on earth on whom my hope might depend.

The most interesting of the remaining elegies is that of William Adams for his mentor Urian Oakes, president of Harvard. It is distinguished not only by the same rich combination of Christian and classical tradition that marks Corlet's work but also by the singularly witty intimacy of the poet's tribute to his subject. Here are ten lines in Latin and a full translation.

Tristia narrantur, miris ferit ictibus aures
mors inopina meas, totos pavor occupat artus,
attonitum reddens animum. Sed nonne fefellit
vox aures? Aures animum? Num dicere vera
fama potest? Heu, vera potest ac dira profari!
Mortuus est Praeses; tremor ima per ossa cucurrit.
Proh Cantabrigiae, proh musis lethifer annus!

. . . .
Heu quam vanus homo! Memor esto tu brevis aevi:
pallida prae foribus Mors est. Resipisce repente,
vive hodie, ne sera nimis sit crastina vita.

Sad news is told; a sudden death strikes my ears
with strange blows, and fear possesses all my limbs,
stunning my mind. But surely the word deceived
the ears, the ears the mind? Surely rumor cannot
speak truth? Alas, it does speak truth, and dire truth!
The President is dead; a trembling runs through the marrow of my bones.
Woe for Cambridge, woe for a year deadly to learning!

Your buildings, Harvard, grow dark with mourning;
The voice of the hall, lifeless, whispers lamentation,
and the tongue of the bell; the wall answers lamenting.
Who can suppress tears? Whose eyes are dry?
Let us weep for the burning anger of injured divinity.
What poem, honored Oakes, can properly adorn
your tomb? Who of us shall be able
to compose a song worthy of the dead President?
Lowly songs obscure lofty praises;
I confess this enterprise surpasses my powers—
it is a hard task, fit for angels' pens.
I cannot pay due tribute to this learned Rector;
but in great matters the desiring shall be enough.
The noble body is to be received by a marble tomb,
the noble names are to be inscribed on marble tablets,
names given by happy omen, not by change:
Urian properly means Uranius, herald of heaven;
powerful in his heavenly speech, this herald raised
tempests in the heart of sinners, as if another water by Orion;
for him shone Urim and blessed Urijah, and
the wondrous teacher was radiant with burning light.
He was like an oak in strength, of solid firmness,
conquering by his robust prayers both men and God.
And many men, under this oak's sheltering branches,
took pleasure, reclining, to pluck the fruits
it bore in abundance, dropping honeyed dews.
Now it lies shattered, struck down by the divine axe;
now the trunk with the spreading branches, the fruits and the leaves
are gone. For man—this is all you need say—
the whole story is "he was born and he died."
How vain and empty man is! Remember your life is short;
pale death is at the door. Come to your senses quickly.
Live today, lest tomorrow's life be too late.

Early lines echo Ovid; later come allusions to Vergil and Exodus. The elegy's last lines are a farrago of allusions to Horace and Martial. The note of Roman epicureanism they evoke is rare in the Puritan elegy, which is seldom a confrontation with inscrutable death.[15] Rather the life of the subject is an *exemplum* to the reader or his death a warning to the community. Adams does touch on these themes in passing, but his exhortation is derived not from the particulars of Oakes's life or death but from the common mortality of human kind. On the other hand, the Roman themes are altered by their Puritan context, which sets resonating in them a spiritual overtone they do not originally possess. In *vive,* "be alive," one hears "live *in Christ*;" from *resipisce*, "come to your senses," one gets not only an echo of Martial, the Roman epicurean philosopher, but also—if one knows the Vulgate, as Adams and his readers surely would have—those who recover themselves (*resipiscant*) from the snares of the devil (2 Timothy 2:26).

I referred above to the "intimacy" of Adams's tribute; what I meant was that Adams's elegy for Oakes was also an imitation of him. Note midway through the elegy the etymological fantasia of puns on Oakes's two names. "Urian" yields its Latin form Uranius ("Heavenly messenger," as Adams explains), Orion, Urim, and Urijah, and Adams finds or makes each name appropriate to Oakes the man. "Oakes," on the other hand, gives only "oak" and thus *quercus*, the Latin word for that tree; but this association permits allusion to a line in Vergil's *Eclogues* (IV:30) in which *quercus* is made much of:

> Et durae quercus sudabunt roscida mella.
> And harsh *oaks* shall exude honeyed dews.

The point is first that such macaronic wit is in Oakes's own manner; Adams has adopted Oakes's style to praise his name. But the imitation is the more precise in that Oakes himself, in his Harvard oration of 1675, had made equally punning use of the same Vergilian passage Adams alludes to here.[16] The deftness of the poet's wit heightens, rather than detracts from, the bereaved student's lamentation for his dead master. Then too, Oakes's elegy for Thomas Shepard is often said to be the best of the Puritan funeral elegies in English: Adams's masterful elegy is an offering to a masterful elegist.

In their wit, their craftsmanship, and their learning, such poems as these seem at first sight evidence for a vision of Puritan literary culture like that offered by Samuel Eliot Morison: "The humanist tradition, one of the noblest inheritances of the English race, went hand in hand with conquering Puritanism into the clearings of the New England wilderness."[17] Morisons's scrupulous research established that Puritans owned and read a great variety of Greek and Roman texts. The poems I have cited establish that Puritans wrote skillful and witty Latin verse stuffed with classical allusions. But they do not establish the *place* of Latin verse in Puritan literary culture, only its presence; nor did Morison's work establish the *relationship* between the humanist tradition and conquering Puritanism, only their coexistence. To discuss the implications of these poems for that relationship, it is necessary to step back, to look not at their individual virtues and vices but at the patterns they make as a collection.

To begin with, the collection is astonishingly small. The bibliography in Harold Jantz's *The First Century of New England Verse* yields about one hundred poems—if, that is, one counts examples of that odd, amphibious form the prose epitaph,[18] poems written in New England by writers who were not Puritans, and poems only partly Latin and mostly English. Leo Kaiser's researches will no doubt add to this number, but he has suggested that they will not add much[19]— no more than a strict definition would take away. Say one hundred poems, then, written between 1620 and 1720: one poem per year. For the same period in England, Leicester Bradner's *Musae Anglicanae*, the standard account of British Latin verse, lists four hundred *publications*.[20] John Milton wrote more lines of Latin verse than all the Puritans of New England in a century. These comparisons do not of course suggest that the Puritans were deficient in energy or inspiration; they do, however, suggest that the writing of Latin verse for the Puritans and the writing of Latin verse for the learned of England and Scotland were activities of a different nature.

Certain traits of the Latin verse the Puritans did write clearly corroborate that suggestion. The Puritans do not write in the lyric meters, but only in elegiac couplets and dactylic hexameters;[21] the humanists were metrical virtuosi, and took pride in their skill as distinguishing them from what they saw as the ignorance of the middle ages, when couplets and hexameters were the only quantitative meters made use of. The Puritans are tolerant of rhyme, which the humanists (and Milton), associating it with medieval accentual meters, regarded as barbarous. The humanists entrust Latin verse with private thoughts; the notable genres of the Puritans' Latin verse are public, and the poems themselves reveal no secrets.[22]

But what is one to make of the Puritans' learned allusiveness? Is not that at least is a humanistic trait, indeed a centrally humanistic trait? The answer to these questions is that one must distinguish between *allusion* and *imitation*; the Puritans share with humanists an enviable familiarity with Greek and Roman literature, but their relation to that literature is different in nature. When humanist writers of Latin verse read the classics, they seize on and imitate everything: phrases, genres, meters, *topoi*, particular scenes and poems, and the styles of individual authors. They write odes in imitation of Horace, eclogues and epics in imitation of Vergil, epigrams in imitation of Martial—indeed they retain these genres even when markedly varying their topics, and produce eclogues on religious subjects and epics on the birth of Christ. They form allegiances and choose sides and find affinities among the Roman poets. One poet is called the Christian Horace, another the Christian Vergil, another the Catullus of the 16th century.[23] It is possible to identify an Ovidian phase in Milton's Latin poetry, and possible to specify where it ends.[24] Nothing in the history of Puritan Latin verse corresponds to any of this. What the Puritans take from Roman literature is phrases. Adams has no particular allegiance to Ovid, and he takes from him neither the genres of epic and love-elegy, nor any of the *topoi* of myth or erotic technique, nor Ovid's habit of compressed and ironic argument, nor the structure of any scene in any of Ovid's poems. What he does take (lines 9–10) is a memorable phrase describing universal lamentation. Ovid is for Adams a source of ornament; and the Puritans generally adorn their verse with classical tags as we adorn our essays with bits of Shakespeare, without any thought of doing either servile or creative homage to Elizabethan drama or the imabic pentameter. In a word: the classics are for the humanists an influence, for the Puritans a resource.[25]

Enough has been said, I think, to establish that the writing of Latin verse was not for the Puritans the same sort of activity it was for the humanists, and to suggest that here, at least, the humanist tradition is distinctly peripheral to conquering Puritanism. It remains to see what sort of activity the Puritans' writing of Latin verse *was*; and the first step in doing that is to consider the most elusive trait of that verse, which is the curious passivity, the inertness, of its Latinity. If on the one hand nothing the Puritans wrote could, as some of Milton's elegies could, be mistaken for the work of a Roman poet, it is on the other hand equally and paradoxically true that little of their Latin verse—little, at any rate, in its Latinity—bears the stamp of early New England. Neologisms are rare, and the vocabulary is small and familiar. Such discussions of local issues and scenes as would necessarily stretch the resources of classical Latin are also rare. With some exceptions (for example, Adams ll. 36–7), the verse is oddly lucid—not, I think, as the result of complex and individual thoughts' having been brought into order, but rather from general and typical thoughts' having been expressed in the familiar words readily available for them. It is exaggerated, but it is perhaps helpful, to say that reading the *corpus* of Puritan Latin verse gives the impression of watching children putting together puzzles made by adults.

Now what is interesting about this trait is not that it once again differentiates the Puritans' Latin verse from that of their humanist contemporaries and pred-ecessors—though it does that—[26]but rather that it so strikingly differentiates the Puritans' Latin verse from the whole of their literature in English. The resources of English Puritan writers tax to the limit. Nathaniel Ward and Edward Taylor seem to have plundered dictionaries. The ceaseless, sinuous, anxious motion of Cotton Mather's prose, the elliptic brevity of Samuel Sewall's, the sensuous abstraction of Jonathan Edward's: these are distinctive and individual shapings of the common language. The curious inertness of its Latin verse is thus no symptom of lethargy in the general New England mind; rather the fact that the Puritans' Latin verse is not the vehicle of the literary energies they possessed suggests that it is not by comparing it with other bodies of literature that it is to be understood.

I shall state my conclusion first and defend it afterwards. What Puritan Latin verse should be compared with is trade-jargon, thieves' argot, and the sacred languages of priests. The anthropologist Arnold Van Gennep's term for the genre to which all these belong is *langues spéciales*; and their common function, he argues, is to assert the coherence of a restricted society within the larger society of which it is a part:

> . . . les langues spéciales ont une raison d'être biologique: elles ne sont
> que l'un des innombrables moyens par lesquels les collectivités de tout

ordre maintiennent leur existence et résistent aux pressions de l'extérieur. Elles sont à la fois un moyen de cohésion pour ceux qui les emploient, et un moyen de défense contre l'étranger. . . .[27]

The first justification of this hypothesis is that it is consistent with the principal oddities already noticed: the small quantity of Latin verse and the inertness of its Latinity. Restricted societies might be expected to yield small quantities of what is in any case a private product. Nor would one expect literary energy to be directed towards what is only superficially and intermittently a literary activity. The more striking justification, however, is that on the basis of this hypothesis one can gather together certain apparently fortuitous traits of this body of verse— indeed the hypothesis enables one to discern them—and perceive them as constituting a harmonious ensemble directed towards a common goal. For example, little Latin verse appears in almanacs or newspapers, little more in broadsides.[28] These are of course the sorts of printed matter read by almost everyone, and thus not the right vehicles for a restricted society's assertion of its coherence. Again, we have already noted that Latin verses often turn up scattered in predominantly English poems; we might now add to the category of these hybrids such common phenomena as Latin anagrams followed by English explanations, Latin epigraphs and *envois*, Latin titles for English poems, Latin poems of diminutive size, and we might now see that if Latin verse is principally a means of asserting coherence, only an assertion is needed— a Latin title is as adequate as the Mason word. We might even make sense of the fact that so many of these Latin scraps occur in the charged, numinous areas of beginnings and endings by recalling the connection of *langues spéciales* with the domain of the sacred.[29]

Two objections may be made, which being answered will become further justifications. The first is that humanist Latin is clearly not a *langue speciale* but a *langue universelle*. This is true, and the theoretical result of writing in Latin is of course an exchange of one's immediate community for the whole learned world. One's ignorant neighbors are shut out, but scholars ignorant of English are embraced. Now in some few cases, it is possible to conceive of Puritan writers of Latin verse as aiming at a European audience, for example, Leonard Hoar in his poem in the Harvard Catalogue for 1674.[30] But in most cases it is not. Poems nine-tenths English and one-tenth Latin, Latin poems in English books, poems left in manuscript: these are not beacons to Europe from the city on a hill. Most Latin poems written by Puritans fall into these categories, and *no* Latin poem appears in a book of Latin poetry. Is it not plausible to suspect that their intended audience is not the larger community but the smaller, not the learned world but the learned world of New England?

The second objection might arise from noting that Puritan Latin verse is chiefly public discourse and contains no secrets. Are *langues spéciales* not above all instruments by which secrets may be transmitted? This objection construes the notion of *langue spéciale* too narrowly. Thieves' argot is meant to keep crimes secret from policemen; but the general function of these languages is to exclude strangers not from the secrets but from the whole life of the restricted society, and their range of subject matter need not be limited to the clandestine. As Van Gennep remarks, ". . . la langue spéciale joue à l'intérieur de la société générale le rôle que chaque langue générale joue vis-à-vis des autres langues générales. C'est l'un des formes de différentiation, formes voulues, et nécessaires à la vie même en société."[31]

All investigations are interminable, and every useful hypothesis raises questions in offering explanations. The most important of the questions raised by the present hypothesis concern the collective portrait of the Puritan Latin poets. What traits, that is, have they in common besides Latinity? What is the nature of the group they compose and assert? Are they, say, Antinomians or Arians, conservatives or liberals, ministers or merchants, Puritans or Yankees? These questions are important because an investigation of them would lead to a better understanding of the numerous and complexly intersecting limiting societies in professedly homogeneous New England. Such an investigation cannot be undertaken here, though I will permit myself to notice the suggestive abundance of Latin verse in the preface to that great tribute to the New England Way constituted by Cotton Mather's *Magnalia*. Rather I should conclude by stressing that the study of Puritan Latin verse does lead precisely to questions about its composers. The writing of Latin verse in the seventeenth century is a singularly artificial task; but even the apparently most detached and cloistered activities, the apparently purest and most self-contained literary exercises, express and fulfill the needs of human beings living in human communities.[32]

NOTES

1. Jantz, *First Century*; Kaiser, "Thirteen Early American Latin Elegies: A Critical Edition," *Humanistica Lovaniensia* 23 (1974), 346–81. See both Jantz and Kaiser for bibliographical information supplementary to that given in the notes.

2. See on the *quaestio* Samuel Eliot Morison, *Harvard College in the Seventeenth Century* (Cambridge, Mass.: Harvard University Press, 1936), I, 160–64.

3. A good handbook for those unfamiliar with the technical terms of classical prosody is the *Princeton Encyclopedia of Poetry and Poetics*.

4. Quoted in Morison, *Harvard*, II, 595. Morison quotes all the extant *quaestio*-verses.

5. Printed in *The Historical Magazine* 4 (1860), 148.

6. *Magnalia*, I, 364. Quotes from the *Magnalia* are taken from the first American edition (Hartford: Roberts and Burr, 1820).

7. Sibley's *Harvard Graduates*, II, 228.

8. Tyler, *History*, p. 87.

9. "Martii 27.1712"; printed as a broadside, but more accessible as reprinted in Samuel Sewall's *Letter-Book MHS Collections* 51–52 (6th Series 1–2), I 315.

10. Sewall, *Diary*, May 18, 1696 (on his son); November 25, 1705 (on the Quebec cross); *Letter-Book* II, 174 (on Father Rasle), II, 178 (on a wedding).

11. Colman. Papers I (at MHS; the poem is in an autograph manuscript).

12. *Magnalia*, II, 27–28.

13. Murdock, *Paul*, p. 84.

14. Kaiser, "Thirteen Elegies," pp. 352, 358–60. All subsequent quotations from Puritan elegy are drawn from Kaiser's article also; his editions are the best we have.

15. Astrid Schmidt-von-Mühlenfels, *Die "Funeral Elegy" Neuenglands*, Beihefte zum Jahrbuch für Amerikastudien 37 (Heidelberg: Carl Winter Universitätsverlag, 1973), p. 92: "[die Elegie] konfrontiert nicht mit der Unerforschlichkeit des Todes." This book is a good example of scholarly indifference to the Puritans' Latin verse; the author is otherwise remarkably thorough, but does not mention a single Latin poem.

16. As Kaiser notes, "Thirteen Elegies," p. 363.

17. Morison, *Life*, p. 55.

18. On this form see John Sparrow's intriguing *Visible Words* (Cambridge: at the University Press, 1969), especially chapter 3, "The Inscription as a Literary Form," pp. 101–35. See also Jantz's article in this collection (chapter 18, above).

19. This assurance came in a private conversation.

20. Bradner, *Musae Anglicanae*, The Modern Language Association of America General Series 10 (New York: The Modern Language Association of America, 1940), pp. 348–64.

21. The one exception is Thomas Bailey's verses (manuscript at the MHS), which refine the rule. They include Sapphics and Asclepiads; but they are distinctly *juvenilia*.

22. My account of the norms of humanist verse here follows Bradner, *Musae Anglicanae*, pp. 10–18.

23. Casimir Sarbiewski is the Christian Horace, Mantuan the Christian Vergil, Giovanni Cotta the sixteenth-century Catullus.

24. See D.P. Harding, *Milton and the Renaissance Ovid*, Illinois Studies in Language and Literature 30:4 (Urbana: Univ. of Illinois Press, 1946).

25. The one exception is a preoccupation with the *Aeneid*. But even here the Puritans are preoccupied not with the poet but with the myth he tells, because in it they see an analogue of their own experience.

26. See Leo Spitzer's immensely insightful "The Problem of Renaissance Latin Poetry," in his *Romanische Literaturstudien* (Tübingen: Max Niemeyer Verlag, 1959), pp. 923–46.

27. Van Gennep, "Essai d'une théorie des langues spéciales," *Revue des études ethnographiques et sociologues*, I (1908), 337.

28. Samuel Sewall is an exception here; he published his poems in newspapers and had them printed as broadsides. In this respect, and in the great diversity and abundance of his compositions (a good many on private subjects), Sewall does seem to be behaving like a humanist. This is consonant with other traits of what one might call Sewall's cultural profile; see the chapter on Sewall in my "Three Early American Diarists" (Ph.D dissertation, Columbia University, 1979).

29. Van Gennep, "Essai," pp. 331–32.

30. Quoted in Morison, *Harvard*, II, 413. To some extent, Latin *prose* was for the Puritans a *langue universelle*; but we do not yet have enough information to see the *range*

of functions Latin prose fulfilled, nor to see which functions were principal, which subordinate.

31. Van Gennep, "Essai," p. 337.

32. My warm thanks to Leo Kaiser. His published contributions to the study of Puritan Latin verse would in any case have put me in his debt; but he also took time to talk with me as I was beginning this study, gave me much valuable information and advice, and graciously provided me with offprints of two of his articles. I think it is fair to say that this essay could not have been written without him.

22 MEDITATIVE POETRY IN NEW ENGLAND

URSULA BRUMM

Although the flourishing of religious meditation in the seventeenth century has long been recognized, the distinctive influence of Protestant meditative thought in England and America has been underestimated in much modern scholarship. This relative neglect has stemmed partly from the influential work of Louis L. Martz,[1] who first proposed in 1954 that Protestant meditative thought and poetry had been largely derivative of Catholic meditative theory before Richard Baxter in his *Saints Everlasting Rest* (1650)[2] established a Protestant theory of meditation. Martz's thesis was that the major metaphysical poets were rather faithfully obeying the rules laid down by Catholic writers about the meaning and aims of meditational exercise; their stipulations about the three stages of memory, understanding, and will; and their even more precise instructions by which the sufferings of Christ were to be relived by the believer: composition of place, the vivid recreation of the events of the Passion before the meditator's eye, and the transference of these events to the believer's heart.

In recent years Martz's assumptions have been challenged by scholars who have pointed out that an independent Protestant tradition of meditation goes back to the beginning of the seventeenth century. This tradition found its first widely read and influential representatives in Joseph Hall's *The Art of Divine Meditation* (1607)[3] and Richard Rogers' *Seaven Treatises* (1603)[4] and was continued by Richard Sibbes, Isaac Ambrose, James Ussher, Richard Baxter, Thomas Hooker, Edmund Calamy, and many others. Rogers explicitly took up the Catholic challenge and gave a detailed summary and critique of the "Papist" authors, especially Parsons and the *Christian Directory*, as an introduction to his own directions on meditation:

> To goe forward therefore, seeing this was one cause why I tooke this worke in hand, because the Iesuites cast in our teeth the want of such bookes, as may direct a Christian aright through his whole course towards the kingdome of heaven, . . . to frame out of the word of God by that little helpe of my knowledge and experience, such a direction for Christians, . . . that hath not onely beene shaped after the rules of the Scripture, but also such as hath beene and is practiced and followed so farre forth, as of sinfull flesh may be looked for, both of minister and people, and

approved of those who have excelled, and gone before many, in both (Third Treatise, "Preface to the Reader").

Not surprisingly, the reader's attention is directed from the Passion of Christ to the word of God and the rules of the Scripture. Rogers focuses on the achievement of redemption, on the gift of grace, and on salvation, rather than on the story of Christ's suffering.[5]

Among the scholars who have challenged Martz's thesis is U. Milo Kaufmann, who sees the Puritan orientation toward *logos* as the main departure from the Catholic tradition.[6] Barbara Kiefer Lewalski contradicts Martz's theory by tracing an independent Protestant tradition of meditation in England. She also challenges Kaufmann's view that Calvinist emphasis on doctrine and *logos* cancelled poetic imagination and insists that Protestant meditation engaged the mind deeply in the effort to search out the motives and motions of the psyche. It thus "contributed to the creation of poetry having a new depth of psychological insight and a new focus upon the symbolic significance of the human individual." She defines three characteristics of Protestant meditation: near identification of sermon and med- itation in method and purpose; insistence upon detailed and forceful "application to the self"; attention to a large number of doctrinal or religious topics, instead of the Passion of Christ, also to occasions of the natural world and events of daily life.[7]

Even earlier Norman Grabo, in "The Art of Puritan Devotion," observed that, long before Baxter, Protestant writers and also American Puritans were concerned with meditative theory and added their own ideas and experience to it. The American Puritans, Grabo maintains, made a considerable contribution to a substantial literature treating the affective side of human experience much more positively than our usual generalizations about Puritans might lead us to expect:

> The art of Puritan devotion was basically a method for channeling emotion into verbal structures—a poetic method—and until the literature that embodies that art is defined and examined precisely and imaginatively, not only our intellectual history, but our literary history as well will remain incomplete.[8]

It would have been an anomaly if during a time of fervent Protestant thought and debate, as was the first half of the seventeenth century, no attention had been given to the idea and practice of meditation. Meditation was indeed much discussed, and as a customary part of man's religious duties, was brought over from England by the first immigrants. From the beginning, there was no doubt among the American Puritans that the efforts and aims of meditative discipline were especially suited to their religious convictions. In a general sense, all Puritan religious works and writings can be said to be the fruits of serious and deliberate thought and contemplation: sermons, prayers, funeral elegies, and religious poetry are the result of meditative endeavour. When in 1666 Samuel Whiting, in Cambridge, Massachusetts, published a volume of sermons under the title *Abraham's Humble Intercession for Sodom, and the Lord's Gracious Concessions in Answer thereunto*—"wherein," as Cotton Mather explains, "he does raise, confirm, and apply *thirty-two* doctrines"—Whiting specified his volume as "Containing sundry Meditations upon Gen. XVIII from VER. XXIII to the end of the Chapter" and in a preface enumerated the purposes of meditations according to Protestant theory. In his biography of Whiting, Mather comments on the benefits of this activity:

> And if meditation (which was one of *Luther's* great things to make a divine) be a thing of no little consequence to make a *Christian*, this must be numbered among the exercises whereby our *Whiting* became very much improved in *christianity*. *Meditation* (which is *Mentis-Dilatio*) daily enriched his mind with the dispositions of Heaven; and having a *walk* for that purpose in his orchard, some of his flock that saw him constantly taking his *turns* in that *walk*, with hand, and eye, and soul, often directed heavenward, would say, *There does our dear pastor walk with God every day*. [p. 458]

By this charming peripatetic scene—the philosophical allusion is doubtlessly intended—Mather skillfully illustrates one of the numerous definitions which Protestant ingenuity had invented for meditation. Like his father, Increase, Cotton Mather published some of his own works as "Meditations," for instance, "Christianus per Ignem. Or, a Disciple WARMING of himself and OWNING of his Lord: With Devout *and* Useful MEDITATIONS, Fetch'd out of the FIRE by a Christian in a *Cold Season*, Sitting before it. A Work Though *never out of Season*, yet more Particularly, designed for the Seasonable and Profitable Entertainment, of them that would well Employ their Leisure by the Fire-Side . . ." (Boston, 1702). The witty title is characteristic of a later Puritan period; it is meant to attract readers who by being entertained and amused will accept advice for recommendable conduct. By using traditional meditation imagery in a facetious mood Mather's friend Nicholas Noyes, pastor at Salem, in a "Praefatory Poem" has given the appropriate valuation of this kind of meditation:

> There is a *Stone* (as I am told)
> That turns *all Metals* into *Gold*
> But I believe, that there is none,
> Save pious *Meditation*. [in Meserole, *Poetry*]

Noyes goes on to explain how all the fireplace paraphernalia and "The *flame*, the *sparks, light, heat,* and *motion,* / Are *Metamorphosed* to *Devotion.*"

In spite of the whimsicality which adorns this popularized form of meditation, a forerunner of the 18th century didactic essay,[9] Cotton Mather was, of course, well aware that meditation was a serious effort of the mind. In writing the biographies of the "eminent divines" who emigrated to the New World, Mather again and again discussed the role of meditation in their lives. In many cases, they had left diaries, journals, or autobiographical reports which confirm their reliance on meditation. About Charles Chauncy, Mather reports: "He was also very much in *meditation,* and in that one important kind and part of it *self-examination;* especially in his preparations for the *Lord's table.* From his *diary* we have recovered a little relating thereunto; and for a *specimen,* the reader shall here have a few of his notes, which he entitled, SELF-TRIALS BEFORE THE SACRAMENT" (p. 424).

As an exercise of self-examination in preparation for the Lord's Supper, an effort to purify oneself from sin and to search for evidences of regeneration, meditation assumes its specifically Puritan significance. It is therefore on this kind of meditative advice that we focus our attention not on meditations as such (texts which are the fruit of meditation), but on books or sermons on the art of meditation. They are Puritan also in the sense that they expect the same high degree of mental effort from all believers, pastors as well as flock, since as regenerate members of the covenant they all have to fulfill the same requirements in order to be worthy participants in the Sacrament of the Lord's Supper.

In his autobiography Thomas Shepard describes the daily meditations he practiced when he experienced his conversion while still at Emmanuel College at Cambridge, England:

> I did therefore set more constantly (viz., 1624, May 3) upon the work of daily meditation, sometimes every morning but constantly every evening before supper, and my chief meditation was about the evil of sin, the terror of God's wrath, day of death, beauty of Christ, the deceitfulness of the heart, etc., but principally I found this my misery: sin was not my greatest evil, did lie light upon me as yet, yet I was much afraid of death and the flames of God's wrath. And this I remember: I never went out to meditate in the fields but I did find the Lord teaching me somewhat of myself or himself or the vanity of the world I never saw before.[10]

"And Isaac went out to the fields to meditate at even tide," Gen. 24,63, to which Shepard refers, is the major biblical authentication of meditation. The detailed discussion of his difficulties and doubts amounts to an example of applied meditation theory.

To explain minutely to his flock the role of meditation within the soul's process toward redemption was the life-long concern of Shepard's father-in-law Thomas Hooker, an effort which was preserved for posterity when, after Hooker's death, notes of his sermons were published in London under the title *The Application of Redemption, By the effectual Work of the Word and Spirit of Christ, for The bringing home of lost Sinners to God, The Ninth and Tenth Books.*[11] Hooker, who had made a reputation for his skill in treating troubled souls and wounded spirits,[12] based his conception on a searching analysis of the soul, or inner self of man, which he understood according to seventeenth-century psychology as the interrelation of understanding, will, and affection, and within this system as a complex communication between the head and the heart.[13]

In that crucial issue of acquiring grace, Hooker, as an orthodox Puritan, steered clear of the heresy of Arminianism; he took, however, the somewhat voluntarist position which insisted on the necessity of "preparing the heart" for Christ. It is within these duties that meditation is assigned its important role. Meditation is considered the means to bring about the contrition of the heart because of sin. Hooker's early work, *The Soules Preparation for Christ, or, A Treatise of Contrition,*[14] "wherein is disclosed How God breaks the Heart and wounds the Soule, in the conversion of a Sinner to Himself" contains the main insights which Hooker later developed and enlarged in the "Tenth Book" of the *Application of Redemption.* "To break the heart" (a reference to Psalm 51, 17) is Hooker's favorite image. It illustrates the doctrine "that serious meditation of our sins by the word of God is a special means to break our hearts for our sinnes." The breaking of the heart is the result of a meditative activity which starts in the mind and carries over to the heart: "Meditation is a serious intention of the mind whereby wee come to search out the truth and settle it effectually upon the heart." This is the decisive step toward salvation: "When the heart is fitted and prepared, the Lord Christ comes immediately into it."[15]

In order to explain this process, and indeed impress his audience with its imperative claim, Hooker has illustrated it with a great number of ingenious images and likenesses, which are partly, it seems, of his own invention, partly taken from the store of meditation discussion. We find in Hooker, for example, the peripatetic comparison which we encountered in Mather's Whiting biography: "I use to compare meditation to perambulation, when men goe the bounds of the parish, they go over every part of it, and see how farre it goes; so meditation is the perambulation of the soule; when the soul looks how far sin goeth and considers the punishment of it, and the plagues that are threatened against it, and the violence in it." The labor of self-examination and the searching out of sin by the meditative effort is dramatized effectively by Hooker as like "a searcher at a sea-port, or Custom House," who unlocks every chest, rummages every corner and takes a light to discover the darkest passages: "So it is with Meditation, it observes the woof and web of wickedness, the full frame of it, ... Meditation goes upon discovery, touches at every coast, observes every creek, maps out the dayly course of mans conversation and disposition."[16]

To illustrate the process of purification and transformation effected by meditation a number of medical images are used: ". . . Meditation is the Medicine, it hath a *Probatum est* upon it, approved by all the Saints and the Cure left upon Record." Also:

> Meditation is this Spiritual Chymistry, or the art of holy Distillation, which draws out the spirits of the poyson and bitterness that is in corruption, Spirituallizeth the plague and venom of the vengeance that attends every transgression; and though it was never so small in the eyes of the world, yet it stings the heart more than the greatest evil which is committed, if not mused on, nor attended.

Hooker is particularly fond of the image of the rack: meditation "holds the heart upon the rack under restless and unsupportable pressures. 2 Pet 2.8." Also: "How we came to grapple with the heart by Meditation we heard before; and because this task is wearisome in itself, and tedious to our corrupt Nature, to be ever raking in the Wound, sets mans heart upon the rack, . . ." Like other meditation theorists, Hooker uses the typological image of the "chewing of the cud" for meditation. All this leads to this end:

> When Meditation hath thus taken hold of the heart, it then drags it to the Throne of Justice, and then drives it to seek out for payment and satisfaction, without which it cannot be eased or delivered. This is the Markstone, within which the bounds and limits of Meditation are to be confined that it may be ordered and acted aright, according to the Method of the Almighty, and a right Rule.[17]

Hooker's "*preaching* was notably set off with a *liveliness* extraordinary," reports Cotton Mather in his biography of Hooker.[18] His power over language, his capacity to explain the secret working of the soul and heart, established his reputation as one of New England's eminent clergymen. His preaching on the process of redemption and on the role of meditation within it stimulated the art and activities of meditation in New England, as is demonstrated by the adoption of his images by later practitioners of meditation.

Zealous Puritans throughout and beyond the seventeenth century practiced meditation in preparation or confirmation of conversion. Yet with some third-generation Puritans like Mather and Noyes, meditation as a term and also as an exercise loses some of its urge and seriousness. Toward the end of the century, the term is not only used in the broad sense of contemplation, but may also refer to didactic or even to "entertaining" considerations. In 1690, Cotton Mather published *Compassion for Communicants. Discourses Upon the Nature, the Design, and the Subject of the Lord's Supper with Devout Methods for, and Approaching to that Blessed Ordinance.*[19] This book, which became very popular, explains the Puritan conception of the Lord's Supper and encourages participation. In a final section, Mather gives advice for "preparation" and formulates questions for self-examination, yet although he uses some of Hooker's images, such as the broken heart, he does not conceive of self-examination as a process of meditation; the term does not appear in his advice. While this omission does not spell the end of serious meditation, it is an indication of its fading significance.[20]

In view of Hooker's powerful, and indeed poetic, meditations on the role of meditation, one is curious to see what kind of meditative poetry was written in New England. The answer is that while most Puritan poetry is contemplative, only a few poets wrote verse that is meditative in the sense of being meant to prepare the heart for the experience of conversion and for the renewal of grace in the Sacrament of the Lord's Supper. Anne Bradstreet wrote serious contemplative poetry on the fate of man in nature, in history, and in New England; she also meditated on "The Vanity of all Worldly Things," or on the antagonism of "The Flesh and the Spirit," and thus on man's ultimate religious fate. She did not, however, use meditation in the preparatory function described by Hooker and other Protestant meditation theorists.

It comes as a surprise to see that among the immigrant generation it is Edward Johnson who tries his hand at this difficult form. In Book III, chapter IX of *Wonder-Working Providence* this dedicated and hot-tempered Puritan man of action wrote poetry which comes very close to the form and spirit of religious meditation. The chapter consists of a long poem, twenty-two stanzas in all; they are broken up into smaller units by five short prose sections, distinguished by the letters A through E, which are in the nature of notes and express the theme and occasion for each preceding section of poetic meditation, a fact which Johnson has emphasized by attaching the appropriate letter to individual stanzas.[21]

The first two stanzas, however, are not by Johnson but seem to have been copied by him from song X in John Dowland's *A Pilgrimes Solace. Wherein is contained Musicall Harmonie of 3. 4. and 5. parts, to be sung and plaid with the Lute and Viols* (London, 1912).[22] Johnson's dependence on Dowland is another indication of the American Puritans' familiarity with a broad spectrum of English life, including its musical culture. While the first two stanzas are a lamentation on sorrow and grief, stanzas three and four address themselves to Christ; they are meditative in the specific religious sense. Since no source in seventeenth-century English poetry has been found, these subsequent stanzas should be regarded as Johnson's.

Beginning with the fifth stanza, references to the experience of the colonists are made—in the second section to sea disasters, in the six stanzas of the third section to "our Land affairs"—and here serious admonishments by a public-minded Christian are stated:

> Lord stay thy hand, and stop my earthly mind,
>   Thy Word, not world, shall be our sole delight,
> C Not Medow ground, but Christs rich pearl wee'l find,
>   Thy Saints imbrace, and not large lands down plight
> Murmure no more will we at yearly pay,
> To help uphold our Government each way;

While the short fourth part of Johnson's meditation continues the theme of an "over-eager desire after the world," the last and longest section laments the death of eminent first-generation immigrants:

> What courage was in Winthrope, it was thine;
>   Shepheards sweet Sermons from thy blessing came,
> [E] Our heavenly Hooker thy grace did refine, . . .

Undoubtedly, therefore, Johnson was aware of Hooker's preaching on redemption. The fourth stanza of the first section expresses the meditative purpose which Hooker formulated. Johnson addresses Christ:

> Thou deepest searcher of each secret thought,
>   Infuse in me thy all-affecting grace,
> [A] So shall my work to good effect be brought,
>   While I peruse my ugly sins a space,
> Whose staining filth so spotted hath my soul,
> That nought can wash, but tears of inward dole.

Johnson's poetic jeremiad, which is both lament and admonition, is in the true nature of meditation by virtue of its concern with individual salvation as well as with Christ's saints in general. Using English meditative poetry as a model and an inspiration, Johnson is to my knowledge the first writer in New England to try his hand at meditative poetry.

By the middle of the 1660s meditating seems to have become popular in New England. In 1666, the same year the meditation-sermons of Whiting were published, a slim volume of verse meditations appeared, the *Daily Meditations* of Philip Pain. The book contains an introductory poem, "The Porch," and a sequence of sixty-four six-line lyrics—four one-stanza meditations for each day from July

19 through August 3, 1666. Leon Howard traced the numerous echoes of English metaphysical poetry in Pain's work. The influence of George Herbert, signalled by the title of "The Porch," is evident throughout the sequence. Howard points out that Pain can hardly be considered a Puritan, although he wrote religious poetry, as well as contemplations about man's mortality, the immediacy of death, and the uncertainty of grace.[23] Christ's help and the hope of grace are regularly invoked, but without attention to the doctrinal system of the redemptive process that was so important to Puritan belief. Pain's fourth meditation of the first day (in Meserole, *Poetry*) is fairly representative of the sequence: starting with an assertion, "This World a Sea of trouble is," it moves to a prayer, "O great God, let me / be kept from sinking into misery," and concludes with a question, "*who can say / That I shall surely live another day.*"

In 1669 the pastor-physician Michael Wigglesworth, already well known for his dramatic poem *The Day of Doom*, published a series of verse meditations which brought him still more fame and went through at least four editions before Edward Taylor started to write his private meditations. Wigglesworth's *Meat Out of the Eater: or, Meditations Concerning the Necessity, End, and Usefulness of Afflictions Unto God's Children* is made up of fifty-three "meditations" or "songs" of an average length of seven to ten eight-line stanzas, written in a somewhat uncertain rhyme scheme of a b a b c d c d (quite often, rhymes are not achieved). The lines have a three-stress beat, except for the third and seventh lines which tend to bear four stresses.[24] If this form seems to be more suited to the dramatic temperament of a ballad than to a meditative mood, it nevertheless serves Wigglesworth well, because he deals with "calamaties," as he likes to call them: the distresses, afflictions, sicknesses, frailties, failures, and miseries of "God's Children." The afflictions of sickness receive particular attention from an author who suffered most of his life from various forms of illness and experienced many calamities because ill health quite often prevented him from doing his job as a pastor. It is interesting to note how his treatment of the Protestant-Puritan notion of sickness as a result of man's depravity, as a symbol of his sinfulness, is balanced by the view that it is an affliction sent by God as a necessary and, in the end, useful affliction which prepares man for salvation.

The poems are clearly the result of meditative endeavor: most stanzas throughout the volume are annotated in the margin with at least one, often up to three, biblical quotations which testify to the author's concentrated attention to God's word. To juxtapose the word of God with the searching out of sin is, according to Hooker and all Protestant meditation theorists, the essential duty of the meditator. Right at the beginning, in the fourth stanza of the first meditation, Wigglesworth signals Richard Baxter as one of his mentors:

> Our way to heavenly Rest,
> Is all against the Stream;
> We must not sail with Wind and Tide
> As too too many dream;

But row against them both,
And many Storms endure;
Till we arrive at that sweet port,
    Where Saints shall rest secure.[25]

There are also unmistakable references to the meditation theory which Hooker formulated in his *Application of Redemption*; Hooker's favorite image of the "broken heart" is taken up several times, as in Meditation III, stanza 10:

Our hearts are over-run
Much like a Fallow-field,
Which must be broke and ploughed up
    Before it Fruit can yield:
Afflictions are God's Plough
Wherewith He breaketh us,
Tears up our *lusts* those noisome *weeds*,
    And fitteth us for Use.[26]

Or the Savior talking in Song X of "Light in Darkness" about his Father:

He will to thee impart
An humble broken heart,
Increase of Spiritual Strength,
And victory at length.[27]

In Wigglesworth's view the saints' way to heavenly rest is not only thorny but accompanied by severe punishment. The first section of *Meat Out of the Eater*, comprising ten meditations and one "Conclusion Hortatory" is subtitled "*Tolle Crucem.* All Christians must be Cross-bearers," and this section is dominated by images of punishment. Besides the cross, "God's Rod," and wrath, such implements of punishment and "chastisement" as the prison, chains, scourge, hunger, thirst, sickness, and suffering are constantly evoked to demonstrate the basic meditation insight:

God doth chastise his own
    In Love, their souls to save:
And lets them not run wild with them:
    That no Correction have.
    Now as the Rod restrains
    From posting down to Hell;
So by the same God doth Excite
    And teach us to do well.

The second section is entitled "Riddles Unriddled, or, Christian Paradoxes."
Nine such riddles, or paradoxes, also called mysteries, are listed; they are the
subtitles to sections in which these paradoxes are treated by meditations or songs:

> Light in Darkness,
>   Sick mens Health,
> Strength in Weakness,
>   Poor mens Wealth,
> In Confinement,
>   Liberty,
> In Solitude,
>   Good Company.
> Joy in Sorrow,
>   Life in Deaths,
> Heavenly Crowns for
>   Thorny Wreaths.

The listing of the nine riddles is irregularly rhymed and reads like a catalogue
poem; the riddles define mysteries of God's providence which Wigglesworth
treats in this order by a varying number of meditations or songs.

A riddle is also indicated by the over-all title *Meat Out of the Eater*. It is the
riddle which Samson puts to the Philistines at his wedding: "Out of the eater
came forth meat, and out of the strong came forth sweetness" (Jud. 14, 14).
The solution—honey came out of the carcass of the lion which Samson slew,
or "rent"—is one of the stark images which appealed to the Puritan imagination,
expressing, as it does, the belief that out of the corruptions of mortality, and
out of a rent heart, may be gained the sweetness of everlasting life. As Wig-
glesworth puts it:

> Droop not faint-hearted man,
>   Thou art not yet undone:
> So long as God himself survives,
>   And is thy Portion.[28]
>   Out of the Eater He
>   Will surely bring forth Meat:
> And Spiritual good more sweet than hony
>   Out of Affliction great.

The nine riddles, or Christian paradoxes, of the second part of *Meat Out of
the Eater* all gain a positive result from their various situations of afflictions:
light from darkness, joy from sorrow, finally "heavenly crowns" in exchange
for "thorny wreaths." Accordingly, tone and imagery in this part are not quite

so menacing as in the first ten meditations. Some of the meditations and songs of the second part are written as dialogues between conflicting forces or parties: between Spirit and Flesh, Faith and Unbelief, Distressed Conscience and Rectified Judgment, between the Soul and the Savior. The hortatory severity of the first part is softened; chastisement is replaced by consolation, God's Rod by the death-conquering sacrifice of Christ which turns anxiety into hope and praise:

> Be cheerful, Suffering Saint,
> Let Nothing cast thee down:
> Our Saviour Christ e're long will turn
> Thy Cross into a Crown.

Wigglesworth's conception is truly Protestant in that it ties meditation to salvation, the infusion of grace and faith. The stages and forms of Christ's suffering are meditated upon as the model and supreme form of suffering which should teach man the relevance of his own afflictions, and at the same time console him with His redemptive power.[29]

> Art thou a prisoner?
> Our Lord himself was Bound,
> Art thou disgrac'd why he was scorn'd,
> And trampled to the ground.
> Blindfolded, spit upon,
> Most wrongfully accused,
> Reviled, mocked, buffeted
> And wickedly abused.
>
> Art thou in poverty?
> Why, Christ himself was poor,
> And had not where to lay his head;
> It's like he gives thee more.
> Art thou in heaviness?
> He was a man of Grief,
> Whose Soul was sorrowful to Death,
> -To purchase our relief.

It can be said that Wigglesworth is overly Puritan in his view of a God of wrath and in his preoccupation with suffering, sickness, and calamities—doubtless a consequence of his own precarious health and the professional and personal troubles he experienced because of it. Descriptions of the miseries of the human condition are more prominent in *Meat Out of the Eater* than the effort to understand and search the heart. His meditations are, in that sense, somewhat more sentimental and passive than Hooker's directives would seem to allow. Wigglesworth is more concerned with bearing the cross than with getting at the bottom of human sinfulness.

Except for the central dogma of Christ's sacrifice, there is little attention to dogmatic structures and intricacies in *Meat Out of the Eater*. Wigglesworth's meditations are both hortatory and consoling;[29] they were, as the contemporary response testifies, a successful effort in pastoral counseling. His verse meditations are not great poetry, but they are far from being mere doggerel. It can be assumed that he chose the verse form because the success of *The Day of Doom* had taught him that his New England readers loved to have their harsh theology in strong beat rhythm and catching rhymes. Of the two alternative forms of meditative effort—the one private, the other directed to an audience—Wigglesworth practiced the second with considerable success. Edward Taylor, on the other hand, consigned his pastoral advice to the sermon and practiced meditation as a purely personal and private labor.

Edward Taylor's *Preparatory Meditations* are the crowning achievement of American Puritan poetry. The ever–expanding Taylor research has brought forth a superabundance of meaning which Taylor's meditative intensity has put into words and images. These meanings cannot here be reproduced or even summed up: some observations are to be made, however, about Taylor's place and role in the Protestant-Puritan meditation tradition. Taylor's meditations were written in preparation for the Sacrament, and they fulfill the classic requirements of self-examination in order to arrive "at a true sight of Sin" and of a comprehensive understanding of the Sacrament of the Lord's Supper in its threefold components: The Fall of man, Christ's sacrifice and the attribution of grace within the cosmic context of God's Glory. True to meditation tradition, the understanding is applied to the heart.

As a Protestant meditator, Taylor based his efforts on the words and images of the Bible, which he explored in their fullest meaning and dimensions. In addition, he placed himself in the meditative tradition by taking up thoughts and definitions contributed by its major representatives. Thus, he makes use of the typological definition of the meditative labor as the "chewing of the cud,"[30] and we encounter in his meditations the metaphoric use of "cordialls," " spices," "chymistry," "conduit," "pipes," and "veans." Food and digestion imagery, abounding in Taylor's meditations, traditionally not only belongs to the interpretation of the Lord's Supper but also, in Protestant meditation theory, serves to explain the meditative process of understanding—a process that "chews upon the things of God," or upon experience, in order to convey the "meat it hath chewed . . . into the heart, and into the will, and into the affections, and into the conversation."[31] This explication is not to suggest that Taylor was in all these instances dependent on other writers; in many cases his images and illustrations clearly had their source in the Bible. Yet it is also evident that Taylor absorbed ideas and their visualization from the tradition of Protestant meditation and developed these to serve his purposes. Within that tradition and the contemporary discussion in the pulpit and the printed page, he chose his own position. In short, the basic principle of Protestant meditative thought, the working arrangement between head and heart, receives ingenious applications in every meditation Taylor wrote.

The two writers who seem to be closest to Taylor's conceptions are Thomas Hooker and Edmund Calamy. Calamy's sermons on meditation were posthumously published by his son, shortly before Taylor left for the New World, as *The Art of Divine Meditation, or, a Discourse of the Nature, Necessity and Excellency thereof, with Motives to, and Rules for the better performance of that most important Christian Duty.*[32] Calamy, like all his colleagues who wrote on this topic, draws on a long history of meditative thought and imagery—from Bernard of Clairvaux via Joseph Hall, Baxter, and Hooker (all of them mentioned). In a very readable text he discusses meditation in depth and with psychological insight. Like Hooker, he uses images and illustrations that engage the reader's imagination, also giving precise instructions to the religious man and, explicitly addressed, the religious woman of his time.

The most vital concern of the meditator is that his "dim eyes," the eyes of fallen man, be cleared. This concern, which Taylor discusses throughout his meditations,[33] is explained by Calamy:

> Another type of this rare grace of Meditation, is that of the Beasts, Ezek. I, that Ezekiel saw, *that had eyes within and without*, Vers. 18., *their wings were full of eyes round about them* . . . for meditation is nothing else but a looking thoroughly into the things of God, *a looking before and behind*, as I may so speak; a meditating Christian is a man full of eyes, that doth not only know God, but sees much of God. [p. 25]

Taylor's relation to the meditative tradition can be documented by a number of significant parallels. Among the rarer similes used for the "sweetness" and fruitfulness of meditative labor is that of a pomander—"and as it is with a pomander," says Calamy, "unless you do rub it, you will never smell the sweetness of it" (p. 33)—which Taylor expresses in his supplication:

> My heart, oh Lord, for thy Pomander gain.
>   Be thou thyselfe my sweet Perfume therein, [I. 2, ll. 19–20]

Taylor's closest affinity is with Calamy's elaborate image of the meditator as a musician:

Oh, it is a hard matter to get our hearts in tune for this duty; as it is with a *Musician*, he hath a great deal of time to string, and to tune his Instrument before he can play; the best Christian is like an Instrument unstrung, and untuned, he had need to take a great deal of time to get his heart in tune for Divine Meditation; the best Christian is like wet wood, which will not burn, you know, without a great deal of blowing; he had need to take a great deal of time to kindle a holy zeal in his heart to God, to blow up the sparks of grace that are in him. [p. 84]

Taylor expressed his unpreparedness with the lament "my Soul is damp Untun'd. My strings are fallen and their screw pins slipt" (II, 152, ll. 1–2), or, as he put it in the last stanza of "The Return":

> Be thou Musician, Lord, Let me be made
>   The well tun'de Instrument thou dost assume.
> And let thy Glory be my Musick plaide.
>   Then let thy Spirit keepe my Strings in tune,
>   Whilst thou art here on Earth below with mee
>   Till I sing Praise in Heaven above with thee. [p. 11, ll. 49–54]

The "Sparke" is also one of Taylor's favorite images, put to a great variety of uses. Calamy likened meditation to "a Divine pair of bellows to blow up the sparks of grace" (p. 55). Taylor used simile in three of his meditations (II. 6; II. 49 and II. 82):

> Then let thy Spirits breath, as Bellows, blow
> That this new kindled Life may flame and glow. [II. 82, ll. 17–18.]

A direct quotation from Hooker is made in this latter meditation: "This thought on, sets my heart upon the Rack" (II. 82, l. 5) echoes Hooker's ". . . sets mans heart upon the rack." "Wrack," "wracks," "wrackt," sometimes predominantly in the meaning of rack, sometimes of wrack, is used in nine meditations. The first stanza of Med. I. 32 (in Meserole, *Poetry*) furnishes an example of the ingenuity with which Taylor developed this image of his complex strategy of fusing images and meaning. Taylor argues with images; he opens the argument by a juxtaposition: "Thy Grace" is "my golden Wrack." This is both a shortcut of Hooker's proposition that meditation "sets man's heart upon the rack" and an extension of its meaning: the rack is grace because grace is the very essence and purpose of meditation. The torture instrument of the rack has become golden by the meditator's strain to understand God's grace and the consequent prospect of its distribution. By this very fact, the "wrack" has been turned into a musical instrument like a harp or virginal, made up of strings on a frame, strings which must be screwed tight in order to be tuned, as the heart of the meditator on the "golden wrack" has to be stretched in order to be in tune for praise. Thus, the meditator's imagination is screwed "into ragged verse," poetry which is fragmentary, worthless, rag-like as well as "racked." Yet, although the poet's fancy is not equal to celestial music on King David's Harp, by persevering effort, "Tuning thy Praises in my feeble minde," the meditator is able to praise God with harmonious music. In this way, Hooker's torture rack and Calamy's musical image, two major definitions of meditational effort, are blended into one complex whole.

"There is no creature but it hath the Image of God upon it" according to Calamy, who considered it "the greatest affront" which man could offer God "not to take spiritual notice of his creatures and not to make a spiritual use of his Creatures," since God has made man "to be the tongue of Praise" for all his creatures and the whole cosmos, including sun, moon, stars, fire, water, snow, rain, and ice. "When we praise God for these things, then *they* praise God when we use them for God, and draw Heavenly things, spiritual instruction out of them." Taylor fulfilled this injunction; he refined it by making full use of both the "book of the Scripture" and "the book of the Creature," as Calamy called it, as well as the insights which mediative thought had assembled about this labor. The sacrament of the Lord's Supper is the living center of Taylor's faith and thought, a feast of supreme meaning in which he sees the essence of Christianity encompassed: Christ crucified and resurrected, the God-man as the highly exalted "relation" who gives man access to God, the Son of God who offers His body and blood as the bread and water of life at a feast of redemption to which He invites sinful man and thereby converts death into eternal life. In this sacrament the central mystery of the Christian religion and the crowning experiences of human life are epitomized. The drama of Adam's fall is reflected in the Sacrament as is the suffering of Christ together with all the types by which he was announced and prefigured.

The classical stages and requirements of Protestant meditation: to learn an awareness of sin, to gain an understanding of God's creation and the conditions of grace, to praise God's glory and grace—all are fulfilled by Taylor in an extraordinary variety of configurations which determine the individual structure of each of his meditations. In fulfilling these tasks Taylor is acutely aware of an incompatibility at the center of meditation as poetry: for, while the meditative labor undertaken in composing each poem is a preparation for the bestowal of grace, the possession of grace is the very basis of the poetic effort and the praise it is required to express. It is a problem of religious as well as aesthetic significance, and Taylor deals with it in every meditation by elaborating the progress from speechlessness to praise:

> When, Lord, I seeke to shew thy praises, then
>   Thy shining Majesty doth stund my minde,
> Encramps my tongue and tongue ties fast my Pen,
>   That all my doings, do not what's designd.
>   My Speeche's Organs are so trancifide
>   My words stand startld, can't thy praises stride. [II. 43, ll. 1–6]

Actually, the fruit of completed meditation is the poet's ability to use his will and affections in a successful appeal for grace and at the same time in praise of God's glory:

> Oh! that my Heart, thy Golden Harp might bee
>   Well tun'd by Glorious Grace, that e'ry string
> Screw'd to the highest pitch, might unto thee
>   All Praises wrapt in sweetest Musick bring.
>   I praise thee, Lord, and better praise thee would
>   If what I had, my heart might ever hold. ["The Experience", ll. 25–30]

Thus, each poem is a new venture in meditation, a new preparation and plea for renewal and confirmation of grace at the sacrament of the Lord's Supper. Taylor made this venture more than two hundred times in poetic form, each time conducting a merciless probing of his mind by exploring the meditative process with singular intensity and profundity. Certainly Edward Taylor was one of the great masters of meditation, which for him meant the concentrated intellectual and emotional effort to understand the mysteries of the Christian religion, his own existence and ultimate destination, and the order of the whole cosmos. Since the tools of this tremendous effort were thought and language, his meditations are among the most intricate and concentrated explorations of word and meaning in all American literature. Moreover, together with Hooker he has added a significant dimension to our understanding of the Puritan psyche by giving passionate expression to its longing for purification and redemption.

NOTES

1. *The Poetry of Meditation* (New Haven and London, 1954), rev. ed. 1962; also Foreword to Stanford, *Taylor*.
2. Abridged with introduction by John T. Wilkinson (London, 1962).
3. *The Works of Joseph Hall*, New Edition, 12 vols. (Oxford, 1837), vol. 6, pp. 47–85.

4. *Seaven Treatises Containing Such Directions as Is Gathered Out of the Holie Scriptures* (London, 1603).

5. Thomas Shepard, in his *Autobiography*, refers to Rogers' *Seven Treatises* and *Practice of Christianity*, "the book which did first work upon my heart," when in 1624 he resolved to meditate every day.

6. *The Pilgrim's Progress and Traditions in Puritan Meditation* (New Haven and London, 1966), p. 126.

7. *Donne's "Anniversaries" and the Poetry of Praise. The Creation of a Symbolic Mode* (Princeton, 1973); also *Poetics*, chapter 5.

8. *Seventeenth-Century News*, 26 (1968), 7–9.

9. *Magnalia Christi Americana*, 2 vols., 2nd ed. (Hartford, 1820), p. 458.

10. *God's Plot. The Paradoxes of Puritan Piety Being the Autobiography & Journal of Thomas Shepard*, ed. with an introduction by Michael McGiffert (Amherst, 1972), p. 42. Mather describes these events on p. 344, *Magnalia* I.

11. (London, 1656); references in this chapter are to 2nd ed. (London, 1659).

12. Cf. Mather's report, *Magnalia* I, 304.

13. Sargent Bush, Jr., *The Writings of Thomas Hooker. Spiritual Adventure in Two Worlds* (Madison, 1980) gives a detailed discussion of Hooker's conception of the soul and preparation of the heart.

14. (London, 1632).

15. *Soules Preparation*, p. 81; *Application of Redemption*, p.210; *Soules Preparation*, p. 166.

16. *Soules Preparation*, p. 83; *Application of Redemption*, p. 214.

17. *Application of Redemption*, pp. 247, 218–19, 276, 273. In typological interpretation, chewing the cud, a faculty of clean beasts, "intimates Meditation ruminating on the Things of God, digesting Spiritual Food, for the Word is compared to Food," Samuel Mather, *The Figures and Types of the Old Testament*, 2nd ed. (London, 1705). This typological definition is used also by Edmund Calamy, who wrote that "a meditating Christian is one that chews the cud, that chews on the Truth of Jesus Christ," and Edward Taylor, both discussed later in this chapter.

18. *Magnalia* I, 306.

19. (Boston, 1690).

20. About early eighteenth-century books and manuals on the Lord's Supper, among them Samuel Willard's private *Some Brief Sacramental Meditations* (1711), see E. Brooks Holifield, *The Covenant Sealed. The Development of Puritan Sacramental Theology in Old and New England, 1570–1720* (New Haven and London, 1974), p. 198.

21. *Johnson's Wonder-Working Providence 1628–1651*, ed. J. Franklin Jameson (New York, 1910), pp. 257–61; reprinted in Silverman, *Poetry*.

22. I am indebted for the discovery of Dowland as a source to Professor Astrid Schmitt-von Mühlenfels. Johnson copied with slight variations the first two of Dowland's three stanzas. The text of this song seems to be by Dowland himself; at least no other origin has been discovered nor identified by E. H. Fellowes, who included the text in *English Madrigal Verse 1588–1632*, 2nd ed. (Oxford, 1929).

23. *Daily Meditations by Philip Pain*, reproduced from the original with an introduction by Leon Howard (San Marino, Calif., 1936). A selection from Pain's Daily Meditations is in Meserole, *Poetry*.

24. (Boston, 1669). References in this chapter are to the fifth edition (Boston, 1717),

"Corrected and Amended by the Author in the Year 1703," as it says on the title page. The designation of some items as "songs" seems to be derived from Deut. 31, 19. Song X of the second section, "A Dialogue or Discourse between the Believing Soul and her Saviour," is in four-line stanzas rhyming a a b b. See chapter 15 for Ramean logic in Wigglesworth's poetry.

25. Other references to "heavenly" or "everlasting rest" are on pp. 6, 69, 83, 124.

26. Hooker employs a similar image when he speaks of "our corruptions" which may be plucked up by the roots (*Application of Redemption*, p. 214).

27. Another reference to Hooker, or perhaps to general sermon or meditation lore, is the striking image that we must not "think to ride to Heaven/Upon a Feather-bed" which Richard Crowder used in the title *No Featherbed to Heaven. A Biography of Michael Wigglesworth* (East Lansing, Mich., 1962). Hooker had used it—"You must not thinke to goe to heaven on a feather-bed"—in *The Christians Two Chiefe Lessons* (London, 1640), p. 64; cf. Bush, *Writings of Thomas Hooker*, p. 151.

28. God as man's "Portion" in Ps. 16, 5; 73, 26; 119, 57; and 142, 5.

29. About Wigglesworth's effort of *consolatio* see also Richard M. Gummere, "Michael Wigglesworth: From Kill-joy to Comforter," *Seven Wise Men of Colonial America* (Cambridge, Mass., 1967).

30. Calamy, pp. 16, 33; Hooker, *Application of Redemption*, p. 218; about "chewing of the cud" see note 17 above.

31. Calamy, p. 28.

32. (London, 1667); reference in this chapter is to an edition published 1680 in London.

33. More than 200 entries for "eye," "eyeballs," "Eyebeams," "eyesight," etc. are in Gene Russeell, *A Concordance to the Poems of Edward Taylor* (Indian Head Inc., 1973).

34. Med. I. 2, ll. 19–20 in Stanford, *Taylor*.

Index